BUILDING STATES AND NATIONS

BUILDING STATES AND NATIONS

Models and Data Resources

Volume I

Edited by

S. N. EISENSTADT

and

STEIN ROKKAN

SAGE PUBLICATIONS / Beverly Hills / London

For information address:

SAGE PUBLICATIONS, INC.
275 South Beverly Drive
Beverly Hills, California 90212

SAGE PUBLICATIONS LTD
St George's House / 44 Hatton Garden
London EC1N 8ER

Printed in the United States of America

International Standard Book Number 0-8039-0244-1

Library of Congress Catalog Card No. 73-77873

FIRST PRINTING

PREFACE

A PROGRAMME FOR COMPARATIVE CROSS-NATIONAL RESEARCH: THE ACTION OF THE INTERNATIONAL SOCIAL SCIENCE COUNCIL

The International Social Science Council was established by UNESCO in 1951 as a central organization for the advancement of projects of cooperation across disciplines and across countries. The Council's mission is to internationalize the social sciences: to help social scientists across all regions link up with each other in their concrete work; exchange information; test out techniques in new settings; compare models, procedures, and findings across cultures and across political systems.

The Council has tried a variety of strategies in its efforts to internationalize the social sciences. In 1962, just over ten years ago, the Council launched a programme to advance joint work on the infrastructure, the methodology and the theory of comparative cross-cultural and cross-national research.

The programme was initially centered on the coordination of efforts to build up data resources for comparative analysis. Publications such as *Comparing Nations,*[1] *Data Archives for the Social Sciences,*[2] and *Quantitative Ecological Analysis,*[3] all helped to generate interest in the development of better infrastructures for cross-national research.

To establish a firmer framework for these efforts of cooperation and coordination, the ISSC in 1966 established a Standing Committee on Social Science Data. This body concerns itself not only with the maintenance of an active network of communication among data archives, but also with technical matters such as the diffusion of management and retrieval systems and of social science computer programs.

The Council took stock of its initial endeavours at an important meeting in Paris in 1965.[4] The scholars assembled strongly recommended that the Council take steps to broaden its programme: it should pay more attention to the methodology of comparisons, and it should help forward efforts of systematic confrontation of theories. To move forward on the methodology front, the Council was able to persuade UNESCO to organize a number of "data confrontation seminars" and training courses designed to acquaint younger research workers with the techniques of cross-national comparison. This programme was later supported under a grant by the Volkswagen Foundation, which allowed the Council to launch a series of summer schools for training in comparative research and also to organize several seminars on problems in the methodology of comparisons and in the development of theories of the sources of variability across cultures and territorial units.

The stock-taking conference in 1965 also strongly recommended that the Council establish close links with historians in exploring the possibilities of systematic comparisons of cultures and systems in greater time depth. During 1966-1967, the Council prepared a plan for a series of encounters between historians and generalizing social scientists over issues in the theory of development. This plan was submitted to UNESCO, and it proved possible to finance a series of seminars and larger conferences on issues of national political development. The first such encounter took place in 1968.[5] This was followed in 1970 by a major cross-regional conference on "State Formation and Nation-Building" in Cérisy-la-Salle in Normandy,[6] by regional conferences in Asia and in Latin America, and by a technical workshop on data resources for historical comparisons of national development.[7]

This series of meetings generated a number of important reports and papers. To ensure wide circulation of these texts, UNESCO published a selection of papers from the Cérisy Conference[8] and asked the International Social Science Council to assemble the broader body of contributions in a separate publication. The task of editing this collection was entrusted to two of the Directors of the UNESCO project, Professors S. N. Eisenstadt and Stein Rokkan. They commissioned a number of additional chapters to fill lacunae and to round off the presentations region by region. They also took steps to prepare an extensive bibliography of the literature on state formation and nation-building.

The results of these various efforts can be studied in the two volumes of this Council publication, *Building States and Nations*. In the first volume the editors have assembled a series of general discussions of *models and concepts* in the study of macro-political change and added a number of papers on the *data resources* for comparative research on such processes. The second volume presents a series of papers on major variations in political development across the world; it is organized by *region* and offers analyses of the sources of diversity within each of the distinctive areas of common cultural and/or political inheritance.

We believe that this collection offers a useful source of information on current thinking and research on national political development, and we hope that the recommendations and the suggestions recorded in this volume will help to give direction and structure to future comparative studies in this field. The International Social Science Council is ready to continue its efforts to advance systematic exchanges and encounters at the borderline between history and social science and will be much encouraged if the work reported on in these pages will inspire new initiatives by younger scholars interested in cross-cultural and cross-national comparisons.

This volume would never have seen the light of day without the help so freely given by so many friends and colleagues. We are particularly indebted to Marie-Anne de Franz of the Department of Social Sciences in UNESCO: as an historian working with social scientists, she believed firmly in our project and helped it forward at every step. We are also most grateful to S. N. Eisenstadt, Rajni Kothari, and Candido Mendes for all they did to advance our project. Among the many who helped us produce this volume in Paris, in Bergen, and at Yale, we would single out for special thanks Elina Almasy, Astrid Blom, Kirsti Saelen, Marianne Serck-Hanssen, Joan Warmbrunn, and Lydia Stevens. We finally wish to thank all the authors for both the quality of their contributions and for their patience in answering our queries and in awaiting publication of these volumes.

Bergen and Paris,   *Samy Friedman*
1 February 1973.   *Stein Rokkan*

NOTES

1. R. L. Merritt and S. Rokkan, eds., Comparing Nations, New Haven, Yale University Press, 1966.
2. S. Rokkan, ed., Data Archives for the Social Sciences, Paris, Mouton, 1966.
3. M. Dogan and S. Rokkan, eds., Quantitative Ecological Analysis in the Social Sciences, Cambridge, Mass., M.I.T. Press, 1969.

4. See Stein Rokkan, ed., Comparative Research Across Cultures and Nations, Paris, Mouton, 1968.

5. See the report by Stein Rokkan in the following chapter.

6. See the report by Stein Rokkan below, and the one by Rajni Kothari in Chapter 3 of this volume.

7. See Chapter 5 of this volume: "Data Resources for Comparative Research on Development: A Review of Recent Efforts," by Stein Rokkan.

8. International Social Science Journal, Vol. 23, No. 3, 1971.

CONTENTS

BUILDING STATES AND NATIONS

INTRODUCTION:

CENTRE-FORMATION, NATION-BUILDING AND CULTURAL DIVERSITY: REPORT ON A UNESCO PROGRAMME

Stein Rokkan

What do we mean when we call a territorial unit a "nation"? Which are the main components in this complex concept and how can we compare territorial units on such possible dimensions of "nation-ness"? Can we fruitfully operate with one concept of "nation-building" across all areas of the world or must we content ourselves with region-specific comparisons? Is the "nation-state" essentially a European and a Western construct or can it also be fruitfully applied in the study of the recent crop of sovereign political units in the Third World? Is "nation-ness" a worthwhile goal of political development or are there alternative, and less costly, solutions to the problems of cultural unification within sovereign territories? These and a host of related issues have been debated by scholars from all world regions within a programme of studies and encounters organized since 1967 by UNESCO in close cooperation with the International Social Science Council.

The programme was initially proposed at a Round Table organized by the International Social Science Council in 1965:[1] the scholars assembled at this meeting reviewed the "state of the art" in comparative studies and strongly recommended that UNESCO take steps to launch a series of cross-regional studies of conditions, strategies, and crises of national development. UNESCO organized a preparatory session on this programme during the World Congress of Political Science at Brussels in September 1967. Participants proposed that UNESCO organize a series of regional workshops on varieties of national development within each major cultural area and also proceed fairly soon to a cross-regional conference on issues of theory and model-building.

The first regional workshop took place at Aspenäsgården near Gothenburg in August 1968. The larger cross-regional conference took place at Cérisy-la-Salle in Normandy in August 1970. Further regional workshops were held in Asia and in Latin America in 1971 and 1972. This report centers on the first two of these encounters.

THE FIRST REGIONAL WORKSHOP: EUROPEAN DEVELOPMENTS IN A WORLD PERSPECTIVE

The Workshop at Aspenäsgården focused on the experiences of the developed nation-states of Western Europe: particularly the Nordic countries and such smaller pluralist democracies as the Netherlands, Belgium, and Switzerland.[2] But these cases of nation-building were not discussed in isolation from the rest of the world. The purpose of the meeting was to ensure a systematic confrontation between the past experiences of the older units and the current experiences of the newer ones. In fact the emphasis throughout was on variations in the cultural, economic, and political conditions for nation-building and on the consequences of this great variability for current policy-making in the developing countries. Obviously only some of the many dimensions of variability could be discussed at this five-day symposium, but at least an attempt was made to set up a common framework for a series of further confrontations of theories and experiences across the major regions of the world.

Historians, political scientists, sociologists and social psychologists from twelve countries and four continents took part in the symposium,[3] which was organized in nine sessions:

1. Models of nation-building:
   the confrontation of theories and data

Three papers had been prepared for discussion at this session: E. Allardt, "A frame of reference for describing evolutionary, structural and institutional characteristics of national societies;" S. Rokkan, "Models and methods in the comparative study of nation-building," and S. Rokkan, "Trends in the development of cross-cultural, cross-societal and cross-national research." Section III of the last-named paper, on "macro-comparisons," was submitted for specific discussion at the Symposium.

2. A comparative study of Nordic social structure

For this session a report had been prepared by Edmund Dahlström on a plan for a cooperative study of the structure of four Nordic societies: Danish, Norwegian, Swedish, and Finnish.

3. Comparative nation-building statistics:
   the Nordic countries

In this session the discussion of strategies in the comparative study of Nordic nation-building was followed up through detailed consideration of the statistical bases for time series analyses of such processes. Birgitta Odén presented an overall review of developments in the production of national statistics in the four Nordic countries and Paavo Seppänen reported on an analysis of correlations among a large number of indicators of social change in Finland from 1910 to 1960.

4. Contrasts in nation-building processes in Europe:
   the Low Countries and Switzerland
   compared with the North

For this session Hans Daalder had prepared an extensive paper: "Nation-building the Dutch way." His presentation was followed up by parallel presentations of the Belgian experience by Val Lorwin and of the Swiss by Jürg Steiner.

5. Cleavage structures and mass politics

This session was introduced by Stein Rokkan and was focused on the model of national mobilization processes spelled out in his article "The structuring of mass politics in the smaller European democracies," *Comparative Studies in Society and History,* vol. 10, 1968, pp. 173-210.

6. Cultural and organizational mobilization

For this session two papers had been presented on nation-building and mass mobilization in Sweden from the 1870s onwards: C. G. Andrae, "The popular movements and the process of mobilization in Sweden," and P. E. Back, "The political role of voluntary associations in Sweden: 1870-1910."

7. Changes in class structure and elite composition

This topic was introduced by Ulf Torgersen. He focused on the development of national markets for the professions and presented an analysis of Norwegian data on cycles in the balance between the output of professionally educated elites and the openings in the governmental and the private job markets. This presentation was followed up through a comparison of time series data on the recruitment of parliamentary personnel in Norway, Sweden, and Switzerland: "Changes in the channels of recruitment to Parliament: tables for three countries," by S. Rokkan and K. Salhus.

8. The distinctiveness of the Western experiences of
   nation building: contrasts and similarities to current
   developments in the Third World

This session wound up the discussion of concepts, models and theories in the study of state formation and nation-building. Abdelkader Zghal presented a paper on "La participation de la paysannerie Maghrévine à la construction nationale." Rajni Kothari compared state formation and nation-building processes in the developed countries of the West with the current efforts to establish viable political systems in other regions of the world and paid particular attention to differences in the linkage between peripheries, autonomous subcultures, territorial and extraterritorial centres. S. N. Eisenstadt summed up the discussion of differences and similarities in processes of political development and outlined a programme for further comparative research.

9. Facilities for comparative research on
   nation-building processes

This final session of the Workshop offered an opportunity for an exchange of experiences and reflections on the establishment of infrastructure facilities for the organization of comparative research on national cultural and political development. Warren Miller reported on his experiences in the organization of a series of files of machine-readable records of the history of the United States since the colonial era: census data, electoral data, biographical elite data, legislative roll call data. Stein Rokkan reported on the parallel development of historical data archives in Norway and showed how such facilities might offer a basis for the testing of alternative models of state formation, nation-building, and mass mobilization.

These nine themes obviously overlapped a great deal. A number of central theoretical points came up again and again throughout the Workshop and could not be exhaustively discussed in any one session. To simplify our report on the proceedings, we shall organize it around four core themes:

I. State-ness and nation-ness: the structure of the centre and the links with the peripheries

Erik Allardt introduced this theme and stressed the need for a conciliation of structural and institutional approaches in the study of political development: it was important to reach agreement on general categories for the mapping of actual or potential oppositions and cleavages within each territorial population, but it was equally important to study the ways in which these oppositions are handled through conflicts and bargains between elite groups and the ways in which conflicts have been resolved and bargains reinforced through the development of institutions. To show how such a conciliation of structural and constitutional approaches might proceed, he presented a two-dimensional model of possible paths of development from the stage of "mechanical" solidarity (characteristic of traditional tribal societies over stages of anomic disintegration) and coercive centralization toward the stage of "organic" solidarity (seen as a hallmark of the integrated pluralist nation-state in Durkheim's analysis). The paths from the initial stage to the final one would vary from case to case and so would the institutional expressions of the strains and compromises at each stage. But the underlying dimensions would still be roughly identical across all cases: the task was to establish measures of such basic dimensions and to work out models of possible configurations for testing against concrete developments. Commenting on the differences between his scheme and the one proposed by Karl Deutsch and the Almond-Pye group, he stressed the need for greater conceptual clarity in the distinctions made between processes of societal development and differentiation on the one hand, and processes of nation-building on the other. He felt very ambivalent about the term "nation-building:" on the one hand, it carried the implication that the aim of all developmental efforts was a unified nation rather than a humane and tolerant society; on the other hand, he recognized that the nation-state, at least in Europe and the West, was the principal agency of social and cultural planning and that effective measures of improvements in material welfare, cultural opportunities and political equality could still be taken only within the historically defined territories of nations.

Stein Rokkan followed up the discussion by presenting a model of four sources of variations in the structuring of territorially defined political organizations:

(1) the distinctiveness, the consolidation and the economic, political, and cultural strength of the *territorial centre;*

(2) the cultural distance of the *peripheries* from the centre and their economic and political resources for resistance against integration and standardization;

(3) the internal strength and the external resource links of *cross-locally organized subcultures* such as churches, sects, castes;

(4) the internal strength and the external resource links of *cross-locally organized economic units,* such as merchant leagues, credit networks, international corporations.

The first of these bore essentially on the same dimension as the "state-ness" variable proposed in an important article by Peter Nettl.[4] It might be operationalized through measures of the corporate distinctiveness of the central and provincial administrative personnel from the established local elite families. The second of the four dimensions focused on the primordial collectivities in the territorial peripheries and bore on processes of assimilation and mobilization: the central time series variables in Karl Deutsch's work on *Nationalism and Social Communication.* These two dimensions could generate a typology for the ordering of empirically given political systems: one might usefully identify a few systems as "full nation-states" in the sense that they were high both on "state-ness" and on "nation-ness," but as soon as the analysis was broadened to cover a larger number of cases it would be essential to distinguish between these two dimensions.

The need for such distinctions had been brought out with great force in the current study by Hans Daalder, Robert Dahl, Val Lorwin and Stein Rokkan of eleven smaller pluralist political systems in Western Europe: the five Nordic countries, the three Benelux countries, Ireland, Switzerland, and Austria. These were all "nation-states" in the commonly accepted terminology but they still differed markedly both in "state-ness" and in "nation-ness:" the weight of the central administrative apparatus varied very much from case to case and there were also clear-cut contrasts in cultural unification, both in terms of the legitimation of official languages and in terms of religious organization. Switzerland, the Netherlands, and Belgium were historically polycephalous systems characterized by weak concentrations of administrative resources: in Arend Lijphart's terminology, they were essentially "consociational" systems[5] developed through alliances between independent cities and provinces. By contrast Austria and the Nordic countries were higher on "state-ness" as well as on "nation-ness:" republican Austria as the metropolis of a decolonized empire; Denmark and Sweden through their continuous histories of dynastic consolidation since the Middle Ages; Norway, Finland and Iceland through the inheritance of stable administrative structures from their earlier superiors and through several waves of national cultural mobilization before and after the achievement of territorial independence. Such contrasts in centre formation and nation-building could only be understood through detailed information on variations in the other two of the four fundamental dimensions of political development: the cultural and the economic dimensions. It was no accident that the three consociational systems had to be developed along the broad "buffer zone" between northern Protestantism and southern counter-Reformation in Europe. Nor was it an accident that they had emerged out of the strong networks of independent cities at the margins of the large continental systems of territorial control. Consociation represented a constructive solution to an inherited configuration of cultural and economic forces: a stronger drive towards administrative centralization. A greater investment of resources in efforts of cultural unification might have disrupted the balance in each system.

This analysis of contrasts in centre formation and nation-building within Europe was developed in further depth in Hans Daalder's paper on the Netherlands and in Val Lorwin's and Jürg Steiner's statements on Belgium and Switzerland. It was further amplified through Edmund Dahlström's presentation of a cooperative project on the basic structures of the Nordic societies. This brought out very clearly the contrasts between the Danish-Norwegian tradition of centralized administration and the Swedish-Finnish style of balanced and differentiated civil service corporations.

In the discussion of these papers, S. N. Eisenstadt recognized the merits of the dimensional model but stressed the crucial importance of empirical testing against *all* cases of territorial political development. He was not against concentrated efforts at region-specific analysis, but he felt convinced that no decisive intellectual payoff could be expected before the models had been reorganized and tested across several regions of the world. He considered it essential to analyze the variations among the many systems that would be coded low on state-ness as well as on nation-ness and he was convinced that this would call for specifications of further dimensions of variation. In a world perspective none of the smaller European polities was particularly low either on state-ness or on nation-ness; they might vary considerably in a European perspective, but they were still nation-states when judged against the majority of the emerging polities of the Third World. In S. N. Eisenstadt's formulation a nation-state was only one species of the genus "modern political system," whose defining characteristics were (a) the high degree of congruence between the cultural and the political identities of the territorial population, (b) the high level of symbolic and affective commitment to the centre as the locus of territorial integration, and (c) the marked emphasis of common politically defined collective goals for all members of the national community. The majority of the world's polities were low on all these three criteria; the question was whether it was still possible to develop a scheme for the identification of alternative paths of modernization for such systems.

II. Economic-cultural alliances and the character of the commitment to the centre

Much of the further discussion of the four-dimensional model outlined by Stein Rokkan was focused on the notion of commitment to the centre.

The four dimensions of the model were meant not only to serve as so many yardsticks for the location of particular systems at particular stages of their development. They also helped to identify the crucial sets of actors in the sequences of conflicts and bargains which brought each system from one stage to the next in its development: the model posited a constellation of structural conflicts and a series of elite efforts of institutionalization.

In the discussion of this scheme, Barrington Moore's thought-provoking comparison of eight cases of coalition formation and polity building received a great deal of attention.[6] In his introductory paper, Stein Rokkan had spelled out the essentials of Moore's model and criticized him on two points: his concentration on alliances among *economic* actors and his refusal to attempt any testing of his model against the evidence for any but the *largest* of the historically given polities. There was general agreement that Moore's analysis had opened a promising avenue of comparative analysis, but there was also consensus on the need to extend the testing of models of this type to polities at all size levels and in all regions. It was recognized that any such attempts at generalization would make it essential to introduce further categories of actors into the model. Torcuato Di Tella reported on efforts in this direction for Latin America and emphasized the importance of such sets of actors as the armed forces, the hierarchies of the Roman Catholic church, and the different monastic orders. This was brought out again with even greater force in the discussion of variations within Europe: to gain any understanding of the processes of centre formation and nation-building, it was essential to analyze not only the conflicts or bargains between landowners and merchants, as Moore had done, but also the arrangements between secular and religious authorities, between majority and minority churches, and between the religious hierarchies and the lower levels of the priesthood.

Hans Daalder explained the roles of the orthodox Calvinist and the Catholic clergy in linking up the traditional peripheries with the growing urban centres in the Netherlands: in the Dutch case, the emergence of the organizationally distinctive subcultures, the *zuilen* (pillars), represented a definite step forward in the integration of a once only loosely federated set of provinces and cities. Val Lorwin analyzed the Belgian case in similar terms: the *verzuiling* of the Belgian political community along lines of religion and Weltanschauung had helped to integrate the linguistically divided population for several decades after the first waves of mass mobilization, but the original zuilen had not proved strong enough to create lasting links of solidarity between the Flemings, the Bruxellois, and the Walloons. Jürg Steiner described the Swiss case in a similar conceptual framework. In his terminology, the Dutch system was one of segmentation along one dominant dimension—denominational commitment and its secularizing complement, the Belgian system one in transition from religious/ideological to linguistic segmentation, and the Swiss system one of multi-dimensional segmentation without any one dominant cleavage line. The Swiss system was one of crisscrossing segmentation along religious, linguistic, geographic and partisan lines. No single dimension was ever allowed to dominate: the quickly settled Sonderbund war, the pressures of the international system and the blessings of steady economic growth had helped to integrate all the overlapping segments into one consociational whole with a minimum of violence. Whether this would last was another matter: to explore the prospects for continued equilibrium or increasing disruption, Jürg Steiner had worked out a feedback model of the Swiss decision-making system and tried to pin down the factors making for integration and *amicabilis compositio* and the factors making for innovation and structural change.

Rajni Kothari stressed the importance of the concept of segmentation for the study of centre formation and nation-building in the Third World. What made most of the Asian and African developments so different from the European was the persistence of autonomous subcultural centres even after great efforts of military, administrative, and economic centralization. The centres in the Third World tended to be weak and divided: they did not possess the surplus of resources required for effective cultural unification, and attempts at nation-building in the European style were most likely to prove self-defeating. The point was further developed by Francis Okediji in his discussion of the Nigerian case.

Rajni Kothari also stressed the importance of the timing of the territorial consolidation efforts. The international economy had been much less centralized during the crucial periods of European nation-building from 1500 to 1900 that it was today. This meant that few of the emerging polities today could develop effective centres of their own. The external centres of the world economy—London, Paris, New York or Washington—counted more than the internal ones. Dahlström did not think this was peculiar to developments in the Third World: in most of the small and the medium-sized nation-states of the West, the decisive line of cleavage tended to be between the elites which derived their principal resources from the national centre and the elites which could command independent resources in the international economic system. Stein Rokkan made it clear that this was his primary rationale for the addition of the fourth dimension in his model: the strength and the external resources of the urban economic networks.

S. N. Eisenstadt agreed that the analysis of the early centre-forming conflicts and alliances might help to explain the style and structuring of domestic politics but did not think it possible to account for the emergence of the centre as such in this way: this could only be done through an analysis of the precontractual norms establishing links of solidarity across local elites within the given territory. The commitment to the territorial centre went beyond purely rational calculations of sectoral payoffs: a centre could survive only if it commanded the loyalty of major elite groups independently of immediate gains to any one set of actors.

III. Stages and sequences of nation-building, elite integration, and mass mobilization

The discussion of centre-forming alliances and subcultural segmentation was closely tied in with a series of reports on stages in the process of nation-building, elite integration, and mass mobilization.

Stein Rokkan reviewed the "crises" paradigm suggested by Almond, Pye, and their associates and pointed to the possibilities of using various crude time series data to identify crucial phases of change in the historical processes of national territorial consolidation in Western Europe. In the Nordic countries the "penetration" challenge was successfully met in the sixteenth and seventeenth centuries. As Birgitta Odén pointed out, the process of nation-building got well under way in the sixteenth century in Sweden through the introduction of direct taxes to the king, the recruitment of peasants to the royal forces, and the acceptance of the norms of "public order" throughout the periphery. Much more intensive research, however, had been carried out on the later phases of development: the broadening of the recruitment to administrative elite positions (the theme of Sten Carlsson's pioneer work on the decline of the estate-structured Swedish society and the emergence of a class-stratified society), the opening up of new channels of access to the national centre, and the mobilization of the underprivileged strata into strong voluntary associations claiming rights of participation in the national system.

Ulf Torgersen reviewed data for Norway on the ways in which the public and private markets for professional elite positions interacted in the nation-building process. He had collected information on the production of lawyers and clergymen and had been able to identify several cycles in the balance between the supply of candidates and the demand for personnel and had correlated this with information on professional discipline and conformity. He had explored the hypothesis that social origins counted less in determining the behaviour of rising elites in a tight market for positions than in an open one: conformity to superiors was much easier to enforce in a buyer's market; while a seller's market would allow much more leeway for the expression of norms inherited from the strata of origin. The main focus of his analysis had been on developments in Norway from 1814 to the 1920s, but he was anxious to explore the implications of this type of market model in the analysis of trends in the recent decades of steady expansion in the professional job markets.

Stein Rokkan reported on a comparative study of the recruitment to parliamentary positions in Norway, Sweden, and Switzerland from the 1860s to the 1920s. He distinguished between an "ancien régime phase" characterized by high barriers against new entrants into elite positions, a "mass mobilization phase" bringing in a broad phalanx of cultural and economic organizations and opening up channels for the rise of new elites from the hitherto underprivileged strata, and finally an "integration phase" characterized by organizational saturation and the establishment of new professional and educational hierarchies. The ancien régime phase lasted much longer in Switzerland than in Norway and in Sweden, and the mass mobilization phase was much shorter. The strong emphasis on peasant representation in the constitutions of the Nordic countries had kept the barriers low enough to encourage the rise of fresh leadership, yet high enough to make necessary the organization of broad cultural, economic, and political movements to fight for further rights in each system.

Two papers on parallel Swedish developments added further depth to this analysis: Pär-Erik Back reported on an analysis of early forms of associational activity from the 1870s onward and showed how the movements at the levels of the privileged strata had opened up channels of "access to the centre" for the national mass organizations which rose to dominance in the end phase of the struggle for universal suffrage. Carl Göran Andrae reported on a large-scale project of data collection on the spread of such mass movements in Sweden: at the Institute of History at Uppsala University a major effort has been made to assemble, from local newspapers, biographical registers and a host of other sources, the fullest possible time series information on the establishment of religious sects and societies, teetotaler lodges and labour unions across all localities in Sweden. This vast archive of machine-readable information would allow a variety of analyses of the processes of mass mobilization and elite integration in Sweden.

S. N. Eisenstadt was very much impressed by the potentialities of such archives for the study of elite integration. He was struck by the overwhelming evidence of the strength of the teetotaler movements in the parties defending the rights of the underprivileged: first the Liberal party, later the Social Democrats. He interpreted the teetotaler movement as a crusade for the legitimation of rising elites: the emphasis on strict sobriety made for solidarity in the fight against the established stratification system and at the same time justified the claims to access to the centre. There were parallel movements in many countries of the Third World, but the centres were too weak and too divided. What distinguished the developments in the North was the early formation of strong centres and the slow but steady opening up of access for further strata and sectors of the national community.

Much of this discussion revolved around the question of the "terminal stage" in the process of nation-building. Warren Miller reported on work at the Survey Research Centre at the University of Michigan on the "nationalization of politics" in the United States and showed how it was possible to develop time series indicators for the increases in the cross-constituency similarities in the swings from election to election. The swings had become less and less determined by local variations ever since the 1890s, but there were still important pockets of localized politics. S. N. Eisenstadt stated that such indicators might well be used as measures of the degree of national unification, but added further criteria: the equalization of the rights of access to the centre, and the build-up of generally available public services. By such criteria several Western European political systems *had* reached the terminal stage of nation-building: they had entered the "post-welfare state" era. The revolt of the students might be interpreted as a characteristic response to these developments: the opening up of full access to the national centre had demystified it and made the fight for rights within the established systems increasingly meaningless. Erik Allardt objected that this might be true for the formal legislative and judicial centres, but not for the educational and the economic subcentres: the fight for rights of participation in schools and universities, in factories and corporations, was far from meaningless. Rajni Kothari emphasized the difficulties of comparing student revolts across countries at different levels of cultural or political integration: in Europe there might be a movement of revulsion against the meaninglessness of the established channels of access; in Asia some students might fight to establish the rights of the peripheries, while others might be mobilized to defend the traditional central elites against the claims of the peripheries.

IV. **Alternatives to the nation-state:**
    the bearing of Western experiences
    on the decisions facing the Third World

The Workshop was again and again brought back to the central question of the uniqueness of the Western experiences of state formation and nation-building: how far *could* the political systems of the Third World repeat the same sequences of institution-building and, even if they could, how far *should* they?

Abdelkader Zghal stressed the importance of the initial structures: on the continent of Europe the legacy of the universal Church and the feudal hierarchies, in the Arab world the tradition of endogamy and parallel cousin marriage and the consequent difficulties of establishing fixed boundaries for tribal alliances. In North Africa there were no fixed boundaries between tribe and nation, the nation and the Maghreb, the Maghreb and the entire Arab World. With the breakdown of traditional structures, only two sets of organization could provide stable bases for nation-building: the party and the Army.

Francis Okediji stressed the weaknesses of the central structures throughout Africa. Nation-building in the European style was a luxury when not a catastrophe. The only solution was federation.

Rajni Kothari expressed profound dissatisfaction with the Western models of political development as they offered very little guidance for the Third World. He had been impressed by the analysis of the multi-cultural nation-states in Europe; these might offer models for some of the Third World countries, but it was essential to recognize the weakness of their territorial centres. In Europe the political centre controlled the subcultural centres; in Asia stability could be achieved only through the coexistence of a multiplicity of autonomous sub-centres. But this was not an all-or-none issue. It should be possible to establish measures of the strength of each centre and to gauge the potentialities for change. The input-output models proposed by Almond and Pye were of little help. What was needed was a macro-sociological model identifying the major dimensions of variation in the inherited structures and in the systems of external pressures at each stage of further development.

Torcuato Di Tella reviewed developments in Latin America and identified as the primary source of instability the low level of commitment to the political centre. Not only was there no legitimate conservation ideology, but the ruling oligarchies had been more concerned to protect their short-term economic interests than to develop strong and legitimate organs of decision-making. The extension of the suffrage to all citizens had proved premature: there was now a widespread revival of corporatist ideas, in fact a return to the *régime censitaire*.

S. N. Eisenstadt summarized the session and agreed that the nation-state could not be taken to be the goal of all political development. The nation-state represented only one of several possible paths of modernization. A modern political system, in this terminology, had three characteristics: (a) it had shed all vestiges of traditional legitimation and was distinctly self-legitimizing; (b) it had established channels of access from all its peripheries to its centre; (c) it was positively oriented toward change. Most of the polities of the Third World were still traditional or transitional but further modernization need not mean nation-building in the European sense. The Western emphasis on the congruity of cultural and political identities made little sense in most of the Third World. The Western emphasis on the supremacy of the political dimension of human life was alien to much of mankind. The statesmen of the Third World might like to call their polities "nation-states," but any comparative analysis would show up profound contrasts to the European developments. What counted was the drive to modernize, not the imitation of Western models. Modern political systems could develop under the aegis of military bureaucracies, city state federations, or peasant republics: the nation-state was not the only model. In exploring the prospects for alternative developments, the European experiences would have to be analyzed in further detail—but element by element, dimension by dimension. This, he took it, was the thrust of the model proposed by Stein Rokkan. What was the meaning of the Reformation in this perspective? It established the supremacy of political identity but it did not win out against the inherited cultural identities throughout Europe. The verzuild countries with their peculiar mix of identities might offer models for the Third World, but their centres were still markedly stronger than the typical Third World centre. Rajni Kothari interjected that this was essentially a matter of the timing of economic versus political development: the centres of the verzuild countries had been strengthened through the autonomous growth of the city economies ahead of the major thrust toward nation-building. In the emerging countries of the Third World, the city economies were stagnant and the state had to tackle issues of economic growth concurrently with its efforts of centre-building.

THE CROSS-REGIONAL CONFERENCE: THE CONFRONTATION OF GENERAL MODELS WITH CONCRETE REALITIES

The discussions at Aspenäsgàrden left a number of general questions for further discussions with scholars from all regions of the world. Was there anything the leaders and the intellectuals of the post-colonial world could learn from the early European experiences of state-building and national unification from the sixteenth to the nineteenth century? What were the principal components of these early developments, and which of the many configurations to be found in Europe suggested the most realistic models for the builders of states and nations in the Third World? Which elements were unique in the early European developments, and which elements suggested themes for detailed comparisons between the Western "then" and the Third World "now"?

These questions were taken up for extensive scrutiny in a conference convened by the UNESCO Department of Social Sciences from 7 to 14 August 1970.[7] The conference was held at a chateau at Cérisy-la-Salle in Normandy and brought together a total of 22 social scientists, sociologists, anthropologists, political scientists, and historians from 17 countries of Europe, North and South America, Asia, and Africa. A total of 19 papers was discussed at the conference—some of them directly commissioned by UNESCO, others prepared independently for parallel purposes.[8]

The conference papers, with authors listed beneath the appropriate heading, were organized as follows around five themes; those marked with * are included in this volume; those marked ** appear in Volume II:

I. *Theories of political development:* changes in focus and perspective, strategies in the construction of cross-regional paradigms and typologies.

Gabriel Almond (Stanford University)
*S. N. Eisenstadt (Hebrew University)
*Stein Rokkan (University of Bergen)
*D. L. Sheth (Centre for the Study of Developing Societies, Delhi)

II. *Variations in state formation and nation-building experiences in Europe*
Gabriel Almond (Stanford University)
**Hans Daalder (University of Leiden)
V. F. Kotok (Soviet Academy of Sciences, Moscow)[9]
**Juan Linz (Yale University)
**Najdan Pasić (University of Belgrade)
Charles Tilly (University of Michigan)

III. *Variations within the continents settled from Europe*
**Kenneth McRae (Carleton University)
Candido Mendes (Rio de Janeiro)
**José Silva Michelena (University of Venezuela)

IV. *Variations within Asia and Africa*
**R. Mukherjee (Indian Statistical Institute, Calcutta) on South Asia
**J. Watanuki (University of Tokyo) on Japan versus Korea
**Ali Mazrui (Makerere University) on the three East African States, Kenya, Tanzania and Uganda (paper presented by Y. Tandon)
**Abdelkader Zghal (University of Tunis) on nation-building in the Maghreb.

V. *Data Resources for Comparative Research on Nation-Building*
Carl-Göran Andrae (University of Uppsala)
Jerome Clubb (Inter-University Consortium for Political Research, Ann Arbor, Michigan)

I. Theories and paradigms

Almost inevitably the first of these five themes proved the dominant one throughout the five days of discussion. There were heated debates over the scientific status and the practical utility of the many variants of "developmental" theory, and there were a series of confrontations between Western "generalizers" and Third World "historicists" over the intellectual payoffs of efforts to construct paradigms for analyses across all regions. Much discussion was devoted to the current attempts at voluntaristic reformulations of earlier theories of development: the emphasis on the margins of choice for the territorial elite, the cost of alternative strategies, the possible scenarios of crises and institutionalizations. The central thrust of Gabriel ALMOND's important theoretical paper was just this: the histories of all territorial political systems should be reanalyzed to pinpoint the crucial "choice points" for decisions on new modes of institutionalization and the sequences of leader interactions at each such point should be described in detail to bring out similarities and differences in the range of possible coalition alternatives as well as in the actual combinations forcing decisions. Parallel attacks on the determinism of the early theories of development were made in the papers by S. N. EISENSTADT and D. L. SHETH: there was no single predetermined path to modernity and there was no single dominant model of the modern polity. The leaders of the developing nations were faced with a variety of alternatives. These might differ in cost to different sections of the populations but there was still a great deal of leeway for rational choice.

The paradigm presented by Stein ROKKAN in his paper might in fact be taken as a checklist for descriptions of such choice situations: what were the typical sequences of challenges faced by territorial leaders in their efforts to consolidate a political system, and which alliance options were open to them at each phase of consolidation? The paradigm posited four central tasks in the process of territorial consolidation: the first of these focused on the formation of a boundary-defining state and the development of an administrative machinery for the control of transactions within the territory or across the boundary. The second concerned the building of institutions for socialization into a territorial political identity, whether through linguistic standardization, through religious unification, or through educational penetration. The third bore on the institutionalization of channels of participation, representation and opposition. The fourth task involved the creation of territorial economic solidarity through measures to equalize benefits and opportunities both across regions and across strata of the population. Each of these phases corresponded with a set of potential coalition partners or potential opponents. The thrust of the argument was that the concrete history of any particular attempt at system-building could be analyzed chronologically, in terms of time lags versus cumulations of phases; structurally, in terms of the persistence versus reversal of initial coalitions. The implications of the model were spelled out for only one region of the world: the territory of Western Christendom after the Schisma of 1054. A few suggestions were made about possible applications to other regions of the world, but these were not fully discussed at the conference. Of the three primary dimensions of the ROKKAN paradigm, the centre-periphery dimension was clearly the one which appealed most directly to the analysts of Third World developments. Again and again, the discussion brought out the weaknesses of the center formation processes in the new nations, the lower levels of differentiation within each center, the greater distances—social and psychological as well as political—to each periphery.

The paper by Abdelkader ZGHAL brought out the uniqueness of the European developments with particular clarity. By contrast to the European nation-states, the states of the Maghreb had never penetrated their total territory nor defined their boundaries administratively or culturally. In fact the Arab word for state, *makhzen,* was identical with the word for *magasin,* shop: the action of government was limited to the imposition of taxes at market places, and there was always a clear-cut distinction between the territories accepting taxation (Bled makhzen) and the territories rejecting the right of the government to impose taxes even though accepting their authority of external representation (Bled siba). There was no state in the full Weberian sense in the Maghreb: the state could not claim a legitimate monopoly on the use of violence since all successful violence was legitimate. Nor were there any nations in the sense of culturally distinctive communities, the religious bonds of the Umma cut across the territorial borders, as did the Arabic language and many of the potential tribal coalitions. Similar points were brought out in other comparisons between Third World areas and Western Europe. European states were formed around centres at a high level of differentiation— economically, because of the early development of the autonomous cities of the trade route belt; culturally, because of the hierarchically organized cross-territorial Church and the standardization of distinctive national languages under the impact of the Reformation and the spread of printing.

II. Variations in state-ness and nation-ness in Europe

The discussion of the contrasts between Western Europe and the Third World led to a general questioning of the goals of political development. Was the ideal-typical unicultural, unilingual nation-state at all a realistic or even desirable model of development for the Third World? Was there in fact any sense in calling the new states "nations?" Did not that very word connote some drive to unify the territorially defined population culturally or linguistically? Some of this discussion obviously hinged on semantics, but the underlying dimensions were clear enough: there was a definite need to distinguish territoriality from common ethnic origins, a shared historical fate, a distinctive religious identity, or a distinctive linguistic standard.

The papers on differentiations within Europe offered ample evidence of the empirical independence of these dimensions. There is no necessary one-to-one fit between territoriality, culture, and language. There are close approximations to congruity in such countries as Sweden, but there are also cases where several political systems are part of the same linguistic community (Austria, Germany, and Alemanic Switzerland), or where the territory is culturally divided although politically unified (the United Kingdom, Belgium, Finland, the Netherlands, Switzerland). Europe in fact does not offer one model for the Third World, but several. This point was brought out with great force by Hans DAALDER in his analysis of the Dutch and Swiss systems. Both were "nations" in the basic sense of shared political identity, but they were plural nations composed of several distinct subcultures. In the Dutch case, the basic dimension of subcultural differentiation was religious and ideological; in the Swiss case, not only religious but also linguistic and territorial.

Much of the discussion of this paper focused on the preconditions for "consociational" solutions of this type. Could Nigeria have avoided a civil war if a model of this type had been inculcated among the leaders? Did not the model presuppose a high level of initial consensus at the level of the leadership and a strengthening of this consensus through a high level of pressure through threats from the international system? The discussion ranged across a wide variety of multicommunal political systems through-out the Third World: Lebanon, India, Malaysia, Indonesia, Madagascar, Guyana, and other cases. It was generally regretted that the question of the possibility and viability of consociational regimes had not been made a major theme of the conference. It was strongly urged that UNESCO organize detailed comparative studies of the conditions making for accommodation or conflict in multicommunal political systems.

Another major focus of discussion in the session on Europe was the balance of nationalities within empires and federations. Juan LINZ analyzed the building of the Spanish state and sought to pinpoint the factors that made it impossible to develop a strong sense of Iberian identity: the dynastic divisions during the Middle Ages, the economic strength of the peripheral cities in Catalonia and the Basque country, the parasitism of the administrative machinery. Najdan PASIC brought out several similarities between Yugoslavia and Spain: the economic strength of the Western periphery in Slovenia opposed the political strength of the Serbian capital much in the way Bilbao and Barcelona counterbalanced Madrid. The Balkans in fact offered a fascinating variety of cases of nation-building around competing centres inherited from disintegrating empires. Much in the way the structure of the Iberian politics reflected alignments of centres and networks during the centuries of conflict between the Christian and the Moslem cultures, the political systems of the Balkans could be analyzed as so many "mixes" of components inherited from the two great empires, the Habsburg and the Ottoman.

In any such study of the breakdowns of empires and the construction of new states, it was essential to analyze the ties of the emerging polity-building elites to the established centres of the empires and to the political resources these elites could draw on as well as their strategies in coalition formation, both externally and internally. The bourgeoisie and the intelligentsia played crucial roles in the channeling of resources from outside centres to internal ones: the first, through its ties to the international commodity and credit markets; and the second, through its ties with the major centres of cultural and ideological innovation. In Yugoslavia, the tensions between West and East reflected differences in access to external resources: the bourgeoisie of Slovenia and Croatia derived its essential strength from its close links to established networks of trade and industry, while the party intelligentsia and the administration in the national centre could essentially rely on a strong internal coalition.

The empire-nation polarity was also brought out in the paper presented by V. F. KOTOK on "Distinctive Features of the Development of Nations and National Statehood within the U.S.S.R." Kotok called for greater conceptual clarity in the analysis of the historical cases of break-up of empires, formation of states, and building of nations. He underscored the multi-dimensionality of the concept "nation." He considered it essential to base analyses on the definition first suggested by Lenin and later laid down in Stalin's work on *Marxism and the Question of the Colonial Nationalities*. In this definition, the nation was a stable but still transitional historical reality: a community of people characterized by the sharing of a distinctive territory, a language, a common economic network, and a common culture. Using this definition, he reviewed in detail the development of the policies of the Russian Empire towards the nationalities of Asia and the fundamental change brought about through the great October Revolution and through the establishment of autonomous republics, territories, and districts within the resulting federation of socialist republics. In conclusion, he offered the prediction that the nationalities question would increasingly lose in importance in the decades to come, both because of the rapid urbanization and industrialization of the peripheral territories and because of the continued strengthening of the networks of cultural communication throughout the Union.

There was less optimism about developments in Africa, Asia and Latin America. The heritage of the colonial empires still weighed heavily on the national elites and made it difficult not only to build up strong administrative centres within the new territories, but even more to unify the territories culturally and linguistically. There were many cases of polycephality reminiscent of the Spanish and the Yugoslav configurations, but the overriding dimension almost invariably tended to be the continued dependence on outside centres, particularly the metropolitan centres of the old empires. Differences in resource endowments between central and peripheral territories could in fact frequently bring about Katanga-type conflicts in the future. These would take the form of disagreements over the control of transactions over the national boundaries, but in fact reflect differences within the national elites in their access to the international city network and its credit resources. This dimension was of crucial importance in any effort to understand the character of the varieties in state-building processes in Europe, quite particularly between West and East. The "openness-closedness" dimension was in fact a primary variable in the "conceptual map" of Europe as presented in the paper by Stein ROKKAN.

III. The settler continents: North and South America

The discussion of the source of variations within Europe naturally led to a consideration of the consequent differences in the character of the European empires overseas: the British, the French, the Iberian.

Kenneth McRAE analyzed the mixture of empirical inheritances in Canada and compared the slow process of independent institutionalization within the Commonwealth with the revolutionary development in the United States and with the long period of stagnation after the formal liberation of all the Latin American states from their Iberian masters. He developed a comparative perspective on the linguistic conflict in Canada and pointed to the important role of the Catholic church in Quebec in preserving the French cultural community intact within the federal structure. The church had maintained its hold on the French peasant communities by controlling their lines of communication with the federal centre. Once these lines of communication were broadened, the linguistic issue was politicized and brought to the centre of national attention. In Latin America, the church had also helped to preserve and to spread the Iberian languages, but there were no serious competitors. With one or two exceptions, none of the Indian languages was standardized for literary use, and the much greater distances between the political centres made any clashes over national languages highly unlikely.

José SILVA MICHELENA emphasized the economic inheritance of the Iberian empires: the state monopolies in trade, the strict regulation of industries, the growth of a parasitic bourgeoisie without entrepreneurial spirit and with very few ties of loyalty to the territorial regime. Candido MENDES developed this point further in an analysis of the Latin American urban network. By contrast to Canada and the United States, no functional federalism had emerged, even in a continent-sized territory such as Brazil. Most of the Latin American republics were markedly mono-cephalic in structure. Even with several cities in the 500,000+ range (e.g.,

Buenos Aires, Rosario, Cordoba in Argentina), there were typically very few middle-sized and small cities in the range 10,000 to 200,000. This reflected the heritage of parasitism: too great an emphasis on access to external resources, not enough on internal production. This heritage was reinforced through the sharing of the same linguistic culture throughout the continent: the bourgeoisie and the intelligentsia were not tied to any one country through their training and their friendship connections. The linguistic-cultural context did not tie anyone except the poorest and the least mobile to his national regime.

IV. Traditions and innovations in Asia and in Africa

By contrast to North and South America, Asia and Africa were only marginally affected by major European settlements. The only politically significant exceptions are Hong Kong, South Africa, Rhodesia, and part of Portuguese Africa. This obviously affected the potentialities for the formation of viable political units and was clearly reflected in the four papers presented on these areas at the Conference.

Joji WATANUKI and Ramkrishna MUKHERJEE focused on the transformation of empires into effective units of modern mass government. Watanuki dealt with Japan and Korea; Mukherjee, with India and other South Asian cases.

Commenting on these papers, S. N. EISENSTADT brought out the marked contrast between Europe and Asia. At least in Western Europe the disintegration of the Roman Empire had left congeries of small principalities and autonomous city-states that were to form a major counterweight against all efforts of bureaucratic centralization and cultural unification throughout the period of state formation and nation-building. In Asia, the Chinese empire never fell apart completely and successive Indian empires did not fragment far enough to allow the growth of independent city economies before the coming of the British Raj. As a consequence there was no equivalent to the Reformation in Asia, and no extensive standardization of vernaculars into national languages on the scale of the European developments. There is, it is true, a remarkable parallel between Japan and England: both on the margins of a great empire, both taking over elements of script and law from the mother empire, both economically innovative. But the contexts differed fundamentally: there was a multiplicity of competing powers of differing sizes and resource bases in Western Europe, but only one dominant empire in East Asia.

The empire-nation-tribe theme was analyzed from yet another perspective in Abdelkader ZGHAL's paper on the Maghreb. In his view, any serious analysis of the traditional processes of state formation in Arab North Africa would have to take as its point of departure the cyclical theory of the fourteenth century philosopher Ibn Khaldun: the states of the Maghreb never built up a cumulative legacy of legitimate rule and orderly administration, but were caught in a constant cycle running from the conquest of the centre by a peripheral tribe, through the establishment of this tribe in the capital and its progressive disintegration under urban conditions, to the conquest of the centre by the next peripheral tribe. By contrast to Europe, the states of the Maghreb had not been able to build up stable administrative structures. The stronger lineage solidarities had prevented the development of rural contractual structures of the Roman-feudal type and the cities had only rarely been able to establish autonomous institutions similar to those in Europe. The Moslem religion and the Arabic language also prevented the growth of any sense of political identity beyond the tribal level. Before the arrival of the French, there were no stable political divisions within the Maghreb—any combination was possible. The current efforts of nation-building were essentially conditioned by the experience of colonization and liberation: the borders were maintained by the international system and the leaders of the new states had to use whatever means were at their disposal to integrate the populations within these borders. This was a situation fundamentally different from the European: in Europe, most states could build on historically established national loyalties; in the Maghreb, the nations had to be built by the states.

This theme was spelled out in further detail by Yash TANDON in his discussion of the paper submitted by Ali MAZRUI on the three states of East Africa—Kenya, Uganda, and Tanzania. Tandon underscored the extraordinary variety of tribal configurations in the states of tropical Africa and found it impossible to accept any uniform goal of modernization for all these states. In fact, the very notion of modernization was without empirical content in the African context. Mazrui had distinguished five dimensions of nation-building in Africa: the quest for a shared language; the development of markets and other organizations for inter-tribal economic exchange; the promotion of various forms of social solidarity across classes and between elites and masses; the routinization of conflict resolution; and, finally, the build-up of a common national memory through the sharing of emotions, experiences, and symbols. These dimensions do not make up a "modernization" package; they vary independently of each other from one configuration to another. Tanzania had been able to move faster towards linguistic unification and economic integration than Kenya and Uganda, because a configuration of many small tribal units was easier to consolidate than a structure of two or three larger units competing for dominance. There were differences in the cost of alternative strategies, but no predetermined outcome. Many of the parameters of each territorial situation were set by the external international system, but there was still a great deal of leeway for active choice and innovative leadership. In many ways this could be seen as an advantage for the newer states: they were less "stuck" in history and could, given favourable circumstances, develop innovative structures so far never tried in the history of polity-building.

V. Strategies of comparative research: model construction and data resource development

The UNESCO Conference registered a wide variety of complaints about current academic effort to study processes of nation-building comparatively: there were too many divergent models, they were too abstract, too difficult to translate into specific requirements for empirical indicators, there was no serious effort to marshall the data series that would be needed to test any of the models even if they were to be made precise enough. Carl-Göran ANDRAE and Jerome CLUBB reported on efforts to build up archives for historical time series data for two countries. Sweden and the United States; but these papers only helped to underscore the enormity of the gap between theory construction and serious comparative research. There was consensus that these problems would have to be dealt with much more systematically in a separate conference with a wider range of papers on the many sets of possible indicators. The UNESCO Conference at Cérisy simply could not have covered all this ground within the time allocated to it. It had stimulated exciting debates on problems of fundamental importance for the future of the Third World, but there was still a vast agenda of unfinished items.

To some of the participants, the conference in fact ended on a note a despair—that there are too many urgent and pressing problems and we had not made any headway toward solving them. To others, the conference simply helped to clarify priorities for further work. To quote the concluding statement of one of the organizers:

The scheme we worked out for this Conference was clearly over-ambitious. We have not covered anywhere near all the variations in state-building histories and we are as disagreed as ever on the possibilities of developing a general theoretical structure for comparisons across all regions of the world. The general theory of development first outlined within the ALMOND-PYE Committee on Comparative Politics has come under heavy attack at our meeting and so have the various alternative formulations of the criteria and the phases of modernization. Our

friends from the Third World have almost unanimously rejected these formulations as parodical products of Western ethnocentrism and have expressed their
misgivings towards all attempts at generalization generated from these fragments
of theory. We have also had a vigorous debate on the moral and the political
definition of the goals of development. What sort of models has the West to offer
to the non-West and which ones are worth considering: the unicultural
nation-state, the multicultural federation, the consociational state, the open
city-state structure of capitalism or the closed autarchic system of some variants
of socialism? Here again we seem to have reached an impasse: some of our friends
from the Third World stress the need for a depluralization as a condition for
territorial consolidation; others stress the importance of developing new concepts
of political community-building, better fitted to the multicultural realities of the
Third World.

On reflection, I believe that these ambiguities and resistances are positive and
potentially innovative. We must not rest satisfied with the formulations that had
grown out of our Western experience. It is high time we urge our friends from the
Third World to develop their own theories and to apply them to the variations
they can observe in the West as well as elsewhere. We must help to spread
entrepreneurship in theory-building. We must be willing to evaluate and test
highly divergent theoretical formulations. This is in fact the rationale for the
programme worked out by the Social Sciences Department in UNESCO. We want
to follow up this cross-regional conference at Cérisy by a series of *region-specific
conferences:* one such has already been planned for Asia, another may take place
in Latin America within the next two or three years. In these conferences we do
not only want to study the within-region variations in nation-building experiences
and strategies, we also hope to encourage fresh theory formulations from the
perspective of each Third World region. We must encourage a "shuttle service"
between efforts of globalization and efforts of regional specification. One
approach worthy of serious consideration is by *pairs of regions:* Asia compared
with Africa, Latin America with North America and so on. What is important is
that we ensure continuity in these scholarly efforts, that we keep up the pressure
to break down the barriers between national and regional traditions of
scholarship. We may have taken on too heavy a task at this one conference, but
there is no reason to feel despondent about the results. We may not have reached
consensus on any line of generalization but we have stimulated fresh thinking
about a number of important issues in comparative political theory, issues of
direct importance to academics, statesmen, and political leaders throughout the
Third World.

NOTES

1. See S. Rokkan, ed., Comparative Research Across Cultures and Nations, Paris,
Mouton, 1968.
2. A report was first published in Social Science Information, Vol. 8, No. 1, pp.
85-99.
3. The participants were: Erik Allardt, Sociology, University of Helsinki, Finland;
Carl-Göran Andrae, History, University of Uppsala, Sweden; Pär-Erik Back, Political
Science, University of Umeá, Sweden; Hans Daalder, Political Science, University of

Leiden, Netherlands; Edmund Dahlström, Sociology, University of Gothenburg, Sweden; S. N. Eisenstadt, Sociology, Hebrew University, Israel; Herbert Kelman, Social Psychology, University of Michigan, U.S.A.; Rajni Kothari, Political Science, Center for the Study of Developing Societies, Delhi, India; Val Lorwin, History, University of Oregon, U.S.A.; Warren Miller, Political Science, University of Michigan, U.S.A.; Birgitta Odén, History, University of Lund, Sweden; Francis Olu, Okediji, Sociology, University of Ibadan, Nigeria; Stein Rokkan, Sociology, University of Bergen, Norway; Paavo Seppänen, Sociology, University of Tampere, Finland; Miroslav Soukup, Czechoslovak Academy of Sciences, Czechoslovakia; Jürg Steiner, Thun, Switzerland; Torcuato Di Tella, Unesco Centre, Rio de Janeiro, Brazil; Ulf Torgersen, University of Oslo, Norway; and Abdelkader Zghal, Centre d'Etudes et de Recherches Economiques et Sociales, Tunisia.

Unesco was represented by Witold Zyss, and the International Social Science Council by Clemens Heller.

4. J. P. Nettl, "The state as a conceptual variable," World Politics, Vol. 20, No. 4, 1968, pp. 559-92.

5. A Lijphart, "Typologies of Democratic Systems," Comparative Political Studies, Vol. 1, No. 1, April 1968, pp. 3-4.

6. B. Moore, Jr., Social Origins of Dictatorship and Democracy: Lord and Peasant in the Making of the Modern World, Boston, Beacon, 1966.

7. A summary report, "State Formation and Nation Building," was published in the Unesco Chronicle, Vol. 17, No. 10, October 1971, pp. 347-54.

8. The participants were: Gabriel Almond, Political Science, Stanford University, U.S.A.; Carl-Göran Andrae, History, University of Uppsala, Sweden; Hanna Bogor-Szego, Hungarian Academy of Sciences, Budapest, Hungary; Jerome Clubb, Inter-University Consortium, University of Michigan, U.S.A.; Hans Daalder, Political Science, University of Leiden, Netherlands; S. N. Eisenstadt, Sociology, Hebrew University, Israel; Rajni Kothari, Centre for the Study of Developing Societies, Delhi, India; V. F. Kotok, Soviet Academy of Sciences, U.S.S.R.; J. W. Lapierre, University of Nice, France; Juan Linz, Sociology and Political Science, Yale University, U.S.A.; Kenneth McRae, Political Science, Carleton University, Canada; Candido Mendes, Brazilian Research Society, Brazil; Warren Miller, Center for Political Research, University of Michigan, U.S.A.; R. K. Mukherjee, Indian Statistical Institute, India; Najdan Pašić, Political Science, University of Belgrade, Yugoslavia; S. Rokkan, Sociology, University of Bergen, Norway; D. L. Sheth, Centre for the Study of Developing Societies, Delhi, India; José Silva Michelena, CENDES, University of Venezuela, Caracas, Venezuela; Yash Tandon, Political Science, Makerere University College, Uganda; Charles Tilly, Sociology, University of Michigan, U.S.A.; Joji Watanuki, Sociology, University of Tokyo, Japan; Abdelkader Zghal, Centre d'Etudes et de Recherches Economiques et Sociales, University of Tunis, Tunisia.

The Department of Social Sciences was represented at the meeting by Dr. Marie-Anne de Franz and Dr. T. Ushida, and the International Social Science Council by the Secretary-General, Dr. Samy Friedman.

9. See International Social Science Journal, Vol. XXIII, No. 3, 1971, pp. 371-83.

I.

CONCEPTS AND MODELS IN THE COMPARATIVE
STUDY OF NATIONAL DEVELOPMENT

CHAPTER I.

VARIETIES OF POLITICAL DEVELOPMENT:
THE THEORETICAL CHALLENGE

S. N. Eisenstadt

S. N. EISENSTADT is Professor of Sociology at the Hebrew University in Jerusalem and has been Visiting Professor at Harvard, M.I.T., and Chicago. He is the author of major works in the field of comparative political development, including *The Political Systems of Empires* and *Modernization: Protest and Change.* He has also edited a number of important collections of contributions to comparative analysis such as *The Protestant Ethic and Modernization* and the large volume of readings in *Political Sociology.*

The discussions at the Cérisy Conference forced a serious reconsideration of the notion of "modernization" and of the theories of change and development centering on modernization concepts. In this introductory chapter I shall try to analyze the difficulties with the early models of modernization and development and to suggest possible new avenues for comparative research on processes of change in political systems.

PART I: PROBLEMS AND CONTROVERSIES IN THE
COMPARATIVE STUDY OF MODERNIZATION.

To what degree is it possible to account for the extraordinary variety of changes in the structure of contemporary societies and polities within one single conceptual framework? The optimism of the fifties has given way to a great deal of scepticism, both about the content of the concept of modernization and about the underlying model of sequential change. The basic assumption of most early modernization studies was that the process would keep going once some initial threshold was reached: once a society had reached some given level of structural differentiation, there was a high probability that it would be able to develop continuously and to cope successfully with change. But the accumulating experience of political processes in the new states of the Third World tended to undermine such notions of unilinear step-by-step development. Quite particularly, there was mounting evidence that the underlying assumption about the consequences of a break with established tradition simply did not fit the facts; it became impossible to maintain that the mere destruction of inherited institutions would necessarily guarantee the development of a new, viable, modern society. To the contrary, very often the mere disruption of traditional settings—be they family, community, or even political settings—tended to lead to disorganization, delinquency, and chaos rather than to the establishment of a viable modern order.

In addition, political scientists realized that in some countries modernization had begun successfully under the aegis of traditional symbols and even traditional elites; many traditional symbols, such as the Crown and the aristocracy in Britain or the traditional symbols of provincial life in the Netherlands, were retained. Even in the many cases in which the initial impetus to modernize was provided by antitraditional elites, these elites tried very soon, if haltingly, to revive the more traditional aspects and symbols of society.[1]

Political scientists also renewed their awareness, albeit dimly at first, rather of the possibility of contradictions between different qualitative aspects of modern life—especially between "rationality" on the one hand, and liberty, justice, or solidarity on the other; they recognized the possibility that traditional societies, by virtue of their traditionality, might be better able to nurture these qualities than modern societies.

Early Criticisms of the Modernization Model

Beyond such general indications of the inadequacy of the overall initial approach toward the process of modernization, several more specific findings indicate that the concrete empirical relations postulated by the initial paradigm of modernization were incorrect.

Research showed that although some minimal development of various socio-demographic and structural indices was necessary for the development of any modern structure, further extension of these indices did not necessarily assure the continued processes of modernization or the creation of viable political or social structures—capable of sustained growth, of dealing with continuously new social, economic, and political problems, or of extending the realms of liberty or rationality.

Thus, in many cases—e.g., several countries in Central and Eastern Europe, Latin America, and Asia—a negative correlation at certain levels seemed to have come about between a high degree of development of various socio-demographic indices, such as the degree of literacy, spread of mass media, formal education, or urbanization, and the institutional ability to sustain growth or to develop libertarian or rational institutions and orientations.

Even more paradoxical were the somewhat later findings that in some cases, in India, for example, a relatively low level of social mobilization and a different sequence of mobilization—especially the greater development of education and mass media as opposed to urbanization and industrialization—were not only compatible with the evolution of a relatively viable modern political entity but might have even contributed to it.

Additional evidence indicated that the prerequisites for development of a relatively high degree of urbanization and industrialization could vary in different contexts; the process need not always follow the European pattern that seemingly had served as the basis of many of the first formulations about such prerequisites.[2]

All of these considerations have contributed to undermining the assumed assurances of growth continuity after the "take-off." In both the economic and the political spheres, it became quite obvious that no such assurances existed.

Criticisms of Conceptions of Transitional Societies and the Problem of Historical Continuity

Recognition of the ambiguities in the concepts about transitional societies and evidence of modernization "breakdowns" followed. These concepts were developed in a modernization studies framework when it first became apparent that many of the usual assumptions in the modernization studies were not upheld in reality.

It became clearer that such breakdowns or stagnations did not necessarily bring about a total collapse of these new regimes or their retreat to some traditional social and political form. These new polities and societies certainly differed in many ways from the "older" (Western) modern ones, and they did not even necessarily develop in the direction of these older ones; yet by no means were they still simply traditional societies. They evinced some capability of reorganization and continuity and developed various internal and external policies that aimed at assuring for themselves the conditions of such continuity, even though not necessarily connected with far-reaching institutional building or with a very active positive attitude to change.

Thus, one of the most important considerations in this context was the growing recognition of what may be called the systemic viability of the so-called transitional systems. This recognition was first most clearly represented in the writings of Fred Riggs, especially in his work on the Sala model (primarily based on his studies of the Philippines and Thailand).[3] In his work Riggs attempted to show how, under the impact of Western modernization forces, a traditional system tends to develop into a new type of social or political system; such a new system, often described as transitional, develops systemic characteristics and properties of its own, creating its own mechanism of stability and self-perpetuation.

These considerations have added a new dimension to the understanding of the variability of modern and modernizing societies. They have led to a growing recognition that societies may develop in many directions and do not necessarily approach some given "end-stage" as envisaged by the initial model of modernization. The result has been increased awareness of the importance of tradition and historical continuities in shaping the directions of change.

Even in the first stages of research on modernization researchers realized that some of the differences between the concrete structural and symbolic contours of different modern societies might be related to different historical traditions, and initially, continuity was perceived in terms of persistence of broad cultural orientations. This approach was very often related to or derived from the "culture and personality" school; it paid relatively little attention to the structural aspects of modern societies.[4] The further development of such research concepts by Almond, Verba, and other members of the SSRC Committee on Comparative Politics provided a very important link between cultural orientations and the more specifically structural aspects of behavior.[5] Later on, recognition grew of the fact that such differences may also persist in some crucial structural areas, such as the rules of the political game or the various aspects of social hierarchy, and that these variations might be influenced by the historical traditions of these societies and might also evince a very large degree of continuity with these traditions.

Perhaps one of the most important—albeit somewhat recent—developments in this context was the growth of the "patrimonialism" concept to describe the political regimes of several new states.[6] The use of the term "patrimonial" to describe these various regimes implied a reaction to the inadequacies of both the central assumptions of the major modernization studies, and the later concepts like "breakdown," "political decay," or "transitional" societies. It emphasized the inadequacy of these assumptions by showing first, that many of these societies and states did not develop in the direction of the advanced nation-states; second, that these regimes were not necessarily in a temporary, transitional phase along an inevitable path to this type of modernity; third, that there was yet some internal "logic" in their development; and last, that at least part of this logic or pattern could be understood from and derived from some aspects of the traditions of these societies.

Criticism of the Dichotomy Between Traditional and Modern Societies and the Ahistoricity Critique

From these internal ambiguities and uncertainties about the nitial model of modernization there developed—beginning in the late 1950s, but gathering special momentum from the mid-sixties on—a series of researches dealing with problems of modernization and developing societies. These research efforts resulted from growing criticisms of initial modernization theories, criticisms that have gradually undermined most of the assumptions of the initial model.

Criticisms came from a great variety of vantage points, but they focused around several basic themes. They touched not only on the concrete problem of development and modernization, but also on some very central problems of sociological analysis. Behind much of the debate, there also loomed clear political-ideological differences, sometimes forcefully expressed.

One critical theme focused on some of the basic "contents" of the initial modernization studies model, especially on the validity of the tradition-modernity dichotomy and the supposed ahistoricity and Western -centeredness of this paradigmatic model—the combination of which might, surprisingly, give rise to strong historicist overtones and implications. Other criticisms were aimed at some of the basic theoretical and analytical assumptions of the model—especially of its "developmental" and evolutionary assumptions on the one hand and its "functional-structural" systematic assumptions on the other.

The dichotomy of traditional versus modern society—as it was presented in the original paradigm of modernization studies—was undermined in several critical areas.

First, it was recognized that even if traditional societies were typologically different from modern ones, they might vary greatly in the degree to which their traditions impeded or facilitated the transition to modernity—thus necessitating a more analytical distinction between different types of elements of traditions.

Second, with emphasis on the distinction between tradition and traditionalism, a concept initially developed by Shils, Hoselitz, and Spengler among others, traditionalism was defined as the more extremist, negative reaction to the impingement of forces of modernity, and tradition was denoted as the general reservoir of behavior and of symbols of a society.[7]

Third, the persistence in modern or modernizing societies of strong traditions—binding ways of behavior rooted in the past and, to some degree, referring to the past—was "rediscovered." Of special importance here was recognition of the great impact exerted by some traditional forces or symbols on some of the most modern types of activities, such as scientific and technological endeavors.[8]

Fourth, and closely connected with the third area, several scholars emphasized—whether in several works of Singer on India or in some of the analyses by the Rudolphs—how traditional forces or groups, be they castes or tribal units, tended to reorganize themselves in new, modern settings in very effective ways.[9]

Fifth, scholars began to note that after the initial phases of independence within many of the new states whose politics were greatly shaped by "Western-ideological" political models, there emerged a new phase in which older, traditional political modes or models tended to assert themselves.[10]

Sixth, partial modernization or development—i.e., development of some institutional or organizational frameworks sharing many characteristics of modern organization—might take place in segregated parts of a still traditional social structure; and such development need not necessarily give rise to an overall change in the direction of modernity, but might even reinforce traditional systems by the infusion of new forms of organization.[11]

The alleged ahistoricity of the modernization model comes from two distinct groups of critics. One stressed evaluation of contemporary developments in various societies in terms of their "unfolding" of inherent traditional forces, rather than in terms of their alleged movement toward a seemingly fixed end-stage of development. The other, and, in a sense, opposite direction of such criticisms tended to stress the specific, unique, historical experience and setting of what has been called the process of modernization. This approach emphasized that the modernization process is not a universal one in which all societies tend naturally to participate or which is inherent in the nature of the development of every society; rather, it represents a unique historical situation connected with the various aspects of European expansion. Hence, its basic characteristics are not universal, but are closely tied to this specific historical situation. This last criticism appeared in two different, yet closely related, guises. One—perhaps best exemplified in the work of Bendix and of Riggs—argued that "modernization" does not display any definite universal systemic, symbolic, and/or structural characteristics; it is basically a specific one-time historical process consisting of the spread of the impact of Western culture throughout the world and the attempts of late-comers to emulate and to catch up with these first models of industrialization, of political unification, and the like.[12]

This second trend is probably best represented in many of the recent Marxist writings on the subject. These works claim that the abstract-analytical categories used in modernization studies and the broad, general distinctions between traditional and modern societies tend to lose sight of the historical setting of the processes they study—specifically, that the processes are part of the expansion of capitalism and of the consequent establishment of a new international system composed of hegemonic and dependent societies.[13]

According to partisans of this approach, the core of the differences between modern and traditional or developed and underdeveloped societies lies in various relations of imperialism and colonialism, of exploitation and "dependency," which stem from the Western capitalistic expansion and which have shaped the very contours of the patterns of development of these societies. The patterns cannot, therefore, be measured according to some seemingly universal characteristics or indices derived from the features of the dominant, hegemonic societies.[14]

The Western-Centricity Critique

Most of the studies that stress the ahistoricity of the model of modernization also tend usually, albeit in different ways, to accuse it of Western-centricity. While many such critics accept Western predominance as the basic factor that determined the structure of the development process, they deny the validity of the Western model as the natural model or the ultimate stage of development toward which all societies will go.

Instead, many critical studies stress the potentiality or possibility of alternative models that may develop according to possibilities inherent both in the traditions of these societies and in changing international constellations, thus emphasizing strongly the themes of the internal viability and developmental autonomy of transitional societies that we have encountered above.[15]

The various criticisms of the combined ahistoricity and Western-centricity of this model, and hence also of its historians, have been most succinctly stated by Ernest Gellner, who pointed out one of the gravest defects of the "once-only, European-parochial, perpetual-progress" way of interpreting transition to modernity. Gellner argues that this approach tends to fuse and confuse several distinct sets of features, such as characteristics specific to the *first* such transition, those specific to the *European* transition, characteristics of *any* transition, and characteristics of a *completed* transition to modernity.[16] Following Gellner, many theorists have also often claimed that the situation of dependency, into which most of these societies were placed by the forces of Western imperialism, has stifled and/or diverted and distorted their material potentials of development.

The Critique of Sociological Assumptions

These criticisms of modernization theory were aimed directly or indirectly at the basic theoretical and analytical assumptions of the modernization model—especially at its systemic and structural-functional, developmental and evolutionary premises.

There were three such major criticisms: One denied the closed systemic interrelations among different aspects of a society, the assumption of the necessary convergence of development or modernization in all institutional spheres of society, and the closely related assumption of universal prerequisites of modernization or development in each such sphere. The second major critical theme—closely related to the allegation of historical closure and Western-centricity—held that the seemingly contentless definition of systemic capacity and growth is in reality bound by the specific premises of the Western-centered model, and does not take into account the variety of other possibilities of systemic expansion between conflicting goals. The third strand assailed the neglect of external factors—especially those concerning international relations, inequality, and dependence between societies.

PART II: PRELIMINARY RECONSTRUCTION OF THE ASSUMPTIONS AND VISION OF MODERNIZATION

As all of these reappraisals have obviously touched on some of the basic assumptions of the initial studies of modernization, it was but natural that many of the scholars who have developed these critical themes and several of the new approaches to the study of contemporary societies, claimed that these criticisms have invalidated the distinction between traditional and modern societies. In order to understand these societies in their contemporary settings, they assert that we must look at each one in terms of its own history and traditions—or in terms of the unique historical international situation.

The evidence presented in the numerous chapters of this work indeed enables us to explore a much more differentiated approach to these problems. This evidence shows first that the differences between societies in traditional and in modern settings, which were often stressed in the initial studies of modernization, are indeed of crucial importance for the understanding of their workings—even if we now define these differences in somewhat different and more sophisticated ways. Second, these differences between traditional and modern societies do coincide or impinge on some of those aspects of social organization where the influence of traditional continuities is most forceful. And third, what may often seem to be the epitome of a traditional society—for instance, ancient symbols of collective identity—are not simple vestiges from the past, but sometimes represent new social, political, and cultural constructs that have developed in response to the exigencies and challenges of the new situation. In the shaping of these responses, various internal and international forces may indeed be of great importance.

Demand-Making for European Social Structures

Thus, the evidence accumulated by different case studies of modernization, and so fully presented in the various chapters of this book, points out that the differences between traditional and modern settings of a given society lie, first of all, in a series of rather concrete problems and organizational features developing within these societies. One can be found in the nature of the problems facing different groups in the society, and in the demands made on their respective centers.

Modern societies, as contrasted with the more traditional systems, have been continuously facing the crucial test of the ability of their central frameworks to "expand." The demands for such expansion could develop in several different, but closely connected and interrelated directions. First, there were the aspirations—mostly of the elites—for the creation or maintenance of new, wider, political frameworks. Second, there were the aspirations or demands for economic and/or administrative development or modernization. Third, the center was asked to respond to new types of demands by various new social groups—especially for the elaboration of new principles of distribution. Fourth, there were the demands of these groups in general, and of various new elites in particular, for incorporation into the center of redefined boundaries and collective symbols, as well as for more active participation in the political process and more direct access to the center.

While the concrete contents of such demands varied greatly according to the various structural conditions (such as urbanization or agrarian change, educational expansion, and the like), still there always tended to develop some more general pattern of demand-making, which is in a sense specific to the modern situations.

The sheer increase in the quantity of such demands was closely related to the potential increase of accessible resources. These demands often took the form of relatively widespread pressure on educational channels of access to bureaucratic or political positions by the wider range of the groups and strata that tended to become politically articulate thereby.

However, the pattern was evidenced not only by a quantitative difference in the level of demand-making. Broader groups tended to make not only segregated demands for concrete benefits based on membership in different ascriptive, closed subcollectivities, but also for access to the center by virtue of membership in the collectivity. These particularistic demands on the center—be they agrarian problems, problems of urbanization, or the rise of new occupational categories—tended to become connected with demands in the symbolic sphere derived from the participatory and consensual orientations inherent in the very premises of modernity. That is, the demands of special interest groups were often translated into generalized themes of protest and thereby into the broader political processes—thus impinging on the very centers of the social and political order. It was around such various demands and around the center's responses to them that some of the major possibilities of conflict, cleavage, and crisis, which could undermine any given regime, tended to develop in these societies.

Organizational Structures

It is not only that the social, political, and economic problems vary between the traditional and modern settings of these societies; the same is true of the organizational structures and resources that develop in these settings to be used by different groups or individuals in coping with such problems. Thus, as has been so often shown in the literature, traditional settings are characterized by relatively less differentiated and specialized organizational structures, while the modern ones are characterized by more differentiated organizational forms of political life, such as bureaucracies, parties, or popular movements, which can be used by the rulers and broader strata of the society alike in order to cope with these problems.

Above all, modern societies and polities are usually characterized by a wider scope and wider boundaries of the political community, which have usually been created by differentially enterprising political and cultural elites.

Thus, within the socio-political sphere, the distinction between a traditional and a modern political or cultural order lies in the extent to which some basic symbolic and cultural premises—with their structural and cultural limitations—are or are not maintained on the central levels of the political and cultural orders. The most important among these premises are the continuing symbolic and cultural differentiation between the center and periphery, and the concomitant limitation on the access of members of broader groups to the political center or centers and on participation within them.

In the cultural sphere, the basic premise common to all traditional societies, however great the difference between them, has been the acceptance of some past event, order, or figure (whether real or symbolic) as the major focus of their collective identity, as the scope and nature of their social and cultural order, as the ultimate legitimizer of change, and as the delineator of the limits of innovation.

The most important structural derivatives of this premise are official, normative limitations on (a) change and innovation; and (b) access to central positions, the incumbents being the only legitimate interpreters of the scope allowed by traditions. These premises were, in traditional regimes, in turn closely connected first with the fact that legitimation of the rulers was couched in basically traditional religious terms. Second, the basic political role of the subject was relatively indistinguishable from his other societal roles, such as, for instance, membership in local kinships or "status" communities. That is, citizens or subjects did not exercise any actual direct or symbolic political rights through a system of voting or franchise.

Different traditional societies did, of course, vary greatly with respect to various aspects of legitimation, as well as with respect to the ways in which they viewed their past—whether, for instance, in mythological, historical, or revelational terms. Whatever these differences, they tend to share the symbolic and structural derivatives or tradition mentioned above.

It is then insofar as such changes in the connotation of tradition on central levels have taken place that we witness the breakthrough, that may be gradual or abrupt, to some sort of modern, or rather post-traditional, socio-political order. The crux of such a breakthrough to modernity lies in the weakening of these normative limitations on the symbolic content of the center: in the legitimate interpretation of past and current events, in the secularization of authority, in the growing emphasis on values of human dignity and social equality, as well as in the growing demands for and possibilities of participation—even if in an intermittent or partial way—of broader groups in the formulation of the society's central symbols and institutions.

Similarities and Differences in Post-Traditional Societies

Many of these differences between traditional and modern social and cultural orders have, of course, been stressed in the initial literature on modernization, yet unlike the classical paradigms of modernization, it is by now clear that development or modernization does not constitute a unilinear demographic, social, economic, or political process that leads—even if haltingly—to some plateau whose basic contours—whatever the differences in detail—will be everywhere the same. Rather, modernization has to be seen as a process or a series of processes with a common core, generating common or similar problems.

These processes of growing differentiation, social mobilization, and breakdown are unparalleled in the history of human societies; they pose, for the societies and groups on which they impinge, certain basic problems of (a) regulating the various continuously developing and newly emerging groups, and mediating the necessarily increasing conflicts that develop among them; (b) integrating these groups within some common institutional framework; and (c) developing some new foci of collective national identity in which tradition, modernity, and change are to some extent combined. But the most common and crucial problem attendant on modernization—in which all these orders tend to merge—is that of developing and maintaining an institutional structure capable of absorbing changes beyond its own initial premises and of dealing with continuously new and changing problems.

Although these processes of change and development and the problems which they tend to raise have some common cores, the structural and cultural conditions under which they arise, and the responses to them, may vary greatly among different societies. These differing conditions and responses are evident not only with regard to the degree of social mobilization and structural differentiation that develop within each of them, but also with regard to symbolic and institutional responses to the impact of modernity.

Above all, these differences are apparent in the various ways in which post-traditional societies coped with the major problems impinging on them; the very basic parameters of modernity or of post-traditionality; the conceptions of the cultural and social orders; the degree of commitment to participate in their formation; the relative autonomy of the individual vis-à-vis these orders; and the relative autonomy of the social, cultural, and political orders. Variations also developed with regard to their systems of stratification—both in the degree of class cleavages and conflicts and in the very conception of social hierarchy, in the attributes according to which different groups and people are evaluated, or in the degree to which conflict is seen as a basic ingredient of such hierarchy.

These differences also tended to arise from the ways in which societies developed modern traditions in their self-conception and historiography, and in the ways in which the parameters of these traditions may be related to the extension of participation, liberty, or justice. Needless to say, such differences all greatly affect the whole process of building the new, post-traditional social, political, and cultural orders.

PART III: CONDITIONS INFLUENCING THE VARIABILITY OF POST-TRADITIONAL SOCIETIES

The symbolic and organizational patterns of different modern or modernizing societies are influenced by many different conditions. Among those of special importance seem to be the following: the level of resources available for mobilization and institution-building, the pattern of impingement of forces of modernity on the respective society, the structure of the situation of change in which they were caught, the different traditions of these societies or civilizations and their premodern socio-economic structures, and the perception by different elites of the possibilities of choice in given historical situations and their ability to implement such choices.

The development of post-traditional orders is often greatly influenced by the ways in which the forces of modernity impinge on these societies. Such a transition or breakthrough to modernity may take place under a variety of conditions. First of all, it may take place under different structural conditions, i.e., in societies with different degress of structural differentiation; and it may greatly vary with respect to the basic institutional spheres on which these forces impinge—the economic and political spheres or those of social organization and stratification, on the center or on the periphery. The transition may also take place in societies whose groups and elites evince different degrees of adaptability or resistance to change, of erosion of wider normative commitments, and of transformative capacities, as well as societies where the new centers evince different degrees or kinds of strength or weakness.

The second broad set of conditions that tend to influence the development of post-traditional socio-political orders are some structural changes created by these impinging forces of modernity. Of special importance seems to be the relative tempo of modernization processes. Thus, for instance, it has been shown that the general tempo of modernization tends greatly to influence its smooth progress. On the whole, the slower the tempo, the smoother the process of modernization because, other conditions being equal, the greater is the ability of the institutional structure to deal with the attendant problems. It has also been shown that the temporal spread of modernization over different institutional spheres usually facilitates the smooth progress of modernization; while the temporal convergence of modernization in several institutional spheres may undermine, through the accumulation of problems and tensions, such a smooth process.[17]

Of great importance here is the structure of the international setting in which the process of modernization takes place, the distribution of political and economic power among the various societies and strata, and the types and processes of dominance and dependence which tend to develop among them.

Last are the broad differences in the antecedent traditional political structure and order. Here indeed many differences from the original European pattern can be discerned, especially, but not only, with regard to their socio-political tradition. Given the great stress on the importance of tradition in recent studies of modernization, it might be worthwhile to dwell in somewhat greater detail on some ways in which the forces of tradition were found to influence the process of modernization, and on the crystallization of different patterns of post-traditional orders.

Impact of Traditional Forces

The importance of forces of tradition became more and more apparent in some of the strikingly similar ways in which central institutions regulated problems in the political sphere and those in the field of social stratification. The "same" societies in their traditional and modern phases handled these problems in parallel fashion, although different traditional and modern societies differed among themselves.

Within the political sphere the most important aspect of continuity involved the nature of political decision centers and innovation. Second in importance were the types of center-periphery relations prevalent within the society; third, the relative emphasis, by the rulers or elites, on different types of center activities; fourth, the types of policies developed by the rulers; and fifth, some aspects of political struggle and organization.

Within the field of stratification, the most important continuities have been the attributes emphasized as constituting the basis of societal evaluation and hierarchy; second, the degree of status autonomy of different groups irrespective of their access to centers of the society; and finally, the degree of broader status association—as against status segregation—of relatively close occupational and professional groups.

We shall briefly and cursorily illustrate such similarities or continuities of social and political organization in "traditional" and "modern" Western European, Russian, and "patrimonial" (especially Southeast Asian) societies in different (traditional and modern) periods of their respective histories.

The Western European Case

Western Europe encompasses, as is so well known, a relatively high number of pluralistic political decision-making centers and innovation sources, localized in varying combinations of executive and legislative organs and articulated by relatively independent political leaders who absorb the impulses for change from various social groups and who mobilize wider support for various goals and policies. In traditional European political systems, these leaders were mostly the rulers, aristocrats, and representatives of other strata, working in different combination, in executive and consultative bodies and in some independent organs of social and political power. In modern systems, the major loci of political decision-making and of institutionalization of political changes and innovations have usually been the legislature, in the executive acting with the legislature, and also in the bureaucracy.[18]

Neither the increasingly important mass parties nor the bureaucracies have monopolized the arena of political discussion, innovation, and decision-making. Executive and legislative organs continue to maintain some of their—at least symbolic—positions of control by serving as the main framework for independent public opinion and leadership, and as the main target areas in which political innovation became institutionalized.

In the sphere of center-periphery relations, these societies have also been continuously characterized by a high degree of commitment to common ideals or goals. The center has successfully permeated the periphery in attempts to mobilize support for the policies of the center, and at the same time the relatively autonomous forces of the periphery have continuously impinged on the center. Accordingly, both traditional leaders (the absolutist and estate-based rulers of Western Europe) as well as the leaders of modern "nation-states" have emphasized the active forging out of new common symbols of cultural and political identity, of collective political goals, and regulation of the relations between different, relatively independent, groups. Similarly, a continuity developed in the pattern of policies which were not only distributive or allocative, but also promotive—i.e., oriented to the creation or promotion of new types of activities and structures or toward providing facilities for the implementation of new goals expressed autonomously by various strata.

All these aspects of political systems were closely connected with emerging patterns of political organization and struggle, characterized in Western Europe by the development of relatively autonomous political groups, such as parties and organs of public opinion, with highly autonomous political goals. These goals were not limited to the struggle for access to goods and the resources of the center, but often involved attempts to influence the very values and structure of the centers—thus proclaiming the autonomy of broader groups as the bearers of those values and attributes which the center claimed to represent. The roots of this tendency are to be found in the awakening possibility of political participation or representation of most groups in the center by virtue of their collective identities. Hence, this growing countrywide "consciousness" was confined not only to the higher groups, but could also be found among the middle or lowest strata.

Unlike the Russian case, there tended to develop a close relationship between family and kinship identity on the one hand, and collective-strata identity on the other. Family and kinship groups constituted very important channels, not only for ideological orientation to high positions, but also for ascriptive transmission of such positions. However, the degree of access of different groups or strata to the center was not ascriptively fixed, but constituted a continuous bone of contention in what one could call "strata-conflict"—i.e., conflict between different strata about their relative prestige standing in general, and about the scope of their participation in the center in particular. Finally—again, very much unlike the Russian case—each such stratum and especially the "middle" ones (but sometimes also the aristocracy) tended to encompass a great variety of occupational positions and organizations, and to link them in some common way of life and in common avenues of access to the center, resulting in broader status association as against relatively narrow status segregation.

The Russian Case

A rather different pattern of organization of the political sphere is that of social stratification in traditional (autocratic) and modern (communist, revolutionary) Russia. This pattern again evinces some crucial continuities across these periods, while at the same time differing markedly from Western European continuities.

In the traditional tsarist setting and in Soviet Russia as well, the executive has predominated over various other organs of political organization, and political innovation has been monopolized by the political elite. The major medium of political innovation and decision-making in the traditional setting was the monarchy and to some degree the upper bureaucracy. In the modern context, the party leadership and to some extent the bureaucracy have held sway, with the legislature performing mainly ritual functions, and the executive (as distinct from the monarchy or party leadership), although important in several aspects, plays mainly only a secondary, routine role.

Similarly center-periphery relations evince here a marked similarity or continuity mainly characterized by a relatively high degree of permeation of the periphery by the center in order to mobilize resources from it and to control its broader, society-wide activities. Especially in the modern revolutionary setting, there have been attempts to mobilize commitment to the goals of the center, but these have been overshadowed at the same time by strict coercive control of the attempts of the periphery to impinge on the center.

We find here also a marked continuity in the relative emphasis by the center on different types of activities—mainly a very strong emphasis, as in Western Europe, on the formation of political and cultural identity and collective goals, but a much higher degree of emphasis on monopolization of force by the center and a much smaller emphasis on the upholding of the internal regulative activities of various groups. Similarly, the policies developed by the traditional and modern Russian centers alike have been mainly regulative and coercively promotive ones, with but little allowance for the autonomous expression of the goals of broader groups.

The pattern of political struggle and organization also evinces a close continuity in different periods of Russian history—and a marked difference, in all these periods, from those patterns prevalent in Western Europe. The Russian model has been characterized on the one hand by a relatively high degree of organized political activity directed by the center, which also used its organs to sound out possible demands on it and to mobilize potential political activities, but at the same time permitting only minimal expression of autonomous demands or activities. On the other hand, these manifestations of tight central control have alternated with extremist political, ideological, and religious rebellious movements.

Continuity can also be found in Russia—in traditional tsarist and modern Soviet Russia alike—with regard to several basic aspects of social stratification. First of all, we note a great similarity in the nature of the dominant attributes. Closely related to this feature is the fact that the elites of these societies tended to encourage the segregation of the lifestyles and participation patterns of different local, occupational, and territorial kinship groups. These elites attempted to minimize the "status" or "class" components of family or kinship group identity and the autonomous standing of the family in the status system.

Similarly, the elites of tsarist and Soviet Russia alike attempted to establish a uniform hierarchy of major positions—especially with regard to the access to the center. They aimed also at making this hierarchy a relatively steep one: within the center, between it and the periphery, and to some degree also among the peripheral groups. They also tended to discourage the development of any countrywide class-consciousness among most groups and strata. Similarly, they tended to minimize the development of semi-normative styles of life in different strata. Thus, they exhibited—in contrast to most European elites—a smaller emphasis on lifestyles and family continuity, a much greater openness towards different new occupational or economic and educational activities, and a greater readiness to approach the modern center, even if only to use it as a basic resource for its own goals.

The outcomes of these stratificational policies can also be discerned in Soviet Russia. Among different occupational groups there has developed a tendency toward social segregation and an emphasis on distinct occupational or professional goals. Such groups often tend to coalesce into relatively closed semistrata, each stressing its separateness from other such groups, even while stressing similar desiderata and especially using the same basic types of institutional commodities and means of exchange. The broader legitimation of the lifestyles of each such subgroup tends to be severely controlled by the central elite.

These tendencies necessarily affect the nature of participation of different status groups in various spheres of social intercourse. Most groups are in principle allowed to participate in different spheres of life, but their success in effecting such participation will greatly depend on their relative standing with regard to the central elite. Participation is relatively common in the ritual-political sphere of life, for instance, or in communal-sporting activities which are controlled by the central elite, but participation is not possible in the more private spheres of each stratum or in the more central spheres of the elite itself.

These general characteristics of the stratification system are paralleled by—or manifest in—some crucial characteristics of the structure of the elites and the professionals alike. We find a high degree of dissociation both among the elite groups themselves and (in most respects) between them and the rest of society, with one elite group always trying to dominate the others. Similarly, the professional groups—not unlike the urban guilds of tsarist times—evince a very small degree of autonomy or of autonomous commitment to a broader social order, a narrow conception of their technical function, together with a high subservience to the state by which they are closely supervised.

The Case of Patrimonial Society

A similar continuity or similarity of some basic aspects of political and social-hierarchical regulation can be found in many of the "patrimonial societies," such as, for instance, the Southeast Asian or Latin American ones.

Political decision-making and innovation here were, in the traditional regimes, vested mostly in the ruling household cliques. In the modern setting, such powers usually reside in the executive branch of the government—whether composed of bureaucratic, army or political cliques and pressure groups. The basic goal of these central elites was and is to maintain their monopoly of central political activities and resources: to limit any independent access of the periphery to such resources and activities and to minimize the direct independent political contact and participation of the periphery in the center, while as the same time maintaining minimal structural interpretation of the periphery. As against these types of activities, the development of collective goals or the active formation of new symbols of collective identity, as well as the regulation of autonomous intergroup relations, tended here to be much weaker goals.

Accordingly, the central elites often developed mostly distributive policies aimed at the accumulation of resources in the hands of the centers and on their possible distribution among the various groups of the society.

Accordingly, also, insofar as the rulers of these regimes engaged in economic policies, they were, to use Hoselitz's nomenclature, mostly of expansive character—i.e., aiming at expansion of control over large territories, rather than intrinsic ones characterized by intensive exploitation within a fixed resource basis. Or, to use K. Polanyi's term: these were mostly redistributive systems. Such distributive and extractive policies— often coupled with the performance of ritual ones, aiming at the maintenance of the harmony between the cosmic and the social orders—were in line with the ideal "image" of the king as the "keeper" of the welfare of the people. These policies also provided the most important resources for the maintenance of the ruler's power in the internal political game.

The relations between the center and the periphery were based on the relatively limited extent of structural and symbolic differences between the center and the broader peripheral groups or regions of society. The links between the center and the periphery that tended to develop in these regimes created little basic structural change within either sector.

The center impinged on the local (rural, urban, or tribal) communities, mainly in its administration of law, attempts to maintain peace, exaction of taxation, and the maintenance of some cultural and/or religious links to the center. But most of these contacts were with very few exceptions effected through the existing local kinship subcenters—territorial and ritual—and were mostly of rather "external" and adaptive character. They did not often create new types of interlinking mechanisms between the center and the periphery. There developed only a few new structural channels which undermined or attempted to change the existing social and cultural patterns of either the center or of the periphery or at least to inject into them new common orientations, as was the case in imperial systems or in the modern nation-states and revolutionary societies.

The preponderance of central activities and policies has greatly influenced the mechanisms of political struggle that were inherent within these centers. The most important of these mechanisms were direct bargaining, regulation of the access to channels of distribution, and of mediation between various groups. The rules of the political game of any such coalitions pertained mostly to mediation, cooptation to—or exclusion from—access to the center and to bureaucratic positions, with but little leeway for the development of autonomous access.

Within these frameworks and patterns of coalition the major means of political struggle tended to become more and more that of cooptation or extension of the clientele networks—often coupled with general popularistic appeals mostly couched in terms of ascriptive symbols or values representing different ethnic, religious, or national communities. These appeals could easily manifest themselves in outbreaks which often served as important signals about the inadequacy of the existing pattern of cooptations.

A similar continuity can be found in the systems of stratification that developed in both traditional and modern patrimonial societies. The bases of evaluation were attributes of relatively closed groups, with a growing awareness of the differences between "modern" and "traditional" being one of the basic distinctions of such attributes. A second basis of such evaluation was control over resources. Last, and only to a relatively smaller degree, was some functional "performance" or "service," as designated by the center, useful as a social stratification criterion.

Given the strong emphasis on such attributes as well as the center's predilection for strong control over those who could facilitate the access to the center, only very weak country-wide strata or class consciousness developed. Instead, smaller groups—territorial, semi-occupational, or local—tended to become major status units, all of them developing rather strong tendencies toward status-segregation with but little autonomous political orientation.

Thus, in common with traditional patrimonial societies, there also tended to develop in these societies a strong emphasis on the combination of "closed" restricted prestige and "power" as the major social orientations of the elites and outsider groups alike. Unlike traditional patrimonial societies, no matter how segregated various status units might have been from each other, there tended to develop among them—especially within the less traditional ones—strong and usually ascriptive orientations and references to the center. Unlike traditional societies, these groups attempted to convert their resources into media that might enable them to participate in the broader political framework of their societies (but mostly through the ascriptive channels of a new center), and these tendencies had many repercussions in the political field.

Cultural and Organizational Continuities: Models of Social Order and Systems of Codes

The preceding illustrations have been drawn only from three types of societies. Similar continuities in the modes of political organization and of social stratification, which at the same time differ greatly from each of those previously discussed, can also be found in other societies—e.g., Japan, Turkey, or China. But even the cursory illustrations presented above suffice to point out the importance of such similarities or continuities between what has often been designated as "tradition" versus what we call "modern" political behavior. In order, however, to be able to identify the mechanisms through which tradition exerts its influence, it is necessary to look closer at the ways in which these similarities or continuities, between the traditional and the modern settings of the "same" society, converge around certain common structural and cultural foci.

Such a closer look indicates these commonalities focus around the regulation and interchange of resources between different groups and organizational subsystems of a society: first, the degree of autonomy allowed to different subgroups and components of a social order in relation to the centers of these societies; and, second, several aspects of the activities engaged in by centers and outsider groups alike.

Certainly, there were some crucial differences between center and subgroups in certain cultural orientations, especially those which focused around the definition of the boundaries of political and cultural collectivities. Second, there were differing conceptions of interrelationships among the cosmic, cultural, social, and political orders and of their mutual relevance. Also, attitudes toward participation in the social and cultural orders ranged from active to passive. Closely related were the different conceptions of change, attitudes toward change and toward the possibility of an active participation in the formation of such changes in the major social and cultural spheres. Finally, the legitimate basis of the social order in general, and the relations between the center and the periphery in particular, were surely a source of conflict between the center and outsider groups.

Of special interest from the point of view of our analysis is that these orientations cut across different levels of structural differentiation and different types of concrete organizational structures, as well as changes of political systems and some of the symbols of collective identity.

To give but a few random illustrations, the preceding analysis has shown that when the social and cultural orders are perceived as relevant to one another and mutually autonomous, the political autonomy of different groups increases, as does the development of independent foci of political struggle. This is exemplified by the Western European case when one of these orders is subsumed under the other (as in Russia) or the more they are dissociated from one another (as in many patrimonial societies not discussed here), the smaller will be the degree of such autonomy. In the first case, the center will tend to permeate the periphery without permitting independent impingement of the periphery on the center; while in the second case there will tend to develop adaptive relations between the center and the periphery.

Similarly the greater the conception of the center as the single focus of broader cultural order, the greater will be the emphasis on functional attributes of status and on closed segregated status groups. The greater the "adaptive" attitude to the center, the greater also will be the degree of status segregation and emphasis on restricted prestige of closed communities. The greater the commitment of broader groups to the social order, the greater will be the permeation of the center into the periphery and the greater the emphasis on attributes of power in the system of stratification. Similarly, the greater the emphasis on autonomous access to the center and of common commitment to a broader social order, the greater also the degree of status association and autonomy.

Orientation Codes

This close relationship between cultural orientations and the various aspects of social organization analyzed above indicates that these are not only general value orientations; rather, they seem to be much closer to what Weber has called "Wirtschaftsethik," (that is, general modes of religious, ethical, or symbolic orientation to a specific institutional sphere and its problems). The evaluation of this sphere in terms of the given premises of tradition regarding the cosmic order and the place of human relations and social existence within such an order, surely produces consequent structural and behavioral derivatives. These codes or orientations provide directives or choices with respect to some of the perennial problems immanent in the nature of human life, and they especially provide the major ways of looking at the basic problems of the social and cultural order and of posing the major questions about them. These codes differ also from the immanent "contents-directed" structures of different symbolic realms or of intellectual creations, as well as from the more or less articulated symbolic models of society.

The expression of these codes is, of course, always couched in symbolic terms and very often their fullest articulation can be found in organized and articulated cultural systems or artifacts—be they philosophic, theological, or architectural. But the internal structure of any such constellation of codes which may be prevalent within a population is seldom identical with such intellectual creations in terms of their own logical dynamics and premises. Whatever systemic or "structural" characteristics these codes or constellations evince is not articulated in terms of purely intellectual models, but in the juxtaposition of their orientations to different levels of problems—those inherent in the systemic problems of social organization and those inherent in the problems of socio-cultural life and existence. Hence, different codes or constellations of such codes may be operative "beneath" similar-looking cultural creations or symbolic, ideal expressions of the proper social and cultural order, whether or not they are expressed in the orthodoxies or heterodoxies of a given culture.

Thus, we might conjecture that the constellation of such codes operative in any society can be seen as an important—perhaps the most important—aspect of its hidden structure: the rules according to which the members of a society operate with regard to some of the most crucial aspects of their social and political systems.

Some support for such conjecture can be found in the fact that there exists a very high degree of correlation between such codes and the various discrete organizational aspects of these societies. For example, the structure of the political process or several aspects of hierarchical organization which were analyzed above manifest underlying codes, as well as the more "basic" aspects of different social systems. Included among these aspects are, above all, the patterns of participation and the nature of their internal and external crises and their ways of coping with them. Moreover, this conjecture is supported by evidence that these codes tend to influence social and political systems in similar ways in "traditional" and "modern" societies alike.

We might again illustrate the ways in which such codes operate by again taking up very cursorily the societies analyzed above.

Western European Codes and Models of Social Order

Thus, for instance, the modern socio-political order which has developed in Western Europe has been characterized by:

(a) a high degree of congruence between the cultural and the political identities of the territorial population;

(b) a high level of symbolic and affective commitments to the political and cultural centers and a close relation between these centers and the more primordial dimensions of human existence;

(c) a marked emphasis on politically defined collective goals for all members of the national community; and

(d) a relatively autonomous access of broad strata to symbols and centers.

It was in close relation to these features that some of the patterns of participation and protest specific to the European scene developed. The most important of these assumptions was that both the political groups and the more autonomous social forces and elites tend to crystallize into the relatively autonomous yet complementary units or forces of "state" and "society." These forces have continuously struggled about their relative importance in the formation of the cultural and political center of the nation-state and in the regulation of access to it. The various processes of structural change and dislocation—which are concomitant with the development of modernization in the periphery—gave rise not only to various concrete problems and demands, but also to a growing quest for participation in the broader social and political order. This quest for participation of the periphery in such social, political, and cultural orders is mostly manifest in the search for access to the respective centers of these orders and societies.

One of the major expressions of this convergence between concrete socio-economic problems and this quest for participation was the development of the conception of "class society:" a society composed of potentially or actually antagonistic classes, each comprising many different occupational groups which are to some degree autonomous, and which strive to influence and change the format and content of the centers of their respective societies through political organization.

Many of these characteristics of the European nation-state resemble those which existed in their premodern socio-political traditions. The most important among these orientations were: strong activism, which came to a large extent from the city-state traditions; the broad and active conception of the political order as related to the cosmic or cultural order derived from many imperial traditions or from the great religions; and the traditions of the autonomous access of different groups to the major attributes of social and cultural orders, which were derived in part at least from the pluralist-feudal structure. This premodern European structure proved to be a fertile ground for a further continuation and expansion of these orientations in the directions specified above—an expansion which was greatly facilitated by the commercial and industrial revolutions, by the development of absolutism, by the transformative effects in the system of value-orientations of Protestantism.

Nonwestern Imperial Codes and Models of Social Order

The other societies studied here did not share several of the orientations of the West European traditional order, which were related to the city-state and to some imperial background settings. Thus, for instance, in Russia, Japan, or China, the pluralistic elements were much weaker than in the feudal or city-states. Their political traditions rarely envisioned the same type of split or dichotomy between state and society as did the European tradition. Instead, they tended to stress the congruent but often passive relations between the cosmic order on the one hand, and the socio-political order on the other. Unlike the Western European tradition, the interrelation between the political and the social orders was not envisaged in terms of an antithesis between these entities. Rather, it was more often stated in terms of the coalescence of these different functions within the same group or organization, centered around a common focus in the cosmic order.

Thus, for instance in Russia, there did not, on the whole, develop either the conception of a relatively autonomous access of the major strata to the political and cultural centers or of the autonomy of the social and cultural orders in relation to the political one.

Accordingly, also, the demands of broader groups for access to the center were, on the whole, couched in terms of possible participation in a social and cultural order as defined by the center, or in attempts to overthrow the existing center and establish a new one similar in its basic characteristics. On the whole, these demands were seldom expressed in terms of autonomous access or continuous struggle with the center about their relative influence in the formation of such an order. Hence there did not develop in these societies the same type of autonomous class society, class-consciousness, and class struggle as in Western Europe.

Of course this does not mean that in these societies the major groups have not been making demands on their respective center. On the contrary, many such demands, especially for greater distribution of resources by the center (demands not very different from demands made on traditional patrimonial rulers), are very often made. But they are not necessarily couched in terms of actual participation in the political-cultural order or focused around the possibility of such participation and of access to it.

Patrimonial Codes and Models of Social Order

A similar continuity can be found in the traditional and modern patrimonial regimes. Both were characterized first by a relatively low level of general commitment to a broader social or cultural order. This order was mostly perceived as something to be mastered or adapted to, but not as commanding a high level of commitment from those who participate in it or who are encompassed by it.

Second, there tended to prevail within these societies a strong emphasis on the givenness of the cultural and social order. There was often a lack of perception displayed toward the possibility of active autonomous participation by any social group in the shaping of the contours of the order—even to the extent that such shaping is possible in traditional systems.

Third, and closely connected with the points above, the concept of tension between a "higher" transcendental order and the social order was missing. Or—when such tension was indeed conceived as a very important element in the religious sphere-proper—the necessity to overcome some tensions through "this worldly" activity (political, economic, or scientific) was not recognized.

The emphasis on autonomous access by the major groups or strata was relatively weak. Such access was usually seen as being mediated by ascriptive individual groups or ritual experts who represented the given order, and who were mostly appointed by the center or subcenters.

Fifth, a rather weak connection was developed between broader universalistic precepts and orientations—be they religious or ideological—and the actual social order. Participation, in most cases, was purely ritualistic.

Sixth, a relatively passive attitude toward the acceptance of the basic premises of the cultural order, a strong emphasis on its givenness (even if given the basic premises of modernity) could be detected.

These perceptions of the social-political order gave rise to a much weaker orientation toward active participation in the centers. At the same time, a great dependence—especially in the broader modern groups—upon the center for provision of resources and the regulation of their own internal affairs was felt. Only a very weak development of autonomous mechanisms of self-regulation took place, as can be seen in the nature of the political demands which tended to develop in these societies.

Truly enough, the demands on the center did not abate in these societies. On the contrary, given the spread of the basic assumptions of modernity, such demands were continuously emerging and tended to become more and more articulated in ways which emphasized the lack of group autonomy and the crucial position of the center in this process. These usually included demands for increasing access to the center and for the distribution of resources from the center. Thus, control of the center was not sought, but changes in its content and symbols or possible creation of new types of social and cultural orders were demanded.

Summary

These characteristics of the various social orders coalesce, in the traditional and modern settings alike, into some broader models of socio-political orders. We could cite, for instance, those which have been designated as "absolutist" and "estate" and "nation-states" models in Western Europe; the autocratic-imperial and revolutionary-class models of

Russia (or China); the patrimonial and neo-patrimonial models discussed above; as well as the Japanese, Indian, Turkish, or many other such models. Each is characterized, as we have seen, by the predominance within it of certain constellations of codes.

Such codes may exist or persist in traditional and modern societies alike, and, insofar as this is the case, they may continue to evince similarities in coping with specific problems, even though the problems themselves, as we have seen above, vary greatly between such settings. Insofar as such similarity exists or persists in the "same" society in different periods of its development—cutting across different levels of social differentiation, changes of regimes, of boundaries, of collectivities, and symbols of collective identity—these constellations of codes may be seen as one crucial aspect of tradition and continuity in these societies.

But it need not be assumed that any specific society must always remain within the same "model"—that it cannot, as it were, change the model according to which its structure is crystallized. Russia, Mexico, Turkey, and Cuba are among the most important examples of such model changes. Such changes may also develop in other countries, and the study of the conditions under which they take place should, of course, constitute part of comparative inquiry about post-traditional socio-political orders. Whatever the results of these inquiries, they will no doubt indicate that the different post-traditional models do not occur through a sort of "natural" unfolding of the traditions of these societies. In all these processes there exist very strong elements of choice. In any such situation, a series of problems always arises for the "society" and for its various elites and groups who must choose from many possible policies or demands. Neither structural developments nor the traditions of a society will predetermine the outcome. In structurally similar situations, there is always some range of possible alternatives, out of which—through the interplay of different forces operating in the situation—some choice is made.

The crystallization of such choices out of various possible alternatives is more easily perceived when it is implemented by a deliberate act of a revolutionary elite. But the process of choosing such alternatives can also be found in less dramatic situations and is manifested in a less concentrated way through the accumulation of dispersed pressures and the subsequent responses of elites, as was often the case in the first phases of modernization in many European countries. Such choices are also most readily visible with respect to the types of political regimes shaped by different constellations of codes: the development of autocratic or revolutionary regimes in modern Russia or China; of parliamentary, presidential, or plebisciterian regimes in the West; of constitutional or autocratic regimes within many of the neo-patrimonial systems.

On a somewhat less fully institutionalized and formal level, such choices crystallize with respect to differing patterns of reconstruction of the traditions in such post-traditional societies, and especially in the ways in which various symbols of collective identity—which develop in response to the impingement of the cultural and political pressures of modernity— are shaped. Is the situation perceived in terms of cultural continuity or discontinuity? How are various "existing" traditions and symbols of collective identity incorporated into these new symbolic frameworks?

Any post-traditional society or polity is influenced by the combination of the major conditions or forces specified above: the level of resources available for mobilization and institution-building; the pattern of impingement of forces of modernity on the respective society; the structure of the situation of change in which they were caught; and the differing traditions of these societies or civilizations as embodied in their "premodern" socio-economic structure. Combinations of these various elements or forces influence different aspects of the contours and of the dynamics of the post-traditional socio-political orders, while each of these forces tends to be more influential with respect to some developmental aspects than with regard to others.

Hypotheses

At this stage, it is not possible to present more than a few preliminary hypotheses with regard to the ways in which such differential influences operate.

It may perhaps be first postulated that the very ability to institutionalize in some viable way any such post-traditional order with its new types of center-periphery relations (and the subsequent ability to cope with continuously emerging conflicts within such an order) are influenced mainly by the respective power relations between the groups participating in this struggle. In this connection, the internal cohesion of the major new elites may be as significant as the degree of solidarity between the predominant elites and the broader social strata.

Second, the concrete political regimes, as well as the patterns of reconstruction of tradition that become institutionalized in a post-traditional society, are mostly influenced by the composition and orientation of these dominant elites.

Third, broader development of models (e.g., nation-state, partimonial, and so on) of post-traditional societies, and the specific types of conflicts to which they are especially sensitive, are shaped by the constellation of codes operating within the respective societies. I am referring here to the conditions under which the potentialities for such conflicts reach specific boiling points which may threaten the stability of these regimes; the ways in which the regimes cope with these problems and conflicts; and especially the ways of incorporating various types of political demands in general and those for growing participation in the political order in particular. The intensity of such conflicts and the perception of their acuteness; the range of flexibility or of rigidity in response to them and the relative importance of regressive and repressive—as against expansive— policies for coping with them, seems to be mostly influenced by the different patterns of tradition in general, and in particular, by new symbols of collective identity that become predominant in a society. On the other hand, the relative balance of forces between groups with different socio-political orientations cannot be discounted.

Further research, basing itself on the papers presented in these two volumes as well as on new data, will provide, we hope, additional possibilities for elaborating and testing these hypotheses. But even at this stage it is important to stress the usefulness of paradigms from sociology in general and those of modernization in particular.[19]

NOTES

1. See S. N. Eisenstadt, Modernization, Protest and Change, Englewood Cliffs, N.J., Prentice-Hall, 1966. Also see Robert Ward and Dankwart A. Rustow, eds., Political Modernization in Japan and Turkey, Princeton, Princeton University Press, 1964, published in the series, "Studies in Political Development."

2. On these developments, see in greater detail, Eisenstadt, op. cit.

3. Fred Riggs, Administration in Developing Countries: The Theory of Prismatic Society, Boston, Houghton Mifflin, 1964. Also see his "Political Aspects of Developmental Change," in A. Gallaher, Jr. (ed.) Perspectives in Developmental Change, Lexington, University of Kentucky Press, 1968, p. 143; "Administrative Development: An Elusive Concept," in John D. Montgomery and William J. Siffin (eds.) Approaches to Development: Politics, Administration and Change, New York, McGraw-Hill, 1966, p. 225; and Thailand: The Modernization of a Traditional Polity, Honolulu, East West Press, 1966.

4. Lucian W. Pye, Politics, Personality and Nation Building: Burma's Search for Identity, New Haven, Conn., Yale University Press, 1962.

5. L. W. Pye and S. Verba, eds., Political Culture and Political Development, Princeton, Princeton University Press, 1965. See also, G. A. Almond and S. Verba, The Civic Culture: Political Attitudes and Democracy in Five Nations, Princeton, Princeton University Press, 1966.

6. See Max Weber, The Theory of Social and Economic Organization, edited by T. Parsons and translated by T. Parsons and A. M. Henderson, New York, Oxford

University Press, 1947; S. N. Eisenstadt, "Patrimonial Systems: Introduction" to ch. V, in S. N. Eisenstadt (ed.) Political Sociology, New York, Basic Books, 1971, p. 146; S. N. Eisenstadt, "Traditional Patrimonialism and Modern Neo-patrimonialism," forthcoming; Guenther Roth, "Personal Rulership, Patrimonialism and Empire Building in the New States," World Politics, Vol. XX, No. 2, January 1968, pp. 194-206; and A. Zolberg, Creating Political Order: The New Party States of West Africa, Chicago, Rand McNally, 1966.

    7. See E. Shils, "Tradition and Liberty: Antimony and Independence," Ethics, Vol. 68, April 1958, pp. 153-65; B. F. Hoselitz, "Tradition and Economic Growth," and Joseph J. Spengler, "Theory, Ideology, Non-Economic Values and Politico-Economic Development," in R. Braibanti and J. J. Spengler (eds.) Tradition, Values and Socio-Economic Development, London, Duke University Press, 1961, pp. 57-85 and pp. 3-57, respectively; and Joseph J. Spengler, "Economic Development, Political Preconditions and Political Consequences," Journal of Politics, Vol. XXII, August 1960, 94-105.

    8. See E. Shils, "Tradition," Comparative Studies in Society and History, Vol. 13, No. 2, April 1971, pp. 122-59; Thomas S. Kuhn, The Structure of Scientific Revolutions, Chicago, University of Chicago Press, 1962; and "Tradition et Continuité," Cahiers Internationaux de Sociologie, Vol. XLIV, January-June 1968, pp. 1-79.

    9. See M. Singer, ed., Traditional India: Structure and Change, Austin, University of Texas Press, 1959; Lloyd and Suzanne Rudolph, "Political Role of India's Caste Associations," Pacific Affairs, Vol. 33, 1960, pp. 5-22; and L. Rudolph, "The Modernity of Tradition," in Bendix (ed.) State and Society, Boston, Little, Brown, 1968, p. 350.

    10. Nur Yalman, "Islamic Reform and the Mystic Tradition in Eastern Turkey," and Ernest Gellner, "The Great Patron. A Reintrepretation of Tribal Rebellions," European Journal of Sociology, Vol. X, No. 1, 1969, pp. 41-61 and pp. 61-70, respectively; and John Waterbury, The Commander of the Faithful, London, Weidenfeld, 1970.

    11. C. S. Whitaker, "A Dysrhythmic Process of Political Change," World Politics, Vol. XIX, January 1967, pp. 190-218.

    12. See R. Bendix, "Tradition and Modernity Reconsidered," Comparative Studies in Society and History, Vol. IX, April 1967, pp. 292-346; and F. Riggs, "Political Aspects of Developmental Change," in A. Gallaher, Jr. (ed.) Perspectives in Developmental Change, Lexington, University of Kentucky Press, 1968, p. 143.

    13. Some of the most important papers representing this point of view have been collected in James D. Cockcraft, André Gunder Fuare, and Dale L. Johnson, Dependence and Underdevelopment—Latin America's Political Economy, New York, Anchor Books, 1972. See also A. G. Frank, Capitalism and Underdevelopment in Latin America, New York, Monthly Review Press, 1967; Pablo Gonzales Casanova, "Les Classiques Latino-Americains et la Sociologie du Développement," Current Sociology, Vol. XVIII, No. 1, 1970, pp. 5-29; Gail Omvedt, "Modernization Theories: The Ideology of Empire," in A. R. Desai (ed.) Essays on Modernization of Underdeveloped Societies, Bombay, Vol. I, 1971, pp. 119-38; S. J. Bodenheimer, "The Ideology of Developmentalism: American Political Science Paradigm—Surrogate for Latin American Studies," Berkeley Journal of Sociology, Vol. 35, 1968, pp. 130-59; and Fernando Henrique Cardoso and Enzo Faletto, Dependencia y Desarollo en America Latina, Mexico City, Siglo XXI Editors, 1969.

14. See Bodenheimer, "The Ideology of Developmentalism," op. cit., and C. Furtado, Obstacles to Development in Latin America, trans. by Charles Ekker, Anchor Books, 1970.

15. See Harry J. Benda, Non-Western Intelligentsias in Political Elites," Australian Journal of Politics and History, Vol. VI, No. 2, November 1960, pp. 205-8; H. Benda, "Decolonization in Indonesia: The Problem of Continuity and Change," American Historical Review, Vol. LXX, July 1965, pp. 1058-73; J. Heesterman, "Tradition and Modernity in India," Bijdragen Tot de Taal Land en Volkenkunde Deel, Vol. 119, 1963, pp. 237-58; and W. F. Wertheim, "The Way Towards Modernity," in Desai, Essays on Modernization of Underdeveloped Societies, op. cit., pp. 76-95.

16. See Ernest Gellner, Thought and Change, London, Weidenfeld & Nicolson, 1969, p. 139.

17. See A. S. Feldman and W. E. Moore, "Industrialism & Industrialization: Convergence & Differentiation," in Transactions of Fifth World Congress of Sociology, 1962, Louvain, International Sociological Association, 1964; John H. Goldthorpe, "Theories of Industrial Society: Reflections on the Recrudescence of Historicism and the Future of Futurology," European Journal of Sociology, Vol. II, No. 2, 1971, pp. 263-88; A. S. Feldman and W. E. Moore, "Are Industrial Societies Becoming Alike?" in Alvin W. Gouldner & S. M. Miller (eds.) Applied Sociology, New York, Free Press, 1965; Stein Rokkan, "The Structuring of Mass Politics in Smaller European Democracies—A Developmental Typology," Comparative Studies in Society and History, Vol. 10, No. 2, 1968, pp. 173-210; M. Olsen, Jr., "Rapid Growth as a Destabilizing Force," Journal of Economic History, Vol. 23, 1963, pp. 529-52; and M. Olsen, Jr., "Some Social and Political Implications of Economic Development," World Politics, Vol. V, No. 17, 1965, pp. 525-54.

18. Carl J. Friedrich, "Political Development and the Objectives of Modern Government," in Ralph Braibanti (ed.) Political and Administrative Development, Durham, N.C., Duke University Press, 1969, pp. 3-107 (Duke University Commonwealth Studies Center Publication 36.)

19. Karl H. Hoerning, Secondary Modernization: Societal Change of Newly Developing Nations. A Theoretical Essay in Comparative Sociology, Denver, University of Denver, 1969-1970. See also Raymond Grew and Sylvia L. Thrupp, "Horizontal History in Search of Vertical Dimensions," Comparative Studies in Society and History, Vol. V, No. 8, 1965-1966, pp. 118-26.

CHAPTER 2

CITIES, STATES, AND NATIONS:
A DIMENSIONAL MODEL FOR THE STUDY
OF CONTRASTS IN DEVELOPMENT

Stein Rokkan

Stein ROKKAN is Professor of Sociology at the University of Bergen and Recurring Visiting Professor of Political Science at Yale. He has been associated with the ISSC programme for the advancement of comparative research since 1962 and is Chairman of the ISSC Committee on Comparative Research. He is currently (1970-1973) President of the International Political Science Association. Among his major publications are: *Party Systems and Voter Alignments; Citizens, Elections, Parties;* and *Comparative Survey Analysis.*

I have tried, in a variety of contexts, to work out schemes for the exploration of the extraordinary contrasts confronting us when we compare political systems across the world: Why are some large, others very small? Why are some highly centralized, others studded with a variety of centres, fulfilling different functions in the total territory? Why are some highly homogeneous in language and in religion, others built up of several distinctive cultural communities? Why do some of them allow extensive traffic of people, commodities, and messages across their borders while others impose stricter measures of economic and/or cultural autarky?[1]

This chapter presents yet another attempt to come to grips with these questions. The result is far from conclusive: each typology, each hypothesis will have to be checked against detailed institutional and statistical data for each territory and evaluated against alternative theoretical schemes. My primary concern is to formulate the rudiments of a "grammar" for the analysis of macro-variations; the detailed confrontations with historical realities will have to be undertaken by pairs and triples of countries.

Territory, Economy, Culture

Any analysis of variations among political systems must start from notions of territory. We cannot study such variations without looking into the structure of the space over which they exert some control: First we have to study their *centres,* the gathering places where the major decisions are made, where the dominant actors in the system, their families, and their friends interact most frequently; next we have to inform ourselves about the areas controlled from these centres, the *peripheries,* the territorial populations dependent in one way or another on the decisions made at such centres; finally, we have to chart the *transactions* among the centres and between centres and peripheries.

Any study of transactions over distances will have to consider firstly the *physical* conditions of transportation and communication—the contours of landscapes, the distances across waters, making for higher or lower barriers between areas of settlement; secondly, the *technological* conditions for movement: horses, ships, canals, paved roads, later railroads, steamers, planes; thirdly, the *military* conditions for expansion versus retrenchment: differences in levels of organization, in skills of strategy and tactics, in the technology of war, all helping to increase or decrease the temptation to conquer territory; fourthly, the *economic* conditions for cross-territory transactions: differences in resource endowments, in production and in markets, making for higher or lower incentives to barter and to trade; and finally, the *cultural* conditions of communication: ethnic affinities or enmities, differences in language, in moral codes, in religion.

Geography and the technology of transportation determine the potential reach of efforts of expansion; the balance of military power, the directions and the character of trade routes, the affinities and the differences in codes of communication determine the actual reach of such efforts.

Successes and failures in the different modes of expansion also help to determine the internal structure of political systems: the longer the lines of command and communication within the system the more differentiated the distributions of roles, the greater the emphasis on skills in the assignment of roles, and the greater the need for codes of honour and trust cutting across the loyalties to kin and to locality.

THREE DIRECTIONS OF DIFFERENTIATION

Talcott Parsons has set out, in his pathbreaking essay on the sociology of the early empires, a simple model positing three directions of differentiation, three types of cross-local organization, and three types of elites (see Figure 1).[2]

The early systems of long-distance territorial control, the empires, emerged with the invention of script; pictograms and alphabetic writing reduced the dependence on oral relays both over time and across space and made it possible to stabilize structures across wide ranges of local communities.[3]

Communication via script had well-known magical and religious functions and helped to legitimize the instituted authorities, but was also of eminently practical importance, both for military and for economic

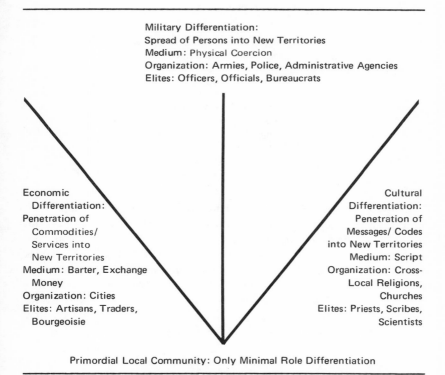

Military Differentiation:
Spread of Persons into New Territories
Medium: Physical Coercion
Organization: Armies, Police, Administrative Agencies
Elites: Officers, Officials, Bureaucrats

Economic
 Differentiation:
Penetration of
 Commodities/
 Services into
 New Territories
Medium: Barter, Exchange
 Money
Organization: Cities
Elites: Artisans, Traders,
 Bourgeoisie

Cultural
Differentiation:
Penetration of
Messages/ Codes
into New Territories
Medium: Script
Organization: Cross-
Local Religions,
Churches
Elites: Priests, Scribes,
Scientists

Primordial Local Community: Only Minimal Role Differentiation

Figure 1: THREE DIRECTIONS OF DIFFERENTIATION IN LARGE-SCALE TERRITORIAL SYSTEMS

organizations. All the early efforts of large-scale territorial organization depended on some form of cultural standardization through the medium of script, but they differed widely in their internal communications structure.

The great archeologist, Henri Franfort, contrasts two models of territorial consolidation: the Mesopotamian conglomerate of self-assertive corporate city communities and the monocephalic empire of the Egyptian pharaohs. The great Mesopotamian invention was the city:

> It is a man-made institution overriding the natural and primordial division of society in families and clans. It asserts that habitat, not kinship, determines one's affinities. The city, moreover, does not recognize outside authority. It may be subjected by a neighbour or ruler; but its loyalty cannot be won by force, for its sovereignty rests with the assembly of its citizens. Thus the early Mesopotamian cities resembled those of Greece, of the Hanseatic League, of Renaissance Italy, in many respects.[4]

By contrast, Egypt developed a dynastic centre in a distinctly agricultural setting:

> In Egypt the great change did not lead to a concentration of social activity in urban centres. It is true that there were cities in Egypt, but, with the single exception of the capital, these were no more than market towns for the countryside. Paradoxically enough, the capital was less permanent than the towns in the provinces, for in principle, it served only a single reign. Each pharaoh took up residence near the site chosen for his tomb. . . . Until the middle of the second millenium B.C. (when Thebes assumed a metropolitan character) there was no truly permanent capital in Egypt, a situation which clearly demonstrates the insignificant role played by the concept of the city in the political thought of the Egyptians. In Mesopotamia, on the other hand, even the most powerful rulers of the land styled themselves rulers of cities, and functioned as such in Akkad or Ur, in Babylon or Assur.[5]

This concept of the city is a fundamental dimension in the comparative history of empire-building. The Egyptian and the Mesopotamian developments represent the two main avenues of territorial expansion: the build-up of military-bureaucratic centres in predominantly agrarian areas versus the creation of agencies for control and adjudication across a network of established cities. The Mesopotamian style predominated in a broad belt from India to the Mediterranean and, later, northward across Europe. The Egyptian style has parallels in China, in the nomadic empires of the Central Asian steppes, in some of the Moslem empires, and in Russia.

The Roman Empire at its height joined resources from both traditions: it controlled a vast network of cities around the Mediterranean and at the same time built up a strong centre for the conquest of territories still at a low level of economic development. And, what was equally important, the Roman Empire also became the essential vehicle for the penetration into new territories of a major script religion, Christianity.

In this way, the Roman Empire for some time drew strength from all of the three basic processes of differentiation: the economic, the military-bureaucratic, and the cultural. The three developments reinforced each other for a while, but generated separate organizational structures with resources of their own. The Western Empire collapsed as a military-administrative structure in the fifth century but the city network was still there and so was the Roman Church and the tradition of long-distance communication via alphabetic script. The Empire broke up as a political system of territorial control, but much of the economic as well as the cultural infrastructure for long-distance communication was left intact, in fact strengthened after the four or five centuries of conflict with Islam, the other empire-building religion in the Mediterranean.

To account for such processes of breakup and reorganization we shall clearly have to add further elements to our initial paradigm. We shall posit three processes of periphery build-up within the territory of disintegrating empires: feudalization, vernacularization, and state-building. The location of these processes can be represented graphically at some halfway point along each of the paths of development (see Figure 2). In the history of the territorial structuring of political systems, it is as important to analyze the processes of retrenchment as it is to study the phases of expansion. The system of states emerging in Europe from the twelfth to the twentieth century can only be understood against the background of the Roman inheritance and the reduction in the range and scope of cross-territorial communications which gradually took place in the wake of the fall of Rome.

The rise of feudal structures is a much-discussed theme in comparative history. Within our simple paradigm, what matters is the rise of intermediary power-holders controlling resources in the primary economy: this "parochialization" of economic and political power was widespread in the territories of the old Empire. But the process was far from uniform throughout Europe; there were few signs of such a process in the territories to the north of the Roman territory, and there were also variations depending on the level of agricultural development and on the degree of exposure to the onslaughts of nomadic raiders and armies. What proved important in the later development of territorial units was the level of resource generation within such concentrated agrarian structures and the strategies adopted by the owners and controllers of land in their dealings with the urban bourgeoisie and with the military-bureaucratic

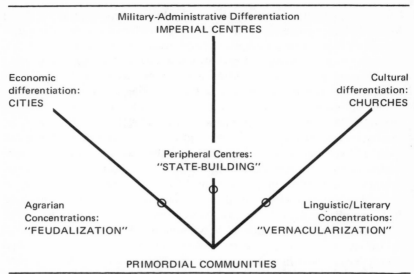

Figure 2: **A PARADIGM FOR THE LOCATION OF BASIC VARIABLES IN ANALYSES OF THE GROWTH AND DISAGGREGATION OF LARGE-SCALE TERRITORIAL SYSTEMS**

agencies of state-building; this concept is the central thrust of Barrington Moore's important work on the development of large-scale territorial units in Europe and in Asia.[6]

Developments were much slower on the cultural front: the Roman Church established itself as the central spiritual authority across all of Western Europe and proved able to maintain its two languages, Greek and Latin, as the dominant standards of elite communication for centuries after the fall of the Western Empire. But as Jack Goody has shown in his penetrating analysis of the social consequences of script, there is a fundamental difference between empires built on idiographic communication and empires using alphabets. In China, it was possible to keep the literati and the gentry integrated across a vast territory varying greatly in its local vernaculars; the idiographs had no direct relation to speech and could be pronounced in all kinds of ways even though conveying the same message. In the Roman Empire, Greek and Latin were maintained for centuries as vehicles of elite communication across Europe, but the alphabetic script opened up possibilities for the direct expression of vernacular languages. There was already a strong flourishing of such vernacular literatures in the Middle Ages, but the decisive break with the Greek and the Latin standards came with the invention of printing and with the Reformation; these developments opened up the floodgates for the mass reproduction of messages in vernaculars and set the stage for the establishment of a variety of national standards of communication in an increasingly fragmented Europe. Gutenberg created an essential technology for the building of nations; the mass reproduction of books, tracts, and broadsheets made it possible to reach new strata within each territorial population and at the same time to confine communication within the limits of the particular vernacular. The Reformation reinforced this process in Northern Europe; it meant much more than a break with Rome in matters of theological doctrine; it strengthened the distinctiveness of each territorial culture by integrating the priesthood into the administrative machinery of the state and by restricting priests to the confines of the given vernacular. In Hirschman's terms, the Reformation built up a wall against cultural "exits" into other territories: this wall was not only an important strategy in legitimizing the new territorial state but in the longer run also a crucial step in preparing the broader population for the use of "voice" within their system.[7]

This process was not uniform, however. The great paradox of European development is that the strongest and the most durable systems emerged at the periphery of the old Empire; the heartlands, and the Italian and German territories remained fragmented and dispersed until the nineteenth century.

To reach some understanding of this paradox we have to reason in several steps:

(1) The heartland of the old Western Empire was studded with cities in a broad trade route belt stretching from the Mediterranean to the east as well as west of the Alps northward to the Rhine and the Danube;

(2) This "city belt" was at the same time the stronghold of the Roman Catholic Church; this territory had a high density of cathedrals, monasteries, and ecclesiastical principalities;

(3) The very density of established centres within this territory made it difficult to single out any one as superior to all others; there was no geography-given core area for the development of a strong territorial system;[8]

(4) The resurrection of the Holy Roman Empire under the leadership of the four German tribes did not help to unify the territory; the emperors were prey to shifting electoral alliances; many of them were mere figureheads and the best and the strongest of them expended their energies in quarrels with the Pope and with the Italian cities;

(5) By contrast, it proved much easier to develop effective core areas at the edges of the city-studded territories of the old Empire; in these regions, centres could be built up under less competition and could achieve command of the resources in peripheral areas too far from the cities in the central trade belt;

(6) The earliest successes in such efforts of system-building at the edges of the old Empire came in the west and in the north, in France, in England, in Scandanavia, later also in Spain; in all these cases the dynasties in the core areas were able to command resources from peripheral territories largely beyond the reach of the cities of the central trade belt;

(7) The second wave of successful centre-building took place on the landward side: first the Habsburgs, with their core area in Austria; then the eastern march of the German Empire; next the Swedes; and finally, and decisively, the Prussians;

(8) The fragmented middle belt of cities and petty states was the scene of endless onslaughts, counter-moves and efforts of reorganization during the long centuries from Charlemagne to Bismarck: firstly, the French monarchs gradually took over the old Lotharington-Burgundian buffer zone from Provence to Flanders and incorporated such typical trade cities as Avignon, Aix, and Lyons; secondly, the key cities to the north of the Alps managed to establish a defense league against all comers and gradually built up the Swiss confederation; similar leagues were established along the Rhine and across the Baltic and the North Sea but never managed to establish themselves as sovereign territorial formations; thirdly, the Habsburgs made a number of encroachments both on the west and on the east of the belt and for some time controlled the crucial territories at the mouth of the Rhine triggering the next successful effort of consociational confederation, the United Netherlands; finally, in the wake of the French Revolution, Napoleon moved across the middle belt both north and south of the Alps and set in motion a series of efforts of unification which ended with the successes of the Prussians and the Piedmontese in 1870.

A CONCEPTUAL MAP OF EUROPE

The result was an extraordinary tangle of territorial structures in Europe: some large, some small, some highly centralized, others made up of differentiated networks of self-reliant cities. The alphabet and the city decided the fate of Europe: the emergence of vernacular standards of communication prepared the ground for the later stages of nation-building at the mass level, and the geography of trade routes made for differences in the resources for state-building between East and West.

The essentials of these differences in the conditions for polity-building can be set out in a conceptual map—a simple two-dimensional typology interpreted within the framework of the topology of Europe.

In this map (Figure 3) the West-East axis differentiates the economic resource bases of the state-building centres: surpluses from a highly monetized economy in the West, surpluses from agricultural labour in the East. The North-South axis measures the conditions for rapid cultural integration: the early closing of the borders in the Protestant North, the continued supraterritoriality of the Church in the Catholic South.

This conceptual map reflects the fundamental asymmetry of the geopolitical structure of Europe: the dominant city network of the politically fragmented trade belt from the Mediterranean toward the North, the strength of the cities in the territories consolidated to the seaward side of this belt, the weakness of the cities in the territories brought together under the strong military centres on the landward Marchland.

This conceptual map is the underlying dimension of Barrington Moore's analysis in *Social Origins*. He does not discuss the middle belt, but his contrast between the seaward powers, England and France, and the landward powers, Prussia and Russia, is directly reflected in the West-East gradient in the map. Essentially this was a contrast in the levels of monetization reached at the time as the decisive consolidation of the territorial centres: England and France during the sixteenth century, Prussia and Russia during the seventeenth and eighteenth centuries. In the West the great surge of commercial activity made it possible for the centre-builders to extract resources in easily convertible currency. In the East, the cities were much weaker partners and could not offer the essential resource base for the building of the military machineries of the new centers at the periphery of the old Europe. The only alternative partners were the owners of land, and the resources they could offer were food and manpower: crofters, tenants, and smallholders in Sweden; serfs in Austria, Prussia, and Russia. This contrast in the resource bases for political consolidation goes far to explain the difference between the Western and the Eastern systems in their internal structure and in the character of the later transition to mass politics. This contrast is the thrust of Moore's detailed analysis. It does not explain all the cases, however, and does not pinpoint the sources of variation on each side; there are important variations both on the seaward and the landward sides, and these can only be understood through an analysis of the other dimensions of the polity, quite particularly the cultural.

In the conceptual map of Europe the West-East axis differentiates conditions of state-building, the South-North axis the conditions of nation-building. In the underlying model of development the Reformation is interpreted as the first major step toward the definition of territorial nations. Lutherans and Calvinists broke with the supraterritoriality of the Roman Church and merged the ecclesiastical bureaucracies with the secular territorial establishments: this action meant a closing of "exit options" on the cultural front, an accentuation of the cultural significance of the borders between territories. The Reformation occurred only a few decades after Gutenberg; the state churches of the Protestant North

THE "STATE-ECONOMY" DIMENSIONS: WEST-EAST AXIS

Territorial Centres City Network	WEAK WEAK Seaward Peripheries	STRONG STRONG Seaward Empire-Nations DISTANT	STRONG STRONG Seaward Empire-Nations CLOSE	WEAK City Integrated into Larger System	STRONG State Consociational Formation	Europe Fragmented until 19th Century	STRONG Landward Empire-Nations CLOSE	WEAK Landward Empire-Nations DISTANT	WEAK Landward Buffers
Protestant State Church	ICELAND NORWAY SCOTLAND WALES	ENGLAND	DENMARK			HANSE GERMANY	PRUSSIA	SWEDEN	FINLAND
Mixed Territories					NETHERLANDS SWITZERLAND	RHINELAND			BALTIC TERRITORIES BOHEMIA
National Catholic	IRELAND BRITTANY		FRANCE	"Lotharingia" BURGUNDY ARELATUM			BAVARIA		POLAND
Counter-Reformation			SPAIN PORTUGAL	CATALONIA	BELGIUM	ITALY	AUSTRIA		HUNGARY

THE "STATE-CULTURE" DIMENSION: SOUTH-NORTH AXIS

Figure 3: A "CONCEPTUAL MAP" OF 16TH-18TH CENTURY WESTERN EUROPE (territories recognized as sovereign, 1648-1789, in italics)

[82]

became major agencies for the standardization of national languages and for the socialization of the masses into unified national cultures. In Catholic Europe the Church remained supraterritorial and did not to the same extent prove an agency of nation-building. True enough, the Catholic Church played a major role in the development of peripheral nationalisms in some of the territories of Counter-Reformation Europe, but these were much later developments; they occurred in the aftermath of the French Revolution and took the form of alliances between the Church and nationalist or secessionist leaders against the rulers at the centre, whether Protestant (Belgium before 1830, Ireland from the 1820s onward), Orthodox (Poland, Lithuania), or simply secularizing (the Carlist wars in Spain). Even in the most loyal of the Counter-Reformation states, the churches remained supraterritorial in outlook and never became central agencies of nation-building in the way the Protestant churches did in the North.[9]

Whether Protestant or Catholic the churches had to work with populations varying widely in their openness to efforts of standardization.

The Völkerwanderung and the struggles of the Middle Ages had produced very different conditions for linguistic unification in the different territories of Europe. The result was a variety of conflicts between claims of territorial control and claims of national identity; there was nowhere a complete fit between the "state" and the "nation," and the conflicts between the two sets of claims were particularly violent in the central trade route belt and in Catholic Europe.

In the Northern Territories the processes of state-building and nation-building tended to proceed *pari passu,* but even in these systems at the edge of the old Empire, claims for territorial control often clashed with claims for separate identities: the English versus the Celts, the Danes versus the Norwegians and the Icelanders, the Swedes versus the Finns. Trade-belt Europe inherited strong linguistic standards from the ancient and the medieval Empires: Italian in the South, German in the North. But there was no corresponding development at the political level; in these territories national identity came first, political unification only much later. In the "Lotharingian-Burgundian" zone between the German reich and the French monarchy the linguistic borders hardly ever followed the territorial frontiers and a variety of developments took place: the Swiss quickly accepted several exoglossic literary standards and never built up a "linguistic nation" of their own; Alsace-Lorraine maintained its Germanic dialect but identified politically with France; Luxembourg also kept its dialect but veered between allegiance to Germany and to France; and Belgium was split between a Flemish-speaking North and a Walloon-speaking South. In the rest of Catholic Europe there were dominant languages at the territorial centres but strong movements of cultural resistance in the peripheries. France went furthest in linguistic standardization but had to keep on "building the nation" in such peripheries as Brittany and Occitania throughout the nineteenth century: the *levée en masse* for the great wars and the nationalization of public education were the decisive vehicles of cultural unification. In Spain the Castilians were never able to build up a unified national culture; the Basque country and Catalonia remained strongholds of regional resistance. Austria tried for centuries to make German the dominant language of Southeast Europe but this drive never succeeded; with the rise of national ideologies this vast empire soon fell apart into a number of territorial fragments, but even these fragments were still torn by cultural conflicts. The contrast between the Austrian and the Prussian strategies is striking: Austria extended the domain of its state apparatus far beyond the borders of the Germanic language community and acquired a multilingual empire; Prussia had also built up its strength on the Eastern marches but in the end turned westward, into the core areas of the ancient German nation. The Catholic power stuck to the supraterritorial ideal; the Protestant power endeavoured to acquire territorial control over the one linguistic community. The struggle between *kleindeutsche* and *gross-deutsche* strategies was a struggle over conceptions of the state and of the nation, a struggle between a political and a cultural conception of territorial community.

VARIATIONS IN THE STRUCTURE OF CITY NETWORKS

We have tried to identify three fundamental dimensions in the tangled histories of the territories of Western Europe: the strength of the city network, the strength of state-building core areas, and the resistance to cultural unification and standardization—to nation-building. These three dimensions combined to produce the extraordinary diversity of political systems in the territories once under the sway of one single empire— variations not only in size, but also in the urban structure and in the cultural balance within each territory. Figure 4 offers a typology of such variations and shows how they can be generated from the proposed conceptual map of Europe.

The city structure of each territory reflects the distances between the state-building core areas and the dominant trade routes: the greater the distance the greater the dominance of the capital city, the shorter the distance the more even the distributions of city strengths whether measured in terms of demographic size or in terms of territorial functions. The territories to the west as well as to the east of the central trade belt are largely monocephalic: they were built up around strong state-building core areas and there was no serious competition from the cities nearer to the old south-north routes. There is an intriguing exception at the Mediterranean end of the belt, however.

The conceptual map focuses on a south-north trade axis but along the Mediterranean littorals there was of course a much older tradition of east-west trade, interrupted, it is true, by the Moslem conquests, but still of vital importance from the time of the Crusades onward.[10]

The Mediterranean territories make up the broad base of our column for "city-state Europe;" at this point there is only a very poor fit between typology and topology. The greater strength of the city-state tradition in the south made it much more difficult to build up dominant core areas for large territorial systems: the result was polycephaly, but of a much more polarized type than further north in Europe.

To clarify this point let us contrast the territorial development in the two southern corners of Western Europe: the Iberian peninsula in the West and the Habsburg territories in the East.

Spain and Austria built up their core strengths as *crusading frontier empires* against the Moslems and the Turks: they both built up their core areas through the mobilization of military-administrative resources against the threatening infidels. But Spain was much closer to the Mediterranean trade belt: Madrid became the dominant political centre but could not compete economically with Barcelona. By contrast, Vienna built itself up as the dominant city on the marchlands; it was too far from the Mediterranean and the South-North trade belt and became overwhelmingly dominant in its territory after the fall of the Habsburg Empire.

This contrast comes out even clearer in a comparison with two other powers bordering on the Mediterranean, France and Yugoslavia. Much like the Spanish dynasties, the French nation-builders had integrated large chunks of the trade route belt in their territories, Burgundy and Provence. But the Ile-de-France core proved able to dominate these economically important peripheries much more effectively than the Castilians were able to control the Catalans. This contrast no doubt reflected differences in the resource balance between the two poles of each system, but it is also clear that there were differences in the cultural thrust of nation-building; French energies centred on the domestic territory, and Spanish energies were expended on empire-building and missionary activities in America.

There is a similar contrast in the southeastern corner of Europe: Austria

SYSTEM CHARACTERISTICS: Size	City Structure	Linguistic Structure	SEAWARD PERIPHERIES: Sovereign After 1814	SEAWARD NATION-STATES: Retrenched Empires	CITY-STATE EUROPE: Early Consociations or Late Unification	LANDWARD NATION-STATES: Retrenched Empires	LANDWARD BUFFERS: Sovereign After 1918
LARGER	MONOCEPHALIC	INTEGRATED		FRANCE (but some resistance among Bretons, Alsatians, Occitans)			(DDR)
		ENDOGLOSSIC PERIPHERIES		UNITED KINGDOM (Welsh, some Gaelic)			
	POLYCEPHALIC	INTEGRATED			GERMAN F.R. and ITALY		
		ENDOGLOSSIC PERIPHERIES		SPAIN			
SMALLER	MONOCEPHALIC	INTEGRATED	ICELAND (Danish never strong)	DENMARK	LUXEMBOURG (but exoglossic standards)	SWEDEN (near-polycephalic) AUSTRIA	
		DIVIDED	NORWAY (two standards, one once close to Danish) IRELAND (Gaelic now very weak)				FINLAND (one endoglossic, one exoglossic standard)
	POLYCEPHALIC	INTEGRATED	PORTUGAL		NETHERLANDS (but religious *Verzuiling*)		
		DIVIDED: Exoglossic Standards			BELGIUM (Flemish, French) SWITZERLAND (German, French, Italian)		(YUGOSLAVIA)

Figure 4: A TYPOLOGY OF THE POLITICAL SYSTEMS OF 20TH-CENTURY WESTERN EUROPE

markedly monocephalic, the much more recent Yugoslavian federation deeply divided economically as well as culturally. The parallels between Yugoslavia and Spain are indeed striking: in both cases there was build-up of a military-administrative centre in the fight against foreign dominance; in both cases there were conflicts between these political centres and the economically stronger cities nearest to the major trade routes. Belgrade and Serbia parallel Madrid and Castilia; Ljubljana and Zagreb parallel Barcelona and Bilbao. In all cases, the economic strength of the peripheral cities reinforce the cultural distinctiveness of their regions; claims for economic autonomy parallel claims for cultural recognition.

The polarization between economic and administrative centres was much less marked in the middle belt from Italy to the North Sea; all these territories developed polycephalic city structures, but the distribution of functions tended to be more diffuse. Italy was unified from a mountain state to the North; the Piedmontese not only led politically but also economically and retained a good deal of control even after the transfer of the capital to Rome. Switzerland and the Netherlands developed remarkably balanced city structures: they stand out, as Daalder has shown, as the two polities in Europe with the most distinctly consociational structure. The basic model underlying these developments was the league of cities, an open contractual organization for the protection of trading privileges and the control of markets. There was a profusion of such leagues in medieval and early modern Germany as well, but these proved geopolitically much less viable.[11]

This vast area of independent cities and petty states could only be unified from outside. The Habsburgs tried to achieve this unification for centuries from their bases in Vienna and later from Brussels, but in vain. The final push toward unification came in three steps: first, the build-up of the Prussian state on the frontier toward the Slavs; next, the reorganization of the German territory under Napoleon and the emergence of a strong nationalist ideology cutting across local loyalties; and, ultimately, the victory of the Prussians over the Austrians and the establishment of a reich covering most of the territories of the German-speaking middle belt.[12] The resulting city structure was markedly polycephalic: Berlin, the political capital, had to compete with the strong centres of the old trade belt to the west. Ironically the defeat of the reich in 1945 again split the Prussian territories from the western city belt; the highly polycephalic Bonn Republic inherited the traditions of the old leagues, the monocephalic DDR conserved a number of the traits of the centralized Prussian monarchy.[13]

THE UNIQUENESS OF THE EUROPEAN CONFIGURATION
AND THE SOURCES OF VARIATIONS
IN THE OTHER WORLD REGIONS

We have argued for the use of a simple grid of variables in the explanation of the many variations in the sequences of state-building and national consolidation in Western Europe. We shall conclude our discussion with a brief and necessarily superficial review of the possibilities of constructing a corresponding grid of variables for the differentiation of sequences of development in the other regions of the world.

In our discussion of the variations within Europe we gave pride of place to four variables: on the cultural side, the independence/dependence of the Church and the conditions for the development of a distinctive national linguistic standard; on the economic side, the level of concentration in the rural economy and the independence/dependence of the city network.

At a higher level of abstraction we can identify four corresponding sets of "master variables," shown in Figure 5.

Let us review these variables in turn and point out the more striking of the overall differences among geocultural areas:

MASTER VARIABLES	GEOCULTURAL AREA
1. Secular-Religious Differentiation[14]	
— Minimal: local religions only	Traditional Tropical Africa
— Intermediate: local religion closely fused with political system	
— no corporate church	Hindu India, Confucian China,
— weakly incorporated	Moslem empires
— Maximal: church differentiated and strongly incorporated	
— separate from society	Buddhist political systems
— closely fused with political system, but supraterritorial	Greek Orthodox Church, Counter-Reformation Roman Catholic Church in Latin American Empires
— supraterritorial organization, potentially in opposition to political authority	Medieval Catholic Church
— nationally fused	Protestant state churches
— separate from national political system	Protestant sects

MASTER VARIABLES	GEOCULTURAL AREA

2. Linguistic Unification Distinctiveness[15]

Low/low

    localized languages, little likelihood of standardization, imperial standard shared with several successor states — Tropical Africa, Latin American countries with large proportions of Indians

Low/medium

    highly diversified several endoglossic, one exoglossic standard — India

Medium/low

    imperial or settler standard near-dominant

      — one standard — Arab states, rest of Latin America, English-speaking settler states

      — several standards — Europe: Switzerland, Belgium; Canada; South Africa

Medium/medium

    one endoglossic, one exoglossic standard — Ireland, Wales, Finland

Medium/high

    major dialectical varieties

      — one — China

      — several — Spain, Norway, Czechoslovakia, Soviet Union

High/medium

    shared endoglossic standard — Austria, Germany, Thailand, Laos

High/high — Japan, homogenous European nation-states

3. Differentiation/Independence of City Networks[16]

    — Low differentiation from rural surroundings, weak networks — Tropical Africa Ibero-American cities outside captaincies, Russian cities[17]

    — High differentiation, network dominated by military/administrative centres — Oriental cities, North African cities, Ibero-American capitals, Prussia, Habsburg Empire

    — High differentiation, largely independent network — Japan (rise of Chonin, 18th century), cities of "trade-belt Europe," English-speaking settler states

MASTER VARIABLES	GEOCULTURAL AREA
4. Concentration/Dispersal of Landholdings	
— No scarcity of land corporate lineage ownership	Traditional Tropical Africa[18]
— Scarcity, narrow-kin inheritance	
— large estates	Asia (must be differentiated), North Africa, Parts of Europe,[19] Ibero-America
— smaller estates	Parts of Europe[20]
freer peasantry	North America

This quick and exceedingly superficial review of major differences among world regions on our four master variables obviously will not take us very far toward the construction of differentiating typologies for use in analyses of the preconditions and sequences of political development. The exercise has helped, however, to bring out with greater clarity the uniqueness of the European configurations.

Let us conclude this chapter by presenting a series of summary formulations of such uniqueness; it is too early to present conclusions from any detailed analysis, but it may be worthwhile, even on this meager basis, to set out, however summarily, a few statements for further elaboration and specification once the fuller variable profiles have been established case by case.

The great paradox of Western Europe was that it developed a number of strong centres of territorial control at the edges of an old empire; the decisive thrusts of state formation and nation-building took place on the peripheries of the territory left without effective control by the disruption of the Western Roman Empire.

	ECONOMY	CULTURE
EXIT VARIABLES: conditioning openness to cross-system transactions	Independence of City Network: Openness of Borders	Differentiation of Secular-Religious Institutions: Closedness vs. Openness Towards External Influence
VOICE VARIABLES: conditioning closeness of ties to territorial system	Separateness and Concentration of Primary Resources	Distinctiveness and Unification of Territorial Language

Figure 5

To this extent there is a tantalizing parallel with developments in the Far East: China, the imperial centre; centripetal Korea, the Asian counterpart to France; the seaward periphery Japan, the equivalent of the "off-shore island" England. But the crucial difference was that the Chinese empire maintained its centres and its borders; the onslaught of the Western powers from the Opium War onward broke up the structure for only brief periods and built up counter-forces making for even greater unification.

What turned out to be crucial in the European development was that the fragmented centre belt was made up of territories at an advanced level of culture, technologically as well as organizationally. Firstly, there was a well-developed agricultural economy, innovative in its technology even during the early Middle Ages;[21] secondly, there was a remarkable network of highly autonomous cities, institutionally distinct from the surrounding agricultural lands,[22] thirdly, these cities as well as the rural areas were linked culturally through a common religion and a cross-territorial corporated church, through the operation of a major organization for long-distance communication, and through craft literacy, in two dominant standard languages, Greek and Latin; and fourthly, the transactions across these varied autonomous territories were controlled under one body of inherited normative precepts, those embodied in long tradition of Roman Law.[23]

At the core of the highly developed region, all attempts at military-administrative centre-building failed until the nineteenth century. The decisive early developments toward a restructuring of the territory took place at the peripheries of the heartland. These attempts might easily have failed as well; many in fact did. Three circumstances contributed decisively to the success of the centre-builders: firstly, the development of literate bureaucracies and legal institutions, largely through the cooperation of the Church with the dynasties of the conquest centres; secondly, the growth of trade and the emergence of new industries, developments which allowed the military-administrative machineries to expand without destroying their resource basis; and thirdly, the emergence of national script and the consequent attempts to unify the peripheral territories culturally around a standard medium of internal communication—this development was pushed one step further at the Reformation, through the break with the cross-territorial Greco-Latin culture, and was accelerated through the invention of printing, through the multiple reproduction of messages without relays.

The extraordinary synchrony of all these developments during the three centuries from 1485 to 1789 goes far to explain the rapid growth of consolidated nation-states on the western and the eastern edges of the

CHALLENGES	SIXTEENTH-EIGHTEENTH CENTURY EUROPE	TWENTIETH CENTURY POSTCOLONIAL SYSTEMS
CONDITIONS OF CENTRE FORMATION: pressures from major centres outside territory	LOW: old Empire, disintegrated, influences from Rome largely cultural, political only in South	HIGH AND DIVERSIFIED: London, Paris, Washington, Moscow, Peking
build-up through wars	FREQUENT	RARE, but exceptions: Vietnam, Israel, Egypt
centre-periphery communications	SLOW: short-distance dependencies favoring integration; slowly expanding literacy favoring integration with national centre	RAPID: long-distance dependencies weaken national centre; increasing exposure of masses to outside communications: radio, films
CULTURAL UNIFICATION: likelihood of development of national linguistic standard	HIGH: outside standards (Latin/Greek), politically/economically weak	LOW: outside standards politically and/or economically strong: role of language of former imperial masters
elite commitment to unified culture	HIGH, OUTSIDE CENTRAL TRADE BELT: early national universities favored development of nation-tied competences (careers in law, education)	LOW: dependence on foreign universities, attraction to alternatives outside [26]

CHALLENGES	SIXTEENTH-EIGHTEENTH CENTURY EUROPE	TWENTIETH CENTURY POSTCOLONIAL SYSTEMS
PARTICIPATION DEMANDS:		
demonstration effects of other regimes	LOW: all regimes restrictive until American/French Revolutions	HIGH: models of universal suffrage politics in Europe and the West
institutional readiness for mass participation	VARYING, BUT TYPICALLY HIGH: historically inherited channels of representation (peasant assemblies, estates-general)	LOW
DISTRIBUTION DEMANDS:		
demonstration effects	LOW	HIGH: welfare states, socialist economies as alternative models
institutional readiness	HIGH: marked build-up of extractive capabilities, potential instruments of redistribution	LOW: state machineries overburdened by other tasks
growth of cultural-national economic solidarity	MARKED: increase in willingness to equalize economic conditions within territory	PROBLEMATIC

[93]

Western Europe core territories. What proved decisive for the further growth of these political systems was the low levels of overall mobilization at the time of state-building; the new linkages were forged at the level of national and local elites; the masses of the peasantry and the urban workers were only gradually brought in. The decisive thrust toward the consolidation of the machineries of territorial control took place before the full monetization of the economy, before mass literacy, before the lower strata could articulate any claims for participation. This gave the national elites time to build up efficient organizations before they had to face the next set of challenges: the strengthening of national identity at the mass level, the opening of channels for mass participation, the development of a sense of national economic solidarity, and the establishment of a workable consensus on the need for a redistribution of resources and benefits. There were important differences in the time sequences of these later crises; we have discussed these in some detail in other contexts.[24] What is important is that the Western nation-states were given a chance to solve some of the worst problems of state-building before they had to face the ordeals of mass politics.[25]

In contrast to these early state-builders, the leaders of the postcolonial polities face a cumulation of challenges in a very different world environment. Let us wind up our analysis by presenting a schematic check list (see below) of such differences in the overall conditions of political action.

These are stark contrasts; the actual gradations are finer, the variations have many more strands to them. The lesson of the analysis is, nevertheless, clear: the European sequence simply cannot be repeated in the newest nations. The new nation-builders have to start out from fundamentally different conditions; they face an entirely different world, but they can learn to develop new combinations of policies from a detailed analysis of the many facets of the European experiences of state-building and national consolidation. They may learn more from the smaller countries than from the large, more from the multicultural consociational polities than from the homogeneous dynastic states, more from the European latecomers than from the old, established nations. What is important is that these experiences be sifted and evaluated, not just case by case, but within an effort of cross-regional systemization. If this chapter helps to initiate discussions along these lines, it will have served its purpose.

NOTES

1. See especially my "Models and Methods in the Comparative Study of Nation-Building," ch. 2 in Citizens, Elections, Parties, Oslo, Norwegian University Press, and New York, McKay, 1970; my "The Growth and Structuring of Mass Politics in Europe," Scandinavian Politics Studies, Vol. 5, 1970, pp. 65-83; and my "Dimensions of State Formation and Nation-Building: A Possible Paradigm for Research and Variations within Europe" in C. Tilly (ed.) The Formation of National States in Western Europe, Princeton, Princeton University Press, forthcoming.

2. Talcott Parsons, Societies: Comparative and Evolutionary Perspectives, Englewood Cliffs, N.J., Prentice-Hall, 1967.

3. See especially H. A. Innes, Empire and Communication, Oxford, Clarendon, 1950 and Jack Goody, ed., Literacy in Transitional Societies, Cambridge, Cambridge University Press, 1967.

4. Henri Franfort, The Birth of Civilization in the Near East, Bloomington, Indiana University Press, 1951, quoted from Doubleday Anchor paperback ed. 1956, p. 77.

5. Ibid., pp. 97-98.

6. Social Origins of Dictatorship and Democracy, Boston, Beacon, 1966.

7. Albert O. Hirschman, Exit, Voice and Loyalty, Cambridge, Harvard University Press, 1970.

8. For an interesting discussion of the differences between the Rhine, the Rhone, and the Seine as possible sites for such core-building efforts, see Laetitia Boehm, Geschichte Burgunds, Stuttgart, Kohlhammer, 1971.

9. The conceptual map presented in Figure 3 covers the territories of the Roman Church only; it does not include the Eastern Territories dominated by the Greek Orthodox Church. No attempt has as yet been made to extend this region-specific model systematically to other areas, but some extensions are quite obvious, e.g., the location of Russia as an "agrarian bureaucracy" in the northeastern corner of the conceptual map, a landward empire isolated from the city networks of the west and "locked in" culturally through the subjugation of the Church to the territorial State. For a broader treatment of the East-West dimension in Europe, see Talcott Parsons, The System of Modern Societies, Englewood Cliffs, N.J., Prentice-Hall, 1971.

10. This is the famous Pirenne thesis: see Mohammed and Charlemagne, London, Allen & Unwin, 1939. For a broader treatment see Fernand Braudel, La Méditerranée et le monde méditerranéen à l'epoque de Philippe II, Paris, Colin, 1949, Première partie, ch. 5 "L'unité humaine: les routes et les villes."

11. For the Netherlands and Switzerland, see the chapter by Daalder in Vol. II of this work. For other leagues, see especially P. Dollinger, La Hanse, Paris, Aubier, 1964; English translation, The German Hansa, London, Macmillan, 1970.

12. For detailed analyses of the alliances which made this transition possible, see Theodore S. Hamerow, The Social Foundations of German Unification, Princeton, N.J., Princeton University Press, Vol. I, 1969; Vol. II, 1972.

13. There is an interesting parallel in the northeast between Sweden and Prussia. the Swedish conquests to the south and west in 1658 created the basis for a more balanced city structure: Scania and Gothenburgh developed important economic

counter-forces against the eastern capital much in the way the Western cities counterbalanced Berlin in the Prussian reich. All these propositions will of course have to be tested against statistical time series for city size rank orders. For possible sources of data for comparative analyses of city networks, see R. Mols, Introduction à la demographie historique des villes d'Europe du XIVe au XVIIIe siècle, Louvain, Publ. Universitaires, 3 vols., 1954-1956. For procedures of computation, see J. R. Gibbs, ed., Urban Research Methods, Princeton, N.J., Van Nostrand, 1961, Ch. 12; and B. Berry, "City Size and Economic Development," Ch. 5 in Leo Jacobson and Ved Prakash, eds., Urbanization and National Development, Beverly Hills, Sage Publications, 1971.

14. This classification relies largely on the distinctions developed by Donald E. Smith, Religion and Political Development, Boston, Little, Brown, 1971.

15. This classification draws in part on the work of Heinrich Kloss, "Notes Concerning a Language–Nation Typology," in J. A. Fishman et al. (ed.) Language Problems of Developing Nations, New York, John Wiley, 1968, pp. 69-86, and on tables assembled by Dankwart Rustow, A World of Nations, Washington, D.C., Brookings Institution, 1968.

16. This crude classification is partly inspired by Weber's treatment in Wirtschaft und Gesellschaft; partly by Fernand Braudel, Civilisation Matérielle et Capitalisme, Paris, Colin, 1967, ch. 8, pp. 397-404.

17. On differences between Russia and Western European cities during the decisive period of state-building, see especially Otto Brunner. "Europäisches und Russisches Bürgertum," pp. 97-115, in Neue Wege der Sozialgeschicte, Göttingen, Vandenhoeck and Ruprecht, 1956, pp. 97-115.

18. This characterization of traditional Tropical Africa is primarily based on J. Goody, "Economy and Feudalism in Africa," Economic History Review, Vol. 22, No. 3, December 1969, pp. 393-504; cf. also "Succession in Contemporary Africa" Arch. Eur. de Sociologie, Vol. 10, No. 1, 1969, pp. 27-40, and Goody's "Uniqueness in the Cultural Conditions for Political Development in Black Africa," in Vol. II of this work.

19. For differentiations within Europe, see especially Folke Dovring, Land and Labour in Europe 1900-1950, The Hague, Nijhoff, 1960 and B. Slichter van Bath, The Agrarian History of Western Europe A.D. 500-1850, London, Arnold, 1963.

20. See note 19.

21. See Slichter van Bath, op. cit., pp. 69-72; also see L. White, "Technology and Invention in the Middle Ages," Speculum, Vol. 15, 1940, pp. 141-59.

22. The distinctiveness of the European city network has been analyzed with great acumen in Brunner, op. cit., ch. II, "Stast und Bürgertum in der Europäischen Geschite," pp. 80-96.

23. See Munroe Smith, The Development of European Law, New York, Columbia University Press, 1928, especially pp. 39-44; P. Koschaker, Europe und das Römische Recht, Munich, Biederstein, 1949, 3rd ed., Beck, 1958; and R. David and J. C. Brierley, Major Legal Systems of the World Today, London, Stevens, 1968, Part I.

24. See my Citizens, Elections, Parties, op. cit., chs. 3-4, also my article, "The Growth and Structuring of Mass Politics in Europe," op. cit.

25. This, of course, is not much more than a reformulation of the argument of Samuel Huntington, Political Order in Changing Societies, New Haven, Conn., Yale University Press, 1968. What we have added is a schema for the analysis of variations

within Europe and some suggestions for parallel differentiations across and within other regions.

26. This point has been brought out with great force by Ronald Dore in his comparison of endoglossic Japan (in this respect a system very similar to the European nation-states) and Latin America. In Japan the closed national culture encouraged the elites to build up their institutions through internal accommodation; in Latin America the cross-national openness of elite structures sharing the same language always allowed escape options. Cf. R. P. Dore, "Latin America and Japan Compared" in John J. Johnson, ed., Continuity and Change in Latin America, Stanford, Stanford University Press, 1964, and the comments by Hirschmann, op. cit., p. 61.

CHAPTER 3

THE CONFRONTATION OF THEORIES WITH NATIONAL REALITIES: REPORT ON AN INTERNATIONAL CONFERENCE

Rajni Kothari

RAJNI KOTHARI is Director of the Centre for the Study of Developing Societies in Delhi and has carried out a series of major empirical studies on India. He is the author of *Politics in India* and edited *Caste in Indian Politics.* He has been active in international comparative projects and has contributed to a great number of journals and symposia. Currently, he is engaged in a study of the future of world order and has just completed a book entitled, *Footsteps into the Future.*

The recent spurt of scholarly interest in the emergence of new "states" and "nations" has given rise, on the one hand, to a renewed interest in the historical study of similar phenomena in older states and, on the other, to a considerable effort at formulating general theories and models which can provide guidelines for an understanding of these phenomena. By and large the initiative for these efforts has come from North American and European scholars. More recently, scholars from the developing nations have also joined in this work. Subsequent cooperation between these two groups of scholars from differing historical backgrounds and socio-cultural contexts has led to a series of questions concerning (a) the relevance of prevailing conceptual frameworks for an explanation of variations in the behavior of social and political phenomena; (b) the empirical validity of these frameworks in different historical settings; (c) the methodological assumptions underlying the whole effort at general theory; and (d) basic

[99]

issues of teleology and directionality, determinacy and choice, in comparative theory.

It was with a view to beginning an exploration of these questions that a Meeting of Experts on Problems of State Formation and Nation-Building was organized by UNESCO at Cérisy-la-Salle (France) in August 1970; its purpose was to expose existing theories and models of state and nation-building to the concrete and diverse experiences of a variety of countries and regions, to examine the empirical validity of these theories and, if possible, to suggest ways of moving towards a more satisfactory model of comparative research. Judging from the papers presented and the discussions that ensued, discontent with existing theoretical formulations is widespread, though it cannot be said that any clear alternative proposals emerged during the meeting.

What I propose to do here is to raise certain unsettled issues in our understanding of state and nation-building, issues that in part arose during the meeting and reflect a growing debate in the literature. My goal will not be to draw up a report in the usual manner, but to draw some meaning out of the many papers and discussions with a view to provoking further thought on problems and controversies that were raised at the Cérisy-la-Salle meeting.

ALTERNATIVE THEORETICAL MODELS

Although there was no clear and systematically articulated confrontation between opposing theoretical standpoints, a variety of alternative models and critiques emerged. The systems theory approach was expanded from its original "structural-functional" premises while still offering an extended rationale for the latter. But both this theory and the systematic methodological-empirical critique of it, plus the fact that no rebuttal of this critique was forthcoming, appeared to put to rest the oft-attacked theory of structural functionalism.

Social Mobilization

Slightly more sympathetic attention was given to the social mobilization theory as propounded by Karl Deutsch and subsequently developed by a number of other authors. Stein Rokkan has considered it at some length in one of his articles that served as a background paper,[1] and in his work *Citizens, Elections, Parties*,[2] in which he presents his more inclusive concept of center-periphery linkages and his phasing of the European nation-building experience. Other participants tried to accommodate this perspective in the approach to a paradigmatic synthesis of a variety of theories of "political development" or as part of an attempt to dimensionalize the nation-building process in Europe on the two major (and relatively independent) dimensions of acquisition of "stateness" on the one hand and "pattern of mobilization" on the other.[3]

That the theory of social mobilization has been highly influential was revealed during the discussions. At the same time serious doubts were raised regarding the viability of this theory as an explanatory model. J. A. Silva Michelena, both in his paper[4] and during the discussion, showed how the package of social mobilization (urbanization, education, industrialization, mass-media exposure), participation, growth of democratic rights and demands, and legitimacy of the political order breaks down in the case of Latin America, partly because it ignores the empirical relationship between agricultural development and land reforms on the one hand and the urbanization-industrialization complex on the other, and partly because it totally ignores the international context of economic dominance and the linkage of the developing political systems to this pattern of dominance-dependence.

> Thus in Latin America new opportunities for participation increased in spite of the prevailing political system. As a result, new loyalties were bestowed almost exclusively on political parties and leaders and not on the system, or else were not generated at all, creating conditions for anomic participation of the urban masses—riots or demonstrations that are not politically goal-directed.[5]

Recent work on the relationship between social mobilization and politicization in the context of India[6] also suggests that the Lerner-Deutsch approach to modernization and social mobilization does not stand up to scrutiny, either as a homogeneous interrelated package of indicators or as a sequence of developments, and that the underlying assumption of a lot of Western theory (according to which the critical development and "inputs" come from society, to which the state responds in the form of "outputs") is also not confirmed by evidence from the new nations, where the major thrust of development consists in the permeation of the social structure from one or more political centers. It shows that the major differentials in the process of development pertain not just to degrees of urbanization, industrialization, and the like, which lead "from tradition to modernity," but rather to the relationship between modernization of the traditional network of society—of agriculture and the rural countryside, of community organization, and of the territorial distribution of a growing population—on the one hand and the growth of a mobile and educated middle class on the other.

The extent to which a political system can answer the needs and demands of a populace depends crucially upon the fit between the size of its urban middle class and the opportunities made available by economic development, and this in turn depends on the rate and character of agricultural development. Agricultural development and land reforms can, of course, also be incorporated in the theory of modernization, but once this is done both the emphasis on some necessary sequence and on "prerequisites" of modernization, as well as the still strong and pervasive dichotomy underlying the theory of modernization, break down. Perhaps much more useful leads can be found in Rokkan's work on the relationship between land and cities, in the recent work of Barrington Moore, Jr.,[7] and in some of the more sophisticated variants of Marxist theory. But these, in turn, suffer from a presumption of socio-economic determination of the political process and leave out the dynamic role of political and intellectual elites in social transformation.

Center and Periphery

Much more relevant to a comparative study of nation-building and state formation is the center-periphery model of political development, though on the whole it has received comparatively less systematic attention among theorists of political development, partly because of its accent on the primacy of the political order over any simple notion of social or economic determinism or "interest aggregation." The most lucid general statement of this concept is to be found in the writings of Edward Shils.[8] But the recent work of Rokkan who has consciously adopted the center-periphery model in his analysis of European development, the general formulations of S. N. Eisenstadt, who seems to carry forward and exemplify the early leads of Shils,[9] the comparative theoretical work of Bendix on nation-building,[10] and the social class analysis of Barrington Moore can all be usefully interpreted through a common conceptual framework of (a) center formation (either through a leading territory or dynasty or a dominant social class); (b) the process of infringement of the center on the periphery (through the play of power and the process of policy-making); and (c) the encroachment of the periphery on the center (through demands on the machinery of the state). My own work on India attempts to view political development as an interaction between the penetration of the center and the response of the periphery to such penetration, mediated by intermediate structures and traditions.[11]

The center-periphery model dominated the discussions at the meeting. But although there was wider acceptance of this model than of any other, there were no clear agreements on its usefulness as an explanatory theory. At best it was seen as an important descriptive and heuristic device. A number of specific questions were raised: What are the territorial implications of the model? If the "center" is a territorial concept, is there a single center or could there be more than one? If there are more than one, in what conceptual interrelationship do they stand? How do these definitions vary with size of the state? What is the degree of social and cultural homogeneity requisite for a center to be accepted as a legitimate locus of authority and loyalty? To the extent that such homogeneity does not exist or there is resistance to the dominant center from regional centers which may conceive of themselves as competing or even "counter-centers," is the former still to be conceived as a center? Examples cited included Canada (English versus French), Belgium (Walloons versus Flemings), Spain (Castilians versus others) and some of the Latin American countries where there was a dualistic or polarized situation in respect of authoritative or legitimate centers. At a somewhat lower key of resistance, there was the question of a special kind of differentiation in which there was a political center and an economic center; what if these were not in the same place? The issue became serious when one of these centers, say the economic center, lay outside the territory of the state, and when its command of resources and network of effective power and influence was such that the economic center became far more potent and powerful than the formally "independent" political center. In such cases, frequently found in the new nations of Latin America, Africa, and some parts of Asia, where did the center lie?

Another set of questions was raised during the meeting which warned against any presumption of stability or continuity in center-periphery analysis as Western theorists applying this framework are prone to hold. (They have done this with almost every conceptual framework though it is not inherent therein.) J. A. Silva Michelena's paper referred at length to the need to take into account the changing class characteristics of ruling elites in any comparative study of nation-building; N. Pašić did the same in discussing the case of the Balkans.[12] As Pašić put it during the discussions, it is necessary to identify the actors, their social composition, their motives, who sides with whom and for what reason. There is need to discern the position of elites and classes, their specific characteristics from one region to another and from one historical phase to another. On the other hand, implicit in Pašić's comments was a rejection of any determination of political positions by reference to class composition, for the same social class may perform wholly different functions. Thus, whereas the bourgeoisie were nation-integrators in France and Germany, they were pitched against integration in Austria and Hungary and later in Yugoslavia where it fell to the Communist Party to lead the movement for national liberation. Nowadays there are quite different sources of nation-builders—intellectual elites, exploited masses without definite class character, and so forth. In some of the new nations the intellectual elite occupying the center played a much more autonomous role. In others, however, the local elites were tied in a dependent economic and political relationship with a center that lay outside the territory. It is necessary, thus, to consider and interpret the problem of relationship between center and periphery in a dynamic way, with special attention to the changing character of both the center and the periphery.

Most of these questions raised definitional and, in part, analytical and interpretive issues, but they also threw up suggestive hypotheses that need to be tested under different conditions and threshholds of statehood and nationhood, economic independence, size of territory, and nature of political system—issues that have so far not been systematically explored in the center-periphery model of nation-building. My attempt to apply the center-periphery conceptual framework to political development in India suggests (a) that large size and cultural heterogeneity necessitate not only the growth of a center which is not just territorial but also has a political-organizational locus (e.g. through a dominant party) but also the need for such a center to enter into a relationship of bargaining and accommodating a large number of intermediate centers which in effect become the loci of institutional and interest aggregation; (b) that such a network of centers makes it incumbent that the process of national integration be conceived not in any linear and centralizing fashion, but rather in terms of a complicated interplay between the persisting autonomy of cultural centers on the one hand and the primacy of the political center in the new scheme of things on the other; (c) that such a framework of integration necessitates a measure of democratic func-tioning, not simply as ideological choice but also as a pragmatic necessity; and (d) that as such a process of integration advances, new conceptual formulations evolve. The concept of "center" moves from being a territorial notion to being a more strictly political notion focusing on a dominant party, coalition, or leadership; the concept of periphery also changes from being territorial to being social in terms of depressed classes, castes, tribes, and so forth; and the concept of nation itself tends to draw its identity less from cultural and linguistic notions which were the origin of national consciousness in many parts of Europe and more from a transcendent notion of statehood which coincides with nationhood.

Underlying all this of course, is the assumption that one is talking of a genuinely independent center, independent not only politically but also economically and culturally. To the extent that such independence is not to be found, the transcendent center may lie outside the national territory. Conceptually, therefore, a far more complex structure of reality is found in which the territorial national center has to be distinguished from the political center (this may be a dominant party or even a single leader within the nation, but it may also be a colonial metropolis or a continental center outside the nation), while the territorial notion of periphery has to be supplemented by a societal or social-class notion of periphery and hence viewed dynamically over time. Furthermore, empirically speaking, there is in all states and nations (except the most primitive ones) likely to be a whole series of centers and peripheries, with a vertical structure of both centrality and peripherality. At the same time, for the concept of center to be meaningful, one has to conceptualize something like the "most central of all centers" which is in effect a notion of a transcendental center the acceptance of whose authority determines its centerness.

When all this is said, however, and in a sense precisely because of the meaningful controversy and dialogue that it generated, the center-periphery framework of a theory of nation-building appears to offer a good way of distinguishing between the variety of nation and state-building experiences before us, ranging all the way from the typical European experiences to the vast variety of experiences going on right now in the so-called Third World. For one thing, it brings to attention the role of political and intellectual elites in nation-building, as autonomous and dynamic agents and not just as simple responding mechanisms to some basic inputs from other segments. On the other hand, it enables us to study many policy and ideological issues without rendering the conceptual framework itself valued-loaded; the problem of peripherality can be conceived as much in social-class terms as in terms of national integration, depending upon the problem under study; the issues of governmental performance, long neglected in political analysis, can be studied as much in respect of equity, distribution, and social justice (along the center-periphery continuum) as it can be studied in respect of political stability and coalition-making between various centers and various peripheries. Above all, this is a framework that is amenable to a variety of methodologies ranging from descriptive typologies and paradigms, to analytical "aids to understanding" through identification of salient parameters of nation-building, to the generation of correlational, sequential, and causal hypotheses that discriminate between different empirical sets of temporal and contextual relationships.

The center-periphery model is, of course, no more than an additional conceptual apparatus to the many that already exist; there is also no doubt that, as it has been developed so far, it raises more questions than it answers. There is little hope of its becoming a unified theory, which is perhaps just as well. All the same, it seems to offer a useful vantage point from which to study developmental processes in politics, and more especially the processes of state and nation-building. Its major attraction, of course, is that it emphasizes the more typically political variables of political change and stability rather than merely seeking explanations from independent variables that lie beyond the political sphere as is the case with most other conceptual models so far.

But in order to turn what is still no more than a mental diagram into an empirically sensitive instrument, the center-periphery theorists have yet a lot more homework to do.

VARIATIONS IN NATION-BUILDING

Apart from some comments on various alternative conceptual schemes of organizing nation-building experiences (an exercise that was not undertaken in any explicit manner), most of the discussions at the meeting were marked by a debate arising out of wide variations in state and nation-building experiences with which different participants were familiar. As the discussions proceeded, however, serious divergencies of viewpoints and perspectives emerged regarding (a) the relevance of general theories based largely on European and North American experience for understanding the course of political development and modernization in the contemporary new nations, (b) the theoretical assumptions underlying the recent interest in deductive model-building as an aid to comparative theory that sought to encompass a wide variety of political entities, and (c) the application of methodological assumptions underlying theories of political development and modernization to a study of concrete historical phenomena such as state formation and nation-building taking place in specific contexts of time and space. The most clear and explicit divergence in viewpoints that emerged was between the scholars from Europe and North America and those from the new nations (including Latin America), although the methodologically specific and middle-range scholars from the Western countries were in a better position to appreciate the empirical perspectives of non-Western experts.

The analysis presented in the regional papers and the discussions that followed showed striking contrasts between the European historical experience in state and nation-building and the contemporary experience in a large part of the developing world. The dimensions of these contrasts were many—in initial conditions and cultural contexts, in timing and sequence, in the impingement of the international system and the role of ideology, and above all in regard to the arenas of decision-making and government-populace relationships. Without doubt there were many important differences among the European countries as was again and again emphasized by Hans Daalder,[13] as also among new nations of the contemporary world in Latin America and Asian countries, or within each of these continents and indeed even within single countries. But the overriding contrasts that emerged were between the historical experiences and contexts of the West and the contemporary experiences and contexts elsewhere. The fact that some among the former "failed," as in the case of Spain and Portugal, or that some among the latter have probably "succeeded" better than others, still does not minimize the overall contrast in conditions, sequences, and social contexts between the early arrivals and the latecomers to independent state and nationhood.

On this there was some agreement, although the committed comparative theorists continued to stretch the relevance and usefulness of the European experience for contemporary nation-builders. Conditions that facilitated European state and nation-building, such as relatively small size of populations, cultural homogeneity, flexibility provided by dynastic wars and an international balance of power, a vast peasant base for resource mobilization, and ample time for a sequential treatment of developmental crises, and a gradual politization of the periphery were specified and stated by both Western and non-Western scholars. The controversy that arose—and remained mostly unsettled—was not so much in regard to particular statements of differential conditions but rather in regard to the scope of prevailing general theories that sought to encompass both historical European and contemporary non-European experiences.

The issues were squarely posed by almost all the scholars from the Third World. One of the participants expressed serious doubts on the utility of deductive models for explaining anything, least of all variations between specific experiences found under specific contexts; there was need to return to the much neglected and often maligned inductive tradition in the social sciences. He illustrated his point by his work on radio listeners and on the relationship between income and satisfaction and the contrast between the conclusions of his empirical investigation and the aggregate ranking presented in the *World Handbook of Political and Social Indicators.*

A participant from Uganda questioned the basic assumptions and definitions underlying the European notion of a centralized state or the contrary conception of consociational democracy, these conceptual formulations were of little consequence to nation-builders of Africa who were trying to forge political authority out of multitribal societies and reconcile whatever authority they could manage to derive with the compelling and simultaneous mandates of mass democracy and a socialist state.

J. A. Silva Michelena from Venezuela questioned the whole theory of modernization which provided the basic mainstay and theoretical rationale of a lot of specific formulations in the literature. These include the theories of national identity (Pye, Rustow), rationalization of authority (Silvert), structural differentiation and social mobilization (Deutsch), political participation (Almond and Verba), the development of political capacity (Eisenstadt), and center-formation and coalition-making (Rokkan, Bendix, Moore). Whereas all these formulations have helped our analytical understanding of some of the interrelationships between society and politics (as for instance through a typology of crises), none of them provides us with an explanatory theory, not to speak of causal theory with predictive power. But the more important point is that these limitations of specific theories derive out of a basic lack in the more general theory of modernization or political development, namely that these are empty concepts, empty of socio-economic content, not informed by any historical points of reference, and always underplaying the structural constraints operating on the political process—social-class structure, the structure of agrarian and industrial relationships, and above all the international structure of dominance and dependence. Lacking a clear theory of the relationship between operating political and economic structures and developmental causation for specific national and international constellations, the modernization paradigm fails to provide an adequate general, or even comparative, theory.

These points were made more vivid by another participant from Latin America. Commenting on the experience of countries in southern Latin America, he elucidated the general critique of modernization theory posed by Silva Michelena by showing how different historical conditions made even some of the most prevalent concepts change their meaning when applied to particular configurations. Thus, for instance, concepts like "people," "elite," and a common "civic" culture as used in social mobilization, participation, and center-periphery theories do not really apply in Latin America due to a very special kind of cultural and political context. The assumption that there is an elite and a mass, that there is a reciprocal flow of primary and secondary messages which lead to a national consensus and a common consciousness and identity, is not very relevant to a historical condition where there is no reciprocity of perspectives and a basic "duality," resulting in a lack of a sense of political community. The prevailing theory of elite hardly applies in a situation where an indigenous entrepreneurial elite did not emerge, where there is a basic structural ambivalence arising out of the frustration of economic dependence and hence the lack of the growth of a genuine national bourgeoisie, and where the middle classes are driven to find their self-esteem and identity by forging a special relationship with the military and merging themselves in the glare and giganticism of their super-cities whose real point of reference—center—lies outside the country. The civic pantheon that emerges is thus highly equivocal, without a clear-cut cultural anchor, and in which the national elites themselves perform no clear-cut roles. Development has thus to be necessarily conceived in discontinuous forms, as rupture points from all that has gone before. Under such cultural conditions it is difficult to see how the existing interrelational models of development can provide any meaningful explanatory leads.

The Latin American experience has of late drawn a great deal of attention, both in the comparative literature and in general theoretical discussions. This was reflected in the meeting too. Of interest were the explanations advanced by scholars from the northern hemisphere. According to them, Latin American intellectual discussion focuses on abstract and symbolic categories rather than on the usual categories of interests, linkages, their articulation and representation. The stress, instead, is on collective representation of wholes. To use Durkheim's analysis, there is greater concern with issues of mechanical solidarity than of organic solidarity. At there is no clear congruence between symbolic categories and social reality, the ideas of intellectuals—which dominate political discourse in these countries—bear little relationship to the interests of specific social groups. A constant concern with legitimacy of regimes leads to a questioning of cultural inheritances and national identities. The problem facing Latin American societies is not so much in respect to goals set before them but rather of frustration with governmental performance, political efficacy, and so forth. A nonacceptance of the "politics of interest" leads to a recourse to symbolic battles. Social mobilization is not conceived in a participatory and representational idiom but rather in terms of overall identities and ideologies. There is here a basic difference in middle-class culture: instead of mobilizing and organizing the rural-ethnic peripheries, there is emphasis on incorporation, identity, and other such themes. Probably all of this is due to a basic lack of authenticity of original culture (unlike in the great Asian and African civilizations), too strong a dependence on the European heritage, and the failure to provide a clear answer to the role and position of the original inhabitants of the continent—the Indians—vis-à-vis Western immigrants in the forging of national identity.

A variant of the same theme dealt with the relevance of Durkheimian categories of division of labor. What one finds in Latin America, it was said, is a different kind of division of labor; neither mechanical nor organic but rather based on linkages at various levels and of various subtypes which do not, however, add up to any total integrated political culture. On this was imposed the ideology of integration in a universalist-transcendental manner and the norms of natural and Roman law, whereas the social reality was more of a patrominal-clientistic kind.

There was some merit in this "psychological" analysis of the Latin American situation; the speakers were no doubt groping in an attempt to come to grips with a baffling cultural phenomenon. At the same time, however, they managed to ignore and get around the more crucial problems of dominance and dependence—economic, intellectual, and ultimately political dependence—raised by Silva Michelena in his paper and in his presentation of a different theoretical approach as initiated in the work of Julian Stuart, the Brazilian scholar. As I see it, the problem of authenticity of culture is closely related to the problem of authority of wrong theories—the theories of national integration and national identity, of interest aggregation, of functional interrelationships and linkages in the framework of a stable aggregate, and of a necessary transition from the absence of such an aggregate to its realization. The style of expressing the two ends of this transition has been generally dichotomous (in spite of universal protestations to the contrary)—from traditionality to modernity, from "communal" to "associational" forms, from "mechanical" to "organic" solidarity, and from Gemeinschaft to Gesellschaft. There is the further assumption that the end-product of each of these transitions was teleologically determined and would be realized in the same way as found in the industrially advanced countries.

These two aspects of intellectual importation—positivist-rationalist theory of structural integration and a philosophical-methodological assumption of teleological progression toward predetermined outcomes —and their normative persistence through pedagogic traditions that are unrelated to the actual configuration of problem situations, account for the ambivalence and equivocation referred to during the discussion. The crisis of universalist aspirations found in several of the underdeveloped areas arises precisely out of their inability to resist being drawn too closely into the intellectual mainstream of the dominant nations. The problems that arise are a consequence of psychological pressures emanating from alien and "half-baked" intellectual traditions on the one hand and the objective conditions of economic and technological dependence on the other. Hence the somewhat better situation found in India or China, which is not merely due to the fact that these are ancient civilizations, which is no doubt true, but also because these nations are too distant and too big to be easily permeated and colonized in any total way as has been the case with large parts of Latin America and Africa, as well as with parts of Southeast Asia.[14] Hence also the great symbolic appeal of Castro in Latin America, Nasser in the Arab world, and Nyerere in black Africa, and of Mao in the whole of the underdeveloped world. One speaker highlighted the peculiar style of Nyerere in asserting his country's political autonomy through an ideological idiom that was at one and the same time expressive of real or mythical continuity of local traditions and assertive of its independence from the dominant norms and traditions emanating from the West The discussion of President Obote's symbolic assertion of Uganda's sovereignty through a dramatized reaction to the intrusion of foreign aircraft underlined the same point. Gandhi in India had again and again asserted such autonomy, employing the devices of both a reinterpretation of tradition and a positive assertion of a futuristic present.

The Indian case was also discussed by both Western and non-Western scholars. I have already mentioned several points above—the role of intermediate and horizontal aggregation and mobilization rather than vertical and total ones, the great importance of demographic (rural-urban) proportions and nation-building under conditions of acute scarcity of economic resources and opportunities, the dissociation between cultural and political wholes, the different meanings attached to concepts of nationhood and national integration, and the important role of intra-national diversities and autonomies in the process of integration. The focus on diversities and variations took the theoretical discussion to a new pitch. The whole issue of teleology was taken up by an Indian participant who asked if we were to presume a common future for all or were there to be different directions along which nations would move despite a common and no doubt comparable heritage of ideas, technologies, and even formal structures of government. The essential tasks in moving from deductive generalizations to empirically sensitive theory, according to him, were twofold: to demarcate the area of choice from the area of determinancy at given points in time and situational context—the essential problem of leadership—and to build into comparative theory the role of normative and value components as against some simple reference to institutionalized structures and functions—the essential problem of ideology. Here the social science endeavor is different from that of the physical sciences (whence social scientists continue to draw their analogies), for it deals with the constant intervention of human agents in the process of history. Theory that is not sensitive to this dynamic and constantly differentiating element in social and political situations would either "condemn" nations to a state of permanent atrophy or make such theory irrelevant to the real actors who are making or unmaking nations. When one participant responded to the criticism of Silva Michelena and others of the prevailing theory of modernization by arguing that the principal components of modernization were now a part of world culture and hence universal, he was asked if the institutional accomplishments of European civilization between the sixteenth and the eighteenth centuries were to be taken as the end points for all that was to come ever after or whether we will leave scope for innovation and creativity to present and future generations. The dangers of a historicist determination in any attempt at general theory (as against a more creative use of history for reorganizing human experience for fulfilling new ends) became evident as the issue was joined.

METHODOLOGICAL ISSUES

As the controversy developed, it became clear that underlying theoretical disagreements there were major differences of a methodological kind. And as the latter were identified and stressed, the issues turned from a simple confrontation between scholars from developed and developing nations to one between the proponents of abstract conceptual models and analytical categories and those whose analyses and critiques were derived from specific empirical observations. The point was brought home that there were two distinct traditions in modern political science itself, one trying to arrange and organize a confused mass of observations through a unified framework of theoretical concepts, analytical categories, and typologies, and the other operating at lower and middle levels of analysis and theory based on systematic observations of a selected cross-section of reality and producing generalizations that are testable. The two are not necessarily contradictory: the former too could lay claim to empirical relevance while the latter aim at continuously moving towards meaningful comparative theory at higher levels of specification. Nonetheless, the emphases are different and hence also the styles and nuances of research methodology. The point of relevance of all this is that a great deal of what passes as general theories (modernization, development, nation-building, and so forth) has very rarely been tested in different contextual and temporal settings while what has in fact been tested are generalizations at rather low levels of theoretical comprehension. There is thus a wide gap here which remains to be bridged before conferences like the one at Cérisy can produce scientific results.

The most comprehensive critique of the tendency at gross theory came from the rapporteur-général of the meeting. He roundly criticized the attempt in much theoretical writing on historical phenomena to impose conceptual frameworks upon empirical reality, to reify concepts and analytical categories, to produce precious little by way of low-level specifications of theoretical problems, to have almost no reference to actual problems encountered by practical men involved in political-historical processes, and instead to be too preoccupied by the analysts' own rather high-level categories and typologies. Another speaker drew attention to the conscious or unconscious incursion of nationalist and ethnocentric biases in such grand theories, and the need perhaps to turn away from imposing a European world view on the study of new nations and rather to utilize the issues and problems that emerge from empirical work in these nations for a more illuminating understanding of European history itself. He dismissed the controversy between global theory and unique explanations and instead called for more meaningful and at the same time more manageable comparisons (such as paired comparisons or comparisons between a limited number of cases).

Methodological issues formed the major thrust of some of the papers presented by non-Western scholars, especially Silva Michelena. Through his critique of the various components of modernization theory, Silva Michelena had shown the importance of structural properties of which both the theoretically posited interrelationships and the conceptually defined indicators are but manifestations. Thus he wanted both to move to a study of more meaningful variables in the context of the developing nations and to test systematically alternative theoretical constructs by detailed empirical studies as have already been undertaken in Brazil.

While conceding that the considerable conceptual and model-building work that had gone on in the United States and elsewhere had promoted a better understanding of certain interrelationships between society and politics (on the assumption that nations can be considered as isolated wholes), Silva Michelena seriously doubted their ability to provide explanations in any systematic way at all. Another speaker drew attention to the same issues by counterposing deductive theory that may at best be a heuristic device and inductive theory which had of necessity to be based on empirical observation, by his further distinction between observation and generalization, and how the latter, when not based systematically on the former, can prove highly fallacious. He also stressed the need to identify conceptual terms (like state and nation, structure and function, masses and elites) in real events, make them context-relevant, and continually interpret them so as to move to valid and tested theory rather than to look for illustrations that exemplify preexisting theory. The same had been highlighted in another paper through a point-by-point critique of systems theory whose preemption of the field of modernization, development, and nation-building studies caused so many of the current problems. Others, like this author, added to this list a whole series of problems germane to any attempt at either comparison or generalization.

CONCLUDING OBSERVATIONS

Many of these criticisms are now well known, but they were raised in a different context at the Cérisy meeting. They were raised in the context of a controversy on the relevance of theoretical concepts and vantage points drawn from the European historical experience to a meaningful explanation of historical phenomena found now and in the future in a major part of the late twentieth-century world. These issues were raised neither in the usual form of an internal dialogue among the current theorists of political development—there is an astounding ignorance among these theorists of the work of scholars from other regions as was manifest from some of the papers presented at the meeting—nor in the form of some naive ideological debate.

Actually, though wholly tentative and exploratory, the controversy that was raised, if properly followed up, can open up a whole vista of theoretical and empirical investigation. To mention a few of the points that need to be followed up, it seems that underlying the so-called gap between theory and data—a continuing problem of all knowledge—one may discern important divergences in theoretical perspectives arising out of different backgrounds of experience, learning, and ideology. It is necessary to explicate systematically these divergences and to build them into comparative analysis. Second, it would be beneficial for all to recognize consciously that the theories of modernization and development have so far, out of necessity and the accidents of their origin, been informed by one major vantage point, namely, that of the European modernization experience. As new vantage points emerge, there will be new theoretical perspectives. It is necessary to recognize this reality and devise theoretical and methodological ways of dealing with it, for otherwise, both the defensive affirmation of a world culture and the charge of ethnocentrism will produce a psychological hiatus that will be difficult to bridge. Third, as we recognize this reality of a confrontation between alternative theoretical perspectives, we must move a significant step forward towards translating our models into sets of testable hypotheses and to test them on the basis of data from a variety of spatial and temporal contexts. Let us recognize that we have not done this in any systematic form so far, nor have we subjected what little has been done to tests of significance and validity. Finally, as we recognize all this and move towards operationalizing these insights into cooperative research under-takings, we must come face to face with the need for another scientific breakthrough in our work. And this is the need to descend from highly inclusive and all-encompassing theory and research models to an emphasis on specificity of phenomena, distinctiveness of concepts, and the testability of theories through a series of observable and measurable relationships. Here perhaps lies a better path to comparative theory—not as elaboration of some overriding general theory through a typology of presumed variations around given categories and indicators, but rather as step by step progression from specific data profiles and theoretical explanations to legitimate comparison and duly tested theory. Theorizing is a legitimate activity provided it follows certain rules of the game. At present the field is replete with irresponsible and casual theorizing without much regard to empirical validity and intellectual relevance. The need now is to move to a more responsible methodological approach.

The Cérisy meeting was a disappointment to those who expected a consensus to emerge on the basis of existing theoretical literature. It was also a disappointment to those who looked for a clear-cut alternative to existing theoretical models to emerge. The usefulness of the meeting lay in other directions—in opening frank dialogue between the theorists from the developed and the developing nations, in acknowledging the importance of contextual variation in the growth of comparative theory, and above all, in making us all humble in face of the fact that we actually know so little about what we so complacently theorize, and of the need to test alternative theories and theoretical perspectives on the basis of a systematic confrontation with data drawn from a variety of historical contexts. It is to be hoped that ten years from now the same issues as were raised at Cérisy can be raised on the basis of a more systematic marshalling of evidence from different regions and, let us also hope, a better recognition of the importance of different vantage points and theoretical perspectives.

NOTES

1. Stein Rokkan, "Models and Methods in the Comparative Study of Nation-Building," Acta Sociologica, Vol. XII, No. 2, 1969.

2. Stein Rokkan, Citizens, Elections, Parties, New York, D. McKay, 1970.

3. A third dimension was also touched upon, that of acquisition of political rights as claims made on the state, as resulting from an interaction between "degree of stateness" and "pattern of mobilization."

4. J.A. Silva Michelena, "Diversities Among Dependent Nations: An Overview of Latin American Developments," in Vol. II of this work.

5. Ibid.

6. Rajni Kothari and Bashiruddin Ahmed, Social Mobilization and Politicization: India's Pattern of Interactions, Centre for the Study of Developing Societies, June 1969 (mimeo). The paper is based on a detailed investigation of a cross-section of the Indian population.

7. Barrington Moore, Jr., Social Origins of Dictatorship and Democracy: Lord and Peasant in the Modern World, Boston, Beacon Press, 1966.

8. Edward Shils, "Center and Periphery," The Logic of Personal Knowledge: Essays Presented to Michael Polani on his Seventieth Birthday, London, 1961.

9. S. N. Eisenstadt, Modernization: Protest and Change, Englewood Cliffs, N.J., Prentice-Hall, 1966.

10. Reinhard Bendix, Nation-Building and Citizenship: Studies of our Changing Social Order, New York, John Wiley, 1964.

11. Cf. my Politics in India, Boston, Little, Brown, and New Delhi, Orient Longmans, 1970.

12. Cf. Chapter 7 in this volume.

13. Cf. Chapter 5 in this volume.

14. In a different context, the same issues were brought out with respect to Japanese dominance in East and Southeast Asia in the paper by Joji Watanuki, of which a revised version appears in Vol. II of this work.

CHAPTER 4

COMPARISONS OF DEVELOPMENTAL PROCESSES
WITHIN AND ACROSS NATION-STATES

D. L. Sheth

D. L. SHETH is Fellow at the Centre for the Study of Developing Societies, Delhi. He was a principal investigator in the International Studies of Values in Politics, sponsored by ISSC, and co-authored the volume *Values and the Active Community*. He has also published papers on Indian political parties and electoral behavior; and he is currently engaged in extensive research on social structure and politics in India, based on sample surveys and aggregate time series data.

Recent discussions on nation-building and state formation processes have, once again, brought into focus the controversy about the possibility of a general theory of political phenomena applicable to various political systems. In contrast to the earlier pursuits of formal theorization, however, the recent efforts concentrate on continuous interaction between data and elements of theory with a view to specifying levels of generalization possible for comparative analyses of a group of political systems or regions.

Earlier, the attempt was toward offering global explanations of assumed differences in the developmental process of different units (societies, cultures, nations, or political systems). The individual cases of developed or underdeveloped units were described either as conforming to or deviating from an ad hoc and evolutionary theory (model) of development. Differences between these units were conceived as differences in the stages of development and were ascribed to the success or failure of a unit in attaining certain economic, cultural, or institutional prerequisites prescribed by formal and definitional requirements of a given model. The generalizations were essentially deductive, where, as Bendix points out, ideal-type abstractions were treated as generalizations, and evidence was sought from the success or failure stories of different cases. Reacting against the crude universalism and ethnocentrism of this approach, the anthropologically oriented scholars came out with a contrary position, treating development as something unique to each socio-cultural unit, explainable only in terms of peculiar characteristics of that unit, but this concept was no less crude; only the ideal type was different.

NEW ISSUES IN COMPARATIVE ANALYSIS ARISING OUT OF THE STUDY OF NEW NATIONS

The empirical context in which the earlier discussions and studies were made has substantially changed since World War II. Numerous new states and nations have appeared on the world's political map in the last two and a half decades. Several of these new territorial entities are, no doubt, struggling to evolve simultaneously the central and unified political authority of a state and the political-cultural identity of a nation. This fact, however, does not necessarily imply that the process of political development is evolutionary and universal. Appreciation of the complexity of this new situation has given rise to several questions concerning comparative analysis of political systems of the world. In a radically changed empirical context of the contemporary world order, what kinds of political systems are these entities heading towards? Are they on the way to developing into the type of nation-states with which we are familiar, or will they cast themselves in new types of political systems (of course, modernizing and developing, but not along exactly the same dimensions as the established nation-states)? In what respects are the processes of political development that went into the shaping of established nation-states comparable to the processes that are under way in the new political entities? Does such a comparison make possible a general theory of the growth of political systems?

While more and more such issues are being identified in the recent discussions on comparative analysis of political systems, they have yet to inform in any rigorous way the formulation of research problems conducive to the construction of a viable general theory. From the search for uniformities which were explained in terms of artifacts or products (outputs) of a universal process of development, the emphasis is now shifting to a search for variations and dissimilarities, perhaps conceding the uniqueness of developmental experience in each country. Though a welcome occurrence for generating new data, it should not undermine the need for and possibility of a general theory of political development. This shift in emphasis, in fact, should point to the complexity of the tasks involved, especially of conceptualization, measurement, and data aggregation, for constructing a more adequate theory that would handle the diagnostic and predictive ends of scientific analysis. Otherwise, there is a danger of replacing the earlier ideology of universalism with that of nationalism and this replacement may turn out to be the same old activity of confusing theorization with ideologization.

The problem, then, is how to reconcile the differences between the "contextualists" who emphasize the "milieu" aspects in comparison and the "universalists" looking for common "patterns" and "sequences," not only with respect to problems but also with respect to institutional and behavioral responses to these problems in the process of political development. A reconciliation of the two approaches is possible, however, if, on the one hand, the deductive model of comparative analysis is replaced by a more complex and differentiated, empirically based theoretical framework that allows examination of competing hypotheses, generation of new data, identification of new dimensions, and the distinction among dimensions along which data aggregation and measurement activities can be carried out in a more fruitful and cumulative manner. On the other hand, the studies emphasizing variations have to be oriented to a theoretical reference of comparative analysis, and their findings have to be in terms of new facts and hypotheses confronting theory. In other words, both the uniformities and the variations in processes of political development should have their place in the same theoretical system, for, in any model of comparison, variations are as vital as uniformities and cannot be treated as exceptions or deviations.

It will be futile, however, to attempt high level generalizations about historical phenomena like nation-building and state formation, still less about the overall process of political development, before the units of comparison are properly described and located on the critical dimensions that enter into these processes, universally for a group of nations and specifically for each. The dimensions have to be identified and distinguished in such a manner that they guide data collection and measurement activities. For example, it needs to be empirically ascertained whether or not the processes of political development in the countries of the Third World converge on the broad dimensions of state formation and nation-building, so that when we extend the earlier typology based on the stages of development of nation-states to the modernization experiences of these new political entities, we are sure of our theoretical ground. If some new and more important variables are found to enter the modernization processes in these countries, their implications for comparative analyses have to be examined. This examination may call for substantial modifications of the present model of comparative analyses (taken largely from the systems theorists), making it more sensitive to both process and context in order to take account of variations and discontinuities in the political development processes of various countries. (For example, in several countries of the Third World, the ascendancy of political processes over age-old social processes may run counter to existing formulations on the evolution of a viable civil society.) Similarly the broad conceptual and methodological presumptions of earlier formulations—such as input-output analysis, developmental "crises" or "sequences"—may need to be freshly thought through in the light of new substantive insights on the historical phenomena of state formation and nation-building. Indeed, as we shall see in what follows, some of the major departures from prevailing formulations are more methodological (in the broadest sense of the term) than substantive.

Although recent theoretical discussions on the comparative study of political development reveal growing awareness of the above issues (Almond, Eisenstadt, Pye, Rokkan, Shils), operationalization of these concerns into specific study designs for comparative analysis lags far behind. For this gap between conceptualization and operationalization to be bridged, two important methodological problems of comparative analysis must be resolved: (i) how to compare processes (as against products and outputs) of political development between countries, so that generalizations can be made about the nature and direction of political development process as it takes place in different political systems; and (ii) how to deal with contextual variations in different political systems so that they can be included in explanations of differences and similarities in the process of political development within and between countries, or groups of countries.

These are two formidable tasks, and have to be tackled simultaneously at the levels of conceptualization and of data aggregation and measurement. In what follows we shall suggest some ways of approaching these problems in the area of comparative study of state formation and nation-building. Our purpose in this chapter is to formulate these problems and some tentative leads out of the present difficulties rather than to offer clear-cut solutions.

MODELS OF POLITICAL SYSTEMS AND POLITICAL DEVELOPMENT IN THE STUDY OF STATE FORMATION AND NATION-BUILDING

Although the recent research interest in the area of state formation and nation-building suggests a renewed concern of social scientists with substantive historical processes, the theoretical models and methodology they apply in these studies are those developed first in the analysis of political systems and then applied to the field of political development. State formation and nation-building are simply considered as constituting two important dimensions of political development, and political development itself is conceived in terms of the earlier model of systems analysis (equilibrium analysis, subsystem autonomy, structural differentiation, functional specialization, and so forth). The studies of state formation and nation-building, therefore, are not viewed as necessitating departure from the traditional theoretical framework of political development studies; they only suggest a choice of certain foci that delimit data requirements to two broad dimensions, namely nation-building and state formation. The framework of comparative analysis adopted in analyzing and interpreting these data is essentially the structural-functional model of political systems analysis.

In this theoretical pursuit, phenomena of state formation and nation-building are viewed as formal characteristics of whole political systems, arising out of interactions among different structural and functional elements constituting these systems. Comparisons are made of different political systems in producing these characteristics, and the political systems are then classified in terms of the degree to which the characteristics obtain in them. The theoretical insight obtained from such comparative analyses is restricted to evaluation of different political systems in their capacity to attain certain systemic goals, and to produce various taxonomies of political systems based on such evaluations.

If comparative political analysis is to serve scientific or even heuristic ends, it should go beyond providing evaluative estimates of products and outputs of political systems. It should also aim at developing diagnostic and predictive capabilities of theoretical models. Comparative studies of state formation and nation-building processes in the old and new nations of the world can provide such an orientation, provided the present classificatory activities and methodological devices based on the structural-functional approach of comparison is carried forward to focus specifically on these historical processes and the peculiar contexts of time and space through which they operate.

This discussion is not to suggest that the conceptual framework of comparative political systems and its application to the new field of political development is not relevant to the studies of state formation and nation-building. It only means that if this framework, as operationalized in structural-functional analysis, is applied uncritically to the studies of state formation and nation-building, it would diminish the promise these studies seem to offer, namely a historical analysis of far-reaching substantive processes of social and political change, and the diagnostic and predictive pay-offs of such analysis. If, on the other hand, these studies are pursued with consciousness of the theoretical and methodological problems they might inherit from the systems approach, they will in fact contribute to a distinctive theory of comparative historical change.

Contemporary processes of state formation and nation-building constitute a distinctive historical phase in human development and call for a historical sensitivity and empathy almost similar to the nineteenth-century analyses of the growth of capitalism and the industrial revolution. Tying such analysis down to a theoretical framework suited to more stable and established systems may prevent the development of new lines of inquiry and approach that are urgently needed.

Admittedly, the systems approach has performed an important role in the initial stage of comparative study of political development, and studies of state formation and nation-building can utilize its theoretical and methodological insights, provided its constraining effects are also realized. This approach has provided a series of abstract and universal categories for ordering and classifying a bewildering variety of socio-political data on widely disparate political entities called nation-states. By conceiving of these entities as political systems, the able practitioners of this approach have evolved taxonomies of types of functions performed by different systems, have charted out certain requisite functions (crises) that all systems shall have to perform to maintain themselves as ongoing political systems, and have also highlighted variations in patterns of interaction among various elements (structural and functional) constituting these systems, and consequences of these variations for different types of systems in determining their levels of political development.

Thus, while the systems approach to the study of political development has no doubt contributed a great deal to the field of comparative political analysis, its almost total predominance in the field may prevent the development of new lines of inquiry and analysis needed for an adequate handling of the historical processes of state formation and nation-building.

It is therefore necessary first to identify the constraining influences of the systems approach for the comparative study of state formation and nation-building. What follows is not a systematic critique of this approach but a few comments organized around certain themes to show how the present orientation of comparative political analysis dominated by this approach can prove restrictive insofar as it bypasses relevant questions and neglects important variables, prevents formulation of alternative hypotheses, undermines the problem of causal relationships between variables, and avoids application of appropriate methodological solutions necessary for the evolution of a truly comparative theory of political development.

CONSTRAINTS ARISING OUT OF THE SYSTEMS APPROACH TO POLITICAL DEVELOPMENT

1. Systems analysis proceeds with the assumption that all territorial entities called nation-states are concrete political systems. The theoretical construct of a political system is taken as an empirical category, a fixed unit of comparison. Accordingly, as ongoing political systems, these entities are viewed as having universally acquired certain formal characteristics of a system. These characteristics pertain to their having interrelated sets of structures and functions oriented to attaining certain systemic goals.

This super-imposition of an analytical category of political system on all legal-territorial entities called nation-states has resulted in a lot of confusion in comparative political analysis about the relationship between form and substance, between processes and products, and between levels of analysis and generalization. In systems analysis, all territorial entities called nation-states become political systems as soon as they come into being. They are treated as composite political wholes comparable with other nation-states that have long been on the scene. They differ among themselves, not in their wholeness, not in possessing formal properties of a political system, but in the degree to which they maintain themselves as ongoing political systems, and in their capacities to deal with their environments. Some political systems may be more efficient in attaining their goals than others, depending on the nature of the arrangement of structural and functional elements within these systems.

Such an approach is more oriented to a general theory of forms of political organizations, and not to explanation of substantive phenomena like state formation and nation-building. The formal categories developed by this approach are indeed helpful in providing a tentative classification of nation-states, but they do not in themselves provide any understanding of the processes and dynamics through which the nebulous entities called nation-states evolve, through time, into politically and culturally cohesive wholes, with well laid out structures, functions, and goals, handling problems of management and performance, and being subjected to further changes or discontinuities in response to new challenges. The systems approach thus poses the danger of bypassing important questions and ignoring the most salient variables of temporal process and situational context.

2. Aside from bypassing important variables, the systems approach to political development produces another constraint: it pertains to the relationship of variables posited in systems analysis.

The primary concern of the systems approach is to evaluate and classify political systems in terms of their capacities to perform certain systemic functions which are oriented to the attainment of certain specific goals. Variations in the arrangements of structural and functional elements would determine variations in capacities of political systems to attain these goals. Attainment of systemic goals is therefore a fixed dependent variable in this scheme of analysis, which may be explained through several variables derived from general parametric elements of a system: structures, functions and processes. Thus the analytical relationship between variables as dependent, intervening, or independent is derived logically from the interrelationship posited between abstract and formal categories prescriptive of definitional requirements of a political system. A substantial number of variables are then specified under each category for purposes of data collection and measurement.

Analyses based on these data, however, are meant to test propositions about logical relationships between formal variables (like structures, functions, and goals) as posited in the model rather than conditions of occurrence and growth of substantive phenomena (like state formation and nation-building). The relationship of variables in such a model is, therefore, assumed to be context-free as well as time-free. The implication of this assumption is that nation-states as ongoing political systems display certain types of interrelationships among elements constituting these systems irrespective of their location in time and space; and the goal of comparative political analysis is to discern these relationships, classify them, and devise tests of validation of general systemic rules governing these interrelationships.

Such a commitment to a logical model of analysis per se produces severe constraints for comparative political analysis when applied to the explanation of substantive empirical phenomena like state formation and nation-building. These constraints pertain to conceptualization of phenomena as well as to finding appropriate methodological solutions to the operationalization of relationships among variables determining the phenomena. Let us examine briefly how these constraints operate in the contemporary studies of comparative political development which, if transferred to the study of state formation and nation-building, would prevent proper conceptualization of these processes as well as application of appropriate methodological solutions needed for a truly empirical comparative theory.

Political development as conceived in the analytical framework of systems analysis consists of a system's efforts to continually attain its goals vis-à-vis its environment. The effort involves continuous rearrangement of its elements by a system, for the environment is not constant and unchanging for any system. Insofar as all political systems are oriented to attainment of certain common goals, the principle guiding such rearrangements is also common for them all. By activating this principle a political system sets itself on a path of political development. Or, to put it differently, the process of political development relates to the operation of certain principles that constantly reconstruct and reorganize structural and functional elements within a system to keep it going in face of changes in its environment. Foremost among these principles is that of differentiation of structures and specialization of functions. Operation of this principle, which may be continuous or intermittent, transforms existing structures and releases new functions to equip the system to cope with such changes in its environment as threaten its survival. In this process of constant reconstruction of its logical elements, a political system develops its organizational form.

Thus the concept of political development as evolved by the systems theorists is an operational construct devised to meet analytical requirements of their model rather than a framework of propositions representing empirical reality. It refers to the formal property of a political system presumed by the model, namely its tendency to attain systemic goals vis-à-vis its environment. This approach was indeed helpful in the initial stage of comparative political analysis insofar as it helped classification of nation-states in terms of the degree of structural differentiation and specialization of functions attained by various political systems. However, it fails to take into account substantive processes of political change through which territorial populations are transformed into viable political entities, possessing institutional and symbolic frameworks necessary to handle emergent problems of management and distribution of political power. More important, it fails to recognize that a dependent phenomenon is not the same thing as a constant but may vary within a system from one point of time to another, and between political systems at a given point of time, just as the plausibility of explanatory (independent) variables would vary in explaining a dependent phenomenon from time to time and from system to system. That is to say, the same variable may behave differently in its influence on dependent phenomena over a period of time within a system and across political systems at a given point of time. The nature of interrelationship between variables, therefore, has to be derived empirically, and not just logically.

Different systems of variables are needed for different phases of political development within a system and for different political systems at different points of time, rather than a single logical model that conceives of dependent-independent relationships in static and formal terms. In a given system of variables an independent variable at one point of time (e.g., exposure to mass media) may acquire a dynamic aspect and rise to the status of a mediating variable that influences the process dimension of the dependent phenomenon more directly. Such a dynamic model may take us away from the long cherished goal of a general theory of political systems, but would bring us nearer to a comparative theory of political development sensitive to empirical reality in time and space. The elements of political development as conceptualized in these systems of variables will be common, but the nature and direction of their interrelationship will be hypothesized differently for each concrete political system and for the time period during which the process is observed. Such methodological exercises, however, can be made possible if political development is viewed as a process at work through time and space, and not just as a realization of certain logical functions.

This neglect of temporal and contextual dimensions in the conceptualization of political development has thus prevented application of appropriate methodological solutions to the problems of comparative political analysis. This occurrence is evident from the fact that contemporary comparative analyses are dominated by those techniques that examine correlative and functional relationships between variables rather than those that can test causal relationships. Massive efforts have been made to compare national level statistics on several countries at a given point of time to establish functional associations among variables of political development. These efforts involve use of sophisticated methods of multivariate analysis. Often inferences are drawn about stages and sequences of political development on the basis of these cross-sectional analyses of various nations. Aggregate values achieved by different countries on identical indicators of political development are taken as measures of their respective levels of political development, where the aggregate values scored by various nations constitute points on an ordinal scale of political development. Thus, countries with low aggregate scores are considered to be at one stage of development, and they reach their next stage when they achieve higher scores possessed by the other set of countries.

Such analyses do not reveal the strength and direction of variables involved in the processes of political development. In order to explore causal relationships between variables, more appropriate techniques of analysis like longitudinal and multiple time-series analyses have to be applied in the study of comparative political development. That such techniques do not attract enough attention from comparative analysts is not accidental. The concept of political development as operationalized in the systems model of comparative analysis prevents if not precludes application of such techniques, insofar as the relationship of variables in this model are not conceived in temporal and contextual terms.

The point of the above discussion is not to suggest definitive and workable methodological solutions to problems of comparative analysis of political development (which cannot be accomplished in the short space of this theoretical chapter), but rather to illustrate how the predominance of systems theory in contemporary comparative analysis has prevented the search for alternative methodological solutions for the analysis of substantial historical processes like state formation and nation-building. This prevention results largely from the fact that the general theory of political systems has preempted the field of comparative political development.

3. The third important constraint of the systems approach to comparative political analysis stems froms its emphasis on the independence and autonomy of structures and functions of a political system over human individuals who have to make specific and time-bound choices affecting the course of political development of the country they live in or manage. That the choice behaviors, attitudes, aspirations, and values of power-holders and of the populace of a country might have important consequences for state formation and nation-building processes in that country is a problem that receives least attention in the structural-functional scheme of analysis. At best such elements of the process are conceived of as performing systemic functions because of certain structural arrangements that make for or prevent adaptation and adjust-ment of a given system to its environment. At worst, they are explained

away as idiosyncratic and irrational elements special to each case which need not be entered into for comparative analysis of political development.

Being primarily concerned with autonomous behavior of macro-structures of total political systems, this approach ignores micro-level problems of policy formation and program execution arising at various levels and in different sectors of social, economic, and political life of a country. Such an orientation prevents proper recognition of the fact that the strides of nation-building activities or relapses into long spells of stagnation, discontinuities, and breakdowns in the life history of a country are largely dependent on specific policy choices of its leadership—its normative orientations and its response to various kinds of information in the form of actions—rather than mere results of certain structural arrangements or functional relationships within a system.

What choices a leadership can make in a given situation is indeed influenced by certain imperatives created by previous choices made by the same leadership or by its predecessors. However, to attribute such a delimitation of choices to autonomous structures—that behave as if they were hidden monsters creating compulsions and directing the choice-behavior of human actors—takes the notion of autonomy of structures to absurd limits. It at least needs to be recognized that choice behavior of human actors is as much dependent on their ability to perceive choices, their normative orientations and realistic calculations about desirable cource of action, as on sytsemic compulsions. A well-informed and determined leadership can convert so-called structural constraints into positive resources for creating new situations.

Thus the focus on the behavior of macro-structures of a total system permits only first-order generalizations; to deduce rules of behavior for micro-level elements from these first-order generalizations is fallacious. It requires an analysis at a different level to be able to talk about how micro-level processes operate and influence the course of political change in the system. Examination of micro-level processes, therefore, should not be merely to illustrate general rules of a system but rather to arrive at second-order generalizations about independent influences of micro-level elements on the processes of social and political change.

In brief, it needs to be recognized that political changes occur and acquire directionality through deliberate choice actions of individual actors managing the system; and rules about behavior of macro-structures refer only to the more durable and rather unchanging features of a system. Change in macro-structures becomes visible only after a long period of specific changes in various elements operating at various micro-levels. This fact is true not only of normal processes of change but also of rapid and so-called revolutionary changes, really end-products of a series of changes going on at the micro-levels of a system which go unnoticed for a long time and are brought to our knowledge retrospectively through careful historical analyses of such events.

Studies of state formation and nation-building can be fruitfully oriented to such analysis. At present it will be sufficient to indicate that although variables of certain types are identified in the systems analysis of political development, some important variables do not enter this analysis, simply because they do not follow from the rules governing formal organization of a total political system. Studies of state formation and nation-building can ill afford to ignore these variables. Illustratively, some of these variables pertain to economic and social planning over time as a major policy instrument of state formation and nation-building; penetration of micro-structures through the policies and dominating personalities of national level elites and responses over time to this penetration through supportive and dissenting behavior; generation and application of new scientific knowledge for the manipulation of environments and management of human affairs (science policy, information processes, institution-building for creation and application of new knowledge); changes in normative orientations of leadership (usually through a generational shift) resulting in reconstruction of developmental goals of a system; and the changes in content and degree of aspirations of populations, which constantly influence and modify elite priorities of developmental goals. Each of these illustrative sets of variables involves (a) relationship between macro- and micro-phenomena and (b) choice sequences of a substantive kind as distinct from sequences based on attainment of formal characteristics of the system.

4. The fourth and last constraint of the systems approach to comparative political analysis that we would like to discuss stems from its much-talked-about "homeostatic" bias. It need not be emphasized that to study problems of survival and maintainance of a political system is the most important and legitimate concern of comparative political analysis, but when this concern operates as a compelling methodological predisposition, it prevents the development of alternative theoretical orientations in comparative analysis.

Although this objection is frequently raised, it is seldom grounded on methodological considerations. Often, it is expressed in the form of a doctrinaire objection by those who suspect ideological underpinnings of the opposite kind in the practitioners of this approach. To hold that those who focus their attention on conditions of stability in a political system are themselves champions of status quo is a crude way of approaching this problem, which may turn an important methodological issue into inconsequential polemics.

It is necessary first to understand the approach for what it is worth. The postulate of homeostasis of a system as applied to comparative political analysis suggests that political systems all have a tendency to attain a state of equilibrium. A system at various points of time, or various systems at a given point of time, may indeed be found in states of disequilibrium (or non-equilibrium), but systems as self-perpetuating entities are ipso facto in constant search of certain regulative and integrative principles that will restore in them the state of equilibrium. How soon and in what manner the equilibrium of a system will be restored and what different types of equilibria different systems can attain will depend on the relationship in which the structural and functional elements of a system stand among each other and vis-à-vis the system as a whole. Thus, changes in the interrelationships between systemic elements (functions), at least those that have implications for states of equilibrium and disequilibrium, do form part of structural-functional analysis; it is not as if the study of change is precluded in this approach. Systems can also be classified by their capacity to attain (move towards) equilibrium, and also by different types of equilibria attained by different systems, but still the primary focus of this approach is undoubtedly on the conditions of stability of a political system.

This orientation operates as a bias when it prevents formulation of a competitive set of hypotheses relating to such changes in political systems which are not directed either towards equilibrium or disequilibrium. All changes in a political system cannot be conceived of as having consequences in terms of equilibrium or disequilibrium. And the changes that different systems have to undergo even to attain stability need not be continuous and have a common directionality. Stability is but one goal of political systems in action. It is misleading to treat all substantive processes and events occurring within these systems as stability functions (or stability dysfunctions)—and that, too, without regard to the time and context in which these occurrences take place.

It is often argued that the knowledge of conditions producing stability also provides a point of reference for studying changes in the system. It is also argued that insofar as systems analysis focuses on the changes that such a system has to undergo (structural-functional prerequisites) to attain equilibrium and the conditions of strains and stresses that constantly disturb the balance (dysfunctions) as much as on conditions that tend to restore the balance (adaptive and regulative functions), it provides an orientation for studying problems of political change.

Both these arguments are indeed valid, but they do not meet the basic criticism of homeostatic bias, which is that all political changes in a system are not directed to restoration or disturbance of an equilibrium, and these changes are not necessarily additive and continuous.

Thus the preoccupation with stability precludes consideration of some important issues relating to the nature and direction of political change. For example, it needs to be empirically examined whether different elements of a nation-state are so interrelated that they converge in producing functions that attain specific systemic goals. Alternatively, if viewed on the temporal dimension and in the context of a specific nation-state, some of these elements may well appear in a relationship of opposition and conflict, or as unrelated and disjunct elements that have not yet acquired salience in the process of political development. Further, it can be hypothesized that it is in the process of management and resolution of conflicts between these various elements—the essence of political power—that political change acquires directionality. Such a notion of political change (as differentiated from systemic change) refers not only to parametric forms of a system, but also to the substantive historical experience of a society in dealing with various problems of development (not merely survival or adaptation), to its failures and achievements in developing institutions for handling problems of management and distribution of political power.

The above discussion of the four constraints—bypassing critical variables of a substantive kind; emphasis on logical rather than empirical relationship between variables; stress on the autonomy of structures and functions rather than on individual actors, thus ignoring the more specific *micro*-changes that ultimately lead to shifts in the *macro*-system; and the homeostatic bias that prevents formulation of alternative sets of hypotheses and methodological devices—reveals some basic inadequacies of the systems approach. These inadequacies become more pronounced in dealing with the problems of comparing processes of political development (the dimension of time) and the problems of the contextual variations that enter into these processes (the dimension of space). We have argued that the systems approach is primarily concerned with a comparative analysis of the development of organizational forms of a political system, and much less with the dynamics of substantive political processes that provide content and direction to political development in various countries. The high level of generality involved in this analysis results in a tendency to abstract away both time and space as elements in political development.

It is further suggested that to have worthwhile comparative studies of state formation and nation-building, not only has the systems approach to be substantially modified but alternative theoretical formulations and methodological solutions also have to be considered, making it possible to ask more significant and relevant questions in the area of state formation and nation-building. For example, it is not enough to ask to what extent different political systems have acquired functional characteristics of statehood and nationhood. More significant questions will be: How are different configurations of political development formed in different countries, and what implications do these different configurations have for processes of state formation and nation-building? What time spans are available or required for different countries to solve specific problems of state formation and nation-building? How do specific policy choices and leadership styles of ruling elites in different countries bring into operation different strategies and courses of action in establishing centers of political authority and mobilizing the peripheries towards these centers? And, in the process of all this, how do elements of political development acquire different significance in different countries and at different points of time?

SOME PREREQUISITES FOR GENERAL AND COMPARATIVE THEORY

If properly conceived, studies of state formation and nation-building processes afford an opportunity to deal with complex questions of comparative political analysis. In the first place, however, it should be recognized that before generalizations about the nature and direction of political processes applicable to a large number of nation-states are made possible, several preparatory research tasks have to be performed. For quite some time, comparative political analysts have had to remain content with an examination of within-country (at most within-region) processes of state formation and nation-building for one or for a small number of comparable units, in order that (i) basic elements of these processes are differentiated from time-bound and unit-specific elements, (ii) configurations of interrelationships among common and differential elements of these processes are identified on a temporal dimension, and (iii) hypotheses are formulated in terms of strength and directionality of these relationships over time for specific countries.

This situation calls for both a time-oriented and a context-sensitive approach to comparative analysis. Processes of state formation and nation-building have to be viewed as concrete historical phenomena and not as perpetual functions of ongoing political systems. In other words, state formation and nation-building processes should be studied as occurrences in time and space and not just as formal characteristics of political systems unbound by temporal and spatial influences. There is no reason why state formation and nation-building processes could not be studied comparatively, treating them as concrete historical phenomena, as indeed was done by our distinctive predecessors in their study of the growth of capitalism and the Industial Revolution. It is here that the systems approach has almost become a blinder: epoch-making historical phenomena with far-reaching consequences for mankind have been reduced to formal taxonomies of classes and categories. This statement does not, of course, mean that comparative analysis should be reduced to studies of social and political history of various countries, or that comparative analysts have to become historians in order to study processes of state formation and nation-building. It only means that several of the hypotheses concerning configurations, directionality, and time sequences of political change have to be tested against historical data of specific countries on a temporal dimension, so that hypotheses about causal interconnections among elements of political development can be formulated. Only then shall we be able to appropriately undertake diagnostic and predictive tasks that lie before us.

Nor should the emphasis on specificity and variations of political processes undermine the need and possibility of a comparative theory of political development. In fact, time-oriented analyses of political development in specific countries have to be carried out in a comparative, analytical framework, so that the findings of these studies yield generalizations about the nature and direction of political development applicable to a number of countries.

In what follows we suggest some tentative leads for a more systematic process and context-oriented framework of comparative analysis. The purpose of this exercise is only to initiate thinking on a program of research oriented to comparative analysis of the processes of state formation and nation-building, not to provide any exhaustive alternative theoretical framework.

Assumption of generality of a phenomenon is a first necessity of comparative analysis. It is assumed that acquisition of territorial sovereignty by political entities is followed by multifarious social, economic, and political changes in a country. The nature and direction of these changes depend on several factors: the point of time at which a country acquires legal sovereignty; the historical processes of establishment of political authority and national identity prior to acquisition of legal sovereignty (the starting point of a country entering processes of political modernization); intrinsic sources of change in the traditional society and value system; the nature of exogenous influences on the traditional social structures, value system, and political organizations. and governmental and elite activities in the sphere of policy-making. These factors can be conceived as broad rubrics of elements constituting processes of state formation and nation-building. Insofar as elements of these rubrics are found to be involved in processes of change in various countries at different points of time, they indicate generality of the phenomenon of state formation and nation-building, but the salience of these elements in influencing these processes will vary from country to country and along the temporal dimension within a country.

The nature of the direction of the processes of change in a particular country or in a time period will depend on how these elements are involved in developmental configurations over a period of time in specific countries. Thus, the patterns of interrelationship of these elements will vary along temporal as well as contextual dimensions. The task of comparative research is to identify developmental configurations for various countries and for different time periods, the direction of relationships among the elements constituting developmental configurations, and the temporal sequences and rates of formation of these configurations.

The central problem, however, is to differentiate developmental configurations as a dependent phenomenon from general processes of economic, social, and political changes; and this problem raises the formidable issue of deciding about the criteria of political development.

While this problem has to be solved before meaningful comparative studies of political development can make their real impact, ambiguity about it is understandable, for it implies a fundamental philosophical problem of social sciences: reconciliation of basic dichotomies of normative versus evaluative and subjective versus objective criteria. Pending agreement on these fundamental issues, comparative political analyses have to proceed by relying on some heuristic devices to differentiate between developmental and nondevelopmental processes of change. One way to get around this problem is to identify consensus among comparative political analysts on the syndromology of developmental processes. Establishing such a consensus itself constitutes a major research effort. Our purpose here is only to illustrate how differential developmental consequences are produced by different combinations of elements in the general process of economic, social, and political change. We shall do this by using implicitly our ad hoc understanding of present consensus on syndromes of political development.

In order to illustrate this configurative approach to comparative political analysis, we may try to cluster elements of the general process of change into relevant rubrics of the process of state formation and nation-building, and to suggest some illustrative hypotheses under each rubric showing how differential involvement of these elements in developmental configurations produce different developmental consequences for different countries.[1]

RUBRICS OF STATE-FORMATION AND NATION-BUILDING

1. Antecedent social structure, value-system, and state of political authority that facilitate or impede the processes of political development. Different types of antecedent states would provide different resources and set different limits to developmental processes of nation-building and center-formation.

Illustrative hypotheses:

(i) Whether in the processes of nation-building the emphasis is laid on integrative activities of nation-building, on legitimacy of the regime, or on governmental performance will depend on whether political authority was fragmentary or centralized in the antecedent state of a country.

(ii) Similarly, whether national identity is forged on singular dimension of ethnicity, religion, or ideology, or on diversified symbols of modernization will depend upon what kind of centers were prominent in the antecedent state of a country.

(iii) A country with a diversified and pluralistic antecedent social structure will provide greater social resources for political mobilization, but whether this will lead to larger identity, reinforce separatist tendencies, or hold these tendencies in abeyance will depend upon the particular integrative strategies adopted by the new agents of change.

2. Exposure to modernizing world impacts and responses thereto. This rubric refers to the intrinsic sources of change and rigidity in a society responding to such exposures. All countries are subject to exogenous influences, but their responses in terms of nation-building vary, depending upon internal capacities of countries to absorb these influences and upon historical circumstances under which these influences operate.

Illustrative hypothesis:

A country that received its modernizing impacts through colonial experience is likely to suffer from a more ambivalent attitude to "Westernized" practices and institutions than a country (like Japan) that frankly undertook the task of Western-style modernization in an attempt to "close the gap" in material welfare and political power.

3. Content of developmental aspirations of populations. In the perspective of contemporary history, populations in all countries aspire to development, but the contents and themes of developmental aspiration will vary with the level of development already attained by a country and, more importantly, along a particular ideology of change propagated in a country. The specific contents and themes of developmental aspirations, therefore, will shape the process of nation-building within a country.

Illustrative hypothesis:

A country with high accent on economic and military power may give rise to a monolithic center, that will have to depend on a continuous renewal of authoritarian symbols of solidarity while suppressing real divisions in society, whereas a country with greater accent on political participation and consensus may involve the state system with integrative preoccupations at various levels and employ a part of national resources in drawing various peripheral groups within the mainstream of national life.

4. Specific problems and challenges (confrontations) that a country faces in the course of its efforts to establish centers of authority. These problems may vary in nature and magnitude for different countries.

Illustrative hypothesis:

A country that is forced to mobilize loyalties and resources for dealing with external or internal threat to security is forced to lay more emphasis on citizen loyalties and national power than on political education and local autonomy.

5. Human agents of change and institutions of social engineering that impart directionality to the process of nation-building. This rubric will include two sets of variables.

First, it will include the actions and attitudes of political leaders, including political activists operating at lower levels as commuters between society and polity, and other specialized elites and publics who participate in the process of nation-building. Relevant here are the strategies and styles these various agents devise in response to different exigencies of support mobilization, involving, on the one hand, reconciliation between the dominant developmental aspirations of the national community at large as perceived by them, and on the other hand, the aspirations and interests of the strata they themselves represent, as exemplified by their values, their beliefs, and their perception of their own roles.

Illustrative hypothesis:

A country that relies heavily on a powerful and "charismatic" leader for undertaking nation-building commitments is likely to give less attention to institutional strategies than will a country whose center is controlled by a more diversified elite structure.

Second, this rubric includes deliberately enacted organizational forms and institutions through which goals of national development are to be achieved. These deliberately devised agencies of change refer to institutional apparatuses of cenralized planning, structures of local governmental administration, political parties, and the like.

Illustrative hypothesis:

In a country where the authoritative agency of change is a bureaucratic or military oligarchy, the leadership is torn between following a radical social ideology and supporting nationalist-chauvinistic urges, whereas in a country where a mass political party has been able to provide the authoritative agency of change, the problem is resolved by making party leadership a symbol of national identity and power. On the other hand, the latter system leads to compromise of radical principles and consequent growth of public cynicism, whereas the former may succeed in creating public awe and enthusiasm for the regime.

We could go on adding to this list of rubrics and of relevant hypotheses regarding the interrelationship of elements within each rubric, but for our purposes, this illustrative listing is sufficient to note that different configurations of developmental elements are formed in different countries and in different time periods of nation-building efforts. The rubrics and hypotheses do no more than provide analytical referents for identifying relevant developmental elements. Specific configurations that are formed in the process of nation-building would draw elements from one, two, or more rubrics and produce differential consequences for political development of specific countries.

Our main interest in undertaking this exercise has been simply to suggest that before generalizations applicable to nation-building processes in various countries are made possible, significant elements of the process have to be identified for different time periods in specific countries. (See the illustrative chart for the single case of India.) Comparative analysis in its "first phase" shall have to be restricted to within-country (or within-region) analysis of nation-building processes over a period of time. Such an analysis will provide ordering of elements along temporal sequences. In the "next phase" of the analysis, more complex comparative designs can be evolved to explain similarities and variations in nation-building processes taking place in various countries.

As we identify research problems and hypotheses along these lines for an increasing number of countries, we shall be able to move from the first to the second phase, and hopefully also from the present rather formal state of comparative theory to formulations that are more sensitive to empirical sequences and more appropriate for diagnostic and predictive ends of scientific analysis.

India: Developmental Configurations Through Time

Time Periods	Changing Problem Contexts	Critical Elements in the Process	Consequences for Nation-Building
1.	Fragmentary political authority: nonterritorial cultural identity of a great tradition.	Colonial rule	Exposure to new ideas and forms: new educational system.	Rise of new Western-educated elites. Territorial consolidation by the colonial regime.
2.	Threat to traditional cultural identity: dissociation of Hindu normative system from great tradition.	Movements of social reforms	Legal and moral protection to new elite by the colonial regime.	Coalition between new indigenous elite and the Raj. Establishment of bureaucratic and judiciary systems based on rule of law.
3.	Growing demands on the new opportunity structure: tenuous coalition between the colonial regime and the new elite.	Expansion of educational and occupational opportunities through establishment of regional centers.	Regime's efforts to include new social classes in the coalition. Enforcement of land reforms and new revenue system.	Crystalization of nationalism-liberalism value complex. Integration of indigenous authority centers within the regime: bureaucratization of governmental roles at local levels.
4.	Questioning of legitimacy of colonial rule: assertion of traditional cultural identity.	Reinterpretation of traditions for cultural self-esteem, economic change and other activities of modernization.	Primacy of political action over social reform activities.	Recruitment of elites from middle-range groups and levels. New channels of political articulation through national party.
5.	Elite-Conflicts: "constitutional" versus mobilizational styles. Breakdown of regime-elite coalition.	Mobilization of peripheral and unorganized social groups for political power: Movement for national independence.	Alienation of reformist elite and ascendency of political activists.	Wide-scale politicization of masses. Legitimation of consent and participation in political decision-making: issue of representation.

Time Periods	Changing Problem Contexts	Critical Elements in the Process		Consequences for Nation-Building
6.	Growth of subnational identities on religious and cultural lines. Colonial regime's efforts to claim support of still left-out peripheries and to protect interests of minorities.	Institutionalization of political participation and subnational conflicts through party-building activities.	Exogenous influences on colonial regime; threat to its imperial power.	Withdrawal of colonial rule; rise of two territorial sovereigns in the subcontinent.
7.	Territorial identification of cultural and political entity vis-à-vis newly grown linguistic and regional identities.	Renewal of central political authority and its legitimacy through coercive and mobilization efforts.	Growth of a new consensus among elites on socialistic and democratic goals of nation-building.	Rise of system of one party dominance. Establishment of federal political authority.
8.	Growing pressures on representational and distributive structures of economic and political power. Challenges to the consensus.	New institutional arrangements to cope with various challenges. Growth of new political parties at regional levels and mobilization of more peripheral groups in organized politics.	Primacy of integrational tasks over performance aspects; emphasis on distributive aspects of economic planning.	Decline of one-party dominance; growing salience of opposition. Increased autonomy of political system, its domination over other systems (economic, educational, etc.)
9.	Reconciling conflicting goals of integration and performance.	Heightened perceptions of disparities and deprivation, as well as of dependence on powerful nations.	Increased reliance on statecraft to solve economic problems; emphasis on independent foreign policy.	New bases of national identity, stress on economic and military power. Ascendency of nationalism.
10.	Breakdown of dominant party consensus and polarization of political parties.	New industrial and agricultural policies.	Relevance of socio-economic cleavages in pursuit of political power.	Rise of coalitional politics. Growth of new centers. Growing accent on issues of performance. Growing fear of electoral reprisal.

NOTE

1. For a more detailed treatment along these lines in the context of the problem of political integration, see D. L. Sheth and Rajni Kothari, "Social Change, Political Integration and the Value Process," paper presented to the International Roundtable on Values in Politics, Dubrovnik, Yugoslavia, 1965 (mimeo). The rubrics and hypotheses presented below have been largely drawn from this paper.

II.

DATA FOR COMPARISONS OF DEVELOPMENTS

CHAPTER 5

DATA RESOURCES FOR COMPARATIVE RESEARCH
ON DEVELOPMENT: A REVIEW OF RECENT EFFORTS

Stein Rokkan

STEIN ROKKAN is Professor of Sociology at the University of Bergen and Recurring
Visiting Professor of Political Science at Yale. He has been associated with the ISSC
programme for the advancement of comparative research since 1962 and is Chairman
of the ISSC Committee on Comparative Research. He is currently (1970-1973)
President of the International Political Science Association. Among his major
publications are: *Party Systems and Voter Alignments; Citizens, Elections, Parties;*
and *Comparative Survey Analysis.*

UNESCO and a number of other international organizations have in
recent years devoted much energy to the study of the social, the cultural,
and the political components of growth. The early emphasis on the purely
economic components has gradually given way to a search for deepened
insight into the dynamics of interaction among a wide range of variables in
the process of national growth: linguistic, religious, and educational
variables as well as characteristics of inherited kinship and stratification
systems, settlement distributions and political structures.

In August 1970, UNESCO organized a conference at Cérisy-la-Salle in
France[1] to review progress toward the formulation of coherent models for
the explanation of such interactions in the process of state formation and
nation-building. A number of models and theory fragments were presented
and confronted with analyses of the sources of variations within and across
the major regions of the world: there were papers not only on Western and

Eastern Europe and the settler-nations in North and South America, but also on East and South Asia, the Maghreb and Tropical Africa. There was much pointed criticism of the Western theories of development and modernization at the conference: the models were too general to be of much use in comparative analyses of concrete historical developments, they rarely helped to generate hypotheses about the sources of variations among the developing areas of the world, and, even when testable hypotheses seemed to have been generated, there was little evidence of willingness to match these efforts on the theory front with corresponding efforts on the data resource front. There was broad consensus at the conference that UNESCO should concentrate in the next round on action to build up data resources for comparative studies of national development: this was seen as a sine qua non for further progress toward an understanding of the extraordinary variations across the world in the interaction among economic, social, cultural, and political components of growth.

As a first step in this direction UNESCO in 1971 asked the International Social Science Council (ISSC) to organize the Workshop on Indicators of National Development to review recent endeavors to build up data resources for comparative time series analyses of processes of change, and to link up this work on historical data with the burgeoning attempts to construct systems of interlocking indicators for the description year by year of the "state of the nation." A plan for a conference along these lines had already been worked out by the ISSC Committee on Comparative Research under a grant from the Stiftung Volkswagenwerk: this effort was later merged with the UNESCO plan and a scheme was worked out for a joint workshop at the University of Lausanne from August 9 to 14, 1971. This venture was also joined by the European Consortium for Political Research (ECPR): this organization was persuaded to join in a tripartite enterprise and to offer funds for the participation of scholars from its member institutions.

The workshop was organized by the ISSC Standing Committee on Comparative Research in close cooperation with UNESCO and the Institute de Science Politique of the University of Lausanne. The meetings took place at the new campus of the University at Dorigny and were attended by forty-four social scientists from fifteen countries: in addition to scholars from eleven European countries there were participants from the United States and from three Latin American countries, Argentina, Brazil, and Mexico.

A total of thirty-eight papers, data inventories and other tabular presentations were prepared for discussion at the workshop. The sessions of the workshop were organized around seven major themes:

1. Core variables in models of development
2. The organization of files for cross-national time-series data
3. Strategies in the analysis of longer versus shorter time series
4. Within-nation versus across-nation variations
5. Strategies of historical-ecological analysis
6. The organization of national historical data archives
7. The establishment of systems of indicators within and across nations

In this brief account, we shall describe a few outstanding examples of innovative work in these fields and spell out the issues confronting the community of scholars in their efforts to build up a better data basis for comparative research as well as for direct advice on alternative policies.

To simplify the account we shall group the themes of the workshop under three headings: first, cross-national historical files; second, within-nation archives; and finally, the transition to social indicator systems.

PRIORITIES IN THE ORGANIZATION OF WORLD-WIDE FILES FOR TIME-SERIES DATA

The workshop offered a first opportunity for a thorough discussion of such large-scale collections of historical statistics and over-time institutional codings as Arthur Banks's *Cross-Polity Time-Series Data,*[2] Kenneth Janda's International Comparative Political Parties project,[3] the Singer-Small *Wages of War* file,[4] and the Zapf-Flora study of quantitative models of modernization (the QUAM project).[5]

The bulk of the discussion during the first half of the workshop focused on these and several smaller collections of comparative time-series data: Why had they been built up the way they were? How could the job have been done differently? What could be done to extend the ranges of the collections, and what criteria should be used in investing further energies in such enterprises? What could be done to improve the precision, the reliability, and the comparability of the data?

The concrete, matter-of-fact presentation of these collections by the scholars who had planned and executed the work made for highly realistic discussions of the possibilities of further action: there was a wide-ranging debate at the beginning of the workshop over the theoretical priorities in the establishment of a data base for comparative histories of development, but there was full awareness of the restrictions imposed on scholars by the inherited systems of governmental bookkeeping. This dependence on the inheritance from the past was in fact a dominant theme at the conference, not only in the sessions devoted directly to time-series analysis but also in the final sessions on systems of social accounting for the future; clearly, to gauge the directions of change in given sets of societies one would have to link up any new indicators with estimates from already inherited statistics. Prima facie, the workshop might seem to fall into two distinct sections: the first devoted to historical time series, the second to the establishment of broad batteries of indicators for the identification of rates and components of ongoing change. In practice the one set of concerns ran into the other set: you could not discuss priorities for time-series work without considering current preoccupations with sources of change in developed as well as developing societies, and you could not discuss the introduction of new indicators without some consideration of possible benchmark data in the statistical records of the past.

Of the four papers presented at the opening of the workshop only two were in fact directly focused on the sources of historical variations in national development. The first of these was the background statement presented by Stein Rokkan: "Dimensions of State Formation and Nation-building."[6] In this paper an attempt was made to specify a paradigm for the exploration of differences in paths of development within Europe; the dimensions of this paradigm were essentially quantifiable and the underlying model could, at least in principle, be tested against historical time-series data. The paradigm cut across a very long span of time, however, and the information at hand differed markedly in coverage, precision, and comparability from period to period. For the early period, from the Reformation to the French Revolution, the model posited interactions among five major sets of variables: the military and the administrative/fiscal strength of each center of territorial consolidation, the concentration of resources in the landed economy, the strength and independence of the territorial Church, and the communication strength of the central elite language versus the peripheral languages within the territory. These were in principle all quantifiable variables, but the time series at hand were very spotty indeed and could only be used as illustrations to support an argument essentially based on qualitative information on elites and their coalitions. The situation for the second period was vastly better: the nineteenth century generated a huge variety of time-series statistics and some of these could clearly be used to test the predictions of the model. But the detailed work of systematic confrontation between the model and the available data case by case had hardly begun, thus forming one major rationale for the organization of the workshop.

Wolfgang Zapf's work with Peter Flora was directly focused on such time-series data for the period of rapid urbanization and industrialization, of accelerated mass education and of formal democratization after 1815. The QUAM project at the University of Frankfurt was essentially geared to the testing of models of modernization and mass mobilization for the century after the Napoleonic wars. The QUAM files did not cover as wide a range of units as the Banks, Flanigan, or Singer collections but they went into much greater detail of conceptual and operational evaluation of each indicator; this was the thrust of Peter Flora's extensive thesis, *"Modernization Processes and Modernization Research,"* presented at the workshop. This thesis was a painstaking *quellenkritische* scrutiny of the statistics for the period 1815-1965 for six major countries for three sets of variables only: there were chapters on indicators of urbanization, education and private as well as public communication for the U.S. and Russia, for Japan and Germany, as well as for France and the British Isles (separate data for England and Wales, Scotland and Ireland). This presentation helped to set the tone for the ensuing discussions; as Banks, Flanigan, Singer, and many others had shown, there were great amounts of data to be assembled but there was a great deal of work still to be done before these data could be accepted as fully worthy of statistical analysis.

The two other papers presented at the opening session had very little in common with these historically focused reports: the one by Peter Heintz went beyond the nation-by-nation approach toward the presentation of a general mathematical model of sources of change in the overall international system; the other, by Erik Allardt, moved below the level of the national system and urged joint consideration of indicators of systems development and indicators of individual development within each system.

Schematically, we present in Figure 1 the range of themes opened up on the first day of the workshop.

Peter Heintz reported on the complex mathematical work undertaken

| | ORIENTATION | |
LEVEL	Historical Development	Policy for Future
International system		Heintz
National system	Rokkan Zapf	
Individual		Allardt

Figure 1

at the University of Zurich and at the Bariloche Foundation in Argentina; his group had in fact submitted a total of six papers to the workshop. Three of these reported directly on the central formal model of reactions to rank disequilibria in the international system; a fourth, by Manfred Dechmann, took up methodological issues in the use of rank indicators ("status lines") in international comparisons; a fifth, by Heide-Birgit Dechmann, dealt with data on communications and interaction within the international system; and a sixth, by Raul Hernandez, focused on technical questions in the archiving and retrieval of international systems data. This effort of theory-building and empirical testing concentrated on the rank profiles of national systems within the total international system; the central hypothesis was that the behaviours of national units could best be accounted for by disequilibria in their rank order positions across selected indicators. So far the effort of empirical testing had been confined to only a few structural variables such as GNP, educational levels, urbanization, and percentages in the different sectors of the economy, but the model could clearly be extended to a wider range of indicators. The Dechmanns had added to the main file of variables a number of interaction data for dyads and other relations: participation in intergovernmental organizations, diplomatic exchanges, alliances, conflicts, military actions, and the like.[7] This work had so far been confined to data for the international system after the Second World War; it was clearly complementary to the extensive efforts of data collection pursued by David Singer and his colleagues on changes in the international system since 1815.

Erik Allardt brought the discussion back to the fundamental concerns of the individual for his welfare and for the realization of his potentials. He questioned the value of many of the overall indicators of national development and urged systematic disaggregation of the totals to gauge their impact on individual welfare and individual growth.

He proposed that all changes registered by overall indicators of development should be evaluated against a set of societal goal criteria. Using as his basis the well-known four-fold classification of needs proposed by Maslow, he suggested that all potential indicators be organized and evaluated within a 4 x 5 grid (see Figure 2).

Erik Allardt strongly urged that theoretically grounded procedures of evaluation of this type be used in establishing priorities of data collection both for analyses of long-term trends and in efforts to guide policies of short-term change. There was a great danger of conservative complacency in the current work of historical data archiving; variables were not interesting just because they happened to be documentable over some period for some countries. Their value could only be established within

GOAL DIMENSIONS	INPUTS Allocations	STRUCTURE		OUTPUTS	
		Differentiation Levels	Conformity Pressures	Societal Goals	Individual Goals
Economy					
Force					
Integrative subsystems					
Knowledge					

Figure 2: PROCESS ELEMENTS

some systematic effort of theory-building. Happily, many of the variables already at hand in the established collections did fit into the 4 x 5 grid; Allardt in fact offered a check list just for this purpose at the end of his paper. But there were many important lacunae and some of the theoretically important variables simply could not be documented with any degree of precision over time; the only hope was that such measures could be indirectly established through sample surveys or other techniques some time in the future.

In the ensuing discussion of the four introductory papers, Rodolfo Stavenhagen added strong support to Allardt. He wanted to give clear priority to the indicators of direct importance in decision-making, whether for the established system or against it, and would specifically call for data on the quality of social relationships. He wanted indicators for the extent of economic, cultural, and political inequalities among individuals, among localities, and among regions, and he wanted data on the character of relations of dominance and dependence in different sectors of the national and the international system.

Peter Flora defended the historical approach and offered a typology of theories of modernization (see Figure 3). There were practical as well as intellectual problems in each of the quadrants of this grid. To the left of the grid, there were all the problems of time-series research: changes in definitions, missing data, reconstruction of series through extrapolation and simulation, smoothing of short-term and long-term trends, tackling of autocorrelations and multicollinearities. On the right-hand side there were all the problems of classification and typology construction: how could one get historians to agree on precise criteria for the coding of institutions and processes within some overall scheme of comparative analysis such as Rokkan's? There were even greater difficulties in the lower quadrants:

	Quantitative		Qualitative	
Descriptive	Developmental trends (e.g., Lerner)	Developmental stages (e.g., Rostow)	Developmental typologies (e.g., Almond/ Powell)	Simple
	Quantitative equations models (e.g., Deutsch)	Causal models	Qualitative typological models (e.g., Rokkan)	
Explanatory		"Problem" theories and "Solution" typologies (e.g., Almond/Pye, Moore)		Complex
	Anglo-American "political arithmetic"		Continental- historical sociology	

Figure 3

what sorts of strategies of theory construction were most likely to pay off? His own inclination was to work toward some combination of typological procedures and causal modeling in the Blalock-Boudon tradition, but much still remained to be done at the level of data assembly and data evaluation. To move faster in this direction he proposed that an international working party be set up to check through the existing cross-national holdings and to decide on procedures of evaluation against primary sources. One possible solution would be an interdisciplinary journal for comparative time-series research; this could give updatings and revisions of time series and help to clear up difficulties of comparative analysis. In the ensuing discussion, it was suggested that part of this task could be taken on, at least for Europe, by the Data Information Service of the European Consortium. It was also suggested that this matter might be taken up with the editors of the "Historical Methods Newsletter."

The further discussions focused on the possibilities of linking up the time-series collections already established, and on the alternative strategies in the analysis of the data in such archives.

There was general agreement that all the collections should be placed in the public domain as quickly as possible to allow further analysis and to ensure critical evaluation of the data. Banks made it clear that the Binghamton collection presented in the extensive compendium *Cross-Polity Time-Series Data* would be available on tape from the Inter-

University Consortium at Ann Arbor. A similar arrangement had already been made for the second edition of the shorter-term series collection prepared at Yale for a broader range of variables.[8] William Flanigan reported on the extensive collection of historical statistics and institutional codings at Minnesota and stated that this collection would also be made accessible to outsiders once an arrangement had been made for consistency checking and documentation, possibly with the Ann Arbor Consortium. Peter Heintz reported on the collections prepared in Zurich and Bariloche on fifty-three nations for the period 1950-1965 and stated that he hoped that these data could be linked up with complementary collections such as Philippe Schmitter's for Latin America; these collections, however, would not be available for some time yet. David Singer reported on the three time-series collections at Michigan and the corresponding analysis projects: (a) the *Wages of War* project on changes in the structure of the international system since 1815, (b) the *Correlates of War* project which brought in a much greater variety of domestic data, and (c) the *Profiles of Nations* project which would offer both synchronic analysis of attributes at a particular time and diachronic analysis of the characteristics of trends and trajectories of change. There was a good deal of overlap with the Banks and the Flanigan-Fogelman collections and it would be highly desirable if funds could be found to link up all these files and cross-check the data against each other.

Kenneth Janda called attention to a number of other projects which ought to be linked up with this effort: the Rummel *Dimensionalities of Nations* collections in Hawaii, the various collections on Africa and Latin America, Anthony Judge's file on international organizations at the UIA (Union of International Associations) in Brussels, the PRIO (International Peace Research Institute) files in Oslo, and so on. He also reported on his own extensive coding operation for 150 political parties in a sample of fifty countries and explained his procedures of information storage and retrieval and his use of z-score techniques in judging the reliability of his codings and in comparing parties and countries. This work was still in progress and the data would probably not be generally available for use by outsiders until 1973.

There was general agreement that steps should be taken, preferably under the aegis of the ISSC, to organize closer cooperation among all scholars responsible for such collections, not only to facilitate exchanges and cross-linkages of data, but, what was even more important, also to ensure systematic evaluations and to establish agreement on priorities in the filling of lacunae in the information grids.

There was, however, some disagreement over strategies. Commenting on the Heintz papers and the Singer-Ray papers, Bruce Russett was struck by the marked difference in styles of theorizing and in the structure of the empirical effort:

Heintz:	Singer:
highly mathematical:	few symbols, mainly
extensive use of	common sense terms;
formal symbols;	
deductive procedure;	inductive procedure;
few variables:	many variables:
highly dependent	only moderately
on each other;	interdependent;
high multicollinearity;	
	directional system:
circular system:	dependent variables;
any variable both	political;
dependent and independent	stress on discovery,
stress on closeness of fit.	on disconfirmation.

In defense of his approach Peter Heintz made it clear that the data base would be expanded in several directions and that the effort of model-building was still under way and had not reached any final form.

The concluding session of this part of the workshop focused on strategies in the comparative analysis of aggregate data for nation-states. Serge Fanchette of UNESCO reviewed the taxonomic procedure used by his group in the Department of Social Sciences for identifying multivariate clusters of countries and for setting targets of development by measuring the distances between each country and its "model" in the given attribute space. C. Richard-Proust of UNRISD reported on the work carried out there on profiles of development; this work focused on the degree of fit among different trend curves country-by-country, and on the identification of conditions for shorter or longer leads or lags and for smaller or larger gaps and imbalances. Kenneth Janda and William Lafferty questioned the rationale of these procedures: they called for greater attention to the contextual meaning of variables and urged that efforts be made to delimit domains of comparability in space as well as in time. Kenneth Janda commented on the procedures used in establishing cross-nationally valid indicators in *Logic of Comparative Social Inquiry* by Przeworski and Teune[9] and suggested that levels of comparability be established by evaluating the means and variances of indicators within and across systems, by using what he termed the z-score technique. William Lafferty warned against worldwide comparisons across all documented periods. It was essential to establish meaningful regions of variation and to use institutional and other contextual information to delimit equivalent periods for time series analysis across systems: examples would be Western European countries between the extension of the suffrage to the working class and the entry of working class parties into government. Commenting on these interventions Serge Fanchette stated that the "Wroclaw" technique of taxonomic analysis in fact could be used to identify such domains of comparability; most of the work of UNESCO was in practice limited to clusters of similar units within one or the other of the major world regions.

ACTION WITHIN EACH NATION-STATE: THE DEVELOPMENT OF FILES BY LOCALITY

The discussion of the comparability of aggregate national statistics naturally led on to a consideration of the internal structure of each of the territorial systems described by such data.

William Lafferty reported in his work on the political effects of industrialization in Denmark, Norway, and Sweden and brought out the crucial importance of variations from level to level in each system; it was essential to analyze the interactions among the national, the organizational, the local, and the individual levels in each case; and any total-system average would be bound to miss a great deal of information.

Richard Rose and Derek Urwin dealt with the internal territorial structure of twenty Western democracies and presented a number of tables for electoral results by regions. Their data showed great variations in party strength among regions but very few cases of regionally dominant parties or regional "one-party rule." They interpreted these findings to suggest a general decline in the importance of territorial conflict in political systems above some minimum level of stability. They also had studied differences between the central city of each national territory and the other areas and found great variations in discrepancy scores; these, however, could not easily be interpreted within any known theory of "centre-periphery" contrasts.

William Flanigan went into further detail in the analysis of urban network structure and reported on the use of a simple index of concentration-dispersion for cities over 100,000 in all countries for the period 1800-1960. The data at hand did not allow a lower uniform cutting point than 100,000, thus obviously limiting the validity of this procedure for smaller countries and making it very difficult to interpret the decade-by-decade correlations found between concentration-dispersion and the stability of pluralistic rule. One result stood out with great clarity, however: increasing concentrations of the city structures in Latin America, and increasing dispersion in a number of Western European countries.

Mattei Dogan reported on his research on regional variations in rural France and showed how it was possible to increase the explanatory power of socio-cultural variables in political analysis by regionalizing the regressions. For instance, the zero-order correlation between occupational class and the Left vote across all the twenty-five hundred rural cantons was only .13; when the same operation was carried out within each department this coefficient rose to .43. This rise suggested that the contextual meaning of the variables changed from department to department or at least from region to region, an important lesson to bear in mind in any cross-local or cross-national analysis.

Juan Linz reported on ecological time-series work in Spain and Italy. The current work on the territorial components of social and political change in the two countries grew out of the model he and Amando de Miguel had prepared in their paper, "The Eight Spains."[10] This work centered heavily on the dual city structure: Madrid versus Barcelona, Rome versus Milan—seen as typical of many Southern European and Mediterranean territories: Lisbon versus Oporto, Belgrade versus Ljubljana, Athens versus Salonika, Ankara versus Istanbul. The task he and his colleagues had set themselves was to document lags and leads in mobilization rates from the late nineteenth century onwards between the economically and the politically advanced regions of each country. This work was still in progress but the data so far assembled promised to add significantly to our understanding of mass political development in the two countries. Concluding his presentation, Juan Linz strongly urged that steps be taken to prepare a series of historical maps of the social structures of the different regions of Europe, at least since the eighteenth century.

The Linz paper gave rise to a great deal of discussion of the low correlations in many areas between industrialization and educational developments. Dogan pointed to the high level of schooling in backward areas of Southern France. Heintz referred to similar situations in Argentina. Linz saw these differences as results of imbalances in the rates of growth between the political-administrative sectors and the economic sectors. This view fitted the distinctions made in the "conceptual map of Europe" presented by Stein Rokkan.

David Cameron, reporting on his work with Richard Hofferbert and others, identified two dimensions of change very similar to Linz's; he called the one "industrialization," the other "integration." These factors were extracted through an analysis of data for administrative subdivisions of five countries: 90 départements in France, 291 districts in India, 32 states in Mexico, 25 cantons in Switzerland, 50 states in the United States. There were occasional difficulties with the interpretation of the integration factors, but the essential message was that processes of mobilization must be analyzed from two major angles: the spread of the political-administrative apparatus of the state and the spread of economic innovations.

The remaining papers on internal differentiations focused on studies within single national settings. Emmanuel Le Roy Ladurie reported on his work with the data from the data from the French Military Archives of the nineteenth century. As he had shown in his article with Paul Dumont in *Daedalus*,[11] it had proved possible to establish a great number of maps for variations by département on the basis of these data. He had now proceeded to analyze a sample of these data at the individual level and could report a number of very interesting results: taking registered delinquency as the dependent variable he had found in a sample of 11,000 conscripts for 1968 that the highest rates were not only to be found among the illiterates and the lowest occupations but quite particularly among the mobile among these, those not born in the locality in which they lived. There was a great deal of interest in these data and Le Roy Ladurie was strongly urged to expand his analyses (a) to cover longer time series, and (b) to bring out the weight of geographical variables.

Roland Ruffieux reported on two analyses of regional development in Switzerland. Both dealt with the Jura issue: one focused on a time-series analysis of mass petitions addressed by the *Jurassiens* to the cantonal government from 1830 to 1890; the other, by Michel Bassand, was an ecological analysis of variations by commune in the Jura area from 1941 to 1960. The Bassand paper brought out with great clarity the stability of the division within the Jura; the two basic dimensions of variation, one socio-economic, the other socio-cultural, remained remarkably constant and the geographical location of the corresponding types of units also stayed very much the same. Contrary to the general assumption, the analysis did not indicate that the increase in separatist attitudes in the Jura was due to rapid social change. On the contrary it appeared that the decisive factor was the slowness of the modernization processes in the Jura as compared with the rest of Berne and Switzerland.

Partly similar in structure was the paper presented by Frank Aarebrot on his analysis of the early processes of mobilization in Norway; this analysis was also concerned with changes over time and made use of regional typologies. The focus of the current analysis was on the "quantum jumps" in turnout rates from 1876 to 1882, but plans had been drawn up for analyses over much longer spans of time.

Possibly the longest time span coverage ever attempted in ecological analysis was that in Leif Lewin's study of electoral data for Sweden from 1887 to 1968. This was limited to the twenty-five län (provinces) but covered a great number of variables. The purpose of the study was to pin down changes in the class basis of the major parties since their emergence at the end of the nineteenth century. This study used a technique of ecological regression derived from Leo Goodman's work; the task was to estimate from the marginal distributions for each unit, the size of the unknown cells in each matrix. The results seemed on the whole acceptable although adjustments would clearly have to be made to take into account extensions of the suffrage and the ensuing spurts of mobilization within the entering strata of the population.

The final session of this part of the workshop was devoted to a discussion of current efforts to build up large-scale computer files of historical-statistical data country by country. Hans Daalder reported on the organization of files of ecological time-series data and of elite biographies at the University of Leiden. Mark Franklin reported on parallel efforts for British data at the University of Strathclyde, and Jerome Clubb reported on the expansion of the historical files of the Inter-University Consortium. There was general agreement that such archives should be built up in all countries, and it was strongly recommended that the ISSC take action to ensure better coordination of such efforts. This coordinating function could be restricted to the purely technical level of coding practices, data management, and retrieval systems, but might also be broadened to cover methodological and theoretical problems of comparative analysis.

FROM HISTORY TO POLICY ANALYSIS: THE LINKS BETWEEN TIME-SERIES ARCHIVING AND THE SOCIAL INDICATORS MOVEMENT

The final section of the workshop centred on the current social indicators movement: how far could the work on historical time series help to supply benchmark data and extrapolations of direct use in the current debate over indicators for policy, and how could retrospective and prospective concerns be fruitfully combined in the evaluation of packages of indicators?

The director of the workshop, Stein Rokkan, underlined the importance of close cooperation between builders of time-series collections and planners of new batteries of indicators; in economics there were very direct links between Kusnetz-type efforts to extract better information from past records and the planning of fresh data collections for the future; there was no reason to think that similar links could not be established within the other social sciences.

It was of some significance that the principal paper on the social indicators movement was given by a leader in the effort to establish time series for historical-sociological analysis in Europe: Wolfgang Zapf presented a critical review of the successive attempts to persuade the U.S. authorities to collect more systematic data for a "social report" on the state of the nation, and also looked into some of the proposals made within the U.N. and the OECD for a standard system of social accounting.[12]

The Zapf paper had originally been written for an audience of German academics and went into considerable detail in accounting for the origins and the peculiarities of the social indicators movement: the revolt against purely monetary economics, against the "numbers magic," against the cult of growth without quality. Zapf traced the history of the movement from the Hoover Committee on Social Trends, and reviewed the contributions of Bertram Gross, the Russell Sage Foundation, the Commission on the Year 2,000, as well as the U.S. government agencies responsible for the first issue of *Towards a Social Report*. He also discussed developments in Europe, quite particularly the comparisons of the "quality of life" in the Federal Republic and the DDR as described in *Bericht der Bundesregierung und Materialien zum Bericht zur Lage der Nation 1971*[13] and the Conference of European Statisticians, *Integrated System of Social and Demographic Statistics*.[14] He saw no clear consensus emerging out of these multiple efforts, but he was convinced that the movement would gain momentum not only nationally but also internationally. In the most immediate future the movement was most likely to help forward a critical attitude to current statistical production schedules: only the economists and the demographers had had much influence on the routine production of public statistics; it was high time that sociologists and political scientists developed criteria for the critique of current statistics and came up with reasoned proposals for improvement and expansion. More research was needed on the "sociology of societal data generation": Why are some areas covered while others are neglected? Why are some statistics used in policy discussions while others go unnoticed? How are pressures for new data generated, and how are decisions made among competing claims? How much data gathering can be done outside official channels, and how does this affect the routinization of governmental procedures? Such questions have not yet been asked systematically across countries. Albert Biderman's work on the sociology of social information in the United States[15] was exemplary and ought to be followed up in many more countries. Generally Zapf expressed scepticism towards the "grand designs" of comprehensive systems of social accounting and urged the completion of series of limited pilot studies across several countries; he singled out as particularly worthy of replication in other countries the Coleman-Rossi Social Accounts Project at Johns Hopkins University, the German two-country comparison *(Materialien zur Lage der Nation),* the British journal, *Social Trends,* and "sociological almanacs" such as the one produced for the United States by Gendell and Zetterberg in 1961.

Eleanor Sheldon of the Russell Sage Foundation reported on the most recent developments in the United States and regretted the parochial character of the work so far carried out in her country. She agreed that much more should be done to establish links with counterparts in other countries but made it clear that much of the impetus behind the movement was specific to the given national system; the demands for new data reflected ongoing struggles over national policies, and these data would of necessity differ from one configuration to another.

Henning Friis of the Danish National Institute of Social Research urged closer cooperation between the archive builders and the social indicators planners. It was important that all those planning fresh data-gathering operations had easy access to the earlier time series and could reanalyze earlier data in designing new instruments. Friis was convinced that the social indicators movement would have its greatest impact through the institutionalization of regular sample surveys on the quality of social conditions. He did not expect that governments could afford or would be willing to add many variables to their censuses or other enumerations, but he did believe that much could be done to improve the statistical coverage through regular surveys. Unfortunately there was as yet very little international cooperation among those who designed governmental sample surveys, but he had hoped that progress could be made through projects currently planned within Scandinavia and the EEC. He also urged that better use be made of the European Coordination Centre for Research and Documentation in Social Sciences in Vienna.

Henry David reported on plans developed within the U.S. National Academy of Sciences/National Research Council for a nongovernmental *International Social Indicators Programme.* This programme would build up a network of communication among research teams and institutions actively engaged in the development and testing of new batteries of indicators, and would seek to link up activities through joint conferences, exchanges of data and personnel, cooperative and comparative studies.

Eleanor Sheldon feared that some of the intellectual quality of the research on indicators would be lost if the movement was internationalized too quickly: she asked those around the table to specify what direct pay-off they saw in a programme such as the one proposed by Henry David.

Erik Allardt agreed that there were dangers in too quick operational-ization across countries. Any international effort in this field should be based on thorough analysis of values and goals, and all proposed indicators should be judged on the basis of their contribution to realistic measure-ment of the extent of realization of such values or goals.

There was the general consensus that all groups concerned with developing indicator programmes in their countries would benefit from some scheme of internationalization, but there were clear preferences for informal networks of research workers genuinely engaged in such work; this point was brought out particularly forcefully by Zapf. Candido Mendes called for international cooperation in the construction of indicator systems for the developing countries and informed the workshop about efforts under way in Latin America. Serge Flanigan said that UNESCO and other U.N. agencies would clearly be interested in helping forward an international programme of this type; he referred quite particularly to the importance of regional-local disaggregation and to the need for a differentiated system of indicators for each level of develop-ment.

The final hour of the workshop was devoted to a general debate on next steps:

(a) There was consensus that the ISSC, the ECPR, and the ICPR should all be asked to take action to ensure better coordination of the current work on the time-series files and to make sure that the available collections be merged for cross-checking, evaluation, and updating;

(b) It was also agreed that steps be taken to establish a forum for exchanges of information about new time series and about current work of evaluation and revision: some of this exchange could be done through the Data Information Service of the ECPR, but other agencies should also be brought in;

(c) It was also recommended that a group be established for the coordination of work on ecological and biographical files; this matter would be taken up both with the ISSC and the ECPR;

(d) There was finally general agreement on the need for some international machinery to ensure better communication among academic social scientists actively engaged in research on systems of social indicators; the workshop agreed to urge the International Social Science Council to explore the possibilities of establishing a pilot programme in this field in close cooperation with UNESCO, OECD, and all national bodies currently promoting such research.

NOTES

1. See the Introduction to this volume and R. Kothari's report in Chapter 3.

2. Cambridge, MIT Press, 1971.

3. A Conceptual Framework for the Comparative Study of Political Parties, Beverly Hills, Sage, 1970.

4. D. Singer and M. Small, The Wages of War 1816-1965: A Statistical Handbook, New York, John Wiley, 1972.

5. W. Zapf and P. Flora, "Some Problems of Time-series Analysis in Research on Modernization," Social Science Information Vol. 10, No. 3, 1971, pp. 53-102, reprinted as Chapter 6 in this volume.

6. To be published in C. Tilley, ed., The Formation of National States in Western Europe, Princeton, Princeton University Press, forthcoming 1973.

7. See Bulletin of the Sociological Institute of the University of Zurich, Vol. 12, February 1969.

8. C. Taylor and M. Hudson, World Handbook of Political and Social Indicators, New Haven, Conn., Yale University Press, 1972 (2nd ed.).

9. A. Przeworski and H. Teune, The Logic of Comparative Social Inquiry, New York, John Wiley, 1970.

10. In R. L. Merritt and S. Rokkan, eds., Comparing Nations, New Haven, Conn., Yale University Press, 1966.

11. "Quantitative and Cartographic Exploitation of French Military Archives 1819-1926," *Daedalus,* Spring 1971, pp. 397-441.

12. Social Science Information, Vol. 11, No. 3/4, pp. 243-77.

13. Bundesministerium für Innerdeutsche Beziehungen, *Bericht der Bundesregierung und Materialien zur Lage der Nation,* Bonn, 1971.

14. R. Stone, *Memorandum* E/CN; 3/394, United Nations Economic and Social Council, 1970.

15. A. Biderman, "Social Indicators and Goals," in R. Bauer (ed.) *Social Indicators,* Cambridge, MIT Press, 1966, pp. 68-153.

CHAPTER 6

DIFFERENCES IN PATHS OF DEVELOPMENT:
AN ANALYSIS FOR TEN COUNTRIES

Wolfgang Zapf
Peter Flora

WOLFGANG ZAPF was Professor of Sociology at the University of Frankfurt through 1972; he is now at the University of Mannheim. He is the author of books on industrial sociology, German elites, and theories of social change (in German). Among his English publications are: "Complex Societies and Social Change" (1968) and "Social Indicators" (1972), both in *Social Science Information.* He is currently engaged in developing a system of social indicators for the German Federal Republic.

PETER FLORA is an associate of Professor Zapf. He has worked for several years on historical indicators of societal development and has recently completed a thesis on modernization research, which will be published in 1973.

Even before the rapid progress of econometrics, attempts were made in the other social sciences to develop procedures appropriate to quantitative analysis and explanation of macro-processes. If we take a new look at the traditions of the *Political arithmetick* and *Staatenkunde* of the seventeenth and eighteenth centuries, we discover that in the early stages of the social sciences no differentiation had yet been made between economic,

AUTHOR'S NOTE: This chapter is a revised version of a paper first presented at the Plenary Session on Nation Building of the Eighth World Congress of Political Science in Munich, September 1970. A shorter version is published in German in Politische Vierteljahresschrift, Vol. 12, 1971.

political, and sociological analysis; and there was no distinction between statistical methodology and substantive research.[1] This retrospective approach does not have the purpose of arguing against the scientific division of labor, but is adopted in order to acquire a more realistic view of what should be done. The task will be to provide the social sciences with a data basis similar to that already available in economics, to match the economic accounting systems with political and social accounting systems,[2] to recover some of the comparative width and historical depth of the classical authors.

TIME SERIES: PROBLEMS OF COLLECTION, CONSTRUCTION, AND ANALYSIS

The New "Data Movement": Cross-national and Time-series Data

The new "data movement" made its breakthrough with the comparative method. Its present position is best documented in works and projects like Banks and Textor's *A Cross-polity Survey*, the *World Handbook of Political and Social Indicators* by Russett et al., Rummel's DON-project, and in such symposia as *Comparing Nations* and *Aggregate Data Analysis.*[3] The authors of these and other works agree not to limit their programme to the collection and analysis of comparative, cross-national data and also to initiate longitudinal research by starting to collect, construct, and analyze time-series, as long as possible. Following this trend, the second edition of the Russett handbook was announced to include short time series covering the period 1950-1965.[4] J. D. Singer has announced a work, *The Wages of War: Longitudinal Profiles, 1816-1965,* which seems to be a decisive step beyond his long term studies on wars and international relations.[5]

In the first edition of the Russett handbook, the analysis was based on " 'stages' of economic and political development" as a substitute for time-series data. Countries were rank ordered according to the variable GNP per capita and then classified into five groups, each typifying a developmental stage. The internal homogeneity of each group was maximized with respect to eight other variables.[6] A more refined substitution for time-series analysis is provided by Adelman and Morris.[7] A factor analysis was carried out on forty-one rank order, quantitative and qualitative variables for seventy-four underdeveloped countries, producing four factors. Factor 1 (which can best be characterized as "breakdown of traditional social organization") "explains" approximately fifty percent of the variance of GNP per capita. Each country's factor score on this factor was calculated and the countries split into three developmental groups (high, medium, low). These groups were then factor-analyzed once more. By this procedure, different interrelations among the same economic, political, social, and cultural variables were detected and found to be characteristic for each developmental stage.

In addition to this difference in the level of methodological refinement the following feature distinguishes the two approaches: Adelman and Morris, for each inductively determined stage, use the complete information of the data collection, whereas Russett (as Lipset earlier[8]) takes only previously selected variables into consideration. It should also be noted that all substitution of cross-national for time-series data presupposes a model of universal stages of development which cannot itself be tested. Therefore the authors hasten to note the limitations of their methods: "A more direct and dependable method for examining stages would be to look at developmental data for many countries over longer periods of time, to substitute longitudinal for cross-national data" (Russett).[9]

2. Some Examples of Time-series Analysis

In order to realize such a programme we fortunately do not have to start from scratch. There are time-series collections and analyses—even outside the field of economics—which are as comprehensive as cross-national studies. Recently, the ambitious goal has been set to improve the standards of cross-national research by carrying out time-series analyses—within the frame of reference of precisely defined theoretical models—of as many indicators as possible, for as many countries as possible, establishing exact references and confidence intervals. Although this may be accepted as a goal, the studies at hand are restricted either to a few variables or to a single country or to a narrowly defined problem or to the use of relatively simple analytical tools.

If by time-series analysis nothing more is meant than "qualitative" interpretation of time-series data, including simple parameters like means, sums, or differences, then Quetelet and Durkheim already did time-series analysis. This kind of descriptive analysis reached a climax between the two World Wars in the works of authors like Ogburn, Sorokin, Wright, and Hart. It is still most impressive to discover the immense historical and comparative material presented for instance in Sorokin's *Social Mobility*.[10] We cannot even superficially report these achievements which make up an important part of the history of quantification in the social sciences.[11] Instead, we will concentrate on some early and some recent approaches to time-series analysis.

(a) Nontechnical Time-series Analyses in Historical Sociology.

For his four monumental volumes, *Social and Cultural Dynamics,* published from 1937 to 1941,[12] Sorokin has compiled long-term, time series covering more than twenty centuries to support the thesis "that no linearism in any form is found to be valid [...] [but] an ever new recurrence of the same patterns.[13] The tables and appendices of volumes two and three are even today a valuable source for time series, particularly with respect to nonecological data.[14] Similarly, the works of Hart[15] are based on time series relevant for a "universal history." Arguing against Sorokin and other cyclical theorists he postulated, first, a law of cultural acceleration, i.e., the acceleration of the rate of material development and, second, a law of logistic surges, i.e., logistic curves of growth with respect to organizational development and culture complexes. The time series he used to support the first law are, e.g., life expectancy, killing capacity, and world speed records; as a basis for the second law, he refers to discoveries, economic crises, and expansion of empires. Today this kind of "quantitative world history" has become suspect and is considered too unspecific and not sufficiently focused on the really interesting mechanisms of change and development. However, we learn from Sorokin and Hart the lesson that a plethora of information is available and can be dug out from our libraries.

(b) Process Models Using Time Series.

A second approach to time-series analysis will be illustrated by two well-known process models tracing the interrelations of various social or political processes with the aid of time series. Let us take two examples from the work of Richardson and Deutsch, both pioneers of modern quantitative macro-theory in the social sciences.[16] L. F. Richardson analyzed time series for armament expenditures of two, three, or more nations or blocs, and developed systems of differential equations to detect the conditions of stability and instability of arms races. Combining data on armament expenditure and foreign trade or on "warlike worktime" and armament expenditure, he constructed theories about interrelations between threats and cooperation and between armament and aggressiveness. These studies have opened a wide field of research; and it is important to note that Richardson succeeded in balancing model-building and theory-testing. K. W. Deutsch, processing time series on population growth, literacy, proportion of speakers of major and minor languages, population in agriculture, urban population, and the like, constructed a model of "critical" relationships between processes of mobilization and processes of assimilation in order to predict tendencies towards equilibrium and disequilibrium in nation-building from different growth rates. His appendices are exemplary for their presentation of sources, data construction, and estimations of confidence.

(c) Factor Analyses of Time Series.

Process models, based on explicitly stated theories, are either tested on time-series data or are constructed to explain specific time series. On the contrary, in factor analysis, large sets of time series are "thrown in" to establish introductive patterns of correlations.

A pioneer in this field was the psychologist R. B. Cattell. By the approach he called "quantitative cultural anthropology," he investigated societies much in the way he had studied personality, coining the term "syntality" for the substratum of emergent societal properties. This approach calls for the use of many and opposed societal characteristics to free the results from idiosyncrasies. Here, we will comment only upon Cattell's longitudinal studies, that he and his collaborators carried out to uncover the "dimensions of social change" (U.S.A., 1845-1945, Great Britain, 1837-1937, and Australia, 1906-1946).[17] The U.S. study started with the collection of more than one hundred time series that after a quality control, were reduced to forty-four series. All data were standardized to a twelve-point scale and submitted to factor analysis with the P-technique (correlation of several variables for one country over time). Formally, the result is five curves representing the "time course of factors"; substantially, beside the major trend-like "factor of progress," the result consists in the detection of four other factors that in part are highly oscillating. Cattell summarizes: "Social change proceeds, or oscillates, along at least four other independent dimensions of transformation beside that of 'progress.' "[18] The study of P. Seppänen[19] on the main transformation processes in Finland, based on a factor analysis of fifty-eight standardized time series from 1911 to 1961, follows Cattell's ideas. Seppänen's innovation consists of the use of the O-technique (correlation of the time points for all variables in one country) which produces independent time periods as factors. Besides factor 1, the total period 1911-1961, the period 1940-1944, 1945-1947, and 1948-1961 turned out to be independent factors.

(d) Correlational and Lead-lag Analyses.

To the authors' knowledge there exists no noneconometric time-series analysis based on complex causal models using partial correlation and dependence coefficients. Correlational analysis, however, is as common as it is controversial, but the causal models used remain only implicit or very simple. Undoubtedly, one of the first substantial time-series analyses with refined statistical methods was that carried out by Udny Yule in 1899.[20] These analyses were an investigation into the causes of changes in pauperism in England between 1871 and 1891, based on data on some six hundred Poor Law unions. His principal aim was to establish whether changes in pauperism had been brought about by changes in administrative procedures or by other causes, e.g., changes in age structure. At the same time he wished to determine the specific weight of each cause. He attempted to answer this question by means of causal interpretation of a correlational and multiple regression analysis of the change rates of all variables, assuming a simple model with independent, additive, and linear causal influences. He discovered that administrative policy had a strong direct influence on changes in pauperism but also that a great part of the variation over time remained unexplained.

Recent examples of correlational analysis are Michael Haas's study of the correlations between indicators of "military behavior" (dependent variables) and of "stress" and "strain" (independent variables) for ten countries in the period 1900-1960[21]; and J. D. Singer's impressive analysis of the relations between indicators of alliance aggregation (independent variables) and of the magnitude, severity, and frequency of war (dependent variables) for the period 1815-1945.[22] Both authors introduce a rudiment of causal reasoning by lagging the independent variables. A further development of this idea is the lead-lag analysis, a method of inductive model-building. Linda Groff planned to make a cross-lagged panel analysis with her time-series data (ninety-three variables—U.S.A., United Kingdom, France, Germany, Japan 1800-1965).[23] This analysis is based on the following principle: if the correlation between X_{t-0} and Y_{t-1} is greater than the corresponding correlation between X_{t-1} and Y_{t-0}, then, one can conclude that the direction of influence is greater from Y to X than from X to Y. In our year-to-year collection (see below), we combined a cross-lagged panel analysis with a correlogram analysis by continually enlarging the time lags, thereby making it possible to detect not only the direction of causal influence but also its course over time.

The Suitability of Methods

Today the statistical methods of time-series analysis have reached a high level of methodological and mathematical refinement,[24] whereas the reliability and accuracy of noneconomic data lag far behind. Therefore, in most cases, we have to go back to the origin of the econometric science to find the methods appropriate to our level of measurement. Already in 1934, S. Kuznets in his article, "Time Series," in the *Encyclopedia of the Social Sciences,* characterized the state of this area of research in a manner still valid for us:

> And while time series analysis is essentially a body of methods of interpreting a historical series as a congeries of changes, each due primarily to a specific group of factors—so that it is presented as a controlled sequence—the resulting generalizations are never so inclusive as to free the investigator from reference to limited historical periods and spatial areas or to relieve him of the obligation of describing fully the basic raw materials, i.e., the historical time series.[25]

In the above-mentioned article, Simon Kuznets outlined the important task of decomposing time-series; it is interesting to compare his statement with the recent formulation of Karl Deutsch:

Kuznets, 1934:

> A more precise formulation [...] would distinguish cumulative, irreversible changes on the one hand and cancelable, reversible changes on the other. The cumulative, irreversible changes are designated secular movements or trends. The cancelable, reversible changes are represented by cyclical movements of various types, distinguished by the period and regularity of the swing: cyclical fluctuations of two to fifteen years of length; seasonal variations of an annual period; and what may be called cycles of highly irregular and on the whole brief duration, the residual changes. The main problem of analysis in connection with these types of temporal change is to define them and to ground them firmly in the already existing knowledge of social phenomena; and to discover a mathematical expression for them which would provide a basis for the statistical procedure of describing the particular group of changes present in any given historical time series.[26]

Deutsch, 1966:

> We will need time series. Here I would suggest that we develop a standard way of describing all time series, by trying to compress every time series into at least four standard components. The first component would be the trend, which is an average trend usually over time. Second is the variance distribution around the trend, and, in the third place, there is a cyclical component. Very often there are fluctuations and it is often possible to model these fluctuations as a simple wave motion or a combination of two or more wave motions. Think, for instance, of economic growth, which is a clear trend but which is modified by regional variance as well as by business cycle fluctuation with a fairly marked periodicity in certain times of history. And finally, the fourth component is the stochastic component, which is a random process superimposed on the whole series.[27]

In our perspective there seem to be—besides the graphical methods of data presentation and crude manipulation (e.g., the comparison or combination of graphical curves, the determination of turning points, and so on)—three phases in the decomposition of time series:

    (a) The testing, determination (by regression analysis), and elimination of a trend;

    (b) The test of randomness after the elimation of the trend;

    (c) The determination of the probable influence of singular important events.

In most cases it will not be possible—beyond a test of randomness—to establish propositions about cyclical movements that are not easily falsified by systematic measurement errors and changes in operational definitions. This situation means that the most advanced methods in econometrics and mathematical statistics, such as spectral analysis,[28] will probably not be appropriate for some time to come.

Many difficulties in the analysis of time series arise from the fact that the individual items of a time series are not statistically independent, i.e., they are autocorrelated. Hence they cannot be treated as if they were the result of random sampling, and many of the classical methods of statistical analysis become inapplicable.[29] Autocorrelation makes it particularly difficult to build and test causal models based on correlation coefficients. One should therefore aim at using methods for the reduction of autocorrelation which are at the same time suitable for the data and allow a causal interpretation of the results. Among the simplest are the following two:

    (a) The use of values produced by the elimination of the trend;

    (b) The use of differences instead of absolute values.

But these methods do not guarantee a reduction of autocorrelation which should therefore in any case be tested. (The Wald-Wolfowitz nonparametric test has the advantage of great simplicity. It is based on all possible permutations of actual observations.)

The strong interrelation between reliability and accuracy of data on the one hand and the possibility of testing causal models on the other confirms the need to improve simultaneously the methods of data collection and construction, and those of causal model building.

Data Collection and Data Construction

In their commentary on the Russett handbook, aptly entitled "Horizontal History in Search of Vertical Dimensions," R. Grew and S. L. Thrupp demanded the "applicability of its methods to still larger periods of time."[30] They criticized Russett's implicit assumption that information gaps were the reason for the lack of time-series analysis and stated that for "some countries this is true, but for the European countries it is not true, and relevant historical research is making headway in Japan, in India, in Mexico and in many other places." Thus, the collection of time series is possible and necessary, since only with the use of time-series data can weak correlations, breaks in a pattern, and deviant cases be appropriately explained. Finally Grew and Thrupp encouragingly call for more cooperation between historians and social scientists:

> One should not claim too much for historical statistics. An attempt to extend into the past the methods here employed for the present would not only raise grave difficulties about the quality of available data and its correct interpretation, but, after all the efforts, many of the results would merely seem to confirm what had been generally assumed, many of the hypotheses suggested would be difficult to subject to proof. Despite all this, historians have a great deal to gain from studying and openly imitating the methods of this book; for here is an approach which should help overcome the easy and false distinction between verbal interpretation and statistics, an approach bound to help define more precisely some significant historical problems. And, whatever its limits, how tremendously useful it would be to have a handbook of historical data similar to this one.[31]

Most certainly, however, neither historians nor historically oriented social scientists can be satisfied with the scope and perspective of official and private statistics, nor with collection and processing of already codified data. There is no question of the importance of work with codified data, but with such data alone, we cannot overcome our well-known biases (e.g., the ecological bias). Besides the task of direct data collection, there is, as Rokkan once stated, that of constructing theoretically important codifications from raw information: "the much more laborious, but possibly more rewarding task of imposing their own classification schemes on the wealth of 'process produced' materials [...], be they biographical records, legislative or ministerial documents, or literary products,"[32] and of developing macroscopic methods of content analysis. In spite of all his theoretical idiosyncrasies, the work of Sorokin remains an outstanding example, especially with regard to the neglected cultural, ideological, and juridical dimensions. As a representative monograph one should remember McClelland's far-reaching work[33] (his well-known n-Achievement index) and in this context, the already highly advanced methods of semiautomatic content analysis.[34]

In cross-national research the construction of "soft data" is often considered to be an adequate procedure to close the data gap (Banks and Textor, Adelman and Morris, Almond and Coleman).[35] Soft data are estimated properties, constructed by experts rating a unit at a time on a given nominal or ordinal scale, e.g., the "importance of the indigenous middle class" in a country, "degree of social tensions," "strength of democratic institutions," "leadership charisma," or "character of the legal system." But here Russett's warning must be remembered: "The Banks-Textor approach has obvious disadvantages in terms of reproducibility."[36]

The difficulties with variables based on evaluation multiply in long time series, but the attempts to quantify qualitative properties and "critical events" can nevertheless be very useful. Furthermore, not all interesting qualitative properties necessitate complicated procedures of evaluation to become amenable to statistical treatment. A very convincing example is J. D. Singer's and M. Small's quantitative description of formal alliances, 1815-1939.[37] Starting with the assumption that "alliance commitments reflect both a congruence of interests among signatories and a constraint of their future freedom of action,"[38] they used an immense number of primary and secondary sources to determine the duration of written alliances between 1815 and 1939 and to classify them according to type of commitment (defense pact, neutrality and nonaggression pact, entente). By cumulating the percentages of nations in the international system (the pre-1920 system being divided in a central and a peripheral system) who were implied in one or more alliances of a given class during each year, they constructed an Alliance Commitment Index for different types of nations and different classes of alliances. Though Singer and Small did not find a consistent pattern of covariation between alliance activity and war, they distinguished three periods (1815-1878, 1879-1919, 1920-1945) showing distinct patterns of type, composition, and duration of alliances on the one hand and of magnitude and severity of war on the other.

A Strategy for Data Collection

Before deciding upon a strategy for data collection one must take into consideration that the major problem to be dealt with does not arise from a scarcity of sources but concerns the choice among abundant data of unequal quality. Of course, there is no ideal strategy to deal with these problems. We will only indicate some of our preferences with regard to starting points and the sequence of steps. In general, we prefer (a) primary sources to secondary sources, (b) historical comparative sources to noncomparative sources, (c) cross-national comparative sources to non-comparative sources, (d) compendia to monographs.

In the first case the distinction pertains to levels of accuracy; in the remaining cases, it concerns choice in a situation of abundance of sources. For our purposes, in contrast with the usage in the historical sciences, we designate a source as "primary" either when we have reasons to assume that the original data had been collected with care and the parameters exactly calculated or when we can reconstruct the collection and calculation process, and thus be able to detect possible errors.

In the last three cases the preferences are by no means absolute since under certain conditions noncomparative sources and monographs may be more reliable and comprehensive than the preferred types of secondary sources. In Appendix 1, we present an outline of types of sources for time-series data. The types listed last become more important the further one goes back in history. Three examples of sources from our own research are given for each type.

At the present stage of research, political scientists and sociologists have to believe in the relative reliability of historical statistics if they want at all to engage in data collection. But in all probability the more promising the use of quantitative data becomes the more it will become necessary to exercise the same critique of sources in time-series analysis as has already been done in the economic and demographic disciplines.[39] Accurate data are even more desirable in time-series analysis than in cross-national analysis, since some inaccurate data do not seriously influence the outcome of a correlational analysis of some dozens of nations whereas in a paired comparison of national development or in the prediction of singular, important events, inaccurate data will almost inevitably lead to wrong conclusions.

The main problems confronting the historical statistician are the systematic errors in data produced by the methods of sampling, collection, and calculation. In most cases his task is limited to finding the direction of error and perhaps estimating its probable range. To fulfill this task he has to gather as much information as possible about the original operational definitions and the actual process of data collection and calculation. For instance, to be able to evaluate the real rate of urbanization in Russia during the last decades before the Revolution of 1917 one should know that in the Russian statistics the administrative definition of cities excluded from the urban population new communities with up to forty thousand inhabitants. In 1897, the official statistics defined 13.4 percent of the population as urban. W. W. Eason indicates an upper limit of 32 percent and estimates 20 percent to be the most likely figure.[40] Last but not least, in collecting data one has to cope with these problems of validity and comparability of data. In order to cope with these problems it would be necessary to collect further qualitative, contextual information in support of the quantitative data. In order to compare, for instance, levels and development rates of the proportion of children enrolled in primary schools between nations and periods, we should at least know what is meant by "primary school" at any given time, what types of schools (public, private, intermediate) are included in the definition, whether the data are based on attendance records or on inscription rolls, and whether the school attendance is part-time or full-time.

The Collection of Time Series: the QUAM-project

We shall report on some of our own efforts in collecting time series relevant for analysis of modernization and societal change. (Examples of analysis are given in the next section.) The acronym QUAM-project stands for QUAntitative Model of Modernization. Our frame of reference is a six-dimensional scheme;[41] our idea is to construct and collect time series to measure the main subdimensions of the modernization process, then to proceed to analyze strategic interrelations and "faults."

Subdimensions of the modernization process
(interaction between all levels)

CULTURE Cultural transformation	Secularization, rationalization, scientific development, ideological changes

SOCIETY
    Polity
    Political development
    Economy
    Economic development
    Social structure
    Social mobilization and integration
	
	State formation, nation-building, partici-
	    pation, redistribution
	Capital accumulation, technical progress,
	    changes in economic structures
	Population growth, urbanization, com-
	    munications development, mobility

PERSONALITY Psychic mobilization	 Empathy, achievement
INTERNATIONAL RELATIONS Transformation	 Power transition, loss of viability

We will briefly describe three of our data collections. First, the decade collection, consisting of thirty-eight indicators of social change for ten societies, from 1820 to 1960 (some indicators for certain countries from 1760), in decade periods; then the year-to-year collection for four societies for the period 1860-1960; and last, the recently started refined collection, consisting of indicators of social mobilization and political development for six societies, 1815-1965, for as many years as data are available.

The Decade Collection

We made this collection in 1967, as a kind of pilot study, after reading the Russett handbook and Grew and Thrupp's commentary. The challenge was: how far can one succeed, by using library sources, in producing comparable time series

(a) of a scope similar to that of the Russett volume,

(b) for a period of at least 150 years, and

(c) for no less than ten societies?

We selected ten "big" countries and grouped them to make possible paired comparisons:

Pioneers	"Super" powers	Early late-comers	Ibero- American	Big underdeveloped
Great Britain	U.S.A.	Germany	Spain	India
France	U.S.S.R.	Japan	Argentina	China

Finally, we retained the following thirty-eight indicators (see Table 1), starting respectively in 1760 (e.g., 06, 27, 37), 1820 (e.g., 09, 13), or 1860 (e.g., 22). As was to be expected, the sources for Great Britain, France, U.S.A., and Germany turned out to be very good in quality and scope, for China very scarce, and for the others medium.

The data are available on punch cards. One set is deposited at the Data Center of the Harvard School of Government. A small sample of results, which will be used for the analysis in the next section, is given in the Appendix tables.

We are certain that this data collection gives a reliable overall impression of the ranges and patterns of developmental and change processes. But upon closer inspection some of the annoying problems peculiar to all series of "straightforward-collected" data become apparent:

– The reliability of the figures, taken one by one, may be highly dubious; very often we get third-hand and fourth-hand data, for which the original source can no longer be consulted.

– It is very difficult to indicate adequately even second-hand sources if there are ten or more needed for one single table.

– Choosing straight decade points might lead you astray if there were "critical events" in between, e.g., the two World Wars.

This is common sense to all experts. However, we have to mention it because of the context of our wishful thinking as to the great possibilities of "fishing for time-series" by means of library research.

TABLE 1
INDICATORS

01	AREAM	Area in thousand square miles	y.[c]
02	EMPIR	Dependent areas in thousand square miles	y.
03	POPUL	Population (in area 01), in hundred thousands	y.
04	EMIGR	Intercontinental emigration, thousands per decade	d.
05	IMMIG	Immigration, thousands per decade	d.
06	BIRTH	Birth rate, per ten thousand inhabitants	a.d.
07	DEATH	Death rate, per ten thousand inhabitants	a.d.
08	LIFEX	Male life expectancy at birth, in years	a.y.
09	RURAL	Rural population in percent of total population	y.
10	URBAN	Population in cities over one hundred thousand, in percent	y.
11	AGRAR	Labor force in agriculture, in percent of labor force	a.y.
12	TERTS	Labor force in tertiary sector, in percent	a.y.
13	INCOM	National income in hundred million U.S. dollars 1952/4	y.
14	I-CAP	National income per capita, in U.S. dollars 1952/4	y.
15	REALI	Real income per capita, in Clark's "international units"	a.d.
16	COALP	Coal production in hundred thousand tons	a.y.
17	STEEL	Steel production in hundred thousand tons	y.
18	ELRGY	Production of electric energy, in hundred million kwh	y.
19	EXPOR	Value of exports in million current U.S. dollars	y.
20	IMPOR	Value of imports in million current U.S. dollars	y.
21	TR-IN	Value of foreign trade, in per mille of national income	a.y.
22	RAILW	Railway mileage, in thousand miles	y.
23	AUTOS	Private automobiles per ten thousand inhabitants	y.
24	MAILS	Letters carried, per capita	y.
25	ILLIT	Illiterates, in percent of population over fourteen years	y.
26	ENROL	Population in primary schools, in per mille	y.
27	CIRCL	Turnover of cabinet ministers[a]	a.d.
28	PRIME	Number of new heads of government, per decade	d.
29	REVOL	Sorokin's index of internal disturbances	d.
30	STRIK	Working days lost by strikes, in thousands	a.d.
31	VOTER	Enfranchised population in percent of total population	y.
32	GOVEX	Central government expenditure, in percent of national income	y.t.
33	MILEX	Military expenditure, in percent of national income	y.t.
34	TROOP	Military forces, in thousands	y.t.
35	NRWAR	Number of wars entered, per decade[b]	d.
36	COMBA	Combatants, average per year, in thousands	a.d.
37	CASUA	War casualties, average per year, in hundreds	a.d.
38	DIPLO	Singer's index of diplomatic representativeness	y.

a. In percent of all positions, average per year.
b. First World War counted 5, Second World War counted 10.
c. y. = year, i.e., indicated year or next best datum; d. = decade, i.e., aggregate for decade or next best period; a.d. = average decade, i.e., average of aggregated years for decade; a.y. = average years, i.e., average of aggregated years, next best to decade; y.t. = year, top, i.e., indicated year, but average in the decades 1910 and 1940 (World Wars).

In spite of our reservations as to the quality of this data collection we have published it in mimeographed form,[42] after adding a correlational analysis of the change (growth) rates.

The Year-to-Year Collection

Ideally, time series of social and political relevance should be collected on a year-to-year basis because only then can we hope to get more than overall trends, and to discover cycles, turning points, and the influence of "critical events." To get accommodated to this task, we collected a small set of indicators "measuring" industrialization, international engagement, and domestic political stability for Great Britain, France, U.S.A., and Germany, for the period 1860-1960. This collection was planned mainly as a technical exercise, but the outcome may be of some theoretical interest. We selected six variables, and calculated and presented them as follows:

(a) Circulation. Ratio of change of cabinet ministers per year. Number of ministerial changes as a percentage of total number of ministerial posts.

(b) Strikes. Number of lost working days per year (for the U.S.A. up to 1923, substituting the number of participating workers).

(c) Index of total exports. Export figures deflated by an index of volume and standardized.

(d) Armament expenditures. In percentage of the central government budget.

(e) Index of income per capita. Per capita income figures deflated and standardized.

(f) Index of total production. Standardized.

Refined Collection

This collection was started at the beginning of 1970 and is still in progress. We plan to collect data for constructing indicators of social mobilization and political development for U.S.A., U.S.S.R., Japan, Germany (Prussia, Germany, West Germany, East Germany), France, and the United Kingdom (England and Wales, Scotland, Ireland, and Northern Ireland) for the period 1815-1965. We collect as many data as possible but, of course, there is no hope to get data for all indicators and all societies on a year-to-year basis. Up to now we have finished our data collection for urbanization, and for development of education and private communication.

This collection is considered as "refined" for three reasons: (a) We try to improve the reliability, validity, and comparability of the data by gathering information about different (operational) definitions and methods of collecting and calculating. We consult a great number of historical monographs to answer questions like the following: what sorts of communities were called towns; who was defined as an illiterate; what types of schools can be classified as primary or secondary; how can we compare different types of mail, and so on. (b) To facilitate future collection we indicate for each specific datum the source(s) and possible estimations and calculations. (c) We refine the indicators themselves by decomposing them into several dimensions. Thus, we show the urbanization process for five categories of communities and the development of education at different levels: illiteracy, primary, secondary, and higher education. We hope that this refinement will improve the detailed analysis of differences and stages in growth and change processes.

Time-series Analysis: Some Examples

We shall present two simple analyses using some selected time series from the QUAM-project and referring to some of the postulates of the first section. The examples mainly serve illustrative purposes, but may also demonstrate the scope and limits of our data collections, and the possibilities of theory-testing by time series. We will first discuss K. W. Deutsch's theory of social mobilization; then D. Lerner's theory of modernization.

K. W. Deutsch's Theory of Mobilization

K. W. Deutsch's article "Social Mobilization and Political Development," well-known as a "modern classic" in the field of quantitative macro-analysis, is focused on cross-national data.[43] We therefore asked ourselves: can this theory be tested with long-term, time-series data, and what will be the result (i.e., how well does it fit the change and developmental processes of already advanced countries.)? We will first summarize the main concepts and propositions of Deutsch's theory, mostly using his own words:

Social mobilization is understood "as one of the major aspects of modernization," as "a recurrent cluster among its consequences," that appear "over a longer period as one of its (modernization's) continuing aspects and as a significant cause, in the well-known pattern of feed-back or circular causation." "Social mobilization is a name given to an overall process of change, which happens to substantial parts of the population in countries which are moving from traditional to modern ways of life." A

TABLE 2
RAPID SOCIAL MOBILIZATION

Symbol of Indicator	Description	Average Annual % of Total Population or Income Added to Category		Decade Growth Rates in %	
		Range	Median	Range	Mean
Group 1:					
dm_1	Shift into any substantial exposure to modernity, including rumors, demonstrations of machinery or merchandise	2.0 to 4.0	3.0		
dm_2	Shift into mass media audience (radio, movies, posters, press)	1.5 to 4.0	2.75		
dm_8	Increase in voting participation	0.2 to 4.0	2.1	2-40	21
dm_6	Increase in literacy	1.0 to 1.4	1.2	10-14	12
dm_3	Change of locality of residence	1.0 to 1.5	1.25		
p	Population growth	(1.9 to 3.3)	(2.6)		
Group 2:					
dm_5	Occupational shift out of agriculture	0.4 to 1.0	0.7	4-10	7
dm_4	Change from rural to urban residence	0.1 to 1.2	0.5	1-12	5
a	Linguistic, cultural or political assimilation	0.5 to 1.0	0.25		
dy	Income growth	(2.0 to 8.0)	(5.0)		
dm_7	Income growth per capita	—	(2.3)		

country undergoing rapid social mobilization approximates the following pattern:

Group 1 indicators may be interpreted as representing "increased demands or burdens upon the government"; group 2 indicators "are related to the capabilities of the government for coping with these burdens. . . ."

In a modern, fully developed country the GNP per capita (m_7) should be above $600; the part of population exposed to modernity (m_1), the mass media audience (m_2), the literates (m_6) should be above 90 percent; persons having changed locality of residence since birth (m_3), urban population (m_4), and population in nonagricultural occupations (m_5) should be above 50 percent. On the contrary, in "an extremely underdeveloped country, such as Ethiopia, m_7 is well below $100 and the remaining indicators may be near 5 percent."

During "the rapid middle stages of the process of social mobilization and economic development—say for a range of between 10 and 80 percent literacy—group 1 indicators, the demands, grow faster than group 2 indicators, the capabilities. If there is no rapid economic growth to meet the new popular needs and aspirations, dissatisfaction, and political and social difficulties are to be expected.

The indicators of the model are more or less interchangeable and should have correlation coefficients of about 0.6 to 0.8, i.e., missing data could be estimated on the basis of available data because social mobilization has to be considered as a coherent process of change.

One should be able to construct for each of the indicators a threshold of significance, below which there is no departure from traditional life, and a threshold of criticality, beyond which there will be obvious social and political spill-over effects.

We will assume that these are the main arguments of Deutsch's theory, and will try to confront them with our time-series data. The decade collection of the QUAM-project does not allow an ideal test, but we will use the available data at least to illustrate testing possibilities. There are no data to measure m_1, m_2, m_3; but we can calculate dm_4, dm_5, dm_6, dm_7 (cf. Table B, Appendix 2). We have to substitute the percentage of enfranchised population for voting participation as a measure of dm_8. Political stability versus instability we hope to measure with data on "circulation" (turnover of cabinet ministers) and data on internal disturbances and strikes. Table B in Appendix 2 summarizes the available data.

Before presenting the results of our analysis, we wish to point to one of its limitations, namely the fact that we have used data concerning big countries, the internal development of which cannot be sufficiently explained without regard to their role in the international system.

(a) The industrial societies have gone through a dilatory and long-term process of social mobilization. Only the U.S.S.R. 1930-1939 and Japan 1900-1939 show coherent mobilization rates corresponding to the order of magnitude of Deutsch's "rapid social mobilization." On the basis of our incomplete information, we have not been able to find such rapid growth rates in India or in China. As for the estimates of what Deutsch calls "range," four out of five growth rates do fit for France 1840-1849, 1860-1869, 1900-1909; U.S.A. 1910-1919; U.S.S.R. 1930-1949; Germany

1870-1879; Japan 1890-1899. From this evidence one might conclude either that Deutsch's growth rates are too high or that they can only be achieved—and this would be an "advantage of backwardness"—when some "pioneer" societies have already completed modernization, i.e., only when developmental models and advanced methods of planning have become available. The cases of Argentina, India, and China up to 1960 argue against the second alternative. Therefore, the mobilization process should be conceived as being slower, more long-termed, and more irregular than postulated; again and again, "prosperity stages" alternate with stages of retardation and stagnation.

(b) A correlational analysis of our data reveals that the process of mobilization is much more unbalanced than implied by Deutsch's theory. There is no correlation coefficient above 0.6, based on data for all the countries; there are only a few exceptions, if one examines the data country by country; for the enfranchisement variable we have found no positive correlations at all. The tendency of the correlation analysis is confirmed by the patterns of the modernity thresholds: relative independence of enfranchisement, elementary education, industrialization, urbanization, and economic development. The length of time between crossing the first and the fifth modernity threshold (i.e., reaching complete modernization as defined above) compares as follows:

Great Britain	ca. 1790 – 1930	140 years
France	1850 – 1930	80 years
U.S.A.	1870 – 1920	50 years
U.S.S.R.	1910 – 1960	50 years
Germany	ca. 1830 – 1950	120 years
Japan	1910 – 1960	50 years

Great Britain is known for her solitary, early urbanization and industrialization with elementary education and enfranchisement conspicuously lagging behind. In Germany (Prussia) we find an "abnormally" early educational development; in France a delayed urbanization. In any case even the comparison of these very simple patterns demonstrates the historical variability of the mobilization process. Our material does not permit an analysis of the thresholds of significance and criticality. We suppose that the idea of thresholds of significance will be found to be sound, but as to the thresholds of criticality we prefer the Almond and Pye concept of differently patterned developmental "crises" during the modernization process.[44]

(c) We analyzed the relationship between social mobilization and political development, postulated by Deutsch, in the following simple manner: we started with two concepts, a concept of social pressure defined by $D > C$ (demands > capabilities), operationalized by $dm_8 + dm_6 > dm_5 + dm_4$, and a concept of political instability, operationalized by a high (i.e., above average) rate of both "circulation" and internal disturbances. Then, we hypothesized that social pressure can be coped with only by an income per capita growth rate (PCI) of ten percent. We deduced the following predictions:

(1) Political instability (I) will be found, if there is social pressure not balanced by income growth (PCI);

(2) In all other cases will be found either circulation or internal disturbances or both below average, which we have indicated as stability (S) including both positive stability (guided change) and negative stability (stagnation).

This gives the following model:

$D > C$	$PCI > 10$ percent	Prediction
–	+	S
–	–	S
+	+	S
+	–	I

This is a very crude theory which does not explain why there is circulation or disturbances above average, and which does not discriminate between the three S-patterns. But we believe it matches the basic idea of Deutsch's theory. In 45 out of 51 cases the predictions turned out to be right; the model rightly predicted the cases of, e.g., Spain 1930-1939 and Argentina *1950-1959*. The six wrong predictions were Great Britain 1920-1929; U.S.A. 1860-1869, *1910-1919;* U.S.S.R. *1860-1869,* 1920-1929; Germany *1920-1929.* It may be worthwhile to note that in the four italicized cases income growth was negative.

To sum up, we evaluate Deutsch's theory and model as basically sound in the political aspects but as biased by a too optimistic conception in the mobilization aspects of long-term modernization. The several mobilization rates seem to be more irregular, more unbalanced, and lower than postulated. If "history repeats itself," the modernization of the present transitional countries will follow at least as many different developmental patterns as did the modernization of the pioneer societies and the early late-comers. Finally then, the model of social mobilization is certainly stimulating and may offer a favorable framework for developmental programmes, but the historical evidence at hand tends to throw more light on "deviant cases."

Daniel Lerner's Theory of Modernization

Daniel Lerner's work on modernization and political development, *The Passing of Traditional Society,* is reputed for its stimulating simplicity, its analytical usefulness, and its relevance for developmental politics.[45] It was an early attempt to construct a model of historical sequences on the basis of cross-national data. Though Lerner's formulations are sometimes inconsistent and vague, mixing correlational and causal language, the essence of the model seems to be the following:

> The secular evolution of a participant society appears to involve a regular sequence of three phases. *Urbanization* comes first, for cities alone have developed the complex of skills and resources which characterize the modern industrial economy. Within this urban matrix develop both of the attributes which distinguish the next two phases—*literacy* and *media growth*. There is a close reciprocal relationship between these, for the literate develop the media which in turn spread literacy. But, historically, literacy performs the key function in the second phase. The capacity to read, at first acquired by relatively few people, equips them to perform the varied tasks required in the modernizing society. Not until the third phase, when the elaborate technology of industrial development is fairly well advanced, does a society begin to produce newspapers, radio networks, and motion pictures on a massive scale. This, in turn, accelerates the spread of literacy. Out of this interaction develop those institutions of participation (e.g., voting) which we find in all advanced societies.[46]
>
> Democratic governance comes late, historically, and appears as a crowning institution of the participant society.[47]

We summarize Lerner's assumptions as follows: The model describes the historical path of Western modernization. It posits a set of components and sequences of global relevance. Hence different developments should be analyzed as deviations from the universal model. (In a later article, however, Lerner expressed some doubts on this point.[48]) It is not only a descriptive but also a causal model containing hypotheses about the "optimum" relationships between urbanization, literacy, and media participation, ostensibly achieved by the modern nations. These hypotheses allow predictions of political disequilibrium in deviant cases.

Lerner tested his model by a correlation analysis based on statistical data for the period shortly after the Second World War for most countries of the world taken from UNESCO and other U.N. sources. He used four indices: *urbanization,* the proportion of the total population living in cities over 50,000; *literacy,* the proportion able to read in one language; *media participation,* the proportion buying newspapers, owning radios, and attending cinemas (combined in a single index); *electoral participation,* the proportion actually voting in national elections. Calculating simple and multiple correlation coefficients (ranging from .61 to .91), he could prove that close relationships exist between these four variables. But his test has two serious shortcomings: first, without a more detailed explication of the model it is impossible to give a causal interpretation of the correlation coefficients, i.e., to distinguish between spurious and causal relations and to determine the paths and weights of causal influences; second, using cross-national data he is unable to test the assumption of a universal model of development and to determine stages and different paths of modernization.

As for the first shortcoming, great improvements have been made through the efforts to develop and test causal models in the tradition of Simon and Blalock.[49] We will discuss only two examples, the analyses of Alker[50] and of McCrone and Cnudde,[51] who illustrate alternatives to Lerner's model. In both articles technical refinement goes hand in hand with a further simplification of the original model. In contrast to Lerner's conception it is assumed first, that the four variables form a closed system (i.e., that no outside variable is significantly correlated with two or more of the four variables); second, that all relationships are linear; and, third, that all relationships are unidirectional.[52] Starting with a simple stage model: $X_1 \rightarrow X_2 \rightarrow X_3 \rightarrow X_4$ (X_1 = urbanization, X_2 = literacy, X_3 = media development, X_4 = political participation) logical alternatives were developed, the only restrictions being that X_1 is always treated as the first and exogenous variable and X_4 as the last and endogenous variable. Various models were then tested step by step and eliminated after calculation of partial correlation, dependence[53] and path[54] coefficients of cross-national data. Finally, two models (shown in Figure 1) seemed to be in accordance with the data.

In both models a strong causal relationship is found between urbanization and education and between education and media development, and a weak direct relationship is found between urbanization and political participation. But, and this fact is somewhat surprising, the

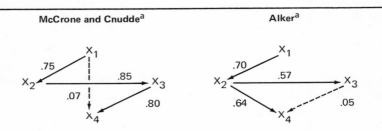

McCrone and Cnudde[a]   Alker[a]

a. The figures (dependence coefficients) indicate the weight of causal influence.

Figure 1

models are clearly contradictory as to the causal importance of media development for political participation. Since we do not know the exact definitions, the samples of countries, and the type of data, we cannot identify the cause of this difference, but we may conclude that a further refinement of the causal models (by enlarging the number of variables and introducing nonlinear and nonadditive relations) will be necessary to produce results of the same level of substantial as well as methodological interest. However, without a corresponding improvement of the data basis, we run the risk of using a razor and an axe at the same time. This danger increases, of course, with the use of time-series data.

With respect to the second shortcoming of Lerner's test—the historical limitation of the data—the analyses by Alker, and McCrone and Cnudde represent no major progress. Although our present data basis is very poor we will try to indicate possibilities which the availability of good time-series will offer for the interpretation of Lerner's model (cf. Tables C to G in Appendix 2). We will take the sample of countries selected for our refined collection and the time period from 1815 to 1914. Our data basis consists of two reasonably reliable and accurate sets of time series on urbanization and the development of primary education (refined collection), a less accurate and incomplete set of time series on the growth of potential and actual voters (decade collection), and some scattered and unreliable data on the development of the circulation of newspapers. The data on electoral participation and enfranchisement could be improved and completed without too many difficulties, but it will probably never be possible to reconstruct the development of the circulation of newspapers, and even the collection and calculation of only certain data would require a special research programme. The incompleteness and lack of accuracy of our data impose limitations on the following short and cautious interpretation.

As far as our sample allows generalizations, the main result seems to be that there is no unique model of modernization (in terms of the four variables) for the Western or—as Lerner generalizes[55]—for modern nations. Perhaps with the exception of the relationship between education and media development, neither the assumed sequence of stages can be found nor, in a stricter sense, any sequence of stages at all. For a demonstration of the first point one should look at the nations leading, in the first half of the nineteenth century, with respect to one of the first three variables. The deviations from the presumed model are striking:

	Urbanization	Education	Political participation
England	*high*	medium	medium
Prussia	low	*high*	low
U.S.A.	low	medium	*high*

A universal stage model obscures the strategic importance of historical points of departure, i.e., of nonadditive and reciprocal relationships, for the different paths of modernization. Thus, to give only one example, we may hypothesize in a very simplified manner that the effects of urbanization and education on democratic development are not additive but—presupposing a low rate of political participation—that a high level or a rapid growth rate of education together with a low level of urbanization (in our example: Prussia 1815-1871, France 1830-1848, Japan 1870-1914) may, at least for some time, even impede a democratic development because the combination probably leads to an authoritarian and centralized school system.

The notion of critical limits, minimum and optimum, which can be determined empirically, is essential to Lerner's conception of developmental stages. He assumes, for instance, that urbanization has a causal influence on the development of literacy only between the critical limits of ten percent and twenty-five percent.[56] This conception, however, is not confirmed by our sample of data. At any fixed level of urbanization the variance of the corresponding education rates is too large to support the idea of critical limits. For example, at the urbanization level of ten percent the rates of primary education range from twelve percent to thirty-seven percent (forty to forty-five percent probably being the optimum).

Lerner's model of modernization may be universal in the sense of a covariance of all four variables between critical limits specified for each nation, but it ignores the decisive differences among modernizing nations concerning the levels and growth rates of the variables and the critical limits and other specifications of the covariance relationships. Stated in the language of the covariance theorem,[57] it is a theory of "within" covariance. Theoretical considerations as well as empirical proofs,[58] however, suggest that the modernization process defined by the sequential growth of Lerner's four variables just consists of a transitional increase of the "between" (nations) covariance.

NOTES

1. Cf. H. R. Alker, "Statistics and Politics," in S. M. Lipset (ed.) Politics and the Social Sciences, New York, Oxford Univ. Press, 1969, especially pp. 245-47.

2. Cf. R. A. Bauer, ed., Social Indicators, Cambridge, M.I.T. Press, 1966.

3. A. S. Banks and R. Textor, A Cross-Polity Survey, Cambridge, M.I.T. Press, 1966; B. M. Russett et al., World Handbook of Political and Social Indicators, New Haven, Conn., Yale Univ. Press, 1964; R. L. Merritt and S. Rokkan, eds., Comparing Nations, New Haven, Conn., Yale Univ. Press, 1966 (cf. pp. 109-29 for a report on Rummel's DON-project); C. L. Taylor, ed., Aggregate Data Analysis: Political and Social Indicators in Cross-National Research, Paris, Humanities Press, International Social Science Council Publication No. 10, 1970.

4. Cf. Taylor, op. cit., p. 263.

5. J. D. Singer and M. Small, The Wages of War, 1816-1965: A Statistical Handbook, New York, John Wiley, 1972.

6. Russett et al., op. cit., pp. 293-303.

7. I. Adelman and C. T. Morris, Society, Politics, and Economic Development, Baltimore, Johns Hopkins Univ. Press, 1967.

8. S. M. Lipset, "Some Social Requisites of Democracy," American Political Science Review, Vol. 53, March 1959, pp. 69-105.

9. Russett et al., op. cit., p. 299.

10. P. A. Sorokin, Social and Cultural Mobility, Glencoe, Ill., Free Press, 1959 (first published, 1927).

11. Cf. P. F. Lazarsfeld, "Notes on the History of Quantification in Sociology," in H. Woolf (ed.) Quantification: A History of the Meaning of Measurement in the Natural and Social Sciences, Indianapolis, Ind., Bobbs-Merrill, 1961.

12. P. A. Sorokin, Social and Cultural Dynamics, New York, Vols 1-3, 1937, Vol. 4, 1941.

13. Sorokin's own statement, cited in H. Becker and H. E. Barnes, Social Thought From Lore to Science, Vol. 2, New York, Peter Smith, 1961, p. 785 (3rd ed.).

14. Examples: indicators of fluctuation of the influence in main systems of truth by twenty-year periods, 580 BC - 1900 AD; fluctuations of the main tendencies in the changes of criminal law; total measure of internal disturbances of Europe from 525 to 1925 by quarter centuries.

15. A summary statement is found in H. Hart, "Social Theory and Social Change," in L. Gross (ed.) Symposium on Sociological Theory, Evanston, Ill., Northwestern Univ. Press, 1959, pp. 196-238.

16. L. F. Richardson, Arms and Insecurity, Pittsburgh and Chicago, Boxwood 1960; K. W. Deutsch, Nationalism and Social Communication: An Inquiry into the Foundations of Nationality, Cambridge, M.I.T. Press, 1953.

17. R. B. Cattell and M. Adelson, "The Dimensions of Social Change in the U.S.A. as Determined by P-technique," Social Forces, Vol. 30, 1951, pp. 190-201; R. B. Cattell, "A Quantitative Analysis of the Changes in the Culture Pattern of Great Britain 1837-1937, by P-technique," Acta Psychologica, Vol. 9, 1953, pp. 99-121; C. A. Gibb, "Changes in the Cultural Pattern of Australia, 1906-1946, as determined by P-technique," Journal of Social Psychology, Vol. 43, 1956, pp. 225-38.

18. Cattell and Adelson, op. cit., p. 200.

19. P. Seppänen, "Muuttuva Yhteiskunta," Sociologia, 1965, pp. 73-89.

20. U. Yule, "An Investigation into the Causes of Changes in Pauperism in England Chiefly During the Last Two Intercensal Decades," Journal of the Royal Statistical Society, Vol. 62, 1899, pp. 249-86.

21. M. Haas, "Social Change and National Aggressiveness, 1900-1960," in J. D. Singer (ed.) Quantitative International Politics: Insights and Evidence, New York, Free Press, 1968, pp. 215-44.

22. J. D. Singer and M. Small, "Alliance Aggregation and the Onset of War, 1815-1945," in Singer, op. cit., pp. 247-86.

23. We do not know if this plan was realized. Cf. L. Groff, Copy of 1st Choice Data for US, UK, FR, Gr, Jp, 1800-1965, Cambridge, Harvard University, 1968 (mimeo).

24. Cf. M. Kendall and A. Stuart, The Advanced Theory of Statistics, Vol. 3, London, Hafner, 1968, (2nd ed.).

25. S. Kuznets, "Time Series," Encyclopedia of the Social Sciences, New York, 1959, p. 630 (13th ed.).

26. Ibid., p. 631.

27. K. W. Deutsch, "The Theoretical Basis of Data Programs," in Merritt and Rokkan, op. cit., p. 52.

28. Kendall and Stuart, op. cit., Ch. 49.

29. Cf. G. Tintner, Econometrics, New York, 1967, Ch. 10 (2nd. ed.).

30. R. Grew and S. L. Thrupp, "Horizontal History in Search of Vertical Dimensions," Comparative Studies in Society and History, Vol. 7, 1966, pp. 258-64.

31. Ibid., p. 263.

32. S. Rokkan, "Methods and Models in the Comparative Study of Nation-Building," in S. Rokkan, ed., Citizens, Elections, Parties, Oslo, 1970, p. 60.

33. D. C. McClelland, The Achieving Society, Princeton, Van Nostrand-Rinehart, 1961.

34. D. M. Ogilvie and L. Woodhead, "The Harvard Need-achievement Dictionary," in P. J. Stone et al. (ed.) General Inquirer: A Computer Approach to Content Analysis, Cambridge, M.I.T. Press, 1966, pp. 191-206.

35. G. A. Almond and J. S. Coleman, eds., The Politics of the Developing Areas, Princeton, Princeton Univ. Press, 1960; especially Coleman's chapter, "The Political Systems of the Developing Areas."

36. Russett et al., op. cit., p. 8.

37. J. D. Singer and M. Small, "Formal Alliances, 1815-1939," Journal of Peace Research, Vol. 1, 1966, pp. 1-32.

38. Ibid., pp. 16-17.

39. Cf. in economy, S. Harris, C. Clark, A. Gerschenkorn, P. A. Baran, A. Bergson, and A. Yugow, "An Appraisal of Russian Economic Statistics," Review of Economics and Statistics, Vol. 39, No. 4, November 1947, pp. 213-46; in demography, G. Ohlin, "No Safety in Numbers: Some Pitfalls of Historical Statistics," in H. Rosovsky (ed.) Industrialization in Two Systems, New York, Wiley, 1966, pp. 68-90.

40. W. W. Eason, Soviet Manpower: The Population and Labor Force of the USSR, New York, Columbia University, 1959 (unpublished dissertation).

41. Note that subcategories of this scheme are taken from Almond, Boulding, McClelland, Lerner, Organski, and Pye, among others.

42. W. Zapf, Indicators of Modernization, 1971 (mimeo).

43. K. W. Deutsch, "Social Mobilization and Political Development," American Political Science Review, Vol. 55, 1961, pp. 493-514.

44. Cf. L. W. Pye, Aspects of Political Development, Boston, Little, Brown, 1966, especially Chapter 3.

45. D. Lerner, The Passing of Traditional Society: Modernizing the Middle East, New York, Free Press, 1966.

46. Ibid., p. 60.

47. Ibid., p. 64.

48. D. Lerner, "Toward a Communication Theory of Modernization," in L. W. Pye (ed.) Communications and Political Development, Princeton, Princeton Univ. Press, 1963, pp. 327-50.

49. Cf. H. A. Simon, Models of Man, New York, 1967; H. M. Blalock, Jr., Causal Inferences in Nonexperimental Research, Chapel Hill, Univ. of North Carolina Press, 1967.

50. H. R. Alker, Jr., "Causal Inference and Political Analysis," in Taylor, op. cit., pp. 209-42.

51. D. J. McCrone and C. F. Cnudde, "Toward a Communication Theory of Democratic Political Development: A Causal Model," American Political Science Review, Vol. 61, 1967, pp. 72-79.

52. Lerner calculated high correlation coefficients between the four variables, per capita income and industrialization (Lerner, op. cit., pp. 62-63); he introduced at least into the relation between urbanization and lieracy critical limits, minimum and optimum (p. 59); and he assumed reciprocal relations: "once the modernization process is started, chicken and egg in fact 'cause' each other to develop" (p. 56).

53. Cf. R. Boudon, L'analyse mathématique des faits sociaux, Paris, 1967, Ch. 3.

54. Cf. K. C. Land, "Principles in Path Analysis," in E. F. Borgatta (ed.) Sociological Methodology 1969, San Francisco, Jossey-Bass, 1969, pp. 3-37; D. R. Heise, "Problems in Path Analysis," in Borgatta (ed.) op. cit., pp. 38-73.

55. Lerner, The Passing of Traditional Society, op. cit., p. 67.

56. Ibid., p. 59.

57. Cf., for an excellent explanation of the covariance theorem, H. R. Alker, Mathematics and Politics, New York, Macmillan, 1968, pp. 96-106.

58. Cf. Russett et al., op. cit., Ch. B2, "Stages of Economic and Political Growth," pp. 293-303, especially p. 294; and our own diagrams of urbanization and the development of primary education, pp. 23-24 and p. 37.

APPENDIX 1. TYPES OF SOURCES FOR TIME-SERIES DATA

1. Historical Statistical Compendia

(a) "Primary" sources

Historical Statistics of the United States, Colonial Times to 1957, Washington, D.C., 1960.

B. R. Mitchell, Abstract of British Historical Statistics, Cambridge, Eng.: Cambridge Univ. Press, 1962.

Annuaire Statistique de la France: Résumé Rétrospectif, Paris, 1966.

(b) "Secondary" sources

W. S. Woytinsky and E. S. Woytinsky, World Population and Production, New York, 1953.

World Commerce and Governments, New York, 1955.

P. Studenski, The Income of Nations, New York, New York Univ. Press, 1958.

S. Kuznets, "Quantitative Aspects of the Economic Growth of Nations," in Economic Development and Cultural Change (various articles).

2. Official international statistical series

Statistique générale du Service Postal dans les Pays de l'Union Postale Universelle, Bern, Bureau International des Postes, 1875.

Statistical Yearbook of the League of Nations, Geneva, 1926-1942/1944.

Statistical Yearbook, New York, United Nations, 1949.

3. Official National Statistical Series

Statistical Abstract for the United Kingdom, London, 1840-1953.

Zeitschrift des Königlich-Preussischen Statistischen Bureaus, Berlin, 1860-1894.

Statistisches Jahrbuch für das Deutsche Reich, Berlin, 1880-1941/1942.

4. Semi-Official Yearbooks and Statistical Series

Almanach de Gotha, Gotha, 1764-1944 (with statistical tables: 1821-1944).

Journal of the Royal Statistical Society, London, 1834.

Statesman's Yearbook, London, 1863.

5. Early Comparative Statistical Compendia

J. E. Wappäus, Handbuch der Geographie und Statistik für die Gebildeten Stände, 6 vols, Leipzig, 1855-1871.

G. F. Kolb, Handbuch der Vergleichenden Statistik der Völkerzustands- und Staatenkunde, Leipzig, 1862.

M. G. Mulhall, The Dictionary of Statistics (4th ed.) London, 1899.

6. Comparative Historical Monographs on Special Issues

E. Levasseur, L'Enseignement Primaire dans les Pays Civilisés, Paris, 1897.
Zur Geschichte und Statistik des Volksschulwesens im In- und Auslande, Vienna, 1898.
A. F. Weber, The Growth of Cities in the Nineteenth Century, New York, 1899.

7. National Historical Monographs on Special Issues

F. Lorimer, The Population of the Soviet Union: History and Prospect, Geneva, 1946.
I. B. Taeuber, The Population of Japan, Princeton, 1958.
N. Hans, History of Russian Educational Policy (1701-1917) (2nd ed.) New York, Russell, 1964.

8. Monographs on Very Limited Issues

C. Woldemar, Zur Geschichte und Statistik der Gelehrten- und
Schulanstalten des Kaiserlichen Russischen Ministeriums für Volksaufklärung,
St. Petersburg, 1865.

APPENDIX 2. TABLES

Notes to Table A

Column 1 Voters. (Our variable 31, Deutsch's indicator m_8.) Enfranchised population in percent of total population. The rates to some extent depend on the respective age structure. As a rule 20-25% equals manhood suffrage with minor qualifications; 25-30%, complete manhood suffrage; 60% and above, universal suffrage differing only according to age qualifications.

SOURCES: Statesman's Ybs; Canton, 1966; Woytinsky, 1955; Braunias, 1932; Bendix, 1965.

Column 2 Literates. (Inversion of our variable 25, Deutsch's indicator m_6.) Percentage of population (mostly over fourteen years old, but sometimes men only) which is not illiterate.

SOURCES: Ann. Stat., 1912; HSUS; Fourastié, 1947; Deutsch, 1960; Russett, 1964; Canton, 1966; UdSSR in Zahlen, 1956; Unesco, 1963.

Column 3 Nonagrar. (Inversion of our variable 11, Deutsch's indicator m_5.) Percentage of labor force not employed in agricutlure.

SOURCES: Gothas; Stateman's Ybs.; Ann. Stat., 1912, 1961; HSUS; Davis, 1954-1955; UdSSR in Zahlen, 1956; Studenski, 1958; WWI; BevPloetz; Weber, 1899; STJB, 1962; Espanà, 1961.

Column 4 Nonrural. (Inversion of our variable 09, Deutsch's indicator m_4.) Percentage of population living outside "rural areas." Definitions of rural areas are differing, e.g., U.S.A. "under 2,500", Germany "under 2,000"; the only available Japanese data refer to communities "under 10,00 inhabitants."

SOURCES: Clark, 1960; Kuznets, 1956-1957; Russett, 1964; Fourastié, 1947; Cipolla, 1964; UdSSR in Zahlen, 1956.

Column 5 Income. (Our variable 14, Deutsch's indicator m_7.) National income per capita, in $U.S. 1952-1954. The figures for Great Britain and all figures from 1860-1960 are Zimmerman's. Other figures are taken from sources indicated below and adjusted. Note that, as a rule, national income is about 80% of GNP.

SOURCES: Zimmerman, 1960, 1964; Clark, 1960; Kuznets, 1956-1957; HSUS; Studenski 1958; Woytinsky, 1953.

Notes to Table B

Columns 1-4. Growth rates per decade in percentage points, calculated from Table A.

Column 5 Income. Percentage growth per decade.

Columns 1-5. The rates that are equal to or higher than the gross rates postulated in Deutsch's model are in italics.

Column 6 Circulation. (Our variable 27.) Turnover of cabinet ministers in percent of total number of cabinet positions: yearly average (circulation per decade being normally ten times higher). The rates that are higher than average for the whole period are in italics.

SOURCE: Minister Ploetz.

Column 7 Disturbances. (Our variable 29.) An index of internal disturbances was calculated from Sorokin's data. Decades which have values higher than the average for the whole period are indicated as high (H), all others being considered as low (L).

SOURCE: Sorokin, Vol. 2.

Column 8 D $>$ C. "Demands higher than capabilities", operationalized by $dm_8 + dm_6$ $> dm_5 + dm_4$ (columns 1-4), is marked by a plus sign (+), all other cases by (−).

Column 9 PCI $>$ 10%. All cases in which per capita income growth per decade is above 10% are indicated by a plus sign (+), all other cases by (−).

Column 10 Predictions. From the comparison of columns 8 and 9 either S (stability or stagnation) or I (political instability) is predicted.

Column 11 Results. Right and false predictions are indicated by (r) or (f).

All figures in brackets are interpolated or estimated. The thresholds of full modernity are graphically indicated by a connecting line—dotted when based on estimated values—resulting in "patterns of full modernization threshold." In accordance with Deutsch the following criteria were applied to determine the thresholds: "Literates," 90% and above; "Nonagrar." and "Nonrural," 50% and above; "Income," per capita national income $500 and more (substituted for Deutsch's U.S. 1957 $600 GNP per capita). The "Voting" (enfranchisement) threshold was arbitrarily fixed at 20% of the population or more.

Notes to Table C

SOURCES: Ann Stat., 1966; Birchenough, 1938; Handbuch Preussen; Hans, 1964; HSUS; Knox, 1953; Levasseur, 1897; McElligott, 1966; Mulhall, 1899; Rosovsky, 1966; STAUK; Statesman's Ybs.; STJDR; Zeitschrift Preussen.

a. In some countries (France, Japan, and Russia), the data refer to school enrollment. In England, Scotland, Ireland, the U.S.A. and Prussia/Germany, the data refer to the actual school attendance which in the nineteenth century was much lower, ranging from 50% to 80% of the pupils on rolls.

England and Scotland: the data before 1885 are reported estimations of all primary scholars; the data after 1885 refer to the number of pupils in inspected schools.

Scotland: the datum for 1846 is possibly unreliable because historians maintain that the Scottish elementary education before 1870 exceeded by far the English (cf. Knox, 1953).

Some of the oscillations may have been produced by estimations of the population from 5 to 24 years of age.

Notes to Table D

SOURCES: ABHS; Ann. Stat., 1966; Bowden, 1937; Cahiers de ISEA; Eason, 1959; Gothas; Hauser, 1957; HSUS; Kolb, 1862; Petermann; Statesman's Ybs.; STJDR; Taeuber, 1959; Wappäus, 1864; Weber, 1899.

a. Russia 1893-1912: population in communities of 30,000 and more inhabitants.

Notes to Table E

SOURCES: Newspapers: Archiv f. Post; Mulhall, 1899; Sautter, 1951; Statesman's Ybs.; STSP. Population: ABHS; Ann. Stat., 1966; Eason, 1959; HSUS; Lorimer, 1946; STJDR; Taeuber, 1959.

a. It is unknown which sort of newspapers are included for each country.

Notes to Table F

SOURCES: See Table E.

a. England and Wales, Scotland, Ireland, United Kingdom, Japan: number of newspaper packets. Because of differences in postal system and method of counting, the data are not comparable among nations; they only give a rough idea of the development within a nation.

Notes to Table G

SOURCES: Political participation: Bendix, 1965; Braunias, 1932; HSUS; Mulhall, 1899; Statesman's Ybs.; STJDR; Woytinsky, 1955. Population: See Table E.

a. Potential voters (enfranchisement): France 1830-1848: less than 1%; Germany 1871-1914: 20-22%; Japan 1889-1914: 2-3%; Russia 1905-1914; unknown, probably less than 0.5%; the differences of enfranchisement between England, Scotland, and Ireland disappeared almost completely after the Franchise Act of 1884.

b. Actual voters (electoral participation).

TABLE A
INDICATORS OF SOCIAL MOBILIZATION AND POLITICAL DEVELOPMENT

Year	1 Voters %	2 Literates %	3 Nonagrar. %	4 Nonrural %	5 Income $
GREAT BRITAIN					
1820				(33)	150
1830	3			(38)	
1840	6	59	77	(44)	180
1850	6	(65)	78	50	240
1860	6	72	81	55	260
1870	6	78	85	62	260
1880	9	86	88	68	310
1890	12	92	90	72	390
1900	12	93	91	78	450
1910	17	94	92	78	510
1920	49	95	93	78	480
1930	53	(96)	93		540
1940	55	(97)	94		680
1950	68	(98)	95	90	780
1960	69	(98)	95		910
FRANCE					
1820	1	40	34	(21)	(165)
1830	1	47	37	22	(185)
1840	(1)	53	40	24	(210)
1850	19	61	50	27	(255)
1860	<	67	55	30	310
1870	<	78	57	35	375
1880	27	83	55	36	380
1890	(27)	90	59	37	455
1900	27	94	67	42	490
1910	29	96	71	(44)	580
1920	29	96	71	46	550
1930	(29)	96	76	52	710
1940		96	76		805
1950	62	97	80	63	730
1960	(62)	(98)	84		930
USA					
1820	(4)		28	7	(280)
1830	(11)		29	9	(265)
1840	(16)		31	11	(320)
1850	(16)		35	15	(380)
1860	17		40	20	430
1870		80	49	26	380
1880	23	83	49	28	570
1890		87	57	35	620

TABLE A (Continued)

Year	1 Voters %	2 Literates %	3 Nonagrar. %	4 Nonrural %	5 Income $
1900	25	89	62	40	890
1910	(25)	92	68	46	1,030
1920	51	94	72	51	1,010
1930		96	77	56	1,200
1940	61	97	82	57	1,175
1950	62	97	88	59	1,860
1960		98	90	70	1,950
USSR					
1820	0			(6)	
1830	0			(7)	
1840	0			(9)	
1850	0		15	(9)	
1860	0	2	(16)	9	95
1870	0	(8)	(17)	11	93
1880	0	(14)	(18)	(12)	115
1890	0	20	(19)	(13)	
1900	0	28	20	(15)	145
1910	23	(28)	25	18	160
1920	42		20	18	
1930	53	56	20		180
1940	57	87	44	32	
1950	65	90	50	43	500
1960	(65)	95	57	49	(600)
PRUSSIA, GERMANY, GFR					
1820		72		(27)	
1830		84		27	
1840		91		27	
1850		96		28	
1860		96		31	160
1870	20	98		32	155
1880	20	98	64	41	230
1890	22	99	69	47	300
1900	20	99	76	54	320
1910	22	99	79	60	380
1920	61	99	82	64	
1930		99	83	67	365
1940		99	86	70	430
1950	67	99	88	71	530
1960	67	99	(90)	76	780

TABLE A (Continued)

Year	1 Voters %	2 Literates %	3 Nonagrar. %	4 Nonrural %	5 Income $
JAPAN					
1820					
1830					
1840					
1850					
1860					40
1870			24		
1880			27		45
1890			33	(15)	
1900	2		41	(20)	65
1910	3	No Data	52	(27)	90
1920	5		59	33	
1930	22		64	41	140
1940			72	50	
1950	51		67	54	180
1960			73		300
SPAIN					
1820					
1830					
1840					
1850		20			
1860		24			
1870		26			
1880		28			
1890		30	31		
1900	No Data	32	33	72	180
1910		36	33	74	200
1920		45	43	77	
1930		55	55	80	250
1940		77	49	82	
1950		86	58	83	230
1960		87	57		340
ARGENTINA					
1820					
1830					
1840					
1850					
1860					
1870		22			
1880					
1890		46			

TABLE A (Continued)

Year	1 Voters %	2 Literates %	3 Nonagrar. %	4 Nonrural %	5 Income $
1900					300
1910	12	65	76		365
1920	17		76	53	
1930	18	78	77		400
1940	21		74		
1950	˙23	87	74	63	460
1960	(50)	86	72	61	460
INDIA					
1820					
1830					
1840					
1850					
1860					48
1870					
1880	No Data	6	49		56
1890		6	43		
1900		6	36		56
1910		7	32		65
1920		8	30	11	
1930		9	30	13	67
1940		15	30	17	
1950		20	31		64
1960	(53)	30	29		70
CHINA					
1820					
1830					
1840					
1850					
1860					44
1870					
1880	No Data	No Data	No Data	No Data	44
1890					
1900					46
1910					47
1920					
1930					49
1940					
1950			(30)		50
1960		(48)	31	(15)	110

TABLE B
PATTERNS OF SOCIAL MOBILIZATION: MODERNITY THRESHOLDS

| Decade | Growth Rates in Percentage Points | | | | | | 7 Distur-bances | 8 D>C | 9 PCI>10% | 10 Prediction | 11 Result |
	1 Voters dm8	2 Literates dm6	3 Nonagrar. dm5	4 Nonrural dm4	5 % Income dm7	6 % Circulation					
GREAT BRITAIN											
1820-1829			ca 1790	5	(10)	30	L				
1830-1839	3	6		6	(10)	34	H				
1840-1849	0	6	1	6	33	24	L	−	+	s	r
1850-1859	0	7	3	5	8	55	L	−	−	s	r
1860-1869	0	6	4	7	0	39	L	−	−	s	r
1870-1879	3	8	3	6	19	19	L	+	+	s	r
1880-1889	3	6	2	4	26	44	L	+	+	s	r
1890-1899	0	1	1	6	15	25	L	−	+	s	r
1900-1909	5	1	1	0	13	32	L	+	+	s	r
1910-1919	32	1	1	0	−6	51	H	+	−	−	r
1920-1929	4	(1)	0	(4)	12	46	H	+	+	s	f
1930-1939	2	(1)	1	(4)	26	49	L	−	+	s	r
1940-1949	13	(0)	1	(4)	15	51	L	+	+	s	r
1950-1959	1	(1)	0	17		44	L			s	r

TABLE B (Continued)

Decade	Growth Rates in Percentage Points					6 % Circulation	7 Distur-bances	8 D > C	9 PCI > 10%	10 Prediction	11 Result
	1 Voters dm8	2 Literates dm6	3 Nonagrar. dm5	4 Nonrural dm4	5 % Income dm7						
FRANCE											
1820-1829	0	7	3	1	13	46	L	+	+	S	r
1830-1839	0	6	3	2	13	89	H	+	+	S	r
1840-1849	19	8	10	3	21	83	H	+	+	S	r
1850-1859	–	6	5	3	22	61	L	–	+	S	r
1860-1869	–	11	5	7	21	27	L	–	+	S	r
1870-1879	(10)	5	–2	1	1	127	H	+	–	–	r
1880-1889	0	7	4	1	20	106	L	+	+	S	r
1890-1899	0	4	6	5	8	115	L	–	–	S	r
1900-1909	3	2	4	2	18	43	H	–	+	S	r
1910-1919	0	0	0	2	–5	114	L	–	–	S	r
1920-1929	0	0	5	6	29	107	H	–	+	S	r
1930-1939	0	0	0	5	13	158	L	–	+	S	r
1940-1949	37	1	4	6	–9	130	H	+	–	–	r
1950-1959	0	1	4		27	102	H				

[198]

TABLE B (Continued)

	1	2	3	4	5	6	7	8	9	10	11
	Voters	Literates	Nonagrar.	Nonrural	% Income	% Circulation	Distur-	D > C	PCI > 10%	Prediction	Result
Decade	dm8	dm6	dm5	dm4	dm7		bances				
UNITED STATES											
1820-1829	(7)		1	2	-5	20			-		
1830-1839	(5)		2	2	20	25			+		
1840-1849	(0)		4	4	19	59			+		
1850-1859	(1)		5	5	13	36			+		
1860-1869	(3)		9	6	-11	52	H	-	-	S	f
1870-1879	(3)	3	0	2	48	26	L	+	+	S	r
1880-1889	(1)	4	8	7	9	47	L	-	-	S	r
1890-1899	(1)	2	5	5	43	31	L	-	+	S	r
1900-1909	(0)	3	6	6	16	34	L	-	+	S	r
1910-1919	(26)	2	4	5	-2	15	H	+	-	-	f
1920-1929	(5)	2	5	5	19	33		-	+	S	r
1930-1939	(5)	1	5	1	-2	16	L	-	-	S	r
1940-1949	1	0	6	2	58	28	H	-	+	S	r
1950-1959	0	1	2	11	5	26	H	-	-	S	r

Growth Rates in Percentage Points

TABLE B (Continued)

Growth Rates in Percentage Points											
	1	2	3	4	5	6	7	8	9	10	11
	Voters	Literates	Nonagrar.	Nonrural	% Income	%	Distur-	D > C	PCI > 10%		
Decade	dm_8	dm_6	dm_5	dm_4	dm_7	Circulation	bances			Prediction	Result
U.S.S.R.											
1820-1829	0			1		13	L				
1830-1839	0			2		10	L				
1840-1849	0			0		5	L				
1850-1859	0		(1)	0		15	L				
1860-1869	0	6	(1)	2	-2	14	L	+	−	−	f
1870-1879	0	6	(1)	1	24	8	H	+	+	S	r
1880-1889	0	6	(1)	1	(13)	20	L	+	+	S	r
1890-1899	0	8	(1)	2	(13)	15	L	+	+	S	r
1900-1909	23	0	5	3	10	41	H	+	−	−	r
1910-1919	19	(14)	-5	0	(6)	96	H	+	−	−	r
1920-1929	9	(14)	0	(7)	(6)	18	H	+	−	−	f
1930-1939	4	31	24	(7)	(90)	32	(L)	+	+	S	r
1940-1949	8	3	6	9	(90)	17	(L)	−	+	S	r
1950-1959	0	5	7	6	(20)	47	(L)	−	+	S	r

TABLE B (Continued)

| Growth Rates in Percentage Points | | | | | | | | | | |
Decade	1 Voters dm8	2 Literates dm6	3 Nonagrar. dm5	4 Nonrural dm4	5 % Income dm7	6 % Circulation	7 Distur-bances	8 D>C	9 PCI>10%	10 Prediction	11 Result
PRUSSIA, GERMANY, GFR											
1820-1829		8		0		6	L				
1830-1839		7		0		13	L				
1840-1849		5		1		58	H				
1850-1859		0		3		20	L				
1860-1869		2		2	-3	18	L				
1870-1879	0	0		9	47	16	L				
1880-1889	2	1	5	6	30	16	L	-	+	S	r
1890-1899	-2	0	7	7	7	16	L	-	-	S	r
1900-1909	2	0	3	6	19	18	L	-	+	S	r
1910-1919	39	0	3	4	(-2)	48	H	+	-	-	r
1920-1929	(2)	0	1	3	(-2)	76	H	-	-	S	f
1930-1939	(2)	0	3	3	18	33	L	-	+	S	r
1840-1849	(2)	0	2	1	22		L	-	+	S	
1950-1959	0	0	0	5	45	12	L	-	+	S	r

[201]

TABLE B (Continued)

JAPAN

Decade	Growth Rates in Percentage Points					6 % Circulation	7 Distur-bances	8 D > C	9 PCI > 10%	10 Prediction	11 Result
	1 Voters dm8	2 Literates dm6	3 Nonagrar. dm5	4 Nonrural dm4	5 % Income dm7						
1820-1829											
1830-1839											
1840-1849											
1850-1859											
1860-1869					(6)						
1870-1879			3		(6)						
1880-1889			6	5	(22)						
1890-1899		No Data	8	7	(22)	No Data	No Data	No Data	No Data	No Data	No Data
1900-1909	1		*11*	6	*38*						
1910-1919	2		7	8	*(28)*						
1920-1929	17		5	9	*(28)*						
1930-1939			8		(14)						
1940-1949	*(28)*		−5	4	(15)						
1950-1959			6		67						

TABLE B (Continued)

	Growth Rates in Percentage Points										
	1	2	3	4	5 %	6 %	7	8	9	10	11
Decade	Voters dm8	Literates dm6	Nonagrar. dm5	Nonrural dm4	Income dm7	Circulation	Distur-bances	D > C	PCI > 10%	Prediction	Result
SPAIN											
1820-1829	No Data					No Data	H	No Data	No Data	No Data	No Data
1830-1839							H				
1840-1849							L				
1850-1859		4		(5)			L				
1860-1869		2		(6)			L				
1870-1879		2		(6)			L				
1880-1889		2		(6)			L				
1890-1899		2	2	(6)			L				
1900-1909		4	0	2	11		L				
1910-1919		9	10	3	(12)		L				
1920-1929		10	12	3	(13)		L				
1930-1939		22	−6	2	(−4)		H				
1940-1949		9	9	1	(−4)		L				
1950-1959		1	−2		48		L				

TABLE B (Continued)

ARGENTINA

	1	2	3	4	5	6	7	8	9	10	11
	Voters	Literates	Nonagrar.	Nonrural	Income	%	Distur-	D > C	PCI > 10%	Prediction	Result
Decade	dm8	dm6	dm5	dm4	dm7	Circulation	bances				
1820-1829											
1830-1839											
1840-1849											
1850-1859											
1860-1869											
1870-1879		(12)									
1880-1889		(12)									
1890-1899		(9)				No Data	No Data	No Data	No Data	No Data	No Data
1900-1909		(10)			21						
1910-1919	5	(6)	0		(5)						
1920-1929	1	(7)	1	(3)	(5)						
1930-1939	3	(4)	-3	(3)	(7)						
1940-1949	2	(5)	0	(4)	(8)						
1950-1959	27	-1	-2	-2	0						

TABLE C

EDUCATION: PUPILS IN PRIMARY SCHOOLS IN PERCENTAGES OF POPULATION IN THE 5 TO 24 YEARS AGE GROUP[a]

Year	England and Wales	Scotland	Ireland	France	Japan	Prussia/ Germany	U.S.A.	Russia
1820	12.4		0.3					
1822						32.3		
1825			1.4			33.9		0.9
1828						37.3		
1829				12.1				
1831						38.7		
1832				16.9				
1834						40.9		
1835			1.8					0.9
1837				22.8		39.9		
1840			2.8	24.3		40.4	12.5	
1843				26.1		38.9		
1844			4.8					
1845								1.0
1846	21.0	18.4			39.2			
1847				28.4				
1849						39.1		
1850				26.4			17.2	
1851			7.7					
1852						39.7		
1854			9.5					
1855						39.4		1.3
1857	25.3							
1858						39.7		
1860							22.0	
1861			10.5	33.3		38.9		
1864		32.0	13.1			37.9		
1865								2.3
1866				34.9				
1867						38.6		
1868					7.0			
1870							23.2	
1871			16.1			40.2		
1872				37.4				
1875							26.2	3.0
1878				37.6	16.4	40.6		
1880				38.5			27.3	
1881			20.9					
1882						39.2		
1885	29.6	27.7	23.1	41.5			29.0	4.0
1886					19.1	41.4		
1890	30.7	30.6	23.6	41.9	20.1		29.3	4.9
1891					20.9	41.8		
1895	34.2	32.4	26.6	41.5	22.2		31.4	
1896						41.6		
1900	35.5	34.0	25.8	42.4			32.3	8.2
1901						41.8		
1902					28.5			
1905	39.0	37.2	28.5	43.2	28.9		32.1	9.1
1906					29.7			
1910	39.0	39.4	29.4	43.8	33.1		32.9	10.8
1911						47.0		
1912				43.8	34.6			11.5
1914	39.2	40.4	31.0		34.6		34.3	11.6

TABLE D

URBANIZATION: POPULATION IN COMMUNITIES OF 20,000 INHABITANTS AND MORE IN PERCENTAGE OF TOTAL POPULATIONS[a]

Year	England and Wales	Scotland	Ireland	France	Japan	Prussia/ Germany	U.S.A.	Russia
1800				6.8			2.4	
1801	16.9	13.8						
1810							3.2	
1811	18.1	16.4						
1820							3.4	2.2
1821	20.6	19.7		7.7				
1830							4.2	
1831	25.0	22.5		7.8	5.1			
1836				8.1				
1840							5.5	
1841	29.0	25.1	5.8	8.8				
1846				9.1		7.0		2.9
1850							9.0	
1851	35.0	27.7	8.8	10.1				
1856				12.5				3.5
1858						8.7		4.2
1860							12.0	
1861	38.2	29.3	9.1	14.0		9.6		4.1
1864						10.3		
1866				14.9				
1867						11.1		4.8
1870							15.1	
1871	42.0	32.1	11.4					
1872				15.8				
1875						14.4		
1876				16.6				
1877					7.6			
1880						16.2	17.2	6.5
1881	48.0	39.5	13.1	17.8	8.5			
1882								6.0
1885						18.4		7.3
1886				19.9				
1889					11.0			
1890						21.9	22.2	
1891	56.4	42.4	15.3	20.6				
1893								6.8
1895						24.6		
1896				22.1				
1897								7.0
1898					13.6			
1900						28.7	26.0	
1901	58.1	45.9	19.8	24.1				
1905						31.9		
1906				24.8				
1909								8.9
1910					18.0	34.6	30.9	
1911	62.1	48.1	21.5	26.2				
1912								10.2

TABLE E

NEWSPAPERS: AVERAGE MONTHLY CIRCULATION PER 1,000 INHABITANTS[a]

Year	England and Wales	Scotland	Ireland	United Kingdom	France	Japan	Germany	U.S.A.	Russia
1801	146	49	30	98					
1810									256
1828									498
1831	197	67	42	134					
1850									1,479
1860									2,367
1864	1,925	729	532	1,533					
1870									2,997
1880									3,703
1882	4,272	3,103	2,117	3,835					
1890				4,002	3,150			2,833	3,648

TABLE F

NEWSPAPERS: NUMBER OF NEWSPAPERS MAILED YEARLY PER 1,000 INHABITANTS[a]

Year	England and Wales	Scotland	Ireland	United Kingdom	France	Japan	Germany	U.S.A.	Russia
1875					5,092	73	6,670		462
1880						241	7,715		852
1885				4,101	9,490	397	9,092		
1890	4,447	4,147	3,518	4,298		1,026	14,000		1,034
1896	3,782	4,067	3,699	3,803		2,047	17,420		1,426
1900						3,050	20,863		1,872
1906	4,248	5,042	4,525	4,361		3,703	24,642		
1910	4,196	5,064	5,039	4,390		3,679	29,022		2,666
1914	4,355	6,109	5,768	4,669	3,791	32,445			

TABLE G

POLITICAL PARTICIPATION: VOTERS OR POTENTIAL VOTERS IN PERCENTAGES OF TOTAL POPULATION

Year	England and Wales[a]	Scotland[a]	Ireland[a]	United Kingdom[a]	France[a]	France[b]	U.S.A.[b]	Germany[a]
1815						4.0		
1824							3.3	
1828							9.4	
1835	4.5	3.0	1.2	3.3				
1840							14.0	
1844							13.8	
1846	5.6	3.4	1.6	3.8				
1848							13.1	
1852					26.5	17.1	12.6	
1856							14.3	
1857					27.1	17.1		
1860							14.9	
1866					26.2	19.1		
1868							15.0	
1871	9.1	7.7	4.2	8.1				
1874								12.5
1876							18.2	
1880							18.2	
1881	9.7	8.3	4.4	8.6				12.9
1884							18.1	
1886				11.2				
1888							18.8	
1889					27.3	20.9		
1890								14.7
1892				11.7			18.4	
1895				11.7				
1896							19.6	
1898					26.7	19.9		
1900				11.9			18.3	
1901					28.2			
1903								16.1
1904							16.5	
1906				12.7				
1907								18.1
1908							16.8	
1909					28.9			
1910				13.0				
1912							15.8	18.6

APPENDIX 3. REFERENCES TO SOURCES

ABHS — Abstracts of British Historical Statistics, edited by B. R. Mitchell, Cambridge, Mass., 1962.

Ann. Stat. — Annuaire Statistique de la France, esp. vols. 1912, 1961, 1966.

Archiv f. Post — Archiv für Post und Telegraphie, edited by Reichspostamt, Berlin.

Bendix, 1965 — Bendix, R., "Die Vergleichende Analyse Historischer Wandlungen," in Kölner Zeitschrift für Soziologie und Sozialpsychologie, vol. 17, No. 3, 1965.

BevPloetz — Bevölkerungs-Ploetz: Raum und Bevölkerung in der Weltgeschichte, edited by Kirsten, Buchholz, Köllmann, vol. 2, Würzburg, 1956.

Birchenough, 1938 — Birchenough, C., History of Elementary Education in England and Wales, London, 1938.

Bowden, 1937 — Bowden, W., M. Karpovich, A. P. Usher, An Economic History of Europe since 1750, New York, 1937.

Braunias, 1932 — Braunias, K., Das Parlamentarische Wahlrecht, Berlin, 1932.

Cahiers de ISEA — Cahiers de l'Institut de Science Economique Appliquée: "Histoire Quantitative de l'Economie Française" 3; "La Population de la France de 1700 à 1959", suppl. 33, 1963.

Cantón, 1966 — Cantón, D., Universal Suffrage as an Agent of Mobilization (mimeo).

Cipolla, 1964 — Cipolla, C. M., The Economic History of World Population, Baltimore, 1964.

Clark, 1960 — Clark, C., The Conditions of Economic Progress, London, 1960.

Davis, 1954-1955 — Davis, K., "Urbanization and the Development of Pre-industrial Areas", Economic Development and Cultural Change, vol. 3, 1954-1955.

Deutsch, 1960 — Deutsch, K. W., "Social Mobilization and Political Development", The American political science review, vol. 55, 1961, p. 493 sq.

Eason, 1959 — Eason, W. W., Soviet Manpower: the Population and Labor Force of the USSR, New York, Columbia University, 1959 (unpublished dissertation).

España, 1961 — Annuario Estadistico de España 1961, Madrid, 1962.

Fourastié, 1947 — Fourastié, J., La Civilisation de 1975, Paris, 1947.

Gothas — Gothaischer Hofkalender (Almanach de Gotha): Gotha 1764-1944, esp. vols 1766, 1776, 1779, 1780, 1785, 1790, 1796, 1810, 1820, 1825, 1830, 1835, 1840, 1845, 1850, 1860, 1870, 1880, 1890, 1900.

Handbuch Preussen   Handbuch für den Preussischen Staat, 3 vols, Berlin, 1888, 1893, 1898.

Hans, 1964   Hans, N., History of Russian Educational Policy (1701-1917), New York, 1964.

Hauser, 1957   Hauser, P. (ed.), Urbanization in Asia and the Far East, Calcutta, 1957.

HSUS   Historical Statistics of the United States: Colonial times to 1957, Washington, 1961.

Knox, 1953   Knox, H. M., Two Hundred and Fifty Years of Scottish Education, Edinburgh, 1953.

Kolb, 1862   Kolb, G. F., Handbuch der Vergleichenden Statistik der Völkerzustands- und Staatenkunde, Leipzig, 1862.

Kuznets, 1956-1957   Kuznets, S., "Levels and Variability of Rates of Growth," Economic Development and Cultural Change, vol. 5, 1956-1957; ibid., appendix: "Quantitative Aspects of the Economic Growth of Nations, II: Industrial Distribution of National Product and Labor Force".

Levasseur, 1897   Levasseur, E., L'Enseignement Primaire dans les Pays Civilisés, Paris, 1897

Lexis, 1904   Lexis, W. (ed.), Das Unterrichtswesen in Deutschen Reich, vol. 3, Berlin, 1904.

Lorimer, 1946   Lorimer, F., The Population of the Soviet Union: History and Prospects, Geneva, 1946.

McElligott, 1966   McElligott, T. J., Education in Ireland, Dublin, 1966.

Minister Ploetz   Regenten und Regierungen der Welt: Minister-Ploetz, edited by B. Spuler, 2 vols, Würzburg, 1962-1964.

Mulhall, 1899   Mulhall, M. G., The Dixtionary of Statistics, London, 1899.

Petermann   Petermann, A. (ed.), Mitteilungen aus Justus Perthes Geographischer Anstalt: Die Bevölkerung der Erde, Gotha, 1872-1931.

Rosovsky, 1966   Rosovsky, H. (ed.), Industrialization in Two Systems, New York, 1966.

Russett, 1964   Russett, M. B. et al., World Handbook of Political and Social Indicators, New Haven, Conn., 1964.

Sautter, 1951   Sautter, K., Geschichte der Deutschen Post, vol. 3, Frankfurt-am-Main, 1951.

Sorokin, Vol. 3   Sorokin, P. A., Social and Cultural Dynamics, vol. 3, New York, 1937.

Stateman's Ybs.   The Statesman's Yearbook, London, 1863 sq., esp. vols 1866, 1871, 1881, 1891, 1901, 1911, 1921, 1931, 1942, 1951, 1961, 1963.

STAUK   Statistical Abstract for the United Kingdom, London, 1840-1853.

STJB   Statistisches Jahrbuch für die Bundesrepublik Deutschland, esp. vols 1952, 1961, 1963.

STJDR	Statistisches Jahrbuch für das Deutsche Reich, Berlin, 1880-1941-1942.
STSP	Statistique Générale du Service Postal dans les Pays de l'Union Générale des Postes, edited by Bureau International des Postes, Bern, 1875 sq.
Studenski, 1958	The income of Nations, New York, 1958.
Taeuber, 1959	Taeuber, I., The Population of Japan, Princeton, N.J. 1959.
UdSSR in Zahlen 56	UdSSR in Zahlen, East-Berlin, 1956.
Unesco 63	Statistical Yearbook 1963, Paris, 1964.
Wappäus, 1864	Wappäus, J. E., Handbuch der Geographie und Statistik des Königreichs Preussen und der Deutschen Mittel- und Kleinstaaten, Leipzig, 1864.
Weber, 1899	Weber, A. F., The Growth of Cities in the Nineteenth Century, Ithaca, New York, 1965 (1st ed., New York, 1899).
Woytinsky, 1953	Woytinsky, W. S. and E. S. Woytinsky, World Population and Production, New York, 1953.
Woytinsky, 1955	Woytinsky, W. S. and E. S. Woytinsky, World Commerce and Governments, New York, 1955.
WWI	Wirtschafts- und Sozialstatistisches Handbuch, edited by B. Gleitze, Cologne, 1960.
Zeitschr. Preussen	Zeitschrift des Königlich-Preussischen Statistischen Bureaus, Berlin, 1860-1894.
Zimmermann, 1960, 1964	Zimmermann, L. J., Arme en Rijke Landen, The Hague, 1960 (2nd ed., 1964).

CHAPTER 7

HISTORICAL PROCESSES OF SOCIAL MOBILIZATION: URBANIZATION AND LITERACY 1850-1965

Peter Flora

PETER FLORA has worked for several years on historical indicators of societal development and has recently completed a thesis on modernization research, which will be published in 1973.

The renaissance of macro-sociology since the late fifties has, to an unprecedented extent, submitted the analysis of societal developments to an increasing division of labor;[1] at the same time it has made it a focus of integrative efforts in the social sciences. This renaissance has resulted not only in a revival, reformulation, and enrichment of "classical" questions but also in concerted attempts to design theories and build models, in a sharpening of the methodological consciousness, and in large-scale efforts to provide an adequate data basis.

QUANTITATIVE-COMPARATIVE RESEARCH IN MODERNIZATION

Today we are confronted with a confusing variety of approaches to the analysis of societal developments. This diversity of approaches can be traced to differing political intentions and theoretical questions, and to

differing methodological and empirical problems. Some of these approaches limit or complement each other, whereas others have a
relationship of indifferent or even hostile coexistence. Nevertheless, the
numerous points of contact and the growing coordination efforts are
evident.[2]

Concerning their formal structure these different approaches can be
arranged on a continuum extending from ideal-typical approaches where
causal relations are theoretically postulated or deduced and empirical data
have an illustrative function, to comparative approaches where causal
relations are defined by statistical models as controlled variance and
empirical data have a systematic function.[3]

The present situation in macro-sociological research requires various
competing approaches all of which are legitimate insofar as they do not try
to screen themselves from falsification. In the long run, however, research
will have to be more systematic-empirical and comparative, since the
application of comparative methods is the prerequisite for every causal
analysis.

Of special importance in this context is the systematic collection of
empirical data and the setting up of data archives. The most important and
extensive project in the field of macro-sociological data collections is still
the Yale Data Program[4] which was started at the beginning of the sixties.
Its enthusiastic as well as critical resonance made it a paradigm for all
current or future work in this field.[5]

The data-collections of the "founding fathers" were almost exclusively
cross-national and only toward the end of the sixties were intensified
efforts made to compile quantitative data reaching far back into the
nineteenth century. Probably the first attempt at such a compilation was
begun by Wolfgang Zapf in 1965. Later it was extended under the title
"QUAM-project" (Quantitative Model of Modernization).[6] These efforts
have reached their present climax in the publication of the CCPR-archive
(Center for Comparative Political Research) of the State University of New
York at Binghamton.[7]

The compilation of historical data collections is an important object of
research on modernization, one of the central problem-areas in macro-
sociology. In the historical sense, modernization designates the epochal
transformation which began in the eighteenth century with the English
Industrial Revolution and the political French Revolution in Western
Europe and which extended all over the world;[8] in a general sense, it
designates the total of developmental processes which characterize the
transition from traditional to complex societies. Common to all modernization theories is the conception of a directed long-term change and a

far-reaching interdependency of the various processes of economic and political development, of social and psychical mobilization, and of cultural and international transformation.[9]

Research on modernization uses a series of model-like simplifications ranging from relatively unsophisticated dichotomies and trichotomies to the analysis of trends and the construction of stages, developmental typologies and causal models, and finally to the more complex cataloguing of the problems which societies face in the process of modernization and of the typical ways they solve these problems. Here the attributes of modernity and the processes and problems of modernization are issues not only of empirical research but also of a critical analysis concerning their ideological implications.

The model-like simplifications call for different methods and pose specific empirical problems. Even today the most sophisticated quantitative-comparative research on modernization is in its theoretical references confined to an analysis of developmental trends in the form of changing aggregate data and to their combination into relatively simple causal-statistical models. This confining is due to the limited scope of the data basis, the restricted possibility of quantifying many variables, the problems of validating the indicators, and the modernization theories themselves which have hardly ever been developed for the purpose of testing them empirically in a systematic way.

Above and beyond the analysis of central developmental trends, quantitative-comparative research on modernization is of a more general descriptive and theory-stimulating significance. Rank-orders, sequences and rates of development, regressional relationships, and the like are often interesting as such and can lead to new questions, tests of basic theoretical assumptions, and discoveries of specific relationships. What has become obvious in the study of economic growth for some time must be regarded as equally valid in the field of macro-sociology:[10] the division of labor has led to a spontaneous development of the data production and to a stronger emphasis on inductive methods in research work. Both can have a stimulating effect on the formulation of theories.

The use of quantitative aggregate data and statistical analysis has gained special importance in one particular field of research on modernization. It is commonly referred to as social mobilization.[11]

LONG-TERM PROCESSES OF SOCIAL MOBILIZATION

The term "social mobilization" was coined by Karl Deutsch.[12] It designates "an overall process of change, which happens to substantial parts of the population in countries which are moving from traditional to modern ways of life"[13] and "in which major clusters of old social, economic and psychological commitments are eroded or broken and people become available for new patterns of socialization and behavior."[14]

> The first and main thing about social mobilization is, however, that it does assume a single underlying process of which particular indicators represent only particular aspects; that these indicators are correlated and to a limited extent interchangeable; and that this complex of processes of social change is significantly correlated with major changes in politics.[15]

Important partial processes of social mobilization, among others, are an increase in horizontal mobility, urbanization and changes of the occupational structure, an increase in the direct demonstration of the attributes of modern forms of living and their spreading through mass media and school-education, and the growing effects of the economic market mechanisms and of political decisions on the national level on broad population strata. Up to now these partial processes could be indicated less in their form and intensity, but in their scope measured by the percentage of the population participating in them or affected by them. Aggregate data and their changes, therefore, form the empirical basis for the analysis of social mobilization.

Probably the first theory of social mobilization was formulated by Daniel Lerner.[16] He developed a four-phase model of successive developmental processes which are causally related in an area lying between threshold values. The four phases are urbanization, the development of literacy, the spreading of mass media, and the increase in political participation. This model attempts to describe the historical path of Western modernization characterized according to Lerner by optimal relations among the individual phases. Thus the model assumes a normative character, and non-Western developments are analysed and assessed as unbalanced deviations. If we ignore this problematic and unnecessary assumption[17] and also the far-reaching but misleading equalization of political participation and democratization, i.e., institutionalized public control of the government, we still have to test to what extent the basic historical assumptions of the model are correct, since these assumptions have been tested only by a cross-national analysis of a larger number of nations around 1950. The third part of this paper will show that the basic assumptions, for the first two phases at least, are not valid.

Social mobilization regularly leads to a change in needs and expectations and thus to an increase in economic and symbolic demands on the central political institutions, demands which constantly threaten to turn into frustration, anomie, and violence. As social mobilization gives rise to new social groups and sharpens the self-awareness of existing ones, it leads to a manifestation of latent, and to an intensification of existing, conflicts. Thus the probability of collective violence increases. It is not surprising at all, therefore, that the relations between the mobilization processes and the forms of political stability and instability are a main theme of the social mobilization literature. The hitherto most convincing formulation of these relationships can be found in Samuel P. Huntington's causal equation-system:[18]

(1) $\dfrac{\text{Social mobilization}}{\text{Economic development}}$ = Social frustration

(2) $\dfrac{\text{Social frustration}}{\text{Mobility opportunities}}$ = Political participation

(3) $\dfrac{\text{Political participation}}{\text{Political institutionalization}}$ = Political instability

Political stability is therefore not only a function of social mobilization and economic development that symbolize the rising of expectations and the satisfaction of needs, it is also a function of the traditional social structure regarding the chances of upward social mobility and the evaluation of economic activity, and a function of the traditional political institutions concerning their adaptability to pressures due to growing political participation. Nevertheless, it is still possible to infer the extent of social frustration, political participation, and political instability directly from the rate of social mobilization, allowing for a higher degree of uncertainty, i.e., a larger proportion of unexplained variance. Since the empirical determination of the mobilization rates is therefore of special importance, an attempt will be made in the third part of this paper to reconstruct the long-term historical rates of two partial processes of social mobilization. To be sure, the empirical research on modernization has still by no means reached a level where such verbal equation systems can be transformed into regression equations with known parameters by developing adequate indicators. Three aspects of the social mobilization literature, in particular, have been criticized:[19] (a) the assumptions, (b) the political implications, and (c) the empirical basis of the models.

(a) The analysts of social mobilization are being reproached for widely neglecting the influence of the international system and the processes within the political system, for regarding politics mainly as a dependent variable, and for giving their models a deterministic character. These reproaches do not, however, rule out either an extension of the models by indicators of the processes in the international and political systems or a refinement of the recursive models by introducing reciprocal relationships.

The criticism of the imputed deterministic character, although due to a misunderstanding of the statistical models, is justified insofar as the importance of the political culture, political elites, and charismatic leaders is largely neglected. To include them in the analysis would probably require a combination of statistical models and qualitative-typological methods.

(b) The criticism of the implicit or explicit conservatism is more serious. It concerns the fact that the stability rather than the performance of the political system,[20] the use of collective violence rather than its political consequences,[21] are at the centre of the analysis. This calls for a shift in theoretical questions.

(c) The criticism of the empirical basis refers to the quantitative-comparative research on modernization in general; in particular it concerns first, the preference given to quantitative aggregate data with limited historical scope; second, the reliability, comparability and reproducibility of the data; third, the validity of the indicators; and fourth, their exchangeability and additivity. The use of national aggregate data restricts the analysis to very general and long-term developments without taking into account important differentiations within society. The breaking up of these aggregate data deserves particular priority and has already shown its fruitfulness in the analysis of mobilization and assimilation processes of linguistic and ethnic groups,[22] and in the analysis of the relationships among mobilization, enfranchisement, electoral participation, and development of political parties.[23]

The use of national aggregate data often leads to "ecological fallacies" (false inferences among different levels of aggregation), so the historical statements on the basis of cross-national data involve the danger of a "historical fallacy."[24] Historical data collections provide the only possibility of avoiding such fallacies. Whereas progress has been made concerning the reliability, comparability, and reproducibility of the data, the problems concerning the validity of the indicators are still largely unsolved. Furthermore, the assumptions of the exchangeability and additivity of indicators are controversial.[25] The following part will show that these assumptions can be made only with considerable reservations.

URBANIZATION AND LITERACY

Two central processes of social mobilization are urbanization and the development of literacy, defined as spatial concentration of the population and as the spreading of the ability to read and write. Attempted here will be an analysis of these two processes by using quantitative aggregate data of ninety-four countries, selected according to specific criteria, in the period from 1850 to 1965.[26]

PETER FLORA [219]

As with most macro-sociological indicators the difficulty of interpreting the rates of urbanization and literacy development must be seen in their ambiguity stemming from the diversity of their correlates. Therefore, every analysis based on quantitative data relating to processes in quite different social contexts has to be based on assumptions about these correlates, assumptions that often enough can claim only a vague plausibility.

As long as this problem of validity cannot be solved more satisfactorily by collecting information on the context of such processes, it seems necessary to restrict oneself to an accurate description and a cautious interpretation. The analysis of the historical processes of urbanization and literacy development is based mainly on the following scatter diagrams where the position of every single country for the years 1850, 1870, 1890, 1910, 1930, 1950, and 1965 has been entered.[27]

In an international perspective, modernization can be understood as a sequence of continually new, increasing, and again decreasing inequalities among national societies. Urbanization and literacy development are two early stages in this process of differentiation.

Quite contrary to the widespread assumption of a strong inter-dependency, of a system of the processes of modernization and the attributes of modernity, the relationship between urbanization and literacy development is by no means uniform and close (see Table 1). The correlation coefficients show that a relationship exists only since the turn of the last century. Even then, however, the relatively high coefficients are a result of similar starting points rather than a measure of the uniformity of later developments, as is demonstrated by the diagrams.[28]

Even more important is that the correlation coefficients do in fact measure the relationship between the two rates in seven historical

TABLE 1
RELATIONSHIP BETWEEN URBANIZATION AND LITERACY DEVELOPMENT IN SEVEN HISTORICAL CROSS-SECTIONS

Year	Correlation Coefficient	Coefficient of Determination	Countries (n)
1850	0.09	0.00	31
1870	0.17	0.03	35
1890	0.51	0.26	48
1910	0.62	0.38	63
1930	0.67	0.45	71
1950	0.69	0.47	88
1965	0.64	0.41	94

1850

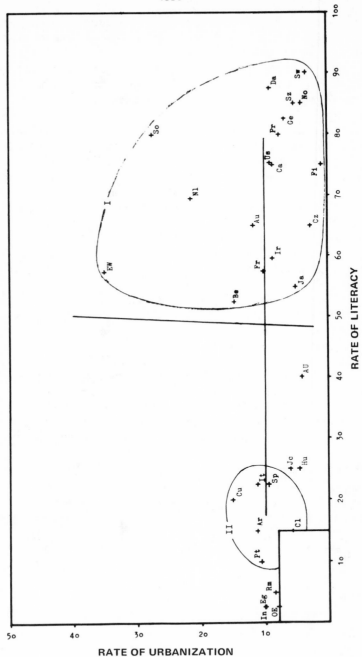

RATE OF LITERACY

RATE OF URBANIZATION

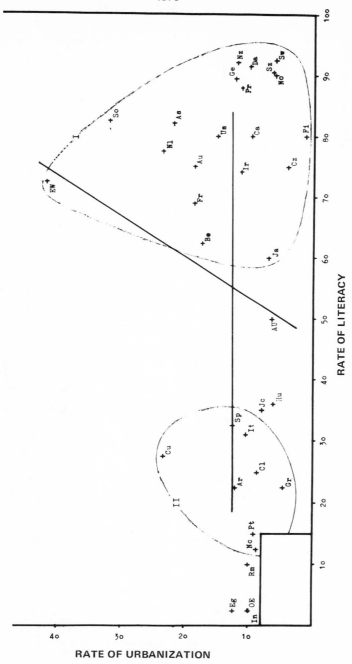

RATE OF LITERACY

RATE OF URBANIZATION

1890

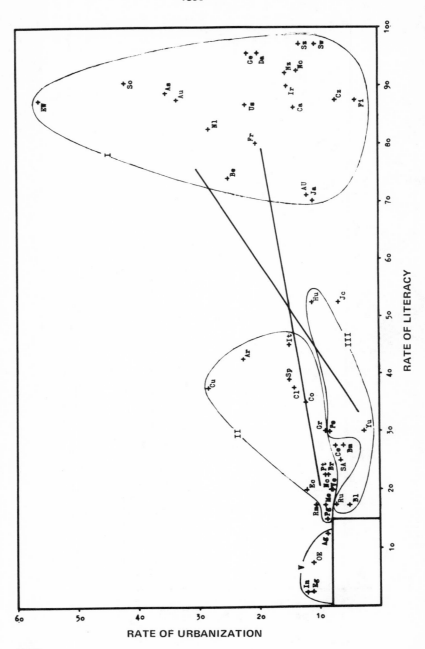

RATE OF LITERACY

RATE OF URBANIZATION

1910

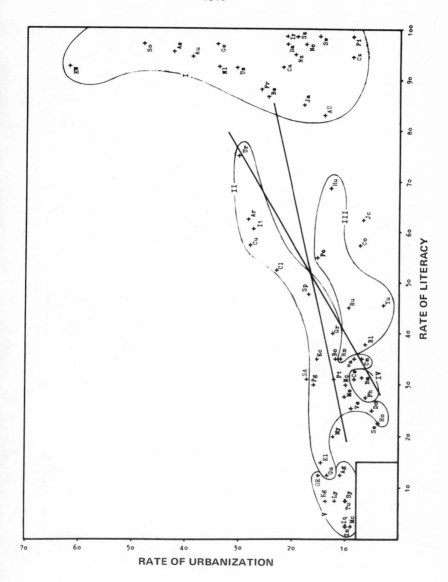

RATE OF LITERACY

RATE OF URBANIZATION

1930

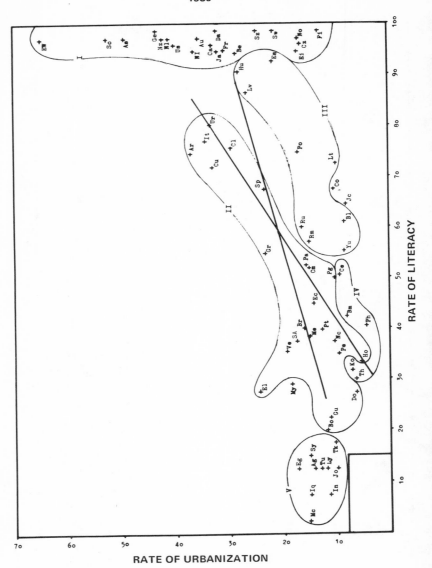

RATE OF LITERACY

RATE OF URBANIZATION

[224]

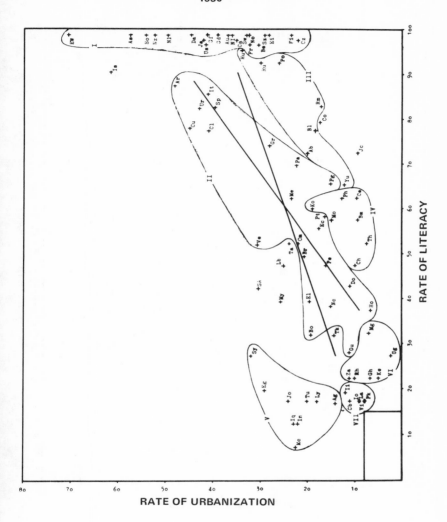

1965

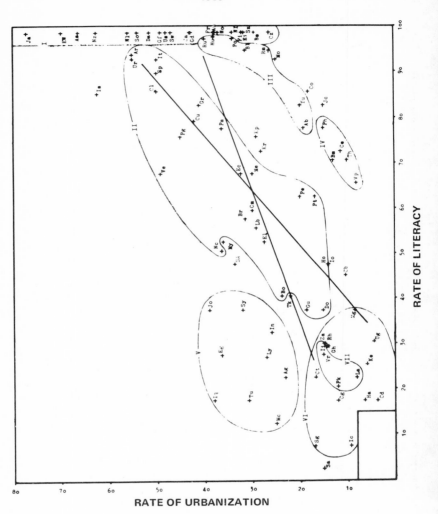

RATE OF LITERACY

RATE OF URBANIZATION

cross-sections, but they conceal the radical change of the developmental relationship in the historical longitudinal section. This reversal of the relationship is the central finding of this analysis.

Whereas the old nations, the countries of Northern, Central, and Western Europe; North America; and Japan are characterized primarily by an early long-term development of literacy that was later followed by an increase in urbanization, this succession of developmental phases has increasingly been reversed in the new nations of Latin America, Asia, and Africa.[29] Since 1850, when enormous differences existed in the educational level and rather insignificant differences existed in the level of urbanization among the various countries, the process of urbanization in general has been much faster than the spreading of literacy (see Table 2).[30]

Undoubtedly there are important regional differences in the relationships among the processes of modernization, e.g., the development of the Eastern and Southeastern European nations and of some Asiatic countries is much more similar to that of the old nations than the development of the Southern European, Latin-American, and Islamic-Arabic countries.[31] Nevertheless, we can speak of a general shift in the relationship between urbanization and literacy development. This shift can be demonstrated most clearly by a comparison of two groups of countries with extreme developmental differences: (A) the predominantly Protestant countries of Northern and Central Europe and of North America (Sw, No, Fi, Da, Pr, Sz, Us, Ca) around 1850,[32] (B) the Islamic countries of the Near East and North Africa (Tk, Sy, Iq, In, Jo, Sa, Eg, Ly, Tu, Ag, Mc) around 1965.[33]

Today the average rate of urbanization in the Islamic countries is five times higher than it was in the Protestant countries around 1850, but the average rate of literacy is still less than one third (see Table 3). The outcome of this comparison suggests that in analysing modernization

TABLE 2
INCREASE IN URBANIZATION AND LITERACY RATES

Year	Index of the Average Rate of:		Countries (n)
	Urbanization	Literacy	
1850	100.0	100.0	31
1870	127.3	113.8	35
1890	151.5	105.9	48
1910	169.7	106.8	63
1930	211.1	122.1	71
1950	252.2	124.7	88
1965	303.8	131.5	94

TABLE 3

**COMPARISON OF URBANIZATION AND LITERACY RATES IN
TWO GROUPS OF COUNTRIES**

Group	Year	% Average Rate of:	
		Urbanization	Literacy
(A)	1850	5.9	81.6
(B)	1965	28.6	25.0

processes in general, differences should be stressed more than common aspects. An emphasis of the latter often stems from a rather simplified thinking in historical dichotomies. This conclusion should be valid whether in the formulation of theories, preference is given to a model of causal interdependency, relating the various developmental processes, as predominantly used in Western research in modernization,[34] or to a model of a causal hierarchy of these processes which is the basis of Marxist theories.[35]

The description of the processes of urbanization and literacy development raises three central questions:

(1) What are the reasons for the early literacy development of the old nations?
(2) How can the rapid urbanization of the new nations be explained?
(3) What are the consequences of the shifting relationship between the two processes of mobilization affecting the stability and efficiency of the political systems?

The data collected for this analysis, of course, allow only some presumptions of possible causes and consequences; at best they can lead to hypotheses which have to be tested later by more extensive empirical research. The following interpretation is based on the scatter diagrams and tries to support the various propositions with additional data or to illustrate them with examples.

Literacy Development in the Old Nations

Contrary to Daniel Lerner's ideas,[36] urbanization cannot be interpreted as the first phase of modernization in the old nations followed by a second phase of literacy development. The growth of larger towns which cannot be identified with urbanization and which preceded the more restricted period of modernization certainly was the historical origin of a higher education breaking the monopoly of sacerdotal and bureaucratic elites, but it was not the origin of a universal spreading of literacy.

Three main factors in different combinations probably explain the large lead of the Central, Western, and Northern European countries; North America; and Japan in the educational development:

(a) the influence of religions whose propagation had an essentially written character,

(b) the institutionalization of political participation on the communal and national level, and

(c) the striving for national self-determination and self-assertion.

(a) There has been a relationship between literacy and religions with a written tradition and propagation in all countries summarized above. It is still valid today, although on a lower level of development, as has been observed in the former English and French colonies.[37] The classic study of Max Weber suggests that among these religions Protestantism in its various manifestations has had the strongest influence. This fact can be strikingly demonstrated by the diagrams: with the exception of England and Wales, all predominantly Protestant countries range before all Catholic countries —even those with the highest levels of literacy. This specific influence was not only the result of the translation of the religious writings into the respective mother tongues, but it was mainly due to the compulsory character which elementary school education assumed. Already in the seventeenth and eighteenth centuries, this character manifested itself in a "right to education" in the Anglo-Saxon countries by obliging communal or national agencies to provide facilities for education; in the German and Scandinavian countries, it manifested itself in the legal obligation to send children to school.[38]

(b) The role of institutionalized political participation cannot fully be proven by the data gathered here, since the predominantly Protestant countries were to a large extent also the countries with the highest levels of institutionalized political participation. At least by some examples, however, the proposition can be illustrated that communal self-government and later the extension of enfranchisement on a national level have considerably accelerated the literacy development: according to the information available, Switzerland, Sweden, and Scotland had the highest literacy rates in Europe in the eighteenth century; the same holds true for the provinces of Tyrol and Vorarlberg in the Austrian monarchy in the nineteenth century; these were all areas with independent peasants and communal self-government;[39] between the electoral reforms of 1832 and 1867/1868 and the most important laws on primary education of 1833 and 1870 in Great Britain, [40] the same direct relation can be found as that between the French Revolution of 1830 and the reform of primary education in 1833.[41] Similar examples can be discovered in countries whose modernization process began later; in Czarist Russia the establishment of self-governing districts after 1864 and the convocation of diets after 1905 had the strongest impetus on the expansion of primary education.[42]

(c) Whereas in the case of the most advanced countries, a combination of Protestantism and self-government might offer a possible explanation for their lead around 1850, it explains the case of Prussia only partially and not at all the large difference between the Catholic countries of France, Austria, and Ireland on the one hand and Spain, Portugal, and Italy on the other. These are cases indicating the influence of a country's position in the international system. For Prussia, France, and Austria, countries at the center of the former system, the development of efficient civil and military bureaucracies and thus of literacy was a necessity of national self-defense and self-assertion. This condition was true to a much less extent for Spain and Portugal after having lost their colonies, and for Italy before gaining national unity. This relationship is further illustrated by the English efforts to accelerate the development of education in the second half of the nineteenth century,[43] the Japanese educational policy after 1868 directed to national strength,[44] and the Russian reform attempts during the Napoleonic Wars and after defeat in the Crimean War.[45]

Ireland, finally, is one of the earliest examples in history of the relationship between the growth of literacy and the striving for cultural self-expression and national independence.[46] It can be assumed that this relationship was the closer the more developed the awareness of cultural individuality and the more the movement for independence led to a mobilization of broad population strata. Therefore, in the nineteenth century, compulsory education became a status symbol of national independence.[47] A comparison of the years when political independence was gained and compulsory education legalized shows clearly the growing importance of this relationship; whereas in the first phase of decolonization in the Latin-American countries, hardly any relationship can be discovered,[48] the disintegration of the Ottoman Empire[49] and the decolonization phase after the Second World War[50] provide sufficient evidence of it.[51]

To what extent and in which form the economic development had an influence on the literacy development of the old nations cannot be answered even approximately by the data collected here. There is no doubt, however, that no direct connection existed between industrialization and literacy development, since the latter began long before the first phase of industrialization in these countries,[52] and as late as 1850 the rates of literacy of the countries with the most advanced industrialization, England and Wales, France, and Belgium, were comparatively low.[53]

Urbanization in the New Nations

The development of the new nations is, as pointed out above, characterized by an overurbanization.[54] Every attempt to explain the differences and the change in urbanization rates is confronted with the difficulty that the changes of these rates cannot be directly interpreted as migration from the country since they are also a function of the population growth,[55] of the differences between the urban and rural birth and death rates, of the immigration and emigration ratio in town and country,[56] and finally of administrative changes of municipal boundaries.

Although we have hardly any information on the above relationships, it is, nevertheless, probably justified to assume that the rapid increase in the urbanization rates is mainly due to an increased rural migration. Three possible factors of this rural migration shall be considered here rudimentarily:

    (a) the economic development in the sense of a sectorial change in the distribution of the labor force,

    (b) the rural overpopulation, and

    (c) the spreading of mass media.

(a) Not surprisingly, a close relationship between the rate of urbanization and the percentages of labor force engaged in nonagricultural and industrial activities respectively could be proven for the '50s. The correlation coefficients for seventy-five countries are 0.78 and 0.67.[57] Deficient information makes corresponding calculations for earlier periods impossible, but those data which are available suggest a similarly close relationship.[58]

This relatively close relation in historical cross-sections, however, is contrasted with a distinct change of the developmental relation in the historical longitudinal section. Compared with the modernization of the old nations, in the new nations, urbanization increasingly surpasses the change of the occupational structure. This fact can be demonstrated by a comparison of two groups of countries: (1) the countries of the Northern Atlantic region between 1850 and 1900,[59] (2) fifty-two countries in the '50s with more than forty percent of the labor force employed in agriculture (see Table 4).[60] Economic development in the sense of a sectoral change of the labor force offers a possible explanation for the urbanization of the old nations and in general for the differences in levels of urbanization of various countries within strictly defined regions. It does not, however, provide any explanation for the historical acceleration of the process of urbanization.

(b) The assumption that urbanization is a consequence of rural

TABLE 4
URBANIZATION AND SECTORAL CHANGE OF THE LABOR
FORCE IN TWO GROUPS OF COUNTRIES

Group	Years	Labor Force Employed in Agriculture (average %)	Rate of Urbanization (average %)
(A)	1850-1900	62	19
(B)	1950-1960	38	19

overpopulation, obvious as it may be, is falsified by the empirical data, at least at first glance: today, with the exception of Egypt, all new nations with the highest density of rural population measured by hectares per capita agricultural population are also among the least urbanized countries.[61]

(c) The interpretation of the accelerated urbanization as a consequence of rapidly rising expectations of the rural population, which can be attributed to a large extent to the unprecedented spreading of mass media, offers perhaps the best explanation. In this context, the classic medium, the newspaper, no longer plays the leading role. Its place has been taken by the radio whose effect is independent of a general literacy. A comparison of the average rate of urbanization and the average number of radios per capita of three different groups of countries:[62] (A) the Latin-American countries, (B) the Islamic-Arabic countries, and (C) some Asiatic countries,[63] provides a first confirmation of the relationship; a more exact empirical proof will be possible only when more data are available on the spreading of mass media in periods further back in history.

Capacities and Demands

In the long run, modernization implies an increase of the capacities of the political system by mobilizing new resources, and simultaneously an

TABLE 5
AVERAGE RATE OF URBANIZATION AND DISTRIBUTION OF
RADIOS IN THREE GROUPS OF COUNTRIES, 1965

Group	Radios per 10,000 Inhabitants (n)	Rate of Urbanization (%)
(A)	1.688	33.2
(B)	1.202	28.6
(C)	.313	12.3

increase of demands due to rising expectations of mobilized population groups. The relation between capacities and demands determines the stability and efficiency of the political system, which leads to the question of how this relation is affected by the historical change of the two mobilization processes, urbanization and literacy development.

According to Karl Deutsch, the first to develop a model of indicators of demands and capacities,[64] urbanization indicates an increase in capacities and the growth of literacy an increase in demands. These assumptions clearly show that the interpretation of these indicators is relatively arbitrary; we have to bear in mind that a change in the rates of urbanization and literacy can indicate both an increase of capacities and of demands and, furthermore, that equal change rates in different contexts can have a divergent meaning. To claim that the different contexts should be taken into account would mean nothing less than to ask for a societal analysis. Compared with this demand only two very modest presumptions shall be made:

(a) Due to the accelerated speed and the changed context, today, the processes of urbanization and literacy development in the new nations in general exert on the political system higher pressures than formerly in the old nations.

(b) Since the nineteenth century the development of literacy has increasingly become a direct indication of the capacities of the political system. The change rates of literacy permit the assumption that these capacities in the new nations are in general not higher today; they are perhaps even lower than those of the old nations between 1850 and 1910.

(a) "The instability of the town" according to a convincing analysis by S. P. Huntington is "an inescapable characteristic of modernization."[65] In the new nations, however, the process of urbanization has accelerated considerably, and it is less synchronized with the sectoral change of the occupational structure. This probably leads to more rapidly increasing pressures on the political system due to the form and scope of political participation and to a lower increase in capacities with regard to economic resources.[66] The growth of literacy in the old nations took place at a time when these societies were hardly urbanized and showed only first signs of a mediated public communication system; it was largely controlled by authoritarian bureaucracies of the state and/or the church and/or by local notables. The growth of literacy in the new nations, on the other hand, was and is preceded increasingly by the mobilization of broad population strata due to the urbanization and the spreading of mass media. This mobilization undoubtedly makes it more difficult to control the destabilizing effects of the literacy development. A correlation of the change rates of primary school enrollment with an index of political instability for 70 countries around 1960 produced the relatively high coefficient of 0.61.[67] Not by chance, therefore, the interpretation of the educational system has undergone a radical change: for a long time it has been considered a predominantly conservative institution preserving and mediating the dominating values, whereas today it is much more regarded one of the central factors of comprehensive processes of change.[68]

(b) Since 1850 the development of primary education has become more and more a national political goal and thus, at the same time, an indication of the capacities of the political system. Compared with the growth of literacy before 1850, the development in the last 115 years undoubtedly has accelerated.[69] In France for instance the rate of literacy rose between 1688 and 1818 from 21 percent to 46 percent,[70] i.e., only by 25 percentage points in 130 years; in England it increased between 1758 and 1834 from 51 percent to 59 percent,[71] i.e., only by 8 percentage points in 76 years. Insofar as the inaccuracy of the data allows any conclusion, this process of development experienced no further acceleration after 1850 as is shown by the comparison (see Table 6) of change rates controlled by the absolute level of literacy.[72]

Bearing in mind the reservations mentioned above, the analysis of the historical processes of urbanization and literacy development shows that the "belated" nations which began their modernization more recently are characterized in general by a much higher mobilization of broad population strata; thus, the political system of these countries is subject to higher pressures whereas the capacities do not increase comparatively. The problems of controlling the mobilization and of institutionalizing political participation, therefore, become a focus of the theoretical and empirical analysis and a starting point of developmental strategies.

TABLE 6
AVERAGE INCREASE OF LITERACY RATES (in percentages)

Period	In Countries with an Average Literacy Rate of		
	10-35%	35-60%	60-85%
1850-1870	5.7	12.2	9.4
1870-1890	10.0	18.3	11.7
1890-1910	9.9	15.1	11.6
1910-1930	15.2	16.3	9.6
1930-1950	14.0	16.1	8.8
1950-1965	9.3	11.8	10.0

NOTES

1. Cf. H. M. Nowotny, Procedures of Macrosociological Research, ch. 1.
2. For example, see G. A. Almond, "Approaches to Developmental Causation."
3. Cf. R. Boudon, L'Analyse Mathématique des Faits Sociaux, ch. 3.
4. See B. M. Russett et al., World Handbook of Political and Social Indicators. Cf. R. L. Merritt and S. Rokkan, Comparing Nations.
5. Cf. C. L. Taylor, Aggregate Data Analysis.
6. See W. Zapf, Materialien zur des Sozialen Wandels; cf. W. Zapf and P. Flora, Some Problems of Time-Series Analysis.
7. See A. S. Banks, Cross-Polity Time-Series Data.
8. Cf. R. Bendix, Nation-Building and Citizenship.
9. See W. Zapf, "Modernisierungstheorien."
10. Cf. S. Kuznets, Modern Economic Growth, p. 31f.
11. Cf. Almond, op. cit., pp. 8-14.
12. See K. W. Deutsch, Nationalism and Social Communication.
13. See K. W. Deutsch, "Social Mobilization and Political Development," p. 493.
14. Ibid., p. 494.
15. Ibid., p. 495.
16. See D. Lerner, The Passing of Traditional Society.
17. In a later article, however, Lerner expressed some doubts on this matter (see Lerner, "Toward a Communication Theory").
18. See S. P. Huntington, Political Order in Changing Societies. Cf. S. M. Lipset, Some Social Requisites of Democracy; J. C. Coleman, "Political System of the Developing Areas"; and P. Cutright, National Political Development.
19. Cf. Almond, op. cit.
20. Cf. P. Cutright, "Political Structure."
21. Cf. B. Moore, Social Origins of Dictatorship, and Zur Geschichte der Politischen Gewalt.
22. See Deutsch, Nationalism and Social Communication.
23. See, for example, S. Rokkan, Citizens, Elections, Parties, chs. 6 and 7.
24. See H. Alker, Mathematics and Politics, p. 101f.
25. Cf. H. Alker, "The Long Road."
26. Find further explanations in the introduction to the Appendix.
27. The positions of the countries, determined by their urbanization and literacy rates, are marked in the scatter diagrams by the abbreviations of their names. A list of these abbreviations can be found in the Appendix. In the scatter diagrams the illiteracy rates (x_i) of the Appendix have been converted into literacy rates ($100 - x_i$). For all rates given as estimated intervals, the mean has been used. The rectangle in the lower left corner of the diagrams (urbanization rate: 0-8%, literacy rate: 0-15%) comprises as a rule all other countries of the world not marked by abbreviations. Exceptions can be found in the tables of the Appendix. The rectangle has not been included in the correlation analysis. Seven regions have been delineated and marked by Roman numerals: (I) Northern, Central, and Western Europe, North America, and Japan; (II) Southern Europe and Latin America; (III) Eastern and South-Eastern Europe; (IV) first group of Asiatic countries; (V) Islamic-Arabic countries; (VI) group of African countries; (VII) second group of Asiatic countries.

28. The Pearson product-moment correlation coefficient is based on the assumptions of a linear regression and a normal marginal distribution of two variables. Since at least the second assumption cannot be made, i.e., the rates of literacy have almost an U-distribution, the correlation coefficients are much too high.

29. The terms "old" and "new" nations are used here as abbreviations only. They do not refer to the status of political independence but to the beginning of the process of modernization.

30. The difference between the two indices of the average rates of urbanization and literacy somewhat overrates the real difference between the rapidity of the two processes of mobilization, for since 1900 an increasing number of countries practically have reached the limit of 100 percent literacy.

31. Compare by using the diagrams the development of the countries in region (I) with those in (III) and (IV) on the one hand and with those in (II) and (V) on the other.

32. In group (A), EW, So, and Nl and in group (B), Lb have been excluded from the comparison as they deviate extremely from the mean of the groups; compare the diagrams for 1850 and 1965.

33. For the following interpretation, compare the diagram for 1850.

34. See, for example, Lerner, The Passing of Traditional Society.

35. See, for example, A. Schaff, "The Marxist Theory."

36. See Lerner, The Passing of Traditional Society.

37. See A. S. Banks and R. B. Textor, A Cross-Polity Survey, p. 14f.

38. Cf. E. Levasseur, L'Enseignement Primaire. In Germany the beginnings of public primary education with partially compulsory character dates back to the second half of the sixteenth century. This development, however, was delayed by the Thirty Years War. Compulsory education was introduced in Wurttemberg in 1649, in Saxony in 1763 for boys and in 1724 for girls, in Prussia in 1717 (partial) and in 1763 (general), in Hesse in 1733. In the first century after the Reformation, the Lutheran Church in Finland made the ability to read a prerequisite for communion, marriage, and the exercise of civic rights. In 1640 the Swedish government decreed that each town had to establish a school; in 1686 the sacristans were obliged to instruct the children, and the ability to read was made a prerequisite for a marriage permit. In 1721 compulsory education was introduced in the royal domains of Denmark, in 1739 in the whole country. In the Anglo-Saxon countries, compulsory education was introduced relatively late: in the U.S.A. between 1852 and 1918, in Canada in 1867, in England and Wales in 1870, in Scotland in 1872; on the other hand a legal claim to education developed very early. In 1647 all communities in American Massachusetts with a certain number of inhabitants were obliged to make school facilities available to all children; until about 1700 in all colonies of New England similar laws existed. In 1696 the Scottish Parliament decided that all parishes should establish schools. In England and Wales the voluntary character of the supply and demand of education has been maintained longer than anywhere else. The religious element in the development of literacy can be found above all in the activity of voluntary organizations established since the end of the seventeenth century with the aim of promoting literacy and religious education.

39. Cf. C. M. Cipolla, Literacy and Development.

40. Cf. S. J. Curtis and M.E.A. Boultwood, An Introductory History.

41. Cf. I. N. Thut and D. Adams, Educational Patterns.

42. Cf. N. Hans, History of Russian Educational Policy.

43. Cf. Curtis and Boultwood, op. cit.

44. Cf. R. P. Dore, Education in Tokugawa Japan; and H. Passin, Society and Education in Japan.

45. Cf. Hans, op. cit.

46. Cf. T. J. MacElligott, Education in Ireland.

47. The development of Finland is probably a comparable example.

48. Country, year when independence was gained/year when compulsory education was introduced: Ha 1806/1874, Pg 1815/1870, Ar 1816/1844, Cl 1818/1860, Cm 1819/1936, Me 1821/1867, Br 1822/1946 (an attempt in 1882 failed), Pe 1824/1901 (in 1828 a legal claim to free primary education became part of the constitution), Bo 1825/1955, Ur 1828/1878, Ve 1830/1893, Ec 1830/1871, Co 1838/1869, Ho 1838/1880, Gu 1839/1945, Nc 1838/1950, El 1841/1950, Do 1844/1917, Cu 1902 (actually independent 1934)/1900, Pa 1903/1903.

49. Country, year when independence was gained/year when compulsory education was introduced: Gr 1830/1834, Rm 1859/1864, Bl 1878/1879, Se 1878/1882, Ab 1913/1921, Sa 1902/-, Eg 1922 (nominally independent)/1923, Iq 1921 (actually independent 1932)/1929, Jo 1946/1952, Sy 1946/1953, Lb 1946/-.

50. Country, year when independence was gained/year when compulsory education was introduced: Asia, Ph 1946/1940, Ii 1947/1950, Pk 1947/-, Ce 1948 (1931 constitution)/1939, Bm 1948/1968(?), Io 1949/1954, Cb 1953/1953 (partial compulsory education since 1911), La 1954/1951, Vr 1954/1952, Vp 1954/1946, My 1957/1966(?); Africa, Ly 1952/before 1969, Mc 1956/before 1969, Tu 1956/before 1969, Sudan 1956/-, Guinea 1958/1959, Ag 1962/1944; fourteen of the twenty-eight African countries which became independent between 1960 and 1966 had introduced compulsory education by 1969.

51. Cf. Levasseur, op. cit.; UNESCO, Statistical Yearbook, and World Survey of Education; and Banks, op. cit.

52. Cf. Cipolla, op. cit.

53. Cf. W. W. Rostow, The Economics of Take-off.

54. Cf. N. V. Sovani, "The Analysis of Over-Urbanization."

55. Ceteris paribus, the growth of population leads to an increase in the rate of urbanization as more towns exceed the limit of 20,000 inhabitants.

56. The urbanization of some countries of Latin America, North America, Australia, and New Zealand was to a large extent the result of the concentration of immigrants in the towns.

57. See B. M. Russett et al., World Handbook . . . , p. 267.

58. Cf. S. Kuznets, Modern Economic Growth. Rank orders of some European and Anglo-Saxon countries around 1900, percent of labor force engaged in nonagricultural activities/rate of urbanization: Great Britain 1/1, Be 2/5, As 3/2, Sz 4/9, Nl 5/3, Fr 6/6, Us 7/4, Da 8/7, No 9/10, Ca 10/8, Sw 11/11.

59. Percent of labor force engaged in nonagricultural activities (year): Great Britain 77 (1841), Fr 57 (1866), Us 49 (1870), Sw 45 (1870), No 51 (1875), Be 76 (1880), Sz 67 (1880), As 74 (1891), Nl 72 (1899), Da 58 (1901), Ca 56 (1901).

60. See Russett, op. cit. La, Ha, Th, Iq, In, Cb, Tk, Ag, Bo, Ab, Ii, Mo, Mc, Gh, Rm, Kr, Sy, Bm, Ch, Gu, Nc, Tu, Yu, Za, Ho, Pk, Bl, Eg, El, Io, Br, Pe, Ph, My, Me, Po, Do, Pg, Co, Cm, Pa, Ec, Ce, Ta, Sp, Jc, Gr, Pt, Ru, Fi, Ve, Cu.

61. Cf. N. Ginsburg, Atlas of Economic Development, p. 48f.

62. Cf. Banks, Cross-Polity Time-Series Data.

63. Ph, Bm, Ce, Th, Sr, Io, Ii, Pk, La, Ch, My.

64. See Deutsch, Social Mobilization and Political Development.

65. See Huntington, op. cit., p. 77.

66. Although comparable historical data are hardly available, one can assume that consequences of this development are an increased urban unemployment and a too rapid growth of the services sector.

67. See Huntington, op. cit., p. 47.

68. Cf. Coleman, Education and Political Development.

69. Cf. Cipolla, op. cit.

70. See M. Fleury and P. Valmary, "Les Progrès . . . ."

71. See W. L. Sargant, "Progress of Elementary Education."

72. The analysis of the change rates calls for extreme caution since the error margins are probably very high. Therefore, no correlation analysis of the change rates has been made.

REFERENCES

Alker, H., "The Long Road to International Relations Theory: Problems of Statistical Nonadditivity," World Politics, Vol. 18, 1966, pp. 623-55.

――― Mathematics and Politics, New York, Macmillan, 1965.

Almond, G. A., "Approaches to Developmental Causation," paper presented at the Eighth World Congress of Political Science, Munich, September 1970.

Banks, A. S., Cross-Polity Time-Series Data, Cambridge, MIT Press, 1971.

――― and R. B. Textor, A Cross-Polity Survey, Cambridge, MIT Press, 1963.

Bendix, R., Nation-Building and Citizenship: Studies in Our Changing Social Order, New York, John Wiley, 1964.

Boudon, R., L'Analyse Mathématique des Faits Sociaux, Paris, Librairie Plon, 1967.

Cipolla, C. M., Literacy and Development in the West, London, Penguin Books, 1969.

Coleman, J. C., Education and Political Development, Princeton, Princeton University Press, 1965.

――― "The Political System of the Developing Areas," in G. A. Almond and J. C. Coleman (eds.) The Politics of the Developing Areas, Princeton, Princeton University Press, 1960.

Cramer, J. F. and G. S. Brown, Contemporary Education, New York, Harcourt, Brace, 1965.

Curtis, S. J. and M.E.A. Boultwood, An Introductory History of English Education, London, University Tutorial Press, 1966.

Cutright, P., "Political Structure, Economic Development, and National Social Security Programs," American Journal of Sociology, Vol. 70, 1965, pp. 537-50.

――― "National Political Development," American Sociological Review, Vol. 28, 1963, pp. 253-64.

Deutsch, K. W., "Social Mobilization and Political Development," American Political Science Review, Vol. 55, 1961, pp. 493-514.

――― Nationalism and Social Communication: An Inquiry into the Foundations of Nationality, Cambridge, MIT Press, 1953.

Dore, R. P., Education in Tokugawa Japan, London, 1965.

Fleury, M. and P. Valmary, "Les Progrès de L'Instruction Elémentaire de Louis XIV à Napoleon III," Population, Vol. 12, 1957, pp. 71-92.

Flora, P., "Indicators of Social Mobilization: Urbanization, Education, Communication," paper presented at the ISSC/ECPR Workshop on Indicators of National Development, Lausanne, August 1971.

Ginsburg, N., Atlas of Economic Development, Chicago, University of Chicago Press, 1961.

Good, H. G., A History of Western Education, New York, Macmillan, 1966.

Hans, N., History of Russian Educational Policy (1701-1917), New York, Russell & Russell, 1964.

Huntington, S. P., Political Order in Changing Societies, New Haven, Conn., Yale University Press, 1968.

Kuznets, S., Modern Economic Growth: Rate, Structure, and Spread, New Haven, Conn., Yale University Press, 1966.

Lerner, D., "Toward a Communication Theory of Modernization," in L. W. Pye (ed.) Communications and Political Development, Princeton, Princeton University Press, 1963.

––– The Passing of Traditional Society: Modernizing the Middle East, New York, Free Press, 1958.

Levasseur, E., L'Enseignement Primaire dans les Pays Civilisés, Paris, Berger-Lerraut, 1897.

Lipset, S. M., "Some Social Requisites of Democracy." American Political Science Review, Vol. 53, 1959, pp. 69-105.

MacElligott, T. J., Education in Ireland, Dublin, Institute of Public Administration, 1966.

Merritt, R. L. and S. Rokkan, Comparing Nations: The Use of Quantitative Data in Cross-National Research. New Haven, Conn., Yale University Press, 1966.

Moore, B., Social Origins of Dictatorship and Democracy: Lord and Peasant in the Making of the Modern World, Boston, Beacon Press, 1966.

––– Zur Geschichte der Politischen Gewalt, Frankfurt am Main, Edition Suhrkamp, 1966.

Nowotny, H. M., "Procedures of Macrosociological Research: An Inductive Analysis of Macrosociological Studies," unpublished thesis, Columbia University, 1969.

Passin, H., Society and Education in Japan, New York, Columbia University Press, 1965.

Rokkan, S., Citizens, Elections, Parties: Approaches to the Comparative Study of the Processes of Development, Oslo, Universitetforlaget, 1970.

Rostow, W. W., The Economics of Take-off into Sustained Growth, London, Macmillan, 1963.

Russett, B. M. et al., World Handbook of Political and Social Indicators, New Haven, Conn., Yale University Press, 1964.

Sargant, W. L., "On the Progress of Elementary Education," Journal of the Statistical Society of London, Vol. 30, 1867, 80-137.

Schaff, A., "The Marxist Theory of Social Development," in R. Aron and B. F. Hoselitz (eds.) Le Développement Social, Paris, Mouton, 1965.

Sovani, N. V., "The Analysis of Over-Urbanization." Economic Development and Cultural Change, Vol. 12, 1964, pp. 113-22.

Taylor, C. L., Aggregate Data Analysis: The Use of Quantitative Data in Cross-National Research, Paris, Mouton, 1967.

Thut, I. N. and D. Adams, Educational Patterns in Contemporary Societies, New York, McGraw-Hill, 1964.

UNESCO, Statistical Yearbook, Vol. 7, 1970.
— — — World Survey of Education, Vol. II, Paris, 1958.
— — — World Illiteracy at Mid-Century, Paris, 1957.
United Nations, Demographic Yearbook, New York, 1948.
Weber, A. F., The Growth of Cities in the Nineteenth Century, Ithaca, N.Y., Cornell
    University Press, 1967.
World's Metropolitan Areas, The, edited by the Institute of International Studies,
    University of California at Berkeley, University of California Press, 1959.
Zapf, W., "Modernisierungstheorien," inaugural speech, Frankfurt, November, 1970.
— — — "Materialien zur Theorie des Sozialen Wandels," unpublished inaugural dis-
    sertation, Konstanz, 1967.
— — — and P. Flora, "Some Problems of Time-Series Analysis in Research on
    Modernization," Social Science Information, Vol. 10, 1971, pp. 53-102.

APPENDIX

Definition

Urbanization is defined as spatial population concentration, whose correlates of behaviour and structure are not part of the definition but a problem of the empirical analysis; the rate of urbanization is the percentage of the total population living in towns with twenty thousand and more inhabitants. Illiteracy is defined as the inability to read or to read and write; the rate of illiteracy is the percentage of the population of five to fifteen and more years, which cannot read and write or can neither read nor write. With reference to the official terminology (cf. UNESCO, World Illiteracy at Mid-Century, 9f.) the ability to read and write is defined in relation to a "relative minimum level" and not to a "functional level."

Comparability

By choosing twenty thousand and more inhabitants as a criterion for a town, an optimum historical and international comparability and, at the same time, a clear differentiation between urban and rural populations according to different criteria is guaranteed. This comparability, however, is impaired by the different methods of determining the boundaries of towns, especially in connection with the development of suburbs and metropolitan areas. In general it can be assumed that the rate of urbanization in the highly developed countries is comparatively too low (cf. The World's Metropolitan Areas). A comparison of the rates of illiteracy is complicated by diverging operational definitions, methods of data-collection and reference groups. The ability to write one's own name as a criterion for literacy results in a lower rate of illiteracy than does the ability to read and write, and the testing of these abilities results in a higher rate of illiteracy than does mere interviewing. The rates of illiteracy for the time before the First World War refer mainly to the ability to read; rates after the First World War refer chiefly to the abilities to read and write. Historical rates of illiteracy are available for the (total) population in the form of census data, and for recruits and brides and bridegrooms in the form of conscription lists and marriage registers. For a society in the phase of primary educational expansion, it can be said, in general, that the rate of illiteracy is lowest in the case of the recruits and highest for the total population, as men of younger age groups have a higher level of education than do women or older groups. Since we have for several countries two or even three different rates of illiteracy (population, recruits, brides and bridegrooms), it is possible to estimate the rate of illiteracy of the population in other countries by using one of the two other rates, assuming that the three rates in all countries are in a comparable relation. The rate of illiteracy of the population varies with the lower age limit which lies here between five and fifteen years. With an age limit between ten and fifteen the variation is relatively small, but with an age limit under ten the rate regularly increases. For some countries, early rates of literacy have been estimated by using information on the development of primary education.

Reliability

The reliability of the data, largely census data, is difficult to assess, but probably it is sufficient for the purpose of this analysis. The higher unreliability of older data is partly neutralized by the relatively small error margins being due to low percentages. To render the data reproducible and accessible to reliability checks, for every single datum, the source(s), specific criteria of the operational definition, and all estimates and calculations are given in the notes.

Representativity

The period presented in 1850 to 1965. It is divided into five sections with twenty years each and one with fifteen years. Though the rates of urbanization of several countries may be reconstructed for the decades between 1800 and 1850, such reconstruction is rarely possible for the rates of illiteracy. With the exception of the city-states for all countries whose population in 1965 was one million or more (cf. United Nations, Demographic Yearbook 1966) and which had formally become independent by that time or earlier (cf. Banks, Cross-Polity Time-Series Data, 297f.), data were collected if only one of the two rates was above the critical value that has been determined as 15 percent for literacy and 8 percent for urbanization. Deviating from this rule the United Kingdom has been divided into England and Wales, Scotland, Ireland, and Northern Ireland respectively; Austria-Hungary into the Austrian empire and the Hungarian kingdom; Sweden and Norway have been analysed separately for the time of their federation. In 1965 between 90 percent and 95 percent of the total population of the world lived in the ninety-four countries covered in this analysis. A list of the countries and the abbreviations of their names used in the diagrams can be found in this Appendix.

Presentation

Table A contains the rates of urbanization, Table B the rates of illiteracy. Figures in brackets point out that the respective areas have not yet become politically independent units. In the case of politically independent countries, the horizontal lines signify that the rates of urbanization and literacy lie below the critical values. Question marks suggest the possibility that the rates were above the critical values at the respective point in time.

TABLE A
RATE OF URBANIZATION

Country	%Population in Towns With 20,000 and More Inhabitants						
	1850	1870	1890	1910	1930	1950	1965
EUROPE							
Albania	—	—	—	—	2.9	20.2	19.1
Austria (Empire)	4.2	6.7	12.0	14.4	—	—	—
Austria (Republic)	(11.8)	(18.6)	(33.7)	(39.0)	35.5	37.0	38.0
Belgium	14.8	17.6	25.1	24.9	28.6	30.6	29.6
Bulgaria	—	—	5.1	6.4	8.5	18.5	31.5
Czechoslovakia	(2.9)	(4.2)	(7.2)	(9.0)	16.6	22.2	26.4
Denmark	9.0	10.1	20.2	21.4	32.0	44.9	51.7
England and Wales	35.0	42.0	56.4	62.1	65.0	70.8	70.0
Estonia	—	—	—	—	21.8	—	—
Finland	(0.0)	(1.4)	(3.9)	(9.0)	13.1	23.7	32.0
France	10.1	18.8	20.6	26.2	30.8	32.4	38.1
Germany	(6.8)	12.5	21.9	34.6	43.4	—	—
GDR	—	—	—	—	—	39.1	42.9
GFR	—	—	—	—	—	41.5	49.2
Greece	—	4.9	9.0	12.7	23.2	28.1	41.1
Hungary	4.6	6.4	11.2	13.0	28.0	34.0	38.0
Ireland	8.8	11.4	15.3	21.5	—	—	—
Eire	—	—	—	—	17.1	28.3	31.8
Northern Ireland	—	—	—	—	36.6	36.0	34.0
Italy	(11.2)	10.6	15.0	27.5	34.5	41.2	50.0
Latvia	—	—	—	—	26.8	—	—
Lithuania	—	—	—	—	10.0	—	—
Netherlands	21.7	23.9	28.3	34.0	41.0	49.7	56.0
Norway	(4.2)	(6.1)	(13.8)	17.8	16.9	32.7	37.0
Poland	—	(5.4)	(8.4)	(15.5)	17.0	26.2	34.1
Portugal	10.6	9.3	9.2	12.3	12.8	16.5	16.9
Prussia	7.8	11.4	—	—	—	—	—
Rumania	(8.6)	10.0	10.7	11.0	15.0	17.2	26.6
Russia	—	—	7.3	9.7	16.4	30.0	40.0
Scotland	27.7	32.1	42.2	48.1	52.8	54.4	54.0
Serbia	—	—	—	4.0	—	—	—
Spain	9.6	12.5	15.0	17.0	23.5	39.8	50.0
Sweden	3.4	6.0	10.8	15.1	21.7	33.0	46.9
Switzerland	5.2	6.6	13.2	19.6	24.9	29.2	31.0
Yugoslavia	—	(1.8)	(2.7)	(3.0)	8.6	12.3	20.2
THE AMERICAS							
Argentina	11.3	12.2	22.8	28.4	37.0	48.3	55.0
Bolivia	—	—	—	—	12.7	19.6	23.9
Brazil	—	—	8.7	12.0	16.0	20.9	31.5
Canada	8.8	9.8	14.2	22.1	33.0	35.1	42.9
Chile	5.9	8.9	14.3	23.1	29.7	41.0	50.0
Columbia	—	—	6.8	7.2	15.0	22.0	30.0

TABLE A (Continued)

Country	%Population in Towns With 20,000 and More Inhabitants						
	1850	1870	1890	1910	1930	1950	1965
THE AMERICAS (Continued)							
Costa Rica	—	—	12.3	7.6	10.6	17.5	18.2
Cuba	(15.0)	(23.5)	(28.5)	28.0	33.0	45.0	42.2
Dominican Republic	—	—	0.0	5.0	6.3	11.1	15.2
Ecuador	—	6.4	12.2	15.4	14.3	17.8	32.5
El Salvador	—	—	—	13.9	24.6	19.8	27.6
Guatemala	—	—	—	13.6	11.2	11.2	18.8
Haiti	—	—	—	—	—	—	6.6
Honduras	—	—	0.0	3.9	5.3	6.8	14.2
Jamaica	(<8.0)	(<8.0)	(7.3)	(6.9)	(8.0)	(9.5)	15.0
Mexico	—	—	9.1	10.3	15.0	23.6	30.0
Nicaragua	—	8.9	8.0	10.1	10.5	15.2	36.4
Panama	—	—	(0.0)	8.5	15.7	22.4	36.4
Paraguay	—	—	8.8	16.1	10.4	15.2	45.1
Peru	—	—	—	4.6	9.7	16.1	20.0
United States	9.0	15.1	22.2	30.9	40.1	41.8	48.0
Uruguay	11.0	20.2	30.4	30.3	33.6	43.0	55.0
Venezuela	—	—	8.0	9.0	19.4	30.9	49.2
ASIA							
Burma	—	(<8.0)	(<8.0)	(<8.0)	(<8.0)	9.6	13.0
Cambodia	—	—	—	—	(?)	11.0	10.6
Ceylon	—	(7.4)	(7.4)	(8.5)	(9.4)	9.8	11.4
China	?	?	<8.0	?	?	10.0	?
Taiwan	—	—	—	—	—	24.0	34.0
India	—	—	—	—	—	12.0	34.0
Indonesia	—	—	—	—	—	9.1	14.0
Iran	>10.0	>10.0	12.0	10.0	11.5	22.0	26.0
Iraq	(?)	(?)	(?)	(>8.0)	(>8.0)	23.0	38.0
Israel	—	—	—	—	—	61.8	62.6
Japan	5.0	7.0	11.0	18.0	32.0	42.2	77.3
Jordan	—	—	—	(?)	(>8.0)	24.1	39.0
Korea	—	—	(<5.0)	(<5.0)	(<8.0)	19.0	—
Korean People's Rep.	—	—	—	—	—	(20.2)	29.0
Korean Republic	—	—	—	—	—	(18.5)	28.0
Laos	—	—	—	—	—	8.0	8.0
Lebanon	(?)	(?)	(?)	(>8.0)	(>8.0)	25.1	29.2
Malaysia	—	—	(?)	(12.5)	(18.5)	(25.9)	36.2
Mongolia	—	—	—	(?)	>8.0	15.0	25.0
Ottoman Empire	8.0	10.0	11.0	15.0	—	—	—
Turkey	—	—	—	—	10.5	14.5	22.0
Pakistan	—	—	—	—	—	7.9	12.0
Philippines	—	—	(5.7)	(6.4)	(4.5)	12.7	15.0
Saudi Arabia	—	—	—	—	—	?	15.0
Syria	(?)	(?)	(?)	(>8.0)	(>8.0)	32.0	32.0
Thailand	—	—	—	—	<8.0	7.6	10.0

TABLE A (Continued)

Country	% Population in Towns with 20,000 and More Inhabitants						
	1850	1870	1890	1910	1930	1950	1965
ASIA (Continued)							
Vietnam	—	—	—	—	(?)	(>8.0)	—
Vietnam People's Rep.	—	—	—	—	—	—	<10.0
Vietnam Republic	—	—	—	—	—	—	15.00
AFRICA							
Algeria	—	—	(8.9)	(11.0)	(14.3)	(14.1)	23.0
Central African Rep.	—	—	—	—	—	—	16.8
Chad	—	—	—	—	—	—	3.9
Congo (Kinshasa)	—	—	—	—	—	—	12.0
Egypt	(>8.0)	(12.6)	(11.2)	(13.8)	(17.4)	29.2	36.5
Ghana	—	—	—	—	—	(6.9)	14.0
Ivory Coast	—	—	—	—	—	—	9.6
Kenya	—	—	—	—	—	(5.0)	5.9
Libya	—	—	(?)	(12.0)	(12.0)	18.0	27.0
Madagascar	—	—	—	—	(<8.0)	(<8.0)	8.6
Morocco	—	—	(?)	(8.0)	(15.3)	(22.7)	25.0
Rhodesia	—	—	—	—	—	(10.0)	14.8
Senegal	—	—	—	—	—	—	16.9
South Africa	—	—	(6.7)	12.5	17.5	30.7	33.8
Tunisia	—	—	(?)	(10.0)	(13.0)	(20.3)	30.8
Uganda	—	—	—	—	—	(<3.0)	<5.0
Zambia	—	—	—	—	—	(11.2)	15.0
OCEANIA							
Australia	—	(22.1)	(35.4)	42.7	49.5	57.8	66.4
New Zealand	—	(12.1)	(15.6)	19.9	42.3	52.6	62.8

TABLE B
RATE OF ILLITERACY

Country	% Population Which Can Neither Read Nor Write						
	1850	1870	1890	1910	1930	1950	1965
EUROPE							
Albania	—	—	(?)	(?)	?	25-30	20-25
Austria (Empire)	55-65	45-55	29	17	—	—	—
Austria (Republic)	(<40)	(<30)	(10-15)	(3-8)	1-5	1-2	1-2
Belgium	45-50	35-40	26	13.4	5.9	3-4	1-2
Bulgaria	—	—	80-85	62.2	37-41	20-25	3-8
Czechoslovakia	(<40)	(<30)	(5-15)	(3-8)	4.1	2-3	1-2
Denmark	10-15	5-12	1-8	1-5	1-2	1-2	1-2
England and Wales	40-45	25-30	10-15	5-10	1-5	1-2	1-2
Estonia	—	—	—	—	5-10	—	—
Finland	(<30)	(<25)	(10-15)	(1.1)	1.0	1-2	1-2
France	40-45	31	18-22	11.9	5.3	3-4	
Germany	(15-20)	8-13	1-8	1-5	1-?		
GDR	—	—	—	—		1-2	1-2
GFR	—	—	—	—	—	1-2	1-2
Greece	—	75-80	68=72	59.7	45.1	25.9	15-20
Hungary	70-80	64	45-50	31.3	9.6	4.7	2-3
Ireland	40.4	25.8	10.1	1.1	—	—	—
Eire	—	—	—	—	3-8	1-2	1-2
Northern Ireland	—	—	—	—	3-8	1-2	1-2
Italy	(75-80)	69	54-56	39.3	23.1	14.4	5-10
Latvia	—	—	—	—	13.5	—	—
Lithuania	—	—	—	—	25-30	—	—
Netherlands	28-33	20-25	15-20	5-10	1-5	1-2	1-2
Norway	(10-20)	(5-15)	(5-10)	1-5	1-5	1-2	1-2
Poland	—	(?)	(?)	(40-50)	25.3	5-10	1-5
Portugal	>85	?	75-80	68.9	60.2	41.7	3-40
Prussia	20	12	—	—	—	—	—
Rumania	>90	>85	80-85	60-70	42.9	17.0	3-8
Russia	—	—	80-85	50-60	35-45	5-10	1-5
Scotland	20	15-20	7-12	1-5	1-5	1-2	1-2
Serbia	—	—	—	75-80	—	—	—
Spain	75-80	65-70	61	52.2	30-35	17.3	8-13
Sweden	10	5-10	1-5	1-2	0.1	1-2	1-2
Switzerland	10-20	7-12	1-5	1-2	1-2	1-2	1-2
Yugoslavia	—	(?)	(65-75)	(52-57)	44.6	34.4	15-20
THE AMERICAS							
Argentina	?	75-80	55-60	35-40	23-28	10-15	4-9
Bolivia	—	—	—	—	75-85	67.9	57-62
Brazil	—	—	75-80	64-66	58-62	50.6	40-45
Canada	(<30)	<25	13.8	5-10	4.3	2-3	1-2
Chile	?	70-80	60-65	45-50	24.4	20-25	12-17

TABLE B (Continued)

Country	% Population Which Can Neither Read Nor Write						
	1850	1870	1890	1910	1930	1950	1965
THE AMERICAS (Continued)							
Columbia	—	—	?	60-70	48.4	45-50	38-43
Costa Rica	—	?	<85	40-50	30-35	20.6	12-17
Cuba	(75-85)	(70-75)	(60-65)	40-45	28.2	21-23	20-22
Dominican Republic	—	—	?	70-80	70-75	57.1	60-65
Ecuador	—	?	<85	60-70	50-60	44.3	30-35
El Salvador	—	—	—	?	72.4	60.6	45-50
Guatemala	—	—	—	>85	75-80	71.9	60-65
Haiti	—	—	—	—	—	—	80-85
Honduras	—	—	?	70-85	66.6	60-65	50-55
Jamaica	(70-80)	(65.0)	(47.5)	(37.7)	(33-38)	(25-30)	15-20
Mexico	—	—	80-85	72.3	61.5	35-40	30-35
Nicaragua	—	>85	<85	65-75	60-65	61.6	47-52
Panama	—	—	(?)	60-70	45-50	30.1	20-25
Paraguay	—	—	?	65-75	45-55	34.2	22-27
Peru	—	—	—	?	60-70	50-55	35-40
United States	24.7	20.0	13.3	7.7	4.3	3-4	1-2
Uruguay	?	?	?	20-30	15-25	15-20	5-10
Venezuela	—	—	80.8	72-77	62-67	47.8	30-35
ASIA							
Burma	—	(?)	(70-75)	(68.6)	(57.6)	40-45	27-32
Cambodia	—	—	—	—	—	(80-85)	50-60
Ceylon	—	(?)	(75-80)	(69.0)	(47-52)	35-40	25-30
China	—	—	?	?	?	50-55	30-35
Taiwan	—	—	—	—	—	45-50	?
India	—	—	—	—	—	80.7	68-73
Indonesia	—	—	—	—	—	80-85	50-55
Iran	>95	>95	>95	>95	>90	85-90	65-70
Iraq	—	—	—	(>95)	(>90)	(>85)	80-85
Israel	—	—	—	—	—	6.3	14-16
Japan	<50	<45	25-35	10-20	3-8	2-3	1-2
Jordan	—	—	—	—	(>85)	80-85	60-65
Korea	—	—	(?)	(?)	(68.2)	35-45	—
Korean People's Rep.	—	—	—	—	—	—	22-27
Korean Republic	—	—	—	—	—	—	25-30
Laos	—	—	—	—	—	(80-85)	75-80
Lebanon	—	—	(?)	(?)	(?)	50-55	42-47
Malaysia	—	—	—	(75-85)	(71.0)	(58-63)	45-50
Mongolia	—	—	—	—	?	40-45	5-10
Ottoman Empire	>95	>95	>90	>85	—	—	—
Turkey	—	—	—	—	80-85	68.1	57-62
Pakistan	—	—	—	—	—	80-85	77-82
Philippines	—	—	(?)	(65-80)	(57-62)	35-40	20-25
Saudi Arabia	—	—	—	—	—	—	>95

TABLE B (Continued)

Country	% Population Which Can Neither Read Nor Write						
	1850	1870	1890	1910	1930	1950	1965
ASIA (Continued)							
Syria	—	—	—	(>90)	(?)	70-75	60-65
Thailand	—	—	—	—	65-75	45-50	27-32
Vietnam	—	—	—	—	—	(80-85)	—
Vietnam People's Rep.	—	—	—	—	—	—	32-37
Vietnam Republic	—	—	—	—	—	—	70-75
AFRICA							
Algeria	—	—	(>85)	(>85)	(>85)	(83.2)	75-80
Central African Rep.	—	—	—	—	—	—	75-80
Chad	—	—	—	—	—	—	80-85
Congo (Kinshasa)	—	—	—	—	—	—	80-85
Egypt	(>95)	(>95)	(>95)	(>90)	(>85)	80.1	70-75
Ghana	—	—	—	—	(?)	(75-80)	68-73
Ivory Coast	—	—	—	—	—	—	>90
Kenya	—	—	—	—	(?)	(75-80)	72-77
Libya	—	—	—	(>90)	(>85)	(80-85)	73.0
Madagascar	—	—	—	—	(?)	(65-70)	60-65
Morocco	—	—	—	(>95)	(>95)	(>90)	>85
Rhodesia	—	—	—	—	(?)	(75-80)	<75
Senegal	—	—	—	—	—	—	>90
South Africa	—	—	(70-80)	68.9	60-65	55-60	50-55
Tunisia	—	—	—	(>90)	(>85)	(80-85)	80-85
Uganda	—	—	—	—	(?)	(70-75)	67-72
Zambia	—	—	—	—	(?)	(75-80)	<75
OCEANIA							
Australia	—	(17.9)	(11.3)	4.5	1-5	1-2	1-2
New Zealand	—	(7.8)	(6.3)	5.0	1-5	1-2	1-2

Notes to Tables A and B

The notes are arranged like the tables: by indicator, continent, country name (abbreviated). They give for every datum in the tables: the exact year of reference **or** (1=1850, 2=1870, 3=1890, 4=1910, 5=1930, 6=1950, 7=1965); the source number(s)—represented by the figure in parentheses; the kind of datum if it is not a census figure (S=estimate, s=author's estimate); and the deviations from specific defining characteristics (urbanization: size of town; illiteracy: age group and defining criterion). If no deviation is mentioned, the rates of urbanization refer to the population in towns with 20,000 and more inhabitants; and the rates of illiteracy refer to the population over fifteen years of age. "Adults" signifies that no clearly definable age group could be reconstructed, but that at least the preschool age group is not included. Two criteria of illiteracy are distinguished: (a) = not able to read, **or** not able to write; and (b) = illiterate in terms of both reading and writing. If nothing else is mentioned, the rates of illiteracy from the following sources refer to the following criteria: (7) = (a); (28 and 29—the estimate for 1950 excepted) = (b); (31) = (b). Source (5) contains no definitional criteria.

Examples

The first note for Table A under the "Europe" heading should be read as follows:

Ab: 1927 (21,XIV); 6,7 (5), 25,000+.

"Ab" is the code abbreviation for Albania—from the List of Countries following these notes. The table datum for the year 1927 is taken from source 21 (Wagner and Supan), volume 14. (Sources are listed by number immediately following the List of Countries.) Also for Albania, data for 1950 (code figure 6) and 1965 (code figure 7) are shown in Table A; these were taken from source 5 (Banks) and refer to Albanian towns with populations of over 25,000.

The first note for Table B under the "Asia" heading should be read as follows:

Bm: 3 (s); 1901 (28), 70.1%; 1911, 1931 (28); 6 (29), S; 7 (s); 1963 (5), 29.0%.

Burma's illiteracy rate in 1890 (code figure 3) has been estimated by the author. The rates for 1901, 1911, and 1931 were taken from source 28 (UNESCO); however, the figure for 1901 refers only to the population over fifteen years of age. The 1950 datum (code figure 6) was an estimate given in source 29, but the 1965 figure (code 7) was estimated by this author. The 1963 datum, from source 5, again refers only to that portion of the population over fifteen years of age. In 1890 and 1965, the figures refer to the proportion of the population which either cannot read or cannot write. Except in 1963—for which definitional criteria are not available, the other given years denote illiteracy in terms of the dual inability to read and write.

Urbanization (Table A)

EUROPE

Ab: 1927 (21,XIV); 6,7 (5), 25,000+. AU (Austrian empire without Hungarian kingdom): 1843 (33); 1869 (14); 3 (33); 4 (5), 25,000+. Au (Republic): 1850-1910: Lower Austria, Upper Austria, Salzburg, Styria, Carinthia, Carniola, Tyrol and Vorarlberg; 1857 (32, vol.IX, pt 1); 1869 (14); 3 (21,IX); 4 (24), 30,000+; 5 (5), 6,7 (s); 1934 (5), 35.6%; 1961 (5), 38.1%. Be: 1846 (33); 1866 (14); 3 (33); 4,5 (5), 25,000+; 1947 (30), 32.0%; 6,7 (5), 25,000+. Bl: 1888 (33)1 4 (5), 25,000+; 1900 (21,XIII), 6.0%; 1905 (21,XIII), 6.6%; 1926 (21,XIV); 1946 (30), 15.2%; 6,7 (s); 1959 (22,1961), 26.4%. Cz: 1850-1910: Bohemia, Moravia, Austrian Silesia; 1857 (32, vol. IV, pt 1); 1869 (14); 3 (21,IX); 4 (s); 4 (24), 7.0%, 30,000+; 5 (21,XIV); 6, 7 (5). Da: 1845 (33); 2 (14); 3 (33); 4 (5), 25,000+; 5 (s); 1925 (21,XIV), 27.6%; 6 (5); 1945 (30), 45.7%; 7 (22, 1968), without suburbs 36.8%. EW: 1851 (33); 1871, 1891, 1911, 1931 (6,17); 1951 (29), 51.9%, 100,000+; 7 (s); 7 (29), 47.8%, 100,000+. Es: 5 (21,XIV). Fi: 1 (32, vol.III, pt 1); 1871 (14); 1889 (24); 4 (s); 1905 (21,XIII), 8.2%; 1928 (21,XIV); 6 (30); 1966 (22,1967). Fr: 1851, 1872, 1891,

1911, 1931 (3); 6 (s); 1946 (3), 31.4%; 1954 (3), 33.4%; 1962 (3). Ge: 1848-52 (32, vol.IV, pt 2), area of the later German Empire without Alsace-Lorraine; 1871, 3, 4, 1933 (27). Gd: 6,7 (26). Gf: 6.7 (25). Gr: 1871 (14); 1889 (33): 1907 (21,XIII); 1928 (21,XIV); 1951 (30); 7 (5). Hu: 1845 (33); 2 (14); 3 (33); 4 (s); 4 (24), 11.1%, 30,000+; 1920 (21,XIV), 19.4%, 12.6%, 50,000+; 5 (s); 5 (24), 21.0%, 50,000+; 6 (s); 1954 (22,1958), 35.8%, 25.8%, 50,000+; 7 (s); 7 (5), 28.0%, 50,000+, Ir: 1851, 1871, 1891 (33); 1911 (24). Ei: 1926 (21, XIV); 1946 (30), 24.3%; 1951 (30); 7 (7). NI: 1926 (21,XIV); 6 (24), 34.2%, 100,000+; 7 (s); 7 (24), 27.6%, 100,000+. It: 1 (32, vol.III, pt 2), partially estimated using the population figures of the towns of 1862 and the population figures of the communities between 1800 and 1868; 1871 (21,IV); 1881 (21,IX), 13.7%; 3 (s); 1901 (21,XIII), 16.3%; 4,5 (5); 1951 (30), 20.4%, 100,000+; 7 (s); 1966 (5), 29.8%, 100,000+; 1810-1910: towns; 1910-1965: communities having more inhabitants than do the towns. Lv: 5 (5). Lt: 1935 (24). NI: 1849 (33); 1869 (14); 1889 (33); 4,5 (s); 4 (5), 38.9%, 25,000+, probably communities and not towns; 5 (5), 49.1%, 25,000+, probably communities; 1920 (21,XIV), 38.9%; 1947 (30); 7 (5), 25,000+. No: 1845 (33); 2 (14); 3 (33); 4 (5), 25,000+; 1929 (21,XIV); 6 (30); 7 (s); 1960 (22,1964), 34.7%, without suburbs 25.3%. Po: 1870-1910: kingdom of Poland; 1871 (14), without suburbs 4.1%; 3 (21,IX); 1908 (24); 5 (s); 1921 (21,XIV), 13.0%, 50,000+; 1931 (5), 12.7%, 50,000+; 6 (22,1963); 1966 (22,1967). Pt: 1857 (33); 2 (5); 3 (33); 4,5 (5); 6 (30); 7 (5). Pr: 1852 (32, vol.IV, pt 2); 1871 (21,III). Rm: 1848-52: (32, vol.III, pt 1), principalities of Moldavia and Wallachia; 1873 (21,III); 3 (33); 4 (5), 25,000+; 5 (s); Old Rumania 1915 (21,XIV), 11.2%; Bucovina 1919 (21,XIV), 11.3%; Bessarabia 1922 (21,XIV), approx. 13.0%; Transylvania 1923 (21,XIV), 12.0%; 5 (5), 12.2%, 50,000; 1948 (30); 1963 (22,1965), without suburbs 21.7%. Ru: 1885 (33); 4 (2); 1926 (23), 12.0%; 1930 (s); 1939 (23), 26.4%, 16.6%, 100,000+; 6,7 (s); 1959 (23), 35.5%, 23.2%, 100,000+; 1967 (19), 27.0%, 100,000+. So: 1851, 1871, 1891 (33); 1911 (24); 1931 (24,30); 1951 (30), 37.6%, 100,000+; 7 (s); 7 (30), 35.5%, 100,000+. Se: 4 (24). Sp: 1857 (33); 2 (s); 1877 (21,VI), 13.9%; 3 (s); 1887 (21,IX), 18.0%, communities that are much larger than towns; 4 (s); 1920 (21,XIV), 18.6%, 15.9%, 30,000+; 5 (s); 5 (24), 20.8%, 30,000+; 6 (30), 30.3%, 50,000+; 7 (s); 7 (5), 40.6%, 50,000+. Sw: 1 (33); 1872 (14); 3 (33); 4 (5), 25,000+; 5 (5); 6 (30); 7 (5). Sz: 1 (33); 2 (14); 1888 (33); 4 (5), 25,000+; 5 (5); 6 (30); 1964 (22,1967), agglomerations of 20,000+: 50.1%. Yu: 1869 (14), Carniola, Dalmatia, Croatia, Slavonia, Serbia, Montenegro; around 1890 (21,IX), same area as 1869 and Bosnia-Herzogovina; 4 (24), same area as 1890; 5 (5); 1948 (30); 7 (5).

THE AMERICAS

Ar: 1 (5); 1869 (14); 3 (33); 4 (5); 25,000+, 26.4%, 50,000+; 5 (s); 5 (5), 32.3%, 50,000+; 1947 (30), 37.2%, 100,000+; 7 (s); 7 (30), 43.1%, 100,000+. Bo: 5,6,7 (5). Br: 1888 (33); 4 (s); 4 (5), 9.8%, 50,000+; 5 (s); 5 (5), 14.0%, 50,000+; 6 (30); 7 (s); 1960 (22,1963), 28.0%. Ca: 1848 (32,vol.I, pt 2); 1871 (14); 1848 and 1871: the provinces of Ontario, Quebec, New Brunswick, Nova Scotia; 1891 (33); 1911 (5), 25,000+; 5 (s); 1931 (5), 26.2%, 50,000+; 1951 (30), 27.5%, 50,000+; 1962 (22,1964). CI: 1 (33); 1865 (14); 1885 (33); 4 (5), 25,000+; 5 (5); 6 (s); 1939 (5), 35.7%, 26.8%, 50,000+; 6 (5), 32.1%, 50,000+; 7 (s); 7 (22,1968), 44.6%, 50,000+. Cm: 1886-95 (33); 4 (5), 25,000+, 3.8%, 50,000+; 5 (s); 5 (5), 12.7%, 50,000+; 6,7 (s); 1956 (22,1958), 26.5%; 1961 (22,1961), 30.9%; 1964 (22,1965), 29.6%. Co: 1892 (33); 4,5 (5); 6 (30); 1967 (22,1968), source (5) gives the deviating value of 30.7% for 1965. Cu: 1,2 (s); 1862 (14), 21.0%; 1887 (33); 4 (5), 25,000+, 26.6%. 50,000+; 5 (s); 5 (5), 31.2%, 50,000+; 5 (s); 1943 (24), 44.2%, main towns, 31.0%, 100,000+, both with suburbs included; 6 (5), 31.5%, 100,000; 7 (22,1968), with suburbs. Do: 3,4 (s), cf. sources (5) and (14); 5 (5); 6 (30); 7 (5). Ec: 2 (14); 1889 (33); 4 (5), 25,000+; 5 (5); 6 (30); 7 (5). El: 4 (5), 25,000+; 5,6,7 (5); source (30) gives the deviating value of 13.0% for 1950. Gu: 4 (5), 25,000+; 5 (5); 6 (30); 7 (5). Ha: 7 (5). Ho: 1889 (33); 4 (5), 25,000+; 5 (5); 6 (30); 7 (5). Jc: 1,2 (s); 1891, 1911 (24); 5,6,7 (s); 1921 (24), 7.3%; 1943 (24), 8.8%; 7 (5), 11.7%, 50,000+. Me: 1889 (33); 4 (5), 25,000+; 5 (s); 5 (5), 11.3%, 50,000+; 6 (22,1953), 18.7%, 50,000+, 15.1%, 100,000+; 7 (s); 7 (30), 20.5%, 100,000+. Nc: 2 (14); 1889 (33); 4 (5), 25,000+; 5 (s), cf.(24); 6 (30); 1964 (24); source (5) gives strongly deviating values for 1930 and 1950. Pa: 3 (s); 4 (5), 25,000+; 5 (5); 6 (30); 7 (5). Pg: 1887 (21,IX); 4

(5), 25,000+; 5 (5); 6 (30); 7 (5). Pe: 1876 (33), 7.8%; 1908 (24); 1928-31 (24); 6 (24); 7 (s); 1961 (24), 26.1%, 28,000+. Us: 1,2,3,4,5,6 (13), 25,000+; 7 (s); 1960 (13), 46.6%, 25,000+, new definition of urban areas. Ur: 1854, 2 (5); 3 (33); 4,5 (5), 25,000+; 6,7 (s); 1953 (24,30), 42.3%, 30,000+; 1963 (24,30), 50.3%, 40,000+. Ve: 1891 (33); 4 (5), 25,000+; 5 (5); 6 (30); 7 (5).

ASIA

Bm: 2,3,4,5 (s); (24), 100,000+: 1891 2.4%, 1911 3.6%, 1931 3.7%; 1953 (11), 5.4%, 100,000+; 7 (s); 7 (5), 8.0%, 100,000+. Cb: 6 (s); 1958 (5), 11.4%; 1966 (5). Ce: 2,3,4,5 1953 (11); 1963 (22,1966). Ch: 3 (s); around 1890 (21,IX), < 5.0%, 100,000+; 6 (11). Ta: 6,7 (s); 6 (24), 17.2%, 100,000+; 7 (30), 29.6%, 100,000+. Ii: 1951 (11); 7 (s); 1961 (22,1965), 8.3%, 100,000+; in 1961 there were 141 towns with 50,000-100,000 inhabitants and 515 towns with 20,000-50,000 inhabitants; the mean values are estimated at 70,000 and 30,000 respectively, therefore the resulting population figure of approx. 25 millions and 5.7% respectively. Io: 6 (11), 7.0%, 100,000+; 7 (s); 1961 (22,1963), 9.8%, 100,000+, In: 1,2 (s); around 1850 (32,vol.II, pt 3), 10-12%; 1865-70 (21,III), 12-20%; 1896 (33); 4,5 (5), 25,000+; 6,7 (s); 6 (11), 18.4%, 50,000+; 1956 (5), 19.1%, 50,000+, (22,1959), 21.1%, 30,000+; 1964 (5), 21.8%, 50,000+. Iq: 3,4,5,6 (s); 1947 (22,1954), 22.3%; 1956 (22,1958), 23.6%, 16.2%, 100,000+; 7 (s); 7 (30), 31.8%, 100,000+; the extremely divergent values in (5) and (30) refer to the administrative units. Is: 1948, 1962 (22, 1964). Jp: 1,2 (s); 1877 (21,VI), 7.6%; 1881 (2), 8.5%; 1889 (2); 4,5, 6 (11); 7 (5). Jo: 5 (s); 1952 (22,1955); 7 (s); 1961 (22,1966), 36.2%, 23.6%, 50,000+; 7 (5), 29.9%, 50,000+. Ko: 3, 1912, 1929 (24); 6 (11). Kp: 6 (11); 7 (s). Kr: 6 (11), 14.7%, 100,000+; 7 (s); 1966 (5), 22.7%, 100,000+. La: 6,7 (s); 7 (s); 1966 (5), 4.6%, 50,000+. Lb: 1949, 7 (5). My: (Singapore included): 4, 5 (s); Malay States (without Singapore) 4 (11), 8.3%, 5 (11), 12.2%, 1947 (11), 17.0%, 7.4%, 100,000+; 1947 (11), 17.9%, 100,000+; 7 (s); Federation of Malaya 1957 (30), 10.8%, 100,000+, pop. 1965 (30), 8,039,000, estimated rate of urbanization 1965 25.0%; Sabah and Sarawak 1960 (30), 6.0%, pop. 1965 (30), 1,364,000, estimated rate of urbanization 1965 8.0%; Singapore pop. 1965 (30), 1,913,500. Mo: 5,6,7 (s); 5 (5), 9.4%, 50,000+; 6 (5), 12.4%, 50,000+; 7 (5), 21.4%, 50,000+. OE: 1,2 (s); around 1870 (21,III), 11.5-18.2%, Europian and Asiatic Turkey; 3,4 (s); 3 (5), 9.2%, 50,000+; 4 (5), 13.1%, 50,000+. Tk: 5 (5), 25,000+; 6 (30); 7 (s); 1962 (5), 17.0%, 50,000+, (22,1964), 19 towns with 30,000-50,000 inhabitants and 11 towns with 25,000-30,000 inhabitants; the mean values are estimated at 37,000 and 27,000 respectively, therefore the resulting population figure of approx. 1 million and 3.4% respectively; 7 (5), 17.8%, 50,000+. Pk: 1951 (11), 5.2%, 100,000+; 7 (s); 7 (5), 7.9%, 100,000+. Ph: 3, 1914, 1931 (24); 6 (11), 5.1%, 100,000+; 7 (s); 1960 (22,1967), 14.2%. Sa: 7 (s); 7 (5), 14.2%, 50,000+. Sy: 4,5,6,7 (s); 1956 (22,1958,1959), 32.6%; 1961 (22,1963), 31.8%. Th: 5 (s); 6 (11); 7 (s); 1960 (22,1963), 8.8%. Vi: 6 (11). Vp: 7 (s); 1960 (24), 7.7%, 100,000+, rural pop. approx. 90%. Vr: 7 (s); 7 (30), 11.3%, 100,000+.

AFRICA

Ag: 1891, 1911, 1931 (24); 1948 (30), 10.6%, 50,000+; 7 (s); 7 (5), 18.4%, 50,000+. Ct: 1966 (22,1967). Ch: 1962 (5). Cg: 7 (s); 1964 (24), 100,000+. Eg: 1 (s); 1871 (14); 3 (33); 1907, 1927 (24); 1947 (30), 22.7%, 50,000+; 7 (s); 7 (5), 29.4%, 50,000+. Gh: 1948 (24); 7 (s); 1960 (24), 11.9%. Ic: 7 (5). Ke: 6 (s); 1962 (21,1965). Ly: 1911, 1931 (24), Tripolitania and Cyrenaica; 1951 (24); 7 (s); 1964 (30), 22.5%, 100,000+. Mg: 5,6 (s); 1960 (5), 7.8%, 25,000+; 7 (5), 25,000+. Mc: 4 (s), cf. (24); 5 (24), French region; 1951 (22,1956), 19.6%, 50,000+; 7 (s); 7 (5), 22.3%, 50,000+. Rh: British Southern Rhodesia 1950 (s), cf. (24); 1964 (24). Sg: 7 (5). SA: 1890-96 (33); 4.5 (s); for these years the figures of white urban population only are available, cf. (24); 1946 (30), 27.4%; 1951 (30); 1963 (22,1964). Tu: 4, 1931 (24); 6 (s); 1946 (30), 19.9%; 1956 (5), 20.8%; 7 (5). Ug: 6,7 (s); 1959 (22,1965), 2.9%. Za: British Northern Rhodesia 1950 (30) African population only; 7 (s); 7 (30), 10.0%, 100,000+.

OCEANIA

As: 1871, 1889 (18); 4,5,6 (5), 25,000+; 1966 (22,1967). Nz: 1871, 1889 (18); 4,5,6,7 (5).

Illiteracy (Table B)

EUROPE

Ab: 6 (29), S; in (5) a deviating value of 53.8% is given; 1955 (31), 28.5%, 9y.+; 7 (s); 1963 (5), 25.0%. AU (Austrian empire without Hungarian kingdom): 1,2 (s), adults; in source (7) an estimated rate of illiteracy of 40-45% is given for 1851; this estimate seems to be much too low, since 49% of the recruits could neither read nor write in 1870 (7,15); the rate of illiteracy of the recruits amounted in 1850 in France to 39% and in Belgium to 44%, the estimated rate of illiteracy of the adult population was 40-45% and 45-50% respectively (7); therefore, the rate of illiteracy of the adult population in Austria around 1870 has been estimated at 45-55%; since public education was started in Austria toward the end of the eighteenth century and only little evidence points at a particularly rapid development between 1850 and 1870, the rate of illiteracy for 1850 has been estimated at 55-65%; 3 (7), 10y.+; in 1880 39% of the recruits were illiterates, in 1890 only 22% (7); 4 (7), 10y.+. Au (republic): 1,2,3,4 (s), 10y.+; the rate of illiteracy around 1900 of the population of 10 and more years in the provinces Lower Austria, Upper Austria, Salzburg, Styria, Carinthia, Tyrol, and Vorarlberg amounted to 6.4% (7); the rates between 1850 and 1910 and for this area are mere estimates; 5 (s), cf. (1); 6 (29), S; 7 (s). Be: 1856 (7), S, adults; 2 (s), 10y.+; the percentage of recruits who could not read and write was: 1850 44%, 1860 39%, 1870 29% and 1880 22% (7); the rate of illiteracy of the population of 10 and more years in 1880 was 31% (7), (b); therefore the rate of illiteracy for 1870 has been estimated at 35-40%; 3 (7), 10y.+, (b); 4,5 (28); 6 (29), S; 1947 (29), 3.3%; 7 (s). Bl: 3 (s); 1893 (12), 84%, total population (?), (b); 1900 (28), 73.6%; 4 (28), 10y.+; 5 (s), 10y.+; interpolated using the values for 1926 (28), 42.9%, 10y.+, and 1934 (28), 35.1%, 10y.+; 6 (29), S; 7 (s); 1963 (5), 7.0%. Cz: 1,2,3,4 (s), 10y.+; around 1900 the rate of illiteracy of the population of 10 and more years in Bohemia, Moravia, and Austrian Silesia was 3.5% (7); the rates for the same area between 1850 and 1910 are mere estimates; for today's area of Czechoslovakia the rates of illiteracy were probably somewhat higher, since the level of education in the new Slovakian and Carpatho-Russian areas in which, in 1921, 26.5% of the population lived (21,XIV) was lower: 1921 (1), 7y.+, (b): Bohemia 2.1%, Moravia 2.6%, Silesia 3.1%, Slovakia 14.7%, Carpatho-Ukraine 50.0%; 5 (29), 10y.+; 6 (29), S; 7 (s); 1963 (5), 1.5%. Da: 1 (s), 10y.+; Prussia had the same rate in 1870 (7); in 1871 in Prussia 12% of the population of 10 and more years were illiterates; therefore the rate of illiteracy in Denmark in 1850 has been estimated at 10-15%; 2,3 (s), 10y.+; in 1881 0.36% of the recruits could not read and 1.73% could not write; 4,5 (s), 10y.+; 1921 (1), 0.1%, population in school age and above; 6 (29), S; 7 (s). EW: 1 (s), adults; source (7) gives an estimated rate of illiteracy of 30-33% for 1851; in 1851, however, 38% of the brides and bridegrooms could not sign their marriage certificates (7); in Italy in 1900 the rate of illiteracy of the brides and bridegrooms was 41% and the rate of the population of 6 and more years was 48% in 1901 (7); therefore, the rate of illiteracy of the adult population in England and Wales in 1850 has been estimated at 40-45%; 2 (s), adults; in 1870 23.5% of the brides and bridegrooms could not sign their marriage certificates (7); in France in 1872 the rate of illiteracy of the brides and bridegrooms was 29% and the rate of the population of 6 and more years 31% (7); therefore, the rate of illiteracy of the adult population in England and Wales in 1870 has been estimated at 25-30%; 3 (s), adults; in 1890 7.5% of the brides and bridegrooms were illiterates (7); therefore, the rate of illiteracy of the population has been estimated at 10-15%; 4,5 (s), adults; in 1924 only 0.34% of the brides and bridegrooms were illiterates (1); 6 (29), S; 7 (s). Es: 5 (s); interpolated using the values for 1922 (29), 11.7%, and 1934 (29), 4.1%. Fi: 1 (s), adults; no quantitative information is available on the illiteracy in Finland at that time, but as the development of primary education began in the first century after the

Reformation and the Lutheran Church made the ability to read a prerequisite for communion, marriage, and exercise of civic rights (15), it can be assumed that the rate of illiteracy in Finland around 1850 was below 30%, cf. also source (7); 2 (s), adults; a decree of 1858 obliged all rural parishes to provide school facilities; they were granted financial support by the government (15); it can be assumed, therefore, that the rate of illiteracy decreased further until 1870; compared to the rate of 1890 a percentage of less than 25% is probable; 3 (s), adults; between 1888 and 1893 5.3% of the recruits could neither read nor write (15); therefore the rate of illiteracy of the adult population has been estimated at 10-15%; 4 (28), (a); 43.6% of the population could read only; 5 (28), (a); 15% of the population could read only; 6 (29), S; 7 (s). Fr: 1 (7), S, adults; 1872 (7), 6y.+, (b); 3 (s), 10y.+; the percentage of brides and bridegrooms who could not sign their marriage certificates was 29% in 1872, 11% in 1890 and 5.5% in 1900 (7); the rate of illiteracy of the population of 10 and more years was 16.5% in 1901 (28); therefore, the rate for 1890 has been estimated with 18-22%; 1911, 1931 (28), 10y.+; 6 (29), S; 7 (s). Ge: 1 (s), adults; comparable rates of illiteracy among the recruits for the time after the foundation of the German Empire show that Prussia had a somewhat higher rate than the average (15); therefore, the rate of illiteracy of the population in the later German Empire without Alsace-Lorraine around 1850 has been estimated at 15-20% somewhat lower than for Prussia with 20% (7); source (18) gives for Germany in 1840 a rate of 18%, but it is not known on which information it is based; 2 (s), 10y.+, cf. the argumentation for 1850; 3,4,5 (s), 10y.+. Gd: 6 (29), S; 7 (s). Gf: 6 (29), S; 7 (s). Gr: 2 (s), adults; 1871 (15), 67% male illiterates, 92% female illiterates; 3 (s), adults; interpolated using the values for 1871 and 1907 (28), 8y.+; 1928 (4,28), 8y.+; 1951 (29); 7 (s); 1961 (31), 19.6%. Hu: 1 (s), 6y.+; 2 (14), 6y.+; since the Hungarian primary school system did not develop more rapidly before the second half of the nineteenth century (15), the rate of illiteracy for 1850 has been estimated at 70-80%; 3 (s), 6y.+; interpolated using the values for 1870 and 1900 (28), 38.6%; 4 (28), 6y.+; for the area of the later Hungary: rate of illiteracy in 1910: 19.7%; 5 (28), 6y.+; 1949 (29); 7 (s); 1960 (31), 3.1%; 1963 (5), 2.5%. Ir: 1851, 1871, 1891, 1911 (16), 5y.+, (a); source (16) gives the absolute figures of all persons who could neither read nor write; they were divided by the figures of the population of 5 and more years (26); the age group 0-4 has been estimated at 11%; the percentage of population who could not read and write was (16): 62.9% in 1851, 44.9% in 1871, 20.2% in 1891 and 5.6% in 1911. Ei: 5 (s), adults; in 1923 2% of the brides and bridegrooms could not sign their marriage certificates (1); 6 (29), S; 7 (s). Nl: 5 (s), adults; in 1923 2.1% of the brides and bridegrooms could not sign their marriage certificates (1); 6,7 (s). It: 1 (7), S, adults; 1871 (7), 6y.+; 1891 (s), 6y.+; interpolated using the values for 1881 (7), 62%, 6y.+, and 1901 (7), 48%, 6y.+; 1911, 1931, 1951 (29); 7 (s); 1961 (5), 8.4%. Lv: 5 (29), 10y.+, (a). Lt: 5 (s); 1923 (29), 32.0%, (a). Nl: 1 (s), 10y.+; between 1846 and 1858 only 22.8% of the recruits could neither read nor write (14); this percentage has been recorded for France around 1870, for Belgium around 1880 and for the Austrian empire around 1890 (7); in the same years the rate of illiteracy of the population of 6 or 10 and more years amounted to 31% in France, to 31% in Belgium, and to 29% in Austria (7); therefore, the rate of illiteracy for the Netherlands in 1850 has been estimated at 28-33%; 2 (s), 10y.+; in 1875 12.3% of the recruits were illiterates (1); 3 (s), 10y.+; in 1890 7.2% of the recruits could neither read nor write (15); in 1900 the rate of illiteracy of the recruits was 6% in France and 12% in Belgium, the rate of illiteracy of the population of 10 and more years was 16.5% and 26% respectively (28,7); therefore, the rate for the Netherlands in 1890 has been estimated at 15-20%; 4,5 (s), 10y.+; 5.4% of the recruits were illiterates in 1905, 0.3% in 1913 and 0.35% in 1923 (1); 6 (29), S; 7 (s). No: 1 (s), adults; since in 1739 and 1741 respectively compulsory education had been introduced in Norway and all parishes were obliged to provide schools, and since the development of the primary school system was similar to that of Sweden and Denmark (15), the rate of illiteracy for 1850 has been estimated at 10-20%, cf. also source (7); 2,3,4,5 (s), adults, cf. source (1); 6 (29), S; 7 (s). Po: 4 (s); 1921 (29), 34.9%; 1931 (29), (a), cf. source (1); 6 (29), S; 7 (s); 1960 (31), 4.7%, 14y.+. Pt: 1,3 (s), 10y.+; interpolated using the values for 1868 (15), 82%, total population, and 1900 (28), 73.4%, 10y.+, (a); 4,5 (29), 10y.+, (a); 6 (31), 10y.+; 7 (s); 1960 (31), 38.1%. Pr: 1849 (7), S, adults; 1871 (7), 10y.+. Rm: 1,2,3 (s), 7y.+; interpolated using the values for 1880 (12), 85%, 7y.+, and 1899 (29), 78.0%, 7y.+; 4 (s), 7y.+; interpolated using the values for 1899 and 1930 (29), 7y.+;

1948 (5); source (29) gives as provisional result of the census the deviating value of 23.1%; 7 (s); 1963 (5), 6.0%. Ru: 3 (s), 9y.+; since the percentage of illiterate recruits decreased between 1890 and 1897 from 68% to 58% (7) and since the educational expansion accelerated only after 1890 (10), the rate of illiteracy of the population of 9 and more years has been estimated at 80-85%; 4 (s), 9y.+; since the percentage of illiterate recruits decreased between 1890 and 1910 very rapidly: 68% in 1890, 58% in 1897, 51% in 1900, 33% in 1913 (7) and since the number of pupils in primary schools trebled: 2.3 million in 1890, 7.4 million in 1910 (10), the rate of illiteracy of the population of 9 and more years has been estimated at 50-60%; this rate amounted in 1920 in the European part of Russia without Wolhynia, Zaporojsk, Podolia, and parts of Witebsk, Tambow, Krementchuk, Poltawa, and Odessa to 59.1% (29); 5 (s), 9y.+; interpolated using the values for 1926 (8), 48.9%, 9y.+, and 1939 (8), 18.8%, 9y.+; 6 (29), S; 7 (s); 1959 (31), 1.5%, 9-49y. So: 1851 (7), S, adults; 2,3 (s), adults; in 1855 17% of the brides and bridegrooms could not sign their marriage certificates, in 1870 15% and in 1890 5.5% (7); therefore the rate of illiteracy of the adult population has been estimated at 15-20% for 1870 and at 7-12% for 1890; 4,5 (s), adults; in 1923 only 0.23% of the brides and bridegrooms were illiterates (1); 6 (29), S; 7 (s). Se: 4 (s), 7y.+; 1900 (28), 79.0%, 7y.+; 1921 (1), Northern Serbia 66%, Southern Serbia 84%, population in school-age and above, (a); since Serbia did not establish a primary school system before 1878 when it gained political independence, compulsory education was introduced in 1882 (15); the rate of illiteracy has been estimated at more than 85% for 1890 and at 75-80% for 1910. Sp: 1 (s), adults; 1857 (7), 75%, S, adults; 2 (s), 10y.+; interpolated using the values for 1860 (7), 76%, total population, 1877 (7), 72%, total population, and 1887 (7), 10y.+, 68%, total population; 4 (28), 10y.+; 5 (s), 10y.+; interpolated using the values for 1920 (28), 44.0%, 10y.+, and 1940 (28), 23.2%, 10y.+; 6 (29), 10y.+, (a); 7 (s); 1960 (31), 13.3%, sample of census results; 1963 (5), 11.0%. Sw: 1 (7), S, adults; 2,3 (s), adults in 1875 only 1% of the recruits could neither read nor write (7); therefore, the rate of illiteracy of the population has been estimated at 5-10%; 3,4 (s), adults; 5 (29); 6 (29), S; 7 (s). Sz: 1,2,3 (s), adults; in Switzerland representative data are lacking for the time before 1880; but since the ability to read and write was already widespread in the sixteenth century and since by the mid-eighteenth century practically every parish possessed a public primary school and since in 1880 only 2.5% of the recruits could neither read nor write (7), the rate of illiteracy of the population in 1850 has been estimated at 10-20%, in 1870 at 7-12% and in 1890 at 1-5%; 4,5 (s), adults; in 1906 and 1916 only 0.39% of the brides and bridegrooms could not sign their marriage certificates (1); 6 (29), S; 7 (s). Yu: 3 (s), 7y.+; 1900 (28), 59.7%, 7y.+, area of today's Yugoslavia; 4 (s), 7/12y.+; 1921 (28), 50.5%, 12y.+; 1931 (28), 11y.+; 1948 (28), 10y.+; 7 (s); 1961 (31), 19.7%, 10y.+.

THE AMERICAS

Ar: 1869 (s), adults; according to source (14) in 1869 20.7% of the total population could read and 17.9% could write; this percentage is considered overrated; however, it includes the children of preschool age; therefore, the rate of illiteracy of the adult population has been estimated at 75-80%; 3 (s), 14y.+; 1895 (28), 53.3, 14y.+; 4 (s), 14y.+; 1914 (28), 35.1%, 14y.+; 5 (s), 14y.+; interpolated using the values for 1914 and 1947 (28), 13.6%, 14y.+; 6 (29), S; 7 (s); 1960 (31), 8.6%, 14y.+, sample of census results. Bo: 5 (s); estimate using the rates of illiteracy of various age groups, census 1950 (29): 35-44y.: 71.4%, 45-54y.: 74.9%, 55-64.: 79.2%, 65y.+: 84.8%; 6 (29); 7 (s); 1962 (5), 60.0%. Br: 3 (s); 3 (1), 85.2%, total population, (a); 1900 (29), 65.3%; 4 (s); 1920 (29), 64.9%; 5 (s); 1940 (29), 56.1%; 6 (29); 7 (s); 1963 (5), 43.0%. Ca: 1,2 (s), adults; since the development of the primary school system in Canada began at the time of colonization, and had a great effect on broad population strata—in 1850 approx. 15% of the population attended public primary schools, in 1880 more than 20% (15; 32, vol. I, pt 2)—the rate of illiteracy has been estimated at less than 30% for 1850 and less than 25% for 1870; 1891 (1), 10y.+, without Indian population, (a); 4 (s), 10y.+; 1911 (28), 11.1%, 5y.+; 1931 (28), 10y.+; 6 (29), S; 7 (s); 1963 (5) 1.5%. Cl: 2 (s), 10y.+; 3 (s), 10y.+; interpolated using the values for 1885 (1), 71.1%, total population, (a), and 1895 (1), 68.1%, total population, (a); 4 (s), 10y.+; 1907 (28), 49.9%, 10y.+, (a); 5 (28), 10y.+, (a); 6 (29), S; 7 (s); 1960 (31), 16.4%; 1963 (5), 14.9%. Cm: 4 (s), 5y.+; 1918 (1), 57.6%, 5y.+, without Indian

population which accounted for approx. 3% of the total population; 1928 (29); 6
(29), S; 7 (s); 1963 (5), 42.0%. Co: 3 (s), adults; in 1886 compulsory education was
introduced (15); 4 (s); estimate using the values for 1927 (29), 34.3%, 9y.+, and the
rates of illiteracy for various age groups, census 1950 (29): 35-44y.: 22.0%, 45-54y.:
23.0%, 55-64y.: 28.4%, 65y.+: 35.7%; 5 (s), 9y.+; 6 (29); 7 (s); 1963 (31), 15.7%.
Cu: 1 (s), 10y.+; 1861 (1), 80.8%, total population, (a); 2 (s), 10y.+; 1887 (1),
72.8%, total population, (a); 3 (s), 10y.+; 1899 (28), 56.9%, 10y.+, (a); 1907 (28),
43.6%, 10y.+, (a); 4 (s), 10y.+; 1931 (28), 10y.+, (a); 6 (s); 1943 (29), 22.2%, (a);
1953 (29), 22.1%; 7 (s); 1963 (5), 21.0%. Do: 4 (s), 13y.+; 1920 (1), 70.1%, 13y.+,
(a); 5 (s); 1935 (29), 73.5%, 7 y.+; 6 (29); 7 (s); 1963 (5), 65.0%. Ec: 3 (s), adults;
since Ecuador had more pupils in primary schools per 100 inhabitants by 1890 than
Chile (15), the rate of illiteracy has been estimated at less than 85%; 4,5 (s); estimate
using the rates of illiteracy for various age groups, census 1950 (29): 35-44y.: 47.7%,
45-54y.: 50.4%, 55-64y.: 54.5%, 65y.+: 61.6%; 6 (29); 7 (s); 1962 (5), 32.7%. El:
5,6 (29); 7 (s); 1961 (31), 52.0%, 10y.+, sample of census results. Gu: 1893 (1),
88.6%, 7y.+, (a); 4 (s); 1921 (1), 86.8%, 7y.+, (a); 5 (s), 7y.+; interpolated using the
values 1921 and 1940 (29), 67.4%, 7y.+; 6 (29), 7y.+; 7 (s); 1963 (5), 65.0%. Ha: 6
(29), 89.5%; 7 (s); 1963 (5), 84.0%. Ho: 4 (s); 5 (29),(a); 6 (29), S; 1945 (29),
63.7%, (a); 7 (s); 1961 (31), 55.0%. Jc: 1 (s); 1861 (1), 68.7%, 5y.+, (a); 1871, 1891,
1911 (1), 5y.+, (a); the percentage of population of 5 and more years who could not
read and write was considerably higher; author's estimates according to source (1):
1861 86.6%, 1871 84.7%, 1891 68.1%, 1911 52.8%, 1921 47.8%; 5 (s), 5y.+;
interpolated using the values for 1921 (1), 39.1%, 5y.+, (a), and 1943 (29), 32.1%,
5y.+, 25.4%, 15y.+, (a); 6 (s), 5y.+; 7 (s); 1960 (31), 18.1%. Me: 3 (s), 10y.+; 1900
(29), 77.7%, 10y.+; 4,5 (29) 10y.+; 6 (29), 43.2%, 6y.+; 7 (s); 1960 (31), 34.6%;
1963 (5), 32.0%. Nc: 2,3 (s); since Nicaragua had more pupils in primary schools per
100 inhabitants in 1890 than Chile (15), the rate of illiteracy has been estimated at
less than 85%; 4,5 (s); estimation using the rates of illiteracy for various age groups,
census 1950 (29): 35-44y.: 62.5%, 45-54y.: 59.9%, 55-64y.: 58.6%, 65y.+: 57.8%; 6
(29); 7 (s); 1963 (31), 50.4%, sample of census results. Pa: 4,5 (s); estimate using the
rates of illiteracy for various age groups, census 1950 (29): 35-44y.: 30.1%, 45-54y.:
43.6%, 55-64y.: 48.5%, 65y.+: 53.7%, 6 (29); 7 (s); 1960 (31), 26.7%; 1963 (5),
24.5%. Pg: 4,5 (s); estimate using the rates of illiteracy for various age groups, census
1950 (29): 35-44y.: 37.1%, 45-54y.: 41.3%, 55-64y.: 53.5%, 65y.+: 63.0%; 6 (29); 7
(s); 1962 (5), 26.7%. Pe: 5 (s); 1940 (29), 57.6%; 6 (29), S; 7 (s); 1961 (31), 39.9%,
17y.+; Us: 1 (s), 10y.+; in source (6) for all whites of 20 and more years an illiteracy
rate of 11.2% is given; the estimate is based on the assumptions that the coloured
population was 100% illiterate and that the population between 10 and 20 years had
approximately the same rate of illiteracy as the population of 20 and more years;
2,3,4,5 (6), 10y.+; 6 (29), S; 7 (s); 1963 (5), 1.5%. Ur: 4,5 (s), adults; in 1920/21
11.8% of the brides and bridegrooms could not sign their marriage certificates (1); in
France the same percentage is found in 1890 and in Ireland in 1900; in these years
the rate of illiteracy of the population of 10 and more years in France was
approximately 20% and the rate of illiteracy of the total population in Ireland was
14% (a) and 21% (b) respectively; therefore, the rate of illiteracy of the adult
population in Uruguay has been estimated at 20-30% for 1910 and at 15-25% for
1930; 6 (29), S; 7 (s); 1963 (5), 9.7%. Ve: 1891 (s), 5y.+; 1891 (1), 83.0%, total
population, (b); the age group 0-4 years has been estimated with 14% of the total
population; 4 (s), 5y.+; 1926 (1), 73.5%, total population, (b); 1926 (s), 69.2%, 5y.+;
5 (s); interpolated using the values for 1926 and 1936 (29), 61.0%; 1941 (29), 58.5%,
6 (29); 7 (s); 1961 (31), 34.2%, sample of census results.

ASIA

Bm: 3 (s); 1901 (28), 70.1%; 1911, 1931 (28); 6 (29), S; 7 (s); 1963 (5), 29.0%. Cb:
6 (29), S; 7 (s); 1963 (5), 56.5%. Ce: 1891 (s), 5y.+; in 1891 63.9% of the male and
94.7% of the female population could not read and write (1); 1911 (28), 5y.+; 1921
(28), 69.0%, 5y.+; 5 (s), 5y.+; interpolated using the values for 1921 and 1946 (28),
42.2%, 5y.+; 6 (29), S; 7 (s); 1963 (5), 29.0%. Ch: 6 (29), S; 7 (s); 1963 (5), 35.0%.
Ta: 6 (s); 1956 (31), 46.1%. Ii: British India (28): 1901 93.5%, 1911 92.7%, 1921
91.4%, 1931 90.4%; 1951 (29); 7 (s); 1961 (31), 72.2%. Io: 6 (29), S; 7 (s); 1961
(31), 57.1%(?), without Western Irian. In: 1,2,3,4,5 (s); 6 (29), S; 7 (s); 1956 (31),

87.2%; 1963 (5), 66.0%(?). Iq: 4,5,6 (s); 1947 (29), 89.1%, 5y.+, (a); 7 (s); 1957
(31), 82.7%, 5y.+; 1963 (5), 83.0%. Is: 1948 (29); 7 (s); 1961 (31), 15.8%, 14y.+;
1963 (5), 15.0%. Jp: 1,1 (s), adults; although Japan did not establish a modern
national school system before 1872, the foundation for this system was laid in the
Tokugawa period; since the middle of the eighteenth century primary education
increasingly spread, and by 1870 there were already 1 million pupils (9,20);
therefore, the rate of illiteracy of the adult population has been estimated at less than
50% for 1850 and at less than 45% for 1870; according to source (12) more than half
of the Japanese population could read and write in 1854 (?); 3 (s), adults; between
1891 and 1893 22% of the recruits on the average could not read or write (15); this
percentage has been observed in France in 1868, in Belgium in 1880 and in Austria in
1890; in these years the rate of illiteracy of the population was 31% in France (6y.+),
31% in Belgium (10y.+) and 29% in Austria (10y.+); therefore the rate of illiteracy in
Japan has been estimated at 25-35% for 1890; 4 (s), adults; as the Japanese primary
school system expanded rapidly since the 80s, and around 1900 already 80% of all
children between 6 and 14 years of age attended school and in 1910 97% (1), the rate
of illiteracy has been estimated with 10-20% for 1910; 5 (s), 15y.+; estimate using
the rates of illiteracy for various age groups, sample survey 1948 (29): 30-34y.: 0.5%,
35-39y.: 0.5%, 40-44y.: 0.7%, 45-49y.: 2.0%, 50-54y.: 3.2%, 55-59y.: 7.7%, 60-64.:
16.8%; in 1925 only 0.88% of the recruits could neither read nor write (1); 6 (29), S;
7 (s); 1963 (5), 1.5%. Jo: 5 (s); 6 (29), S; 7 (s); 1961 (31), 67.6%. Ko: 5 (29); 6 (s);
source (29) gives the improbable estimation of 60-65%; Korean People's Republic
1956 (5), 30.0%; Korean Republic 1955 (5), 31.0%; source (31) gives for 1955 the
deviating value of 23.2%, but 29.4% for 1960. Kp: 7 (s); 1963 (5), 25.0%. Kr: 7 (s);
1963 (5), 29.0%. La: 6 (29), S; 7 (s); 1963 (5), 78.0%. Lb: 6 (29), S; 7 (s); 1963 (5),
45.0%. My (Singapore included): 4 (s); 1921 (1), 57.6%, 5y.+, urban population in
the Strait Settlements, the federated Malay States, Jahore and Kelanta with 883,000
inhabitants; total population of British Malaya: 3,358,000; assuming that the rural
population not covered was 100% illiterate, the rate of illiteracy would amount to
86.5%, assuming 90% and 80% illiterates respectively it would amount to 79.6% and
72.6% respectively; therefore, the rate of illiteracy has been estimated at 70-85% for
1921 and at 75-85% for 1910; 1931 (29); 6 (s); Federation of Malaya 1950 (29), S,
60-65%; Singapore 1950 (29), S, 50-55%; 7 (s); Federation of Malaya 1957 (31),
53.0%; Sabah 1960 (31), 76.5%; Sarawak 1960 (31), 78.5%; Singapore 1957 (31),
50.2%; Malaysia 1963 (5), 48.0%. Mo: 6,7 (s); there are extremely divergent rates of
illiteracy available on Mongolia: (5): 1950 82.5%, 1963 80.8%; (29): 1950 40-45%;
(31): 1956 4.6%, 9-50y.; the author's estimates refer to (29) and (31). OE: 1,2,3,4
(s). Tk: 5 (s); 1935 (29), 81.3%; 6 (29); 7 (s); 1960 (31), 61.9%; 1963 (5), 60.5%.
Pk: 6 (29), S; 1951 (29), 86.1%, total population; 7 (s); 1961 (31), 81.2%. Ph: 4 (s);
1918 (1), 50.8%, 10y.+, native Christian population, about 90% of the total
population, (a); 1921(?) (1), 63%, S; 5 (s); estimate using the value of 1939 (29),
52.3%, and the rates of illiteracy for various age groups, census 1948 (29): 35-44y.:
42.7%, 45-54y.: 56.0%, 55-64y.: 67.2%, 65y.+: 77.8%; 6 (29), S; 1948 (29), 40.0%;
7 (s); 1960 (31), 28.1%; 1963 (5), 22.0%. Sa: 7 (s); 1963 (5), 97.0%. Sy: 6 (29), S; 7
(s); 1960 (31), 64.4%, 10y.+, without Bedouin population, about 7.5% of the total
population; 1963 (5), 63.4%. Th: since the primary school system developed only
after the school law of 1923 (1), the rate of illiteracy has been estimated at more
than 85% for 1910; 5 (s); estimate using the value of 1937 (29), 68.8, and the rates
of illiteracy for various age groups, census 1947 (29): 25-34y.: 46.0%, 35-44y.:
59.1%, 45-54y.: 68.5%, 55-64y.: 73.1%, 65y.+: 77.5%; 6 (29), S; 1947 (29), 48.0%;
7 (s); 1960 (31), 32.3%; 1963 (5), 30.0%. Vi: 6 (29), S. Vp: 7 (s); 1960 (31), 35.5%,
12y.+; 1963 (5), 35.0%. Vr: 7 (s); 1963 (5), 75.0%.

AFRICA

Ag: 3,4,5 (s); 1948 (31), 10y.+; 7 (s); 1963 (5), 79.0%. Ct: 7 (s); 1963 (5), 77.0%.
Cd: 7 (s); 1963 (5), 82.0%. Cg: source (29) gives the improbable estimation of
60-65%; 7 (s); 1963 (5), 83.0%. Eg: 1,2,3,4,5 (s); 1907 (29), 92.8%; 1927 (29),
86.6%; 1937 (29), 86.6%; 1947 (29); 7 (s); 1963 (5), 72.4%. Gh: 6 (29), S; 7 (s);
1963 (5), 72.0%. Ic: 7 (s); 1963 (5), 92.0%. Ke: 6 (29), S; 7 (s); 1963 (5), 75.0%. Ly:

4,5,6 (s); 1954 (22,1968), 78.5%; 1964 (22,1968). Mg: 6 (29), S; 1953 (29), 66.5%, 14y.+, sample survey; 7 (s); 1963 (5), 63.0%. Mc: 3,4,5,6,7 (s); 1960 (31), 86.2%, sample of census results. Rh: 6 (29), S; 7 (s). Sg: 7 (s); 1960/61 (31), 94.4% SA: 3 (s); 1904 (28), 65.4%; 1911 (28); 5 (s); estimate using values calculated according to source (28): rate of illiteracy of the white and Bantu population (about 90% of the total population) 1921 66.1%, 1946 54.9%; the rate of illiteracy of the white population of 10 and more years was 2.1% in 1918 and has been estimated at 2% for 1921 and 1946; white population 1921: 1,519,000 (24) and 1946: 2,372,000 (24); the age group 0-9 years has been estimated at 22%; rate of illiteracy of the total Bantu population 1921: 90.3%, and of the Bantu population of 10 and more years 1946: 72.4%; Bantu population 1921: 4,697,000; the age groups 0-4 and 5-9 years have been estimated at 14% and 13% respectively, the corresponding rates of illiteracy at 100% and 90%; 6 (29), S; 7 (s); 1963 (5), 55.0%. Tu: 4,5 (s); 6 (29), S; 7 (s); 1956 (31), 84.2%, 10y.+, sample of census results; 1963 (5), 83.0%. Ug: 6 (29), S; 7 (s); 1963 (5), 71.0%. Za: 6 (29), S; 7 (s).

OCEANIA

As: 1871, 1891, 1911 (s), 5y.+, (a); 1871 (1), total population, 26.9%, (a), 37.6%, (b); 1891 (1), total population, 21.1%, (a), 15.4%, (b); 1911 (1), total population, 15.0%, (a), 15.4%, (b); the age group 0-4 years has been estimated with 11%; 5,6,7 (s). Nz: 1874, 1891, 1911 (1), 5y.+, (a); 1874 (1), 17.2%, 5y.+, (b); 1891 (1), 10.7%, 5y.+, (b); 1911 (1), 5.8%, 5y.+, (b); 5,6,7 (s).

LIST OF COUNTRIES

1	Ab	Albania	54	Ke	Kenya
2	Ag	Algeria	55	Ko	Korea
3	Ar	Argentina	56	Kp	Korean People's Rep.
4	As	Australia	57	Kr	Korean Rep.
5	AU	Austria (Empire)	58	La	Laos
6	Au	Austria (Republic)	59	Lv	Latvia
7	Be	Belgium	60	Lb	Lebanon
8	Bo	Bolivia	61	Ly	Libya
9	Br	Brazil	62	Lt	Lithuania
10	Bl	Bulgaria	63	Mg	Madagascar
11	Bm	Burma	64	My	Malaysia
12	Cb	Cambodia	65	Me	Mexico
13	Ca	Canada	66	Mo	Mongolia
14	Ct	Central Afr. Rep.	67	Mc	Morocco
15	Ce	Ceylon	68	Nl	Netherlands
16	Cd	Chad	69	Nz	New Zealand
17	Cl	Chile	70	Nc	Nicaragua
18	Ch	China	71	NI	Northern Ireland
19	Cm	Columbia	72	No	Norway
20	Cg	Congo (Kinshasa)	73	OE	Ottoman Empire
21	Co	Costa Rica	74	Pk	Pakistan
22	Cu	Cuba	75	Pa	Panama
23	Cz	Czechoslovakia	76	Pg	Paraguay
24	Da	Denmark	77	Pe	Peru
25	Do	Dominican Rep.	78	Ph	Philippines
26	Ec	Ecuador	79	Po	Poland
27	Eg	Egypt	80	Pt	Portugal
28	Ei	Eire	81	Pr	Prussia
29	El	El Salvador	82	Rh	Rhodesia
30	EW	England and Wales	83	Rm	Rumania
31	Es	Estonia	84	Ru	Russia
32	Fi	Finland	85	Sa	Saudi Arabia
33	Fr	France	86	So	Scotland
34	Ge	Germany	87	Sg	Senegal
35	Gd	GDR	88	Se	Serbia
36	Gf	GFR	89	Sp	Spain
37	Gh	Ghana	90	SA	South Africa
38	Gr	Greece	91	Sw	Sweden
39	Gu	Guatemala	92	Sz	Switzerland
40	Ha	Haiti	93	Sy	Syria
41	Ho	Honduras	94	Ta	Taiwan
42	Hu	Hungary	95	Th	Thailand
43	Ii	India	96	Tu	Tunisia
44	Io	Indonesia	97	Tk	Turkey
45	In	Iran	98	Ug	Uganda
46	Iq	Iraq	99	Us	United States
47	Ir	Ireland	100	Ur	Uruguay
48	Is	Israel	101	Ve	Venezuela
49	It	Italy	102	Vi	Vietnam
50	Iv	Ivory Coast	103	Vp	Vietnam People's Rep.
51	Jc	Jamaica	104	Vr	Vietnam Rep.
52	Jp	Japan	105	Yu	Yugoslavia
53	Jo	Jordan	106	Za	Zambia

Sources for Appendix Tables

(1) Abel, J. F. and N. J. Bond, Illiteracy in the Several Countries of the World, Washington, D.C., Department of the Interior, Bureau of Education, Bulletin No. 4, 1929.
(2) Almanach de Gotha, 1850-.
(3) Annuaire Statistique de la France, Résumé Retrospectif, Paris, 1966.
(4) Apercu de la Démographie des Divers Pays du Monde, La Haye, L'Office Permanent de l'Institut International de Statistique, Van Stockum & Fils, 1925 and 1930.
(5) Banks A. S., Cross-Polity Time-Series Data, Cambridge, MIT Press, 1971.
(6) Bowden W.; M. Karpovich; and A. P. Usher, An Economic History of Europe Since 1750, New York, 1937.
(7) Cipolla, C. M., Literacy and Development in the West, London, Penguin Books, 1969.
(8) DeWitt, N., Education and Professional Employment in the U.S.S.R., Washington, D.C., National Science Foundation, 1961.
(9) Dore, R. P., Education in Tokugawa Japan, London, 1965.
(10) Hans, N., History of Russian Educational Policy (1701-1917), New York, Russell & Russell, 1964.
(11) Hauser, P. M., Urbanization in Asia and the Far East, Calcutta, UNESCO, 1957.
(12) Hickmann, L.; M. Baumann; F. Borschitzky; and V. Zwilling, "Das Volksschulwesen in den Ubrigen Culturstaaten der Erde," in der Sonderausstellungs-Commission "Jugendhalle," Zur Geschicte und Statistik des Volksschulwesens im In- und Auslande, Vienna, Verlag der Sonderausstellungs-Commission "Jugendhalle," 1898.
(13) Historical Statistics of the United States-Colonial Times to 1957, Washington, D.C., 1961.
(14) Kolb, G. F., Handbuch der Vergleichenden Statistik, Leipzig, Arthur Felix, 1875.
(15) Levasseur, E., L'Enseignement Primaire dans les Pays Civilisés, Paris, Berger-Lerraut, 1897.
(16) MacElligott, T. J., Education in Ireland, Dublin, Institute of Public Administration, 1966.
(17) Mitchell, B. R., Abstract of British Historical Statistics, Cambridge, Cambridge University Press, 1962.
(18) Mulhall, M. G., The Dictionary of Statistics, London, 1899.
(19) Naroolnoc Chozjajstvo, SSR (Volkswirtschaft der UdSSR), Moscow, 1968.
(20) Passin, H., Society and Education in Japan, New York, Columbia University Press, 1965.
(21) Wagner, H. and A. Supan, Die Bevölkerung der Erde, I-XIV, supplements to A. Petermann (ed.) Mitteilungen aus Justus Perthes'Geographischer Anstalt, Gotha, 1872-1931.
(22) Petermann's Geographische Mitteilungen, Gotha/Leipzig, 1946-.
(23) Selegen, G. V., "The First Report on the Recent Population Census in the Soviet Union," Population Studies, Vol. 14, 1960, pp. 17-27.
(24) Statesman's Yearbook, The, London, 1864-.
(25) Statistisches Jahrbuch für die Bundesrepublik Deutschland, Stuttgart.
(26) Statistisches Jahrbuch für die Deutsche Demokratische Republik, Ost-Berlin.
(27) Statistisches Jahrbuch für das Deutsche Reich, Berlin, 1880-1941/42.
(28) UNESCO, Progress of Literacy in Various Countries, Paris, 1953.
(29) UNESCO, World Illiteracy at Mid-Century, Paris, 1957.
(30) United Nations, Demographic Yearbook, New York, 1948-.
(31) United Nations, Statistical Yearbook, New York, 1948-.
(32) Wäppaus, J. E., Handbuch der Geographie und Statistik, Vol. I, pt 2, Nord-Amerika, Leipzig, Verlag der Hinrichs' schen Buchhandlung, 1855; Vol. II, pt 3, Asien, Leipzig, 1864; Vol. III, pt 1, Ost- und Nordeuropa, Leipzig 1858-63; Vol. III, pt 2, West-und Südeuropa, Leipzig 1862-71; Vol. IV, pt 1, Osterreich, Leipzig, 1861; Vol. IV, pt 2, Das Königreich Preussen und die Deutschen Mittel- und Kleinstaaten, Leipzig, 1864.
(33) Weber, A. F., The Growth of Cities in the Nineteenth Century, Ithaca, N.Y., Cornell University Press, 1967.

CHAPTER 8

INDIVIDUAL NEEDS, SOCIAL STRUCTURES, AND INDICATORS OF NATIONAL DEVELOPMENT

Erik Allardt

ERIK ALLARDT is Research Professor of Sociology at the University of Helsinki. He has carried out extensive research on social structure and politics in Finland and has taken an active part in international collaborative ventures. He is currently engaged in a comparative sample survey of welfare and marginality in the four Nordic countries: Denmark, Finland, Norway, and Sweden.

The social indicator movement has markedly increased the collection of measures of national development. For most governmental and semi-governmental agencies, indicator data are a stimulus to theory generation and are therefore useful to policy-makers.[1] Current work on indicators demonstrates a growing responsiveness to social needs, not only by governments but also among social scientists, and therefore is a welcome development. However, the demands for easy applicability, high accessibility, and speed in obtaining information tend to divorce these operations from ongoing sociological and politological theorizing. In this way, the work on indicators tends to proceed in too great isolation from the existing body of findings and theoretical propositions.

There are, perhaps, even more serious drawbacks. Related to the atheoretical nature of much work on social indicators is a focus on accessible quantitative information. This focus can lead not only to neglect of theoretically interesting problems but to an exclusive focus on existing social structures. By basing the selection of indicators on theoretical frames of reference it may become possible to point not only toward new policy options but toward new possibilities for societal development.

This chapter attempts to relate some of the objectives of social indicators to sociological distinctions and theory. Although definitely worthwhile, trying to operationalize all variables suggested, in some cases, may be hard to do quantitatively in terms of existing statistical data and time series. As indicated above, it is less fruitful and perhaps even misleading to establish profiles of national development exclusively on the basis of existing time series: sole reliance on existing statistics may lead to questionable conservative bias. Also vested interests may be at work in the production of statistics, or in neglecting to produce certain kinds of statistics.

There are also practical reasons for attempting to select indicators on the basis of a theoretically grounded frame of reference. The application of a theoretical scheme permits economy in selecting indicators of national development. Modern computer facilities make it possible to shop around for indicators from all kinds of statistical sources. Small research outfits and individuals do not always have these resources. The scheme presented here was originally devised as one possible point of departure for a small-scale comparison of the Scandinavian countries.

BASIC CATEGORIES OF NATIONS AS SYSTEMS

The scheme for selecting indicators of comparative national development will be presented in the form of a 4x5 table obtained by cross-classifying two kinds of categories. The first set of categories will be called "elements of society," and the second set "goal dimensions."

The point of departure is a notion of national societies as systems in which there are "inputs" and "outputs."[2]

The inputs consist of the allocations of resources societies make for the economy, for the security of members, for socialization, welfare, and the like. The first societal element is thus labeled "societal allocations." The outputs of a society consist of goals actually attained. Outputs and goals, however, can be assessed in various ways. This author takes the conscious and deliberate stand that outputs have to be assessed in terms of the needs of "individuals." The work on indicators of national development must be seen as part of a significant effort to offer guidelines for social policy. Indicators bear on incentives to action. Under such circumstances a systematic consideration of individual needs becomes all the more important. The second element of a society is therefore called "individual goals."

Nevertheless it is a fact that many allocations in existing societies are made to the fulfillment of societal goals such as economic growth, modernization, and increase in political participation. There is hardly any one-to-one correspondence between individual and societal goals, but the latter may be viewed as a means to attain the former. Our third element is, then, "societal goals."

In recent discussions it often has been pointed out that it is difficult to combine a structural and an institutional approach in the study of societies. In Etzioni's terminology, there are approaches stressing "ongoing change" as more or less blind outcomes of factors in the social structure, as well as approaches concerned with "guided change" as the results of the planning and cybernatorial capacities of societies.[3] Here, ideas from both traditions are to be incorporated in the classificatory scheme. Societies cannot be described in terms of inputs-outputs or allocations-goals only. They also have a social structure, and some structural dimensions ought to be included among the elements of society. There are many kinds of structural dimensions but two very basic patterns in the structure of any society are differentiation on one hand, and conformity on the other.[4] Our fourth element is differentiation, and it displays itself in division of labor, administrative differentiation, amount of communication, and so on. The fifth element consists of structural properties exerting pressures toward conformity. Such pressures exist in forms such as ascriptive solidarities, centralized power, and inequalities on the basis of social class.

National societies are thus envisaged as systems in which societal allocations are inputs. The inputs pass through the social structure, described in terms of the degree of differentiation and the pressures toward uniformity, and result in outputs that can be assessed in terms of societal and individual goals. The five elements of society can thus be presented in the following order: societal allocations (inputs), differentiation, pressures toward conformity, societal goals, and individual goals.

SOCIETAL GOAL DIMENSIONS

Here, the goal dimensions are constructed with two considerations in mind. They should somehow correspond to the basic needs of individuals, but they should also be related to those institutional arrangements by which societies show responsiveness to individual needs. Since the point of departure is that goals ought to be assessed in terms of the basic needs of the individuals, a classification of basic needs is required. Abram Maslow's well-known classification of needs is used for several reasons:[5] (1) the

TABLE 1
ELEMENTS OF SOCEITY

Goal Dimensions	Societal Allocations	Differentiation	Pressures Toward Conformity	Societal Goals	Individual Goals
Economy	Investments for economy and social policy	Technological differentiation (division of labor)	Equality-inequality (Class)	Economic prosperity and growth	Satisfaction of physiological needs
Force	Investments for the political system, defense, diplomacy, and the legal order	Administrative differentiation	Centralization-decentralization (Political power)	Political efficiency	Satisfaction of safety needs
Integrative Subsystems	Investments for family, religion, the associational network, and social relief	Differentiation according to groups of different kinds (religion, region ethnicity, etc.)	Strength of ascriptive roles (Status)	Political participation	Satisfaction of needs for belonging and esteem
Knowledge	Investments for education, artistic production, and play	Differentiation of communication patterns	Hegemony-diversity	Modernization (= the use of knowledge in planning)	Satisfaction of needs for self-actualization

needs listed by Maslow are basic in the sense that they cannot be reduced to each other; (2) Maslow's classification of needs in terms of a hierarchy of prepotency indicates, in contrast to other motivational theories, how needs are interrelated in a dynamic fashion; and (3) Maslow's need classification is formulated in such a fashion that it becomes possible to discuss the responsiveness of society to the basic needs. There are institutions related to man's basic physiological needs (economy), to his safety needs (force), to his social needs for belonging and esteem (subsystems of integration), and to his needs for self-actualization (knowledge). The goal dimensions roughly corresponding to both basic needs and institutions responding to them will be labeled "economy," "force," "integrative subsystems," and "knowledge." These terms are not precisely defined, but it should be noted that they are listed with the point of departure in Maslow's categorization of basic needs. Thus, knowledge does not only refer to technical, instrumental knowledge but also to the expressive, artistic, and spontaneous play with symbols. Economy does not refer only to the maintenance of basic production but to all economic arrangements pertinent to the satisfaction of men's basic physiological needs.

The classification of goal dimensions resembles other similar classifications. Thus, Stein Rokkan discusses nation-building processes with the point of departure in four dimensions: economy, force, culture, and law.[6] In this chapter, law is included under the heading of force, and knowledge, being a central factor in modern development, is introduced as a separate category.

When cross-classifying the elements of society and the goal dimensions, the list of theoretical variables shown in Table 1 is obtained.

SOCIETAL PROCESSES

Although in the first place the scheme presented in Table 1 should be looked upon as a system for selecting variables for comparative national development, it is devised under the assumption that it enables a study of societal and political processes. Some assumptions of processes are by definition already built into the model. It is assumed that there is a production process in society transforming inputs into outputs. Likewise, there is a process in the opposite direction converging outputs into inputs. Outputs satisfying the needs of individuals, such as the production of goods, education, and so on, become in the next stage inputs which are processed anew through the system. Other processes have to be studied empirically.

Of course an infinite number of feedback processes occurs, and it will take much work to distinguish the most important of them. The assumption is that the crucial feedback processes can be described with a point of departure being in the frustration of the basic needs. These frustrations will have different effects under different structural conditions, and they will affect both the inputs and the structural properties. Some feedback processes are of a rather uncomplicated nature and will affect mainly the inputs or the societal allocations. In times when national safety is threatened, there usually will be relatively more allocations to defense than to other goal dimensions, but in such situations, solutions may also be found in peace-creating activities. In any case, the most complicated and the most interesting feedback processes are those which produce changes in the patterns of differentiation and the degree of pressures toward conformity, but they remain to be studied and worked out.

One final comment about developmental processes should be made. Developmental models are often designed in such a fashion that some stages are considered to be final stages or at least the most advanced states of development. Such is not the case here. Although it may be assumed that a state of self-actualization is an ultimate individual goal, no single box in the table stands alone for the good of society or for the society worth striving to achieve. The aim is satisfaction of needs of individuals, and this aim may be approached under different combinations of conditions. For instance, depending on other factors, basic needs may be best satisfied under different degrees of centralization-decentralization. It should be noted that in Maslow's theory the need for self-actualization comes into the foreground only if the other hierarchically lower needs are satisfied. This condition is also one of the definitive advantages of the Maslowian classification. It focuses on the total man. Used with the notion of responsiveness of institutions, it discourages advocacy of too simplistic societal solutions.

THE INDICATORS

The two categories, elements of society and goal dimensions, are not defined so precisely that the theoretical variables indicated in Table 1 can be said to derive from the basic dimensions alone. It is obvious that additional considerations have influenced the labeling of the theoretical variables. It is, therefore, appropriate to make some additional comments about the indicators suggested. An important consideration on all counts is that the variables suggested are relevant for studying either the fulfillment of individual needs or the effects of frustration of these needs on central political and nation-building processes.

Societal Allocations

The societal allocations can to some extent be assessed through allocations in the budgets of the national states. The allocations in the economic realm are not measured only through capital investments for production but also through budget allocations in the field of social policy, such as measures against unemployment, pension plans, and the like. The societal allocations cannot be studied solely through state budgets; private investments also should be accounted for. In the realm of allocations for integrative subsystems, many societal allocations can hardly be measured in terms of money alone.

Differentiation

According to several master theories of societal change, division of labor is a central fact in society. The pattern of differentiation in a society is sometimes treated as a single major variable, but it seems crucial to distinguish between different kinds of differentiation. In several developmental models, such as Rokkan's model on nation-building, differentiation in different realms defines the phases of development.[7] Here, we distinguish between technological differentiation (division of labor), administrative differentiation, differentiation of integrative subsystems based on ascription (religion, region), and differentiation of communication patterns.

Pressures Toward Conformity

Pressures toward conformity always indicate that there are strong social norms that are strictly enforced. Such pressures always relate to power, but power can be exerted by various means and through various sanctions. On the macro-sociological level, some of the most important forms of pressure toward uniformity are based upon inequality of an economic and political kind. The traditional Weberian division into class, party, and status stands for important variations in the kind of pressures exerted. This division has here been supplemented by a fourth kind of pressure, labeled "hegemony." The term hegemony has been frequently used in the New Left critique of capitalist society, meaning that despite formal rights to free expression, the socializing agencies display and enforce norms of only a certain kind, and/or meaning that one kind of ideology or outlook completely dominates all important communications media. Irrespective of the merit of this particular critique of capitalist society, that hegemony apparently stands for one important kind of pressure toward conformity on the macro-level. Strong hegemony can be said to have prevailed in many religiously based state formations such as that in Calvin's Geneva. It seems obvious that a state of hegemony can exist and be enforced in modern states in which, despite rights to free expression, governments or powerful groups can dominate the communications content through major access to communication channels.

Societal Goals

The goals distinguished according to the scheme presented here are economic growth, political efficiency, political participation, and modernization. Political efficiency refers here mainly to arrangements for and responsiveness to the feelings of safety of the citizens. Also, the term modernization has been given a meaning more specific than usually has been the case. Modernization is related to the application of knowledge, and more specifically, modernization indicates the adaptation of institutions to changing functions based on a systematic use of increasing knowledge.[8]

Individual Goals

In recent discussion of the nature of "level of living," the definition of this concept has been based on the concept of "need." Thus, for instance, in a report by UNRISD, the level of living was defined as "the level of satisfaction of the needs of the population assured by the flow of goods and services enjoyed in a unit of time."[9] In a OECD report, the level of living was defined as "the extent to which all the overall needs of the population are satisfied."[10] Such a definition has been criticized on the grounds that a level of living concept based on needs overemphasizes man as a passive consumer. An alternative general definition defines the level of living in terms of "command of resources." An individual's level of living is defined by his command of money, ownership, energy, security, and social relations by which he can master his own conditions of living. Such a definition has been suggested by Titmuss,[11] and it has been used by the Swedish Commission for the study of low-income groups.[12] However, it seems important on the theoretical level to stress the satisfaction of needs as the ultimate goal whereas command of resources, of course, is a central means to attain this goal. When needs are operationalized for comparisons on the macro-level, it is often necessary to use command of resources as the operational measure.

The Swedish Commission for the study of low income groups, which has been commendably and unusually explicit in stating its premises, stresses as its point of departure a notion of "bad conditions" in contrast to a notion of "the good society." It is said that politicians and decision-makers can agree at least to some extent on what constitutes "bad conditions," whereas their views concerning the good society are strongly divergent.[13] Certainly the same argument applies largely to the reports prepared by UNRISD. However, it should be noted that the distinction between bad conditions and the good society does not appear relevant when needs form the point of departure. The goal is to satisfy the individual needs, and a good society does so, but there are hardly any other ways to study need fulfillment than by relating needs to frustrations, and accordingly, to bad conditions. Lists of basic needs have often been criticized by stating that needs are created by society or by saying that needs are culturally defined, and that the level of optimal need satisfaction consequently varies from time to time. This is, in fact, the reason why an assessment of needs and their fulfillment have to be put in a system analysis frame of reference. Needs, their satisfaction and frustration, have to be studied through the feedbacks produced by different kinds of societal arrangements and allocations. This requirement is another reason why the work on indicators or the formulation of national goals have to be put in a theoretical framework relating different kinds of phenomena to each other. A level of need satisfaction defined once and for all has hardly any specific meaning.

SUGGESTIONS OF VARIABLES

It was stated in the beginning of this chapter that it might not be possible to find quantitative measures for all the theoretical indicators in existing statistical sources. It was also pointed out that this problem is not only a liability but an asset as well. Nevertheless, the suggestions are made with some existing statistical sources or some possibilities in mind. Some of the variables are found either in Russett's world handbook[14] or in the Zapf-Flora collection of indicators of national development.[15] In this context, the latter is a more important source since it gives the data in the form of time series, whereas the former gives only one set of values per indicator. These two sources will be noted in brackets if the variables suggested are to be found in them.

There is today a wealth of files of indicators and time series describing national development.[16] Some of the variables listed here may be found in these sources. It is nevertheless a fact that many variables, important on both theoretical and political grounds, are missing from existing files. With this fact in mind, we may make some very tentative suggestions in the form of a list of variables.

SOCIETAL ALLOCATIONS

Economy:

- Capital investments
- Total population (Zapf/Flora, Russett)
- Wage and salary earners in proportion to working-age population (Russett)
- Expenditure of central and local government on social security in percentage of all expenditures (partly in Russett)
- Production of electric energy (Zapf/Flora)

FORCE

- Expenditure on defense in percentage of GNP (Russett)
- Military forces (Zapf/Flora)
- Central government expenditure in percent of GNP (Russett)
- Expenditure on police forces and internal order
- Index of diplomatic representativeness (Zapf/Flora)

INTEGRATIVE SUBSYSTEMS

- Expenditures of local government in comparison with central government
- Number of voluntary associations
- Expenditure of central government toward the support of voluntary associations
- The expenditures of religious bodies
- Marriages per 1,000 population aged 15-44 (Russett)
- Average size of household

KNOWLEDGE

- National expenditure on education
- National expenditure for higher education

- Students enrolled in higher education (Russett)
- Government expenditure for libraries
- (a measure of societal allocations for facilities in sports)
- (a measure of societal allocations for art, painting, sculpture, traditional handicraft, music, theatre, literature)

DIFFERENTIATION

Technological differentiation:

- Labor force in agriculture (Zapf/Flora, Russett)
- Labor force in tertiary sector (Zapf/Flora)
- Percentage of population in cities (Zapf/Flora, Russett)

Administrative differentiation:

- Number of civil servants
- Revenue of central government as a percentage of GNP (Russett)
- Degrees in social science in percentage of all academic degrees

Differentiation according to integrative subsystems:

- Number of individuals of other race or language than dominant population (partly in Russett)
- Number of religious bodies with one percent or more of total population
- Number of votes for religious, regional, racial, or linguistic parties (partly in Russett)

Differentiation of communication patterns:

- Numbers of letters sent per capita (Zapf/Flora, Russett)
- Number of newspapers per 10,000 of population
- Daily newspaper circulation per 1,000 population (Russett)

PRESSURES TOWARD UNIFORMITY

Inequality of class:

- Distribution of agricultural land (Russett)
- Distribution of income (Russett)
- Distribution of ownership of nonagricultural means of production

Political power:

- Exchange in positions of cabinet ministers (Zapf/Flora)
- Number of members in parliament from other than the largest party
- Number of political prisoners in proportion to total population (Russett)

Status:

- Proportion of civil servants appointed for life
- Number of decorations and honorary titles given by the central government
- Female wage and salary earners as a percentage of working-age population (Russett)

Hegemony:

- Proportion of newspapers not controlled by the largest political party
- Daily newspaper circulation–proportions controlled by socialist and bourgeois parties
- (some measure of governmental influence in television and broadcasting)

SOCIETAL GOALS

Economic prosperity and growth:

- Gross national product per capita (Zapf/Flora, Russett)
- Annual growth of GNP per capita (Russett)
- Unemployed as percentage of working-age population (Russett)

Political efficiency:

- Index of internal disturbances (Zapf/Flora)
- Total major crimes in proportion to population
- By strikes, lost working days (Zapf/Flora)

Political participation:

- Votes in national elections as a percentage of voting-age population (Russett)
- Some measures of regional differences in voting participation
- (some measure of worker's participation in management)

Modernization:

- Cutright welfare index
- Number of new industries
- Number of new disciplines (departments, chairs) at the universities per annum

INDIVIDUAL GOALS

Physiological needs:

- Private consumption as a percentage of GNP (Russett)
- (existence of substandard housing)
- (number of poor by some standard, or some measure of the nutritional level)

Safety needs:

- Inhabitants per physician (Russett)
- Number of people killed, assaulted, or robbed
- Life expectancy (Russett)

Needs for belonging and esteem:

- Number of politically prohibited organizations
- Proportion of schools based on religion or language other than those of dominant group
- (some measure of the number of isolated individuals)

Needs for self-actualization[17] (hard to find any adequate measures):

- Proportion of young people in each age class graduating from high school (as education supposedly increases possibilities for self-actualization)
- (some measure of alienation or the absence of alienation)
- (some measure of freedom to choose among jobs available)

It seems, of course, somewhat presumptious to present such a list of variables without presenting actual data. On the other hand, in the course of the process of suggesting variables, it becomes obvious that many important problems and realms seldom are covered in the work on national indicators. The variables suggested here are only to be considered as some examples indicating possibilities of an operationalization of the theoretical indicators. Some of the variables are not very well fitted to the theoretical indicators, and in some cases it has not been possible to suggest adequate operationalizations on the basis of existing data. It can hardly be overstressed that the work on national indicators should not only apply existing statistics but should also address itself to a redirection of the production of statistical data. Statistical information on the need satisfaction of individuals, on one hand, and to their frustrations and sufferings on the other, can certainly be made available to a much higher degree than hitherto has been the case.

This chapter is a very preliminary and sketchy attempt to stress some objectives in the work on indicators of national development. These objectives can be restated as follows:

(1) It appears important to select indicators on the basis of systematic and explicit theoretical schemes.

(2) A systems theoretical approach seems to be fruitful in the theoretical groundwork for selecting indicators.

(3) It is important to try to combine an institutional approach (societies are systems with inputs aiming at certain outputs) with a structural approach (societies have more or less distinct structures).

(4) It seems fruitful to try to account for both societal and individual goals in aiming at finding indicators.

(5) In order to be able to inquire into the responsiveness of societies, it is fruitful to define individual goals in terms of basic human needs. Human needs, however, cannot be assessed once and for all.

To a large extent, needs are both created by the society and culturally defined meaning that the satisfaction and frustration of needs have to be studied in a systematic context in which societal feedback processes are considered. Thus, a study of needs as individual goals presupposes a theoretical frame by which feedback processes can be analyzed.

NOTES

1. In "The Market for Policy Indicators," Richard Rose has analyzed the relationship between the production of indicators and their utility for policy-makers; see his paper for the British SSRC Conference on Social Indicators, April 1971.

2. The author has been influenced by Jerald Hage (Department of Sociology, University of Wisconsin) who in several unpublished papers has discussed his work toward a system analysis of societies. The indicators chosen are different from Hage's, and most of the systems-theoretical implications are not important here, but Hage's nevertheless have been an important source of stimulation.

3. Amitai Etzioni, "Toward a Macrosociology," in J. C. McKinney and E. A. Tiryakin (eds.) Theoretical Sociology, New York: Appleton-Century-Crofts, 1970, pp. 76-77.

4. Erik Allardt, "Types of Protests and Alienation," in E. Allardt and S. Rokkan (eds.), Mass Politics (New York: Free Press, 1970) pp. 45-49.

5. Abraham Maslow, "A Theory of Human Motivation," Psychological Review, Vol. 50, 1943, pp. 370-96.

6. Stein Rokkan, "Dimensions of State Formation and Nation-Building: A Possible Paradigm for Research on Variations Within Europe" (mimeo), 1971, in C. Tilly (ed.) The Formation of National States in Western Europe, Princeton, Princeton University Press, forthcoming, 1973.

7. Ibid.

8. C. E. Black, The Dynamics of Modernization, New York, Harper & Row, 1966.

9. The Level of Living Index, UNRISD, IWP/66/3.

10. Measurement of Changes in National Levels of Living, Social Affairs Division of OECD, MS/S/67, 126.

11. R. M. Titmuss, Essays on the Welfare State, London, George Allen & Unwin, 1958.

12. Sten Johansson, Om Levnadsniväundersökningen, Stockholm, Allmänna Förlaget, 1970, pp. 24-25.

13. Ibid., pp. 29-30.

14. Bruce M. Russett et al., World Handbook of Political and Social Indicators, New Haven, Conn., Yale University Press, 1964.

15. The information about Zapf's and Flora's collection is from European

ERIK ALLARDT [273]

Political Data, Newsletter No. 1, April 1971, published by the European Consortium for Political Research, pp. 14-16.

16. A very extensive national source has been compiled by Paavo Seppänen about Finnish society (Paavo Seppänen, "Suomalainen yhteiskunta, Sosiaalinen muutos aikasarjoina," Research Reports, Institute of Sociology, University of Helsinki, No. 166, 1971). It contains 419 different time series with values for each year between 1911 and 1961 although complete yearly data have not been found for all of them. Despite the extensiveness of this source, many of the variables needed in terms of the theoretical scheme in this chapter are not contained in Seppänen's file.

17. The problematic feature with the category of self-actualization is that it seems unreasonable to demand that self-actualization should have any clear external expressions.

III.

BUILDING STATES AND NATIONS:
A SELECTIVE BIBLIOGRAPHY OF THE
RESEARCH LITERATURE BY
THEME AND BY COUNTRY

BUILDING STATES AND NATIONS:
A SELECTIVE BIBLIOGRAPHY OF THE RESEARCH LITERATURE BY THEME AND BY COUNTRY

Stein Rokkan, Kirsti Saelen, and Joan Warmbrunn

INTRODUCTORY NOTE

The literature on state formation and nation-building knows no bounds. A complete bibliography across all the known political systems is simply inconceivable: it would have to assemble writings on every aspect of the organization of administrative machineries and of the cultural integration of territorial populations across all regions of the world. Any bibliographical review of these central themes in the history of mankind must of necessity be highly selective: it has to pick its way through vast masses of information and cannot stick to the same criteria of selection across the entire world.

This bibliography is selective both by *theme* and by *country*. In the first part we present a selection of the comparative literature: conceptual, methodological, and theoretical as well as substantive analyses across a variety of concrete histories. In the second half of the bibliography, we offer a few central references to the literature on each of the historically known cases of state formation and nation-building since the Middle Ages. These country-by-country selections vary enormously in scope. In the case of the largest and the best-known political systems, we have been very restrictive and have only rarely included general historical accounts of developments; we have tried to limit ourselves to pinpointed analyses of distinctive developments and persistent problems of consolidation within each system. In the case of smaller, less-known systems, particularly the newer states of the Third World, we have had to cite general works of history and overall presentations of the political systems when we could not find any explicit analyses of state-building processes and problems of cultural unification.

The result is a very uneven bibliography: it covers a wide range of the recent literature within comparative politics, but it is quite spotty in its coverage of particular countries. To some degree, this unevenness reflects variations in the actual extent of efforts of analytical research, but it is equally clear that our linguistic limitations have counted heavily in

[277]

reducing our access to important sources of information. We nevertheless hope that students will find this bibliography of some use as an initial guide to this vast literature.

This deliberately restricted bibliography owes much to the work of Karl Deutsch and Richard Merritt; their ̦ interdisciplinary bibliography of *Nationalism and National Development* (see Section 1.4 below) is an indispensable tool. Our only justification for adding this further bibliography to theirs is the difference in perspective: their focus is on attitudes and ideologies of national identity; ours, on the structural conditions for system-building and on the strategies of consolidation and integration. There is of necessity some overlap between the two bibliographies, but we still think that the differences in perspective, in format, and in timing justify separate publication.

The bibliography is organized in seven sections. The first two sections cite selected writings on the central concepts of and attempts at generalized model-building. Sections 3 and 4 offer an assortment of references for analyses of narrower facets of state-building and nation-building. Section 5 focuses on the distinctive characteristics of developments within each major region of the world and on the broader cultural setting for polity-building in each territory. Our classification of regions reflects the historical heritages from the great empires of the past and conforms to the general structure of this volume and to the basic logic of a number of the analyses of differences in styles of center-building and cultural unification. The same principle is used in the organization of information by country in Section 6: each of the current political systems is grouped within regions of common imperial heritage. In some cases, at the margin between several historical empires, this type of hierarchical classification obviously makes for arbitrariness. We still hope that it will prove easy for readers to find their way in the bibliography. They may find further help in the literature cited in the seventh and last section of the bibliography, which reviews efforts to build up better resources for information on developments in all these countries.

The basic structure of the classification scheme can be read from the following table:

Section 1.   TERMINOLOGICAL AND CONCEPTUAL ANALYSES

          1.1   General analyses
          1.2   Specific analyses of concepts of "state"
          1.3   Specific analyses of concepts of "nation," "nationality," and "nationalism"
          1.4   "Nation-building": introductory discussions, surveys, collections, bibliographies

6.815	Haiti
6.816	Jamaica
6.817	Puerto Rico
6.818	Trinidad and Tobago
6.82	Central America
6.821	Costa Rica
6.822	El Salvador
6.823	Guatemala
6.824	Honduras
6.825	Mexico
6.826	Nicaragua
6.827	Panama
6.83	Spanish South America
6.831	Argentina
6.832	Bolivia
6.833	Chile
6.834	Colombia
6.835	Ecuador
6.836	Paraguay
6.837	Peru
6.838	Uruguay
6.839	Venezuela
6.84	The Portuguese Empire: Brazil
6.9	Tropical Africa
6.91	British Africa
6.911	British West Africa
6.9111	Gambia
6.9112	Ghana
6.9113	Nigeria
6.9114	Sierra Leone
6.912	British East Africa
6.9121	Kenya
6.9122	Malawi
6.9123	Rhodesia
6.9124	Somalia
6.9125	Sudan
6.9126	Tanzania
6.9127	Uganda
6.9128	Zambia
6.913	Mauritius
6.92	British-Dutch South Africa
6.921	South Africa
6.922	Botswana
6.923	Lesotho
6.924	Southwest Africa (Namibia)
6.925	Swaziland
6.93	French Africa
6.931	French West Africa
6.9311	Dahomey

1. TERMINOLOGICAL AND CONCEPTUAL ANALYSES

1.1 General Analyses

AKZIN, Benjamin. *State and Nation* (London: Hutchinson, 1964). Useful review of analytical distinctions, giving particular attention to Jewish nationality-statehood issues.

BENDIX, Reinhard, ed. *State and Society: A Reader in Comparative Political Sociology* (Boston: Little, Brown, 1968). A handy collection of classic treatments of the state-nation problematic.

CARR, Edward H. *Nationalism and After* (London: Macmillan, 1945). A major analytical contribution.

DE JOUVENEL, Bertrand. *De la Souveraineté* (Paris: Genin, 1955). An insightful analysis of central concepts.

DEUTSCH, Karl W. *Nationalism and Social Communication: An Inquiry into the Foundation of Nationality* (Cambridge, Mass.: MIT Press, 1953). 2nd ed., Cambridge: MIT Press, 1966. A seminal work.

DEUTSCH, Karl W. *Nationalism and its Alternatives* (New York: Knopf, 1969). A collection of essays.

EMERSON, Rupert. *From Empire to Nation: The Rise to Self-Assertion of Asian and African Peoples* (Cambridge, Mass.: Harvard Univ. Press, 1960). A useful review of developments in the Third World with thorough discussions of concepts.

FROHLICH, Dieter. *Nationalismus und Nationalstaat in Entwicklungsländern* (Nationalism and Nation-state in developing countries) (Meisenheim: Verlag Anton Hain, 1970).

GLENN, Edmund S. "The Two Faces of Nationalism." Comparative Political Studies 3, no. 3 (October 1970): 347-66.

JENNINGS, William Ivor. *The Approach to Selfgovernment* (Cambridge, Eng.: Cambridge Univ. Press, 1956). A lawyer's comments on the transition from colonial status.

KELSEN, H. *Der Soziologische und der Juristische Staatsbegriff* (The sociological and the legal conception of the state) (Tübingen: Mohr, 1922). A classical analysis of central concepts.

LENIN, Vladimir I. *The State and Revolution: Marxist Teaching on the State and the Task of the Proletariat in the Revolution* (London: Allen and Unwin, 1919). German ed., Berlin-Wilmersdorf: Verlag Die Aktion, 1918. A classic of revolutionary thought.

MACIVER, Robert M. *The Modern State* (London: Oxford Univ. Press, 1932). A scholarly discussion of central concepts.

MALINOWSKI, Bronislav. "Tribe-nation and Tribe-state," in *Freedom and Civilization* (New York: Roy, 1944). An anthropological perspective.

MARAVALL, J. A. "The Origins of the Modern State." Cahiers d'Histoire Mondiale 6 (1961): 789-808.

MARITAIN, Jacques. *Man and the State* (Chicago: Chicago Univ. Press, 1951). A Thomist analysis.

MEINECKE, Friedrich. See Section 6.41.

NETTL, J. Peter. "The state as a conceptual variable." World Politics 20, No. 4 (July 1968): 559-92. An insightful discussion of key concepts.

NIEBUHR, Reinhold. *The Structure of Nations and Empires* (New York: Scribner's, 1959).

REJAI, Mostafa and Cynthia H. ENLOE. "Nation-States and State-Nations." International Studies Quarterly 13, no. 2 (June 1969): 149-58.

SEIPEL, Ignaz. *Nation und Staat* (Nation and State) (Vienna: W. Braumüller, 1916). An important statement by an Austrian Catholic thinker.

SIEGFRIED, André. *L'âme des Peuples* (Paris: Hachette, 1950). English ed., *Nations Have Souls* (New York: Putnam, 1952).

SULZBACH, Walter. *Imperialismus und Nationalbewusstsein* (Imperialism and National Consciousness) (Frankfurt: Europäische Verlagsanstalt, 1959).

TAYLOR, Griffith. *Environment and Nation* (Chicago: Chicago University Press, 1936).

WEBER, Max. *Wirtschaft und Gesellschaft* (Economy and Society). Originally published 1922; 4th ed. in 2 vol. by J. Winckelmann (Tübingen: Mohr, 1956); English translation *Economy and Society*. 3 vols. Introduction by G. Roth (New York: Bedminster, 1960). The classic analysis of concepts and interrelations in political sociology.

WIATR, Jerzy J. *Narod i Panstwo. Socjologiczne Aspektry Kwestü Narodowcj*

(Nation and State. Sociological Aspects of the National Question) (Warsaw: Academy of Sciences, 1969).

1.2 Specific Analyses of Concepts of "State"

BORSCH, Herbert V. *Obrigkeit und Widerstand. Zur Politischen Soziologies des Beamtentums* (Public Authority and Opposition. Towards a Political Sociology of the Civil Service) (Tübingen: Mohr, 1954).

BRUNNER, Otto. "Moderner Verfassungsbegriff und Mittelalterliche Verfassungsgeschichte" (The Modern Concept of Constitution and Constitutional History of the Middle Ages). *Mitteilungen des Osterreichischen Instituts für Geschichte,* Ergänzungsband 14, 1939.

BRUNNER, Otto. *Neue Wege der Sozialgeschichte* (New Trends in Social History) (Göttingen: Vandenhoeck u. Ruprecht, 1956). Important essays on the characteristics of the modern state.

DE JOUVENEL, Bertrand. *Du Pouvoir. Histoire Naturelle de sa Croissance* (Geneva: Ed. du Cheval Ailé, 1945). English ed., *On Power, Its Nature and the History of Its Growth* (New York: Viking Press, 1949). A major contribution to the analysis and interpretation of central lines of thinking.

DENNERT, Jürgen. *Ursprung und Begriff der Souveränität* (The Origin and the Concept of Sovereignty) (Stuttgart: Fischer, 1964). A contribution to the history of ideas about the state.

GOODY, Jack. "The Myth of a State." Journal of Modern African Studies 6, no. 4 (December 1968): 461-73. Interesting analysis based on developments in Ghana at the fall of Nkrumah.

HARTUNG, Fritz. *Staatsbildende Kräfte der Neuzeit* (Agencies of state building in modern times) (Berlin: Duncker & Humbolt, 1961).

——— and Roland MOUSNIER. "Quelques Problèmes Concernant la Monarchie Absolue." X Congresso Internazionale di Scienze Storiche, Relazioni 4, Florence (1955): 1-55. Important analysis of the concept of state in the absolutist era.

HINTZE, Otto. *Gesammelte Abhandlungen* (Collected works). Edited by Gerhard Oestrich (Göttingen: Vandenhoeck, 1962-1964). Contains all of Hintze's important articles on the development of the European state system.

HOFMANN, Hans Hubert, ed. *Die Entstehung des Modernen Souveränen Staates* (The Origin of the Modern Sovereign State) (Köln, Berlin: Kiepenheuer & Witsch, 1967). A useful reader.

KEMP, T. *Theories of Imperialism* (London: Dobson, 1967). Marxist survey of theories of imperialism.

KERN, Ernst. *Moderner Staat und Staatsbegriff. Eine Untersuchung über die Grundlagen und die Entwicklung des Kontinental-europäischen Staates* (The Modern State and Concept of State. An Inquiry Into the Foundations and Development of the Continental European States) (Hamburg: Rechts- und Staatswissenschaftlicher Verlag, 1949).

KIENAST, Walter. "Die Anfänge des Europäischen Staatensystems im Späten Mittelalter" (The Beginnings of the European State System in the Later Middle Ages). Historische Zeitschrift 153, no. 2 (1936): 229-71.

KOEBNER, R. *Empire* (Cambridge, Eng.: Cambridge University Press, 1961).

——— and H. SCHMIDT. *Imperialism: The Story and Significance of a Political Word 1840-1960* (Cambridge, Eng.: Cambridge University Press, 1964).

LASKI, Harold J. *The State in Theory and Practice* (New York: Viking, 1938).
LUBASZ, Heinz. *The Development of the Modern State* (New York: Macmillan, 1964).
MAGER, W. *Zur Entstehung des Modernen Staatsbegriff* (The Genesis of the Modern Concept of State) (Wiesbaden: F. Steiner, 1968).
MEINECKE, Friedrich. *Die Idee der Staatsräson* (The Idea of Raison D'état) (Munich-Berlin: Oldenbourge, 1925). A classic treatise on the rise of the modern state.
RAUMER, K. von. "Absoluter Staat, Korporative Libertät, Persönliche Freiheit" (Absolute State, Corporative Liberty, Individual Freedom). Historische Zeitschrift 183 (1957): 55-96. An important discussion of the conflict between absolutism and estate representation.

1.3 Specific analyses of concepts of "nation," "nationality," and "nationalism"

ARGYLE, W. J. "European Nationalism and African Tribalism." In *Tradition and Transition in East Africe,* edited by P. H. Gulliver, pp. 41-57 (Los Angeles: University of California Press, 1969).
BAUER, Otto. *Die Nationalitätenfrage und die Sozialdemokratie.* 2nd ed. (Vienna" Volksbuchhandlung, 1924). The classic study of conditions in the Habsburg Empire by a leading Socialist theoretician.
BLOOM, Solomon F. *The World of Nations: A Study of the National Implications in the Work of Karl Marx* (New York: Columbia University Press, 1941).
BOERSNER, D. *The Bolsheviks and the National and Colonial Question* (Paris: Minard, 1957).
BOROCHOV, B. *Nationalism and the Class Struggle: A Marxian Approach to the Jewish Problem. Selected Writings* (New York: Zion of America, 1937).
CONZE, Werner. "Nation und Gesellschaft. Zwei Grundbegriffe der revolutionären Epoche" (Nation and Society. Two Fundamental Concepts of the Revolutionary Era). Historische Zeitschrift 198 (1964): 1-16.
DALBERG-ACTON, John Emerich Edward. "Nationality," Chapter IX of *The History of Freedom and Other Essays* (London: Macmillan, 1907, reprinted 1919). Also in *Essays on Freedom and Power* (Boston: Beacon, 1948). An important essay first written in 1862.
DAVIS, Horace B. *Nationalism and Socialism. Marxist and Labor Theories of Nationalism to 1917* (New York: Monthly Review Press, 1967).
DECHMANN, M. et al. "A Typology of Nations." Soziologisches Institut der Universität Zürich. Bulletin 11, (December 1968): 1-72.
DELDS, Joseph T. *La Nation* (Montréal: Ed. de L'Arbre, 194).
DUIJKER, H.L.J. and N. H. FRIJDA. *National Character and National Stereotypes* (Amsterdam: North Holland, 1960). A useful trend report and bibliography.
FISHMAN, J. A. "Nationality-Nationalism and Nation-Nationalism." In *Language Problems of Developing Nations,* edited by J. A. Fishman, C. A. Ferguson, and J. D. Gupta (New York: John Wiley, 1968).
HOBSBAWM, Eric. "Some Reflections on Nationalism." In *Imagination and Precision in the Social Sciences. Essays in Memory of Peter Nettl,* edited by T. J. Nossiter, A. H. Hanson, and Stein Rokkan, pp. 385-406 (London: Faber, 1972).
JOHANNET, René. *Le Principe des Nationalités* (Paris: Nouvelle Librairie Internationelle, 1918).

KEDOURIE, Elie. *Nationalism* (New York: Praeger, 1961).

KOPPELMANN, Heinrich L. *Nation, Sprache und Nationalismus* (Nation, language and nationalism) (Leiden: A. W. Sÿthoff, 1956).

LEMBERG, Eugen. "Die Geburt der Nationen: Um eine Theorie des Nationalismus" (The Birth of Nations: On a Theory of Nationalism). Studium Generale 15 (1962): 301-09.

LOT, Ferdinand. "Qu'est-ce qu'une Nation" Mercure de France 306 (May 1949): 29-46.

LOW, Alfred D. *Lenin on the question of nationality* (New York: Bookman, 1958).

MACDONALD, Malcolm H. "Marx, Engels and the National Question." Thesis, Harvard University, 1939.

MARX, Karl. *On Colonialism and Modernization*. Edited with an introduction by Shlomo Avineri (Garden City, N.Y. Doubleday, 1969). A handy collection of Marx's writings on the national question.

MENDES, Candido. *Nacionalismo e Desenvolvimento* (Nationalism and development) (Rio de Janeiro: Instituto Brasileiro de Estudoa Afro-Asiàticos, 1963). An important Brazilian study.

PLAMENATZ, John. *On Alien Rule and Self-Government* (London: Longmans, 1960).

RENAN, Ernest. *Qu'est-ce qu'une Nation* (Paris: Calman-Lévy, 1882), numerous editions. The classic statement in the conflict between French and German conceptions of "nation."

RODINSON, Maxime. "Le Marxisme et la Nation." L'Homme et la Société 7 (January-March, 1968): 131-49.

ROTBERG, Robert I. "African Nationalism: Concept or Confusion." Journal of Modern African Studies 4, no. 1 (1966): 33-46.

RUSTOW, Dankwart A. "Nation." In *International Encyclopedia of the Social Sciences* (New York: Macmillan and Free Press, 1968).

SMITH, Anthony D. *Theories of Nationalism* (London: Duckworth, 1971).

SNYDER, Louis. *The New Nationalism* (New Brunswick: Rutgers University Press, 1968).

STALIN, Josef V. *Marxism and the National and Colonial Question*. English ed. (London and New York: International Publishers, 1935).

SULZBACH, Walter. "Zur Definition und Psychologie von 'Nation' und 'National-bewusstsein, '" (Towards the Definition and Psychology of "Nation" and "National Consciousness"). Politische Vierteljahresschift 3 (June 1962): 139-58.

TAJFEL, H. "Aspects of National and Ethnic Loyalty." Social Science Information 9, no. 3 (June 1970): 119-44.

TANGA, L. "Intégration Politique et Nationalisme." Etudes Congolaises 11, no. 4 (October-December 1968): 72-84.

VAN DEN BERGHE, P. L. *Race and racism* (New York: John Wiley, 1967).

VAN GENNEP, A. *Traité Comparatif des Nationalités* (Paris, Payot, 1922).

VOSSLER, Otto. *Der Nationalgedanke von Rousseau bis Ranke* (The National Idea from Rousseau to Ranke) (Munich: Oldenbourg, 1937).

WEILENMANN, Hermann. "The Interlocking of Nation and Personality Structure." In *Nation Building,* edited by Karl W. Deutsch and William J. Foltz (New York: Atherton, 1963).

WINTERNITZ, J. *Marxism and Nationality* (London: Lawrence and Wishart, 1946).

ZIEGLER, Heinz O. *Die Moderne Nation: Ein Beitrag zur Politischen Soziologie* (The

Modern Nation: A Contribution to Political Sociology) (Tübingen: Mohr, 1931).
See also Section 5.7, HODGKIN, 1956.

1.4 "Nation-building": introductory discussions, surveys, collections, bibliographies

ABDEL-MALEK, A. "Esquisse d'une Typologie des Formations Nationales dans les Trois Continents." Paper presented to World Congress of Sociology 6, Evian, September 4-11, 1966. Published in Cahiers Internationaux de Sociologie 14, no. 42 (January-June 1967): 49-57.

––– "Sociologie du Développement National: Problèmes de Conceptualisation." Revue de l'Institut de Sociologie, Université de Bruxelles 2, no. 3 (1967): 249-64.

ALMOND, Gabriel and James S. COLEMAN, eds. *The Politics of the Developing Areas* (Princeton: Princeton University Press, 1960).

BELL, W. and E. FREEMAN, Eds. *Ethnicity and Nation-Building* (Beverly Hills: Sage Publications, 1972).

BENDIX, Reinhard. *Nation-Building and Citizenship: Studies of Our Changing Social Order* (New York: John Wiley, 1964; paperback ed., Garden City: Doubleday Anchor, 1969).

DEUTSCH, Karl W. *Interdisciplinary Bibliography on Nationalism.* (Cambridge, Mass.: MIT Press, 1956). A brief bibliography, successor to K. S. Pinson (below), forerunner to the major 1970 bibliography by Deutsch and Merritt.

––– and William J. FOLTZ, eds. *Nation-building* (New York: Atherton, 1963). A collection of essays organized by world region.

DEUTSCH, Karl W. and Richard MERRITT. *Nationalism and National Development: An Interdisciplinary Bibliography* (Cambridge, Mass.: MIT Press, 1970). Computer-produced bibliography with extensive KWIC index. A major reference tool.

PINSON, K. E. *A Bibliographical Introduction to Nationalism* (New York: Columbia University Press, 1935).

ROKKAN, Stein. "Models and Methods in the Comparative Study of Nation-Building." Acta Sociologica 12, no. 2 (1969): 53-73; reprinted in Stein Rokkan *Citizens, Elections, Parties* (Oslo: Universitets-forlaget, 1970) pp. 46-71 and also with some amendments, in *Imagination and Precision in the Social Sciences. Essays in Memory of Peter Nettl,* edited by T. J. Nossiter, A. H. Hanson, and Stein Rokkan (London: Faber, 1972), pp. 121-56.

––– "State Formation and Nation-Building." UNESCO Chronicle 17, no. 10 (October 1971): 347-54. Reprint of report on UNESCO Conference, Cérisy, 1970. Partly integrated into the Introduction to this volume.

––– "Centre Formation, Nation-Building and Cultural Diversity: Report on a Symposium Organized by Unesco." Social Science Info. 8, no. 1 (1969): 85-99. Partly integrated into the introduction to this volume.

RUSTOW, Dankwart A. *A World of Nations: Problems of Political Modernization* (Washington, D.C.: Brookings, 1967).

SICARD, E. "Elements Principaux des Constructions Nationales." L'Année Sociologique, Troisième série, vol. 18 (Paris: Presses Universitaires de Frances, 1967).

2. MODELS OF NATIONAL DEVELOPMENT

2.1 Strategies of theory construction and comparative analysis

ASHER, Robert E. *Development of the Emerging Countries: An Agenda for Research* (Washington, D.C.: Brookings, 1963).

BENDIX, Reinhard and Günther ROTH. *Scholarship and Partisanship. Essays on Max WEBER* (Berkeley: University of California Press, 1971).

GALLAHER, A., Jr., ed. *Perspectives in Developmental Change* (Lexington: University of Kentucky Press, 1968).

GERHARD, Dietrich. *Alte und Neue Wege Vergleichender Geschichtesbetrachtung* (Old and New Approaches to Comparative History) (Göttingen: Vandenhoeck & Ruprecht, 1962).

GREW, Raymond and Sylvia L. THRUPP. "Horizontal Theory in Search of Vertical Dimensions." Comparative Studies in Society and History 8 (January 1966): 258-64. An important review of the RUSSETT *World Handbook* (see Section 7).

HOLT, R. T. and John TURNER, eds. *The Methodology of Comparative Research* (New York: Free Press, 1970).

HOPKINS, Raymond F. "Aggregate Data and the Study of Political Development." Journal of Politics 31 (February 1969): 71-94.

HUNTINGTON, Samuel P. "The Change to Change: Modernization, Development and Politics." Comparative Politics 3, no. 3 (April 1971): 283-322. A provocative critique related to the change of perspective discussed in Chapter 1 by S. N. Eisenstadt.

MARSH, Robert M. *Comparative Sociology: A Codification of Cross-Societal Analysis* (New York: Harcourt Brace, 1967).

MERRITT, Richard L. *Systematic Approaches to Comparative Politics.* (Chicago: Rand McNally, 1969).

––– and Stein ROKKAN, eds. *Comparing Nations* (New Haven, Conn.: Yale University Press, 1966). A collection of essays on problems of cross-national aggregate analysis.

MOORE, Wilbert. "Social Change and Comparative Studies." International Social Science Journal 15, no. 4 (1963): 549-58.

MUKHERJEE, Ramkrishna. "Some Observations on the Diachronic and Synchronic Aspects of Social Change." Social Science Information 7, no. 1 (1968): 31-55.

RUSTOW, Dankwart A. "Modernization and Comparative Politics: Prospects in Research and Theory. Comparative Politics 1, no. 1 (October 1968): 37-51.

SALOMON, Lester M. "Comparative History and the Theory of Modernization." World Politics 23, no. 1 (October 1970): 83-103.

SCOTT, Andrew M.; William A. LUCAS; and Trudi M. LUCAS. *Simulation and National Development* (New York: John Wiley, 1966).

TAYLOR, C. L., ed. *Aggregate Data Analysis* (Paris: Mouton, 1968). A follow-up volume from Merritt and Rokkan, this section.

2.2 General models of change, modernization, differentiation

ALMOND, G. A. *Political Development: Essays in Heuristic Theory* (Boston: Little, Brown, 1970).

APTER, David. "Nationalism, Government and Economic Growth." Economic Development and Cultural Change 7 (January 1959): 117-36.

BAILEY, F. G. *Tribe, Caste, and Nation* (Manchester: Manchester University Press, 1960).

BARBER, Bernard and Alex INKELES, eds. *Stability and Social Change* (Boston: Little, Brown, 1971).

BARNETT, H. G. *Innovation: The Basis of Cultural Change* (New York: McGraw-Hill, 1953).

BOULDING, Kenneth. *The Meaning of the 20th Century, the Entropy Trap* (New York: Harper, 1965).

BENDIX, Reinhard. "Tradition and Modernity Reconsidered." Comparative Studies in Society and History 9 (April 1967): 293-346.

BERRIEN, Kenneth. *General and Social Systems* (New Brunswick, N.J.: Rutgers University Press, 1968).

BLACK, Cyril E. *The Dynamics of Modernization: A Study in Comparative History* (New York: Harper, 1966).

BRUNNER, Ronald D. and Garry D. BREWER. *Organized Complexity: Empirical Theories of Political Development* (New York: Free Press, 1971). Proposes a simulation technique for the study of processes of change over time. Data for the Philippines and Turkey.

BURY, J. B. *The Idea of Progress* (London: Macmillan, 1932). A classic statement.

DEUTSCH, Karl W. "Social Mobilization and Political Development." American Political Science Review 55, no. 3 (September 1961): 493-514. A seminal article proposing a paradigm for studies of change in subject peripheries.

DEUTSCH, Karl W. *The Nerves of Government: Models of Political Communication and Control* (Glencoe, Ill.: Free Press, 1963). A cybernetic model for the study of system differentiation.

DURKHEIM, Emile. *De la Division du Travail Social. Etude sur l'organisation des Societés superieures* (Paris: Alcan, 1893). A sociological classic, proposes a basic model of differentiation.

EISENSTADT, Shmuel N., ed. *Readings in Social Evolution and Development* (New York: Pergamon, 1970).

——— "Some Observations on the Dynamics of Traditions." Comparative Studies in Society and History 11, no. 4 (October 1969): 451-75.

——— "Some New Looks at the Problem of Relations Between Traditional Societies and Modernization." Economic Development and Cultural Change 16, no. 3 (April 1968): 436-49.

——— "Reflections on a Theory of Modernization." In *Nations by Design: Institution Building in Africa,* edited by Arnold Rivkin (Garden City, N.Y.: Anchor Books, 1968).

——— "Breakdowns of Modernization." Economic Development and Cultural Change 12 (July 1964): 345-67.

——— "Social Change, Differentiation and Evolution." American Sociological Review 24 (June 1964): 375-86.

——— "Institutionalization and Change." American Sociological Review 24 (April 1964): 235-47.

——— *Essays on Sociological Aspects of Political and Economic Development* (New York: Humanities Press, 1964).

——— "Initial Institutional Patterns of Political Modernization." Civilisations 12 (1962): 461-72.

FAVRET, J. "Le Traditionalisme par Excès de Modernité." Archives Européennes de Sociologie 8, no. 1 (1967): 71-93.

FRIED, Morton H. *The Evolution of Political Society. An Essay in Political Anthropology* (New York: Random House, 1967). An insightful discussion of levels of development.

GEERTZ, Clifford. *Old Societies and New States: The Quest for Modernity in Asia and Africa* (New York: Free Press, 1963).

GERMANI, Gino. "Stages of Modernization." International Journal 24, no. 3 (Summer 1969): 463-548.

――― *Politica y Sociedad en una Epoca de Transicion: de la Sociedad Tradicional a la sociedad de masas* (Politics and Society in an Age of Transition: From a Traditional Society to a Mass Society) (Buenos Aires: Paidos, 1965). An important study of developments in Latin America.

GLUCKMAN, M. *Politics, Law and Ritual in Tribal Society* (Oxford: Blackwell, 1965).

GUSFIELD, Joseph R. "Tradition and Modernity: Misplaced Polarities in the Study of Social Change." American Journal of Sociology 72 (January 1966): 351-62.

HART, H. "Social Theory and Social Change." *Symposium on Sociological Theory,* edited by L. Gross, pp. 196-238 (Evanston, Ill.: Row, Peterson, 1959).

HIMMELSTRAND, Ulf. "Conflict, Conflict Resolution and Nation-Building in the Transition from Tribal 'Mechanical' Solidarities, to the 'Organic' Solidarity of Modern (or Future) Multi-Tribal Societies." Paper VI presented to World Congress of Sociology, Evian, September 4-11, 1966.

HIRSCHMAN, A. O. *Exit, Voice and Loyalty* (Cambridge, Mass.: Harvard University Press, 1970). A pathbreaking study of differences in styles of system-building.

INKELES, Alex. "Making Man Modern: On the Causes and Consequences of Individual Change in Six Developing Countries." American Journal of Sociology 75 (September 1969): 208-25.

JAGUARIBE, Hélio. *Economic and Political Development* (New Haven, Conn.: Yale University Press, 1968). A Brazilian study.

KISHIMOTO, Hideo. "Modernization versus Westernization in the East." Journal of World History 7 (1963).

KOTHARI, Rajni. "Tradition and Modernity Revisited." Government and Opposition 3 (Summer 1968): 273-93.

LERNER, Daniel. *The Passing of Traditional Society: Modernizing the Middle East* (Glencoe, Ill.: Free Press, 1963). A classic study, proposes a paradigm for analyses of change in peripheries.

LEVY, Marion Joseph, Jr. *Modernization and the Structure of Societies: A Setting for International Affairs.* 2 vols. (Princeton: N.J.: Princeton University Press, 1966).

――― *The Structure of Society* (Princeton: Princeton University Press, 1952).

MAZRUI, Ali A. "From Social Darwinism to Current Theories of Modernization." World Politics 19, no. 2 (January 1967): 69-83.

McCLELLAND, D. C. *The Achieving Society* (Princeton: Princeton University Press, 1961). A major contribution to the psychological study of determinants of change.

NANDY, K. S. "Is Modernization Westernization? What About Easternization and Traditionalization? " Paper presented to World Congress of Sociology, Evian, September 4-11, 1966.

NETTL, J. P. and Roland ROBERTSON. *International Systems and the Modernization of Societies* (London: Faber, 1968).

PARSONS, Talcott. *Societies: Comparative and Evolutionary Perspectives* (Englewood Cliffs, N.J.: Prentice-Hall, 1967). A pathbreaking study of the early empires; proposes a general model of differentiation.

――― "Evolutionary Universals in Society." American Sociological Review (June 1964): 339-57.

――― and Neil J. SMELSER. *Economy and Society: A Study in the Integration of Economic and Social Theory* (New York: Free Press, 1956).

REDFIELD, R. *The Primitive World and its Transformations* (Ithaca, New York: Cornell University Press, 1953).

RUDOLPH, Lloyd and Suzanne RUDOLPH. *The Modernity of Tradition* (Chicago: University of Chicago Press, 1967).

SELSAM, H.; D. GOLDWAY; and H. MARTEL, eds. *Dynamics of Social Change: A Reader in Marxist Social Science, From the Writings of Marx, Engels and Lenin* (New York: International Publishers, 1970).

SILVERT, K. H., ed. *Discussion at Bellagio: The Political Alternatives of Development* (New York: American Universities Field Staff, 1964).

SOROKIN, P. A. *Social and Cultural Dynamics: A Study in Major Systems of Art, Truth, Ethics, Law and Social Relationships.* 4 vols. (New York: American Book Co., 1937-41). A classic study in comparative quantitative history.

TAX, Sol, ed. *The Evolution of Man: Man, Culture, and Society* (Chicago: Chicago University Press, 1960).

ZOLLSCHAN, George K. and Walter HIRSCH, eds. *Explorations in Social Change* (Boston: Houghton Mifflin, 1964).

See also Section 5.6 RIBEIRO, 1969, 1971.

2.3 Models of national economic development

ADELMAN, I. and C. T. MORRIS. *Society, Politics, and Economic Development* (Baltimore: Johns Hopkins Press, 1967)

EISENSTADT, S. N. *Essays on Social and Political Aspects of Economic Development* (The Hague: Mouton, 1958).

FURTADO, Celso. *Dialéctica del Desarrollo* (The Dialectics of Development) (Mexico: Fondo de Cultura Economica, 1965).

――― *Development and Underdevelopment* (Berkeley: University of California Press, 1964).

GERSCHENKRON, Alexander. *Economic Backwardness in Historical Perspective* (Cambridge, Mass.: Harvard University Press, 1962).

HAGEN, Everett E. *The Economics of Development* (Homewood, Ill.: H. D. Irwin, 1968).

――― *On the Theory of Social Change: How Economic Growth Begins* (Homewood, Ill.: Dorsey Press, 1962).

HIGGINS, Benjamin. *Economic Development: Principles, Problems and Policies* (New York: Norton, 1959, 1968).

HIRSCHMAN, Albert O. *The Strategy of Economic Development* (New Haven, Conn.: Yale University Press, 1958; paperback 1961). A much-quoted critique of notions of "balanced" growth.

HOSELITZ, Berthold. *Theories of Economic Growth* (Glencoe, Ill.: Free Press, 1960).

——— ed. *The Progress of Underdeveloped Areas.* (Chicago: Chicago University Press, 1952).

KILBY, Peter, ed. *Entrepreneurship and Economic Development* (New York: Free Press, 1971).

KUZNETS, Simon Smith. *Modern Economic Growth: Rate, Structure and Spread* (New Haven, Conn.: Yale University Press, 1966).

——— *Economic Growth and Structure* (New York: Norton, 1965).

LEIBERSTEIN, Harvey. *Economic Backwardness and Economic Growth: Studies in the Theory of Economic Development* (New York: John Wiley, 1967).

ROBINSON, E.A.G., ed. *Economic Consequences of the Size of Nations* (London: Macmillan, 1960).

ROSTOW, W. W. *Stages of Economic Growth: A Non-Communist Manifesto* (Cambridge, Eng.: Cambridge University Press, 1960).

2.4 Models of national political development

ALMOND, Gabriel A. "Political Systems and Political Change." American Behavioral Scientist 6 (June 1963): 3-10.

——— and G. B. POWELL. *Comparative Politics: A Developmental Approach* (Boston: Little, Brown, 1966).

ALMOND, Gabriel A. and Sidney VERBA. *The Civic Culture: Political Attitudes and Democracy in Five Nations* (Princeton: Princeton University Press, 1963).

ANDERSON, Charles W.; Fred R. VON DER MEHDEN; and Crawford YOUNG. *Issues of Political Development* (Englewood Cliffs, N.J.: Prentice-Hall, 1967).

APTER, David E. *Choice and the Politics of Allocation* (New Haven, Conn.: Yale University Press, 1971).

——— *The Politics of Modernization* (Chicago: Phoenix Books, 1965).

BAYNE, E. A. *Four Ways of Politics: State and Nation in Italy, Somalia, Israel, Iran: The Dynamics of Political Participation as exhibited in Four Countries Caught Up in the Process of Modernization* (New York: American Universities Field Staff, 1965).

BINDER, L.; J. S. COLEMAN; et al., eds. *Crises and Sequences in Political Development* (Princeton: Princeton University Press, 1971). A collection of theoretical essays based on the work of the Committee on Comparative Politics of the American Social Science Research Council.

BRAIBANTI, R. and J. J. SPENGLER, eds. *Tradition, Values, and Socioeconomic Development* (Durham, N.C.: Duke University Press, 1964).

BRINTON, Crane. *The Anatomy of Revolution.* Revised edition (New York: Random House, 1960).

CARDOSO, Fernando Henrique. *Politique et Développement dans les Societés Dépendentes* (Paris, Ed. Anthropos, 1971).

CORNBLIT, O. et al. "A Model for Political Change in Latin America." Social Science Information 7, no. 2 (1968): 13-48.

CUTRIGHT, Phillips. "National Political Development: Measurement and Analysis." American Sociological Review 23 (1963): 253-64. A well-known attempt at quantitative comparative analysis.

——— and James A. WILEY. *Modernization and Political Representation: 1927-66* (Beverly Hills: Sage, forthcoming).

DAHL, Robert A. *Polyarchy: Participation and Opposition* (New Haven and London:

Yale University Press, 1971). An important comparative analysis of the conditions for pluralist development.

DIAMANT, Alfred. "The Nature of Political Development." In *Political Development and Social Change,* edited by Jason L. Finkle and Richard Gable (New York: John Wiley, 1966).

EASTON, David. *A Systems Analysis of Political Life* (New York: John Wiley, 1965).

EISENSTADT, Shmuel N. *Modernization: Protest and Change* (Englewood Cliffs, N.J.: Prentice-Hall, 1966).

EMERSON, Rupert. *Political Modernization in the Single-Party System* (Denver: Denver University Press, 1963-64).

——— "Nationalism and Political Development." Journal of Politics 22 (February 1960): 3-28.

ETZIONI, Amitai. *The Active Society* (New York: Free Press, 1968). A general theoretical statement.

FINER, Herman J. *Theory and Practice of Modern Government* (New York: Henry Holt, 1949). A classic treatise on variations in development in Europe and the West.

FINKLE, Jason L. and Richard W. GABLE, eds. *Political Development and Social Change* (New York: John Wiley, 1966).

FRIEDRICH, Carl Joachim. *Man and His Government: An Empirical Study of Politics* (New York: McGraw-Hill, 1963).

GREGG, Phillip M. and Arthur S. BANKS. "Dimensions of Political Systems: Factor Analysis of a Cross-polity Survey." American Political Science Review 59 (September 1965): 602-14. Based on Banks and Textor; see Section 7.

HALLGARTEN, George W. F. *Why Dictators: The Causes and Forms of Tyrannical Rule Since 600 B.C.* (New York: Macmillan, 1954).

HALPERN, Manfred. "Toward Further Modernization of the Study of New Nations." World Politics 17 (October 1964): 157-81.

HARRIS, Richard. *Independence and After: Revolution in Underdeveloped Countries* (London: Oxford University Press, 1962).

HEARD, Kenneth A. *Political Systems in Multiracial Societies* (Johannesburg: South African Institute of Race Relations, 1961).

HOROWITZ, Irving Louis. *Three worlds of development: The Theory and Practice of International Stratification* (New York: Oxford University Press, 1966).

HUNTINGTON, Samuel P. "Political Development and Political Decay." World Politics 17, no. 3 (April 1965): 386-430. A much-debated analysis of development in new states. Revised version published in

——— *Political Order in Changing Societies* (New Haven and London: Yale University Press, 1968).

JOHNSON, Chalmers. *Revolutionary Change* (Boston: Little, Brown, 1966).

——— *Revolution and the Social System* (Stanford: Hoover Institution, 1964).

——— *Peasant Nationalism and Communist Power* (Stanford: Stanford University Press, 1962).

KAUTSKY, John H., ed. *Political Change in Underdeveloped Countries: Nationalism and Communism* (New York: John Wiley, 1962).

KEBSCHULL, Harvey G. *Politics in Transitional Societies: The Challenge of Change in Asia, Africa and Latin America.* (New York: Appleton-Century-Crofts, 1968).

LA PALOMBARA, Joseph. "Political Power and Political Development." Yale Law

Journal 78 (June 1969): 1253-75. Review article centering on Huntington in this section.

——— and Myron WEINER, eds. *Political Parties and Political Development* (Princeton: Princeton University Press, 1966).

LASSWELL, Harold D. "The Policy Sciences of Development." World Politics 17 (January 1965): 286-310.

LIJPHART, Arend. "Typologies of Democratic Systems." Comparative Political Studies 1, no. 1 (1968): 3-44.

LIPSET, Seymour M. and Stein ROKKAN, eds. *Party Systems and Voter Alignments* (New York: Free Press, 1967). Introduction presents developmental model of cleavage structures; see Rokkan in this section.

LORWIN, Val R. "The Comparative Analysis of Historical Change: Nation-Building in the Western World." International Social Science Journal 17 (1965): 594-606. Reprinted in S. ROKKAN, ed. *Comparative Research Across Cultures and Nations* (Paris: Mouton, 1968).

McCRONE, D. J. and C. F. CNUDDE. "Toward a Communications Theory of Democratic Political Development: A Causal Model." American Political Science Review 61 (1967): 72-79.

MEHDEN, Fred R. von der. *Politics of the Developing Nations.* 2nd ed. (Englewood Cliffs, N.J.: Prentice-Hall, 1969).

MERKL, Peter H. *Modern Comparative Politics* (New York: Holt, Rinehart and Winston, 1970). A textbook.

MERRITT, Richard L. "Systems and the Disintegration of Empires." General Systems: Yearbook of the Society for General Systems Research 8 (1963): 91-103.

MICHELENA, José A. Silva. *The Illusion of Democracy in Dependent Nations* (Cambridge, Mass.: MIT Press, forthcoming).

MILLIKAN, Max and Donald L. BLACKMER, eds. *The Emerging Nations: Their Growth and United States Policy* (Boston: Little, Brown, 1961).

MONTGOMERY, John D. "The Quest for Political Development." Comparative Politics 1 (January 1969): 285-95.

OLSON, Mancur, Jr. "Rapid Growth as a Destabilizing Force." Journal of Economic History 23 (December 1963).

ORGANSKI, A.F.K. *The Stages of Political Development* (New York: Knopf, 1965).

PACKENHAM, Robert A. "Approaches to the Study of Political Development." World Politics 17, no. 1 (October 1964): 108-20.

PIPKIN, Charles W. *Social Politics and Modern Democracies.* 2 vols. (New York: Macmillan, 1931).

PYE, Lucian W. *Aspects of Political Development* (Boston: Little, Brown, 1966). A collection of essays by a leading theoretician.

——— and Sidney VERBA, eds. *Political Culture and Political Development* (Princeton: Princeton University Press, 1965). A volume in the series of the Committee on Comparative Politics.

RIGGS, Fred W. "The Dialectics of Developmental Conflict." *Comparative Political Studies* 1 (July 1968).

——— *Administration in Developing Countries: The Theory of Prismatic Society* (Boston: Houghton Mifflin, 1964).

RIVKIN, Arnold. "The Politics of Nation-Building: Problems and Preconditions." Journal of International Affairs 16, no. 2 (1962): 131-43.

ROKKAN, Stein. "Dimensions of State Formation and Nation-Building: A Possible Paradigm on Variations Within Europe." In *The Formation of National States in Western Europe,* edited by C. Tilly (Princeton: Princeton University Press, forthcoming 1973).

––– "The Growth and Structuring of Mass Politics." *Scandinavian Political Studies* 5 (1970): 65-83. A proposal for paired comparisons of national political developments.

––– *Citizens, Elections, Parties* (Oslo: Universitetsforlaget, 1970; New York: McKay, 1970). A collection of papers centering on problems of national political development, mass politics and citizen participation.

RUSTOW, Dankwart A. "Communism and Change." In *Change in Communist Systems,* edited by Chalmers Johnson (Stanford: Stanford University Press, 1970).

––– "Transitions to Democracy: Toward a Dynamic Model." Comparative Politics 2 (April 1970): 337-63.

SCOTT, Roger. *The Politics of New States* (London: Allen and Unwin, 1970).

SHANNON, Lyle William. "Socio-economic Development and Political Status." Social Problems 7 (Fall 1959): 157-69.

––– "Is Level of Development Related to Capacity for Self-government?" American Journal of Economics and Sociology 17 (July 1958): 367-81.

SHILS, Edward. *Political Development in the New States* (The Hague: Mouton, 1962).

SILVERT, Kalman H. et al., eds. *Expectant Peoples: Nationalism and Development.* (New York: Random House, 1963).

STALEY, Eugene. *The Future of Underdeveloped Countries: Political Implications of Economic Development.* Revised edition (New York: Praeger, 1961).

SUTTON, Frank X. "Social Theory and Comparative Politics." In *Comparative Politics: A Reader,* edited by Harry Eckstein and David Apter (New York: Free Press, 1963). A seminal statement on the links between changes in social structure and political development.

THORNTON, Thomas Perry, ed. *The Third World in Soviet Perspective* (Princeton: Princeton University Press, 1964).

TILLY, C., ed. *The Formation of National States in Western Europe* (Princeton: Princeton University Press, forthcoming 1973). A collection of papers on aspects of state-building in Europe 1500-1800.

ULAM, Adam B. *The Unfinished Revolution* (New York: Random House, 1960). Comparative analysis of developments in Communist nations.

VORYS, Karl von. "New Nations: The Problem of Political Development." Annals of the American Academy of Political and Social Science (March 1965): 1-149.

WALLERSTEIN, I. M., ed. *Social Change: The Colonial Situation* (New York: John Wiley, 1966).

WEINER, Myron, ed. *Modernization: The Dynamics of Growth* (New York: Basic Books, 1966).

WHITAKER, C. S., Jr. "A Dysrhythmic Process of Political Change." World Politics 19, no. 2 (January 1967): 190-217.

WOLF, Eric. *Peasant Wars in the Twentieth Century* (New York: Harper, 1970). Anthropological analysis of centre-periphery conflicts in Mexico, Russia, China, Vietnam, Algeria, and Cuba.

ZIMMERMAN, L. J. *Arme en Rijke Landen* (Poor and Rich Countries) (The Hague: Albani, 1960; 2nd ed., 1964).

ZIPF, George Kingsley. *National Unity and Disunity: The Nation as a Bio-social Organism* (Bloomington, Ind.: Principia Press, 1944).

3. MAJOR AGENCIES OF TERRITORIAL CONSOLIDATION AND UNIFICATION

3.1 The role of dynasties and centre-forming networks

BLOCH, Marc. *Les Rois Thaumaturges. Etude Sur le Caractère Surnaturel Attribué à la Puissance Royale en France et en Angleterre* (Paris: 1924, reprinted Colin, 1961).

EISENSTADT, Shmuel N. "Traditional Patrimonialism and Modern Neo-patrimonialism." In *Sociological Studies—Social Change,* edited by J. S. Jackson (London: Cambridge University Press, forthcoming).

GOODY, Jack, ed. *Succession to High Office (Cambridge: Cambridge University Press, 1966).*

KANTOROWICZ, H. The King's Two Bodies (Princeton: Princeton University Press, 1957).

KRADER, L. *Formation of the State* (Englewood Cliffs, N.J.: Prentice-Hall, 1968).

MOORE, Barrington, Jr. *Social Origins of Dictatorship and Democracy: Lord and Peasant in the Modern World* (Boston: Beacon Press, 1966). A major comparative study.

ROTH, G. "Personal Rulership, Patrimonialism and Empirebuilding in the New States." Paper presented to World Congress of Sociology 6, Evian, September 4-11, 1966. Expanded version in R. Bendix and G. Roth. *Scholarship and Partisanship. Essays on Max Weber* (Berkeley: University of California Press, 1971).

SHILS, Edward. "Centre and Periphery." In *The Logic of Personal Knowledge: Essays Presented to Michael Polanyi on his Seventieth Birthday* (London: Routledge and Kegan Paul, 1962).

WITTFOGEL, Karl A. *Oriental Despotism* (New Haven, Conn.: Yale University Press, 1957). A provocative study of the "hydraulic" societies from Egypt to China: power based on control of irrigation works.

3.2 Military agencies

ANDRZEJEWSKI, Stanislav. *Military Organization and Society* (London: Routledge and Kegan Paul, 1954).

BERGER, Morroc. *Military Elite and Social Change* (Princeton: Princeton University, Center for International Studies, 1960).

DAALDER, Hans. *The Role of the Military in the Emerging Countries* (The Hague: Mouton, 1962).

FINER, S. K. *The Man on Horseback: The Role of the Military in Politics* (London: Pall Mall, 1962).

FRIED, Morton H. "Warfare, Military Organization, and the Evolution of Society." Anthropologica 3 (1961): 134-47.

GUTTERIDGE, William. *Armed Forces in the New States* (London: Oxford University Press, 1962).

HOWARD, Michael, ed. *Soldiers and Governments: Nine Studies in Civil-Military Relations* (London: Eyre & Spottiswoode, 1957).

HUNTINGTON, Samuel P. *The Soldier and the State: The Theory and Politics of Civil-Military Relations* (New York: Vintage Books, 1964).

JANOWITZ, Morris. *The Military in the Political Development of the New Nations* (Chicago: University of Chicago Press, 1964).

JOHNSON, John J., ed. *The Role of the Military in Underdeveloped Countries* (Princeton: Princeton University Press, 1962).

LISSAK, Moshe. "Center and Periphery in Developing Countries and Prototypes of Military Elites." Studies in Comparative International Development 5, no. 7 (1969-70).

NORDLINGER, Eric A. "Soldiers in the Mufti: The Impact of Military Rule upon Economic and Social Change in the Non-Western States." American Political Science Review 64, no. 4 (December 1970): 1131-48.

POPPER, Frank J. "Internal War as a Stimulant of Political Development." Comparative Political Studies, January 1971, pp. 413-23.

RAND CORPORATION, ed. *The Role of the Military in Underdeveloped Countries* (Princeton: Princeton University Press, 1962).

ROBERTS, Michael. *The Military Revolution: 1560-1660* (Belfast: Queen's University, 1962).

3.3 Administrative agencies

ALDERFELD, M. F. *Public Administration in Newer Nations* (New York: Praeger, 1966).

––– *Local Government in Developing Countries* (New York: McGraw-Hill, 1964).

BARKER, Ernest. *The Development of Administration, Conscription, Taxation, Social Services and Education.* European Civilization, edited by E. Eyre, Vol. V (Oxford: Oxford University Press, 1930).2nd ed., *The Development of the Public Services in Western Europe 1660-1930* (New York: Oxford University Press, 1945).

BELOFF, Max. *The Age of Absolutism, 1660-1815* (London: Hutchinson's University Library, 1954).

EISENSTADT, S. N. "Bureaucracy and Political Development." In *Bureaucracy and Political Development,* edited by Joseph Lapalombara (Princeton: Princeton University Press, 1963).

EISENSTADT, S. N. "Problems of Emerging Bureaucracies in Developing States." In *Industrialization and Society,* edited by B. Hoselitz and W. E. Moore (The Hague: Mouton, 1963).

FRIEDRICH, Carl J. *The Age of the Baroque: 1610-1660* (New York: Harper, 1952).

HECKSCHER, Eli. *Mercantilism* (London: Allen and Unwin, 1935). A classic treatise on the economics of state-building.

HOLT, Robert T. and John E. TURNER. *The Political Basis of Economic Development: An Exploration in Comparative Political Analysis* (Princeton, N.J.: Van Nostrand, 1966). A comparison of the role of the state in the economies of England, France, China, and Japan.

KLAVEREN, Jacob van. "Die Historische Erscheinung der Korruption in Ihrem Zusammenhang mit der Staats-und Gesellschaftsstruktur Betrachtet" (The Historical Emergence of Corruption in the Context of the Structure of State and Society). Vierteljahrschrift für Sozial-und Wirtschaftgeschichte, vols. 44 (1957), 45 (1958), 46 (1959).

――― "Fiskalismus–Mercantilismus–Korruption. Drei Aspekte der Finanz-und Wirtschaftspolitik Während des Ancien Régime" ("Fiscalism"–Mercantilism–Corruption. Three Aspects of Financial and Economic Policy During the Ancien Régime). Vierteljahrschrift für Sozial-und Wirtschaftgeschichte 47 (1960): 333-53.

LA PALOMBARA, Joseph, ed. *Bureaucracy and Political Development* (Princeton: Princeton University Press, 1963; paperback ed., 1967). Contains extensive bibliography on relationships between administration and development.

MONTGOMERY, J. and W. SIFFIN, eds. *Approaches to Development: Politics, Administration, and Change* (New York: McGraw, 1966).

MOUSNIER, Roland. *Les XVIe et XVIIe Siècles.* 3rd rev. ed. (Paris: Presses Universitaires de France, 1961).

PALMER, R. R. *The Age of the Democratic Revolution, the Challenge.* 2 vols. (Princeton: Princeton University Press, 1959).

RIGGS, Fred W. *Administration in Developing Countries: The Theory of Prismatic Society* (Boston: Houghton Mifflin, 1964).

――― ed. *Frontiers of Development Administration* (Durham, N.C.: Duke University Press, 1970).

3.4 The role of cities

ADAMS, Robert M. *The Evolution of Urban Society* (Chicago: Aldine, 1966).

BERRY, Brian J.L. "City Size Distributions and Economic Development." Economic Development and Cultural Change 9, no. 3 (1961): 573-88.

BERRY, Brian J.L. "City Size and Economic Development: Conceptual Synthesis and Policy Problems." In *Urbanization and national development,* edited by Leo Jakobson and Ved Prakase, pp. 111-55 (Beverly Hills: Sage, 1971).

BROWNINER, H. L. and Jack GIBBS. *Urban Research Methods* (Princeton: Van Nostrand, 1967). Chapter on "rank-size" problem.

BRUNNER, Otto. "Europäisches und Russisches Bürgertum" (European and Russian bourgeoisie). In *Neue Wege der Sozialgeschichte,* edited by Otto Brunner (Göttingen: Vandenhoeck and Ruprecth, 1956).

CASTELLS, Manuel. "Structures Sociales et Processus d'Urbanization: Analyse Comparative Intersociétale." Annales 25, no. 4 (1970): 1155-99.

COMHAIRE, Jean L. and Werner J. CAHNMAN. *How Cities Grew: The Historical Sociology of Cities* (Madison, N.Y.: Florham Park Press, 1959).

DAVIS, Kingsley. "Urbanization and the Development of Pre-industrial Areas." Economic Development and Cultural Change 3 (1954/55).

DEUTSCH, K. and H. WEILENMANN. "The Swiss City Canton: a Political Invention." Comparative Studies in Society and History 7, no. 4 (1965): 393-408.

GUTKIND, E. A. *The International History of City Development.* 2 vols. (New York: Free Press, 1964-65).

HOSELITZ, Bert F. "Generative and parasitic cities." Economic Development and Cultural Change 3 (1955): 278-94.

MORSE, Richard M. "Trends and Issues in Latin American Urban Research, 1965-1970." Latin American Research Review 6, no. 2 (1971): 19-75.

PIRENNE, Henri. *Medieval Cities* (Princeton: Princeton University Press, 1925; paperback ed., 1969). French original published in Brussels in 1927.

RIVKIN, M. D. "Urbanization and National Development: Some Approaches to the Dilemma." Socio-Economic Planning Science 1, no. 2 (December 1967): 117-42.

ROBINSON, Ronald, ed. *Industrialization in Developing Countries* (Cambridge: Cambridge University Overseas Studies Committee, 1965).

RODWIN, Lloyd. *Nations and Cities* (Boston: Houghton Mifflin, 1970).

VAPÑARSKY, Cesar. "On Rank-size Distributions of Cities: An Ecological Approach." Economic Development and Cultural Change 17, no. 4 (1969): 584-95.

WEBER, A. F. *The Growth of Cities in the Nineteenth Century* (New York: Macmillan 1899; current ed., Ithaca: Cornell University Press, 1965).

WEBER, Max. *The City* (New York: Free Press, 1958; paperback ed., 1966). Translated from "Die Stadt," originally published as part of Weber, Max. *Wirtschaft und Gesellschaft* (Tübingen: Mohr, 1922).

ZIPF, George Kingsley. *National Unity and Disunity* (Indiana: Principia Press, 1941).

See also Section 5.3, HAUSER.

3.5 The integration of peripheries: transportation networks and communication barriers

CHATTOPADHYAY, Gouranga and Barun DE. "Problems of Tribal Integration to Urban Industrial Society: A Theoretical Approach." Economic and Political Weekly, Bombay 4, no. 52 (1985-1994).

INNES, H. A. *Empire and Communication* (Oxford: Clarendon, 1950).

LERNER, Daniel. "Some Comments on Center-Periphery Relations." In *Comparing Nations*, edited by Richard L. Merritt and Stein Rokkan (New Haven and London: Yale University Press, 1966).

ULLMAN, E. "Regional Development and the Geography of Concentration." Papers and Proceedings of the Regional Science Association 4 (1958): 179-98.

WEBER, Max Maria. *Nationalität und Eisenbahn-politik* (Nationality and railroad politics) (Vienna: A. Harlteben's Verlag, 1876).

See also Section 6.9121, SOJA.

3.6 The integration of peripheries: dual economics and urban-rural economic linkages

BOEKE, Julius Herman. *Economics and Economic Policy of Dual Societies, as Exemplified by Indonesia* (New York: Institute of Pacific Relations, 1953; Harleem: H. D. Tjeenk Willink, 1953).

DOVRING, Folke. *Land and Labour in Europe 1900-1950* (The Hague: Mouton, 1956; 3rd ed., 1965).

FRIED, Morton H. "Land Tenure, Geography and Ecology in the Contact of Cultures." American Journal of Economics and Sociology 11 (1952): 391-412.

HUNTER, Gay. *Modernizing Peasant Societies: A Comparative Study in Asia and Africa* (New York: Oxford University Press, 1969).

MELLOR, John W. *The Economics of Agricultural Development* (Ithaca, N.Y.: Cornell University Press, 1966).

MILLIKAN, Max and David HAPGOOD, eds. *No Easy Harvest: The Dilemma of Agriculture in Underdeveloped Countries* (Boston: Little, Brown, 1967). A study from the Center for International Studies, MIT.

POIRIER, J. "Note sur la Spécificité des Nations Duelles." Paper presented to the World Congress of Sociology, Evian, September 4-11, 1966.

ROSOVSKY, Henry. "Peasants and the State." World Politics 9, no. 1 (October 1956): 129-39.

WOLF, Eric. *Peasants* (Englewood Cliffs, N.J.: Prentice-Hall, 1966).

SLICHER VAN BATH, B. H. *The Agrarian History of Western Europe A.D. 500-1850* (London: Arnold, 1963).

3.7 Ethnic stratification and the integration of elites

BELL, Wendell and Walter FREEMAN, eds. *Ethnicity and Nation-Building: Comparative International and Historical Perspectives* (Beverly Hills: Sage, 1972).

BOTTOMORE, T. B. *Elites and Society* (London: C. A. Watts, 1964).

DEAN, Vera Micheles. *Builders of Emerging Nations* (New York: Holt, Rinehart and Winston, 1961).

KELLER, Suzanne, *Beyond the Ruling Class* (New York: Random, 1963).

SHIBUTANI, Tamotsu and Kian M. KWAN. *Ethnic Stratification: A Comparative Approach* (New York: Macmillan, 1965).

SILVERT, Kalman. "National Values, Development, and Leaders and Followers." International Social Science Journal 15 (1963): 560-70.

3.8 Trans-territorial transactions: economic integration and dependence

AMIN, Semir. *L'accumulation à l'Echelle Mondiale: Critique de la Théorie de Sous-Développement* (Paris: Anthropos, 1970).

BALASSA, Bela. *The Theory of Economic Integration* (Homewood, Ill.: Irwin, 1961).

CARDOSO, F. H. and L. FALETTO. *Dependencia y Desarollo en Americana Latina* (Mexico: Siglo XXI, 1969).

DOS SANTOS, T. "The Structure of Dependence" American Economic Review, Papers and Proceedings, May 1970.

GALTUNG, Johan. "A Structural Theory of Imperialism." Journal of Peace Res. 2 (1971): 81-118.

JALEE, Pierre. *L'Impérialisme en 1970* (Paris: Mospéro, 1970).

——— *Le Pillage du Tiers Monde* (Paris: Mospéro, 1965). English translation, *The Pillage of the Third World* (New York: Monthly Review Press, 1969).

See also Section 5.6, FRANK.

3.9 Trans-territorial transactions: political integration

BELL, J. Bowyer. "Contemporary Revolutionary Organizations." International Organization 30, no. 3 (Summer 1971).

DEUTSCH, Karl W. et al. *Political Community and the North Atlantic Area:*

International Organization in the Light of Historical Experience (Princeton: Princeton University Press, 1957).

ETZIONI, Amitai. *Political Unification* (New York: Holt, Rinehart and Winston, 1965).

HAAS, Ernst B. *The Uniting of Europe* (Stanford: Stanford University Press, 1958).

JACOB, P. and J. TOSCANO, eds. *The Integration of Political Communities* (Philadelphia: Lippincott, 1964).

MERRITT, Richard L. "Distance and Interaction Among Political Communities." General Systems: Yearbook of the Society for General Systems Research 9 (1964): 255-63.

RUSSETT, B. *International Regions and the International System* (Chicago: Rand McNally, 1968).

4. NATION-BUILDING AND CULTURAL STANDARDIZATION

4.1 General analyses

KUSHNER, Gilbert et al. *What Accounts for Sociocultural change?* (Chapel Hill, N.C.: Institute for Research in Social Sciences, 1962).

MANNERS, Robert A., ed. *Process and Pattern in Culture* (Chicago: Aldine, 1964).

MEAD, Margaret. *Continuities in Cultural Evolution* (New Haven, Conn.: Yale University Press, 1964).

SCHNEIDER, Louis, ed. *Religion, Culture and Society* (New York: John Wiley, 1964).

SHILS, Edward. "Primordial, Personal, Sacred and Civil Ties." British Journal of Sociology 8, no. 2 (June 1957): 130-45.

SILVERT, K. H. "The Costs of Anti-nationalism." In *Expectant Peoples: Nationalism and Development,* edited by K. H. Silvert, pp. 347-72 (New York: Random, 1963).

STEWARD, Julian H. *Theory of Culture Change* (Urbana: University of Illinois Press, 1955).

WHITE, Leslie. *The Evolution of Culture* (New York: McGraw-Hill, 1959).

4.2 The role of language: unification versus differentiation

CENTER FOR APPLIED LINGUISTICS. *Second Language Learning as a Factor in National Development in Asia, Africa, and Latin America* (Washington, D.C., 1961).

CIPOLLA, Carlo M. *Literacy and Development in the West* (Harmondsworth: Penguin, 1969).

DAUZAT, Albert. *L'Europe Linguistique* (Paris: Bibliothèque Scientifique, 1940).

ELWERT, Th. *Das Zweisprachige Individium* (The Bilinguistical individual) (Wiesbaden: F. Steiner, 1960).

FISHMAN, Joshua A., ed. *Readings in the Sociology of Language* (The Hague and Paris: Mouton, 1968).

FISHMAN, J. A.; C. A. FERGUSON; and J. D. GUPTA, eds. *Language Problems of Developing Nation* (New York: John Wiley, 1968).

FLORA, Peter. "Historische Prozesse Sozialer Mobilisierung: Urbanisierung und

Alphabetisierung, 1850-1965" (Historical Processes of Social Mobilization: Urbanization and Literacy Development, 1850-1965). Zeitschrift für Soziologue 1, no. 2 (April 1972): 85-117. Revised version in Chapter 7 in Volume 1 of this work.

GOODY, Jack, ed. *Literacy in Traditional Societies* (Cambridge, Eng.: Cambridge University Press, 1968).

GOODY, Jack and I. WATT. "The Consequences of Literacy." Comparative Studies in Society and History 5, no. 3 (1963): 304-45, later revised in Goody, this subsection.

HANSEGARD, Nils Erik. *Tvåspråkighet eller halvspåkighet?* (Bilingualism or Half-lingualism?) (Stockholm: Aldus, 1968).

HAUGEN, Einar. "Dialect, Language and Nation." American Anthropologist 68, no. 4 (August 1966): 922-35.

——— "Linguistics and Language Planning." In *Sociolinguistics: Proceedings of the UCLA Sociolinguistics Conference, 1964,* edited by William Bright (The Hague: Mouton, 1966).

HENLE, P. *Language, Thought and Culture* (Ann Arbor: University of Michigan Press, 1958).

HERAUD, Guy. *Peuples et Langues d'Europe* (Paris: Ed. Denoël, 1966).

HYMES, Dell, ed. *Pidginization and Creolization of Languages* (Cambridge, Eng.: Cambridge University Press, 1970).

JESPERSEN, Otto. *Mankind, Nation and Individual from a Linguistic Point of View* (Cambridge, Mass.: Harvard University Press, 1925).

KLOSS, Heinz. "Notes Concerning a Language–Nation Typology." In *Language Problems of Developing Nations,* edited by J. A. Fishman et al., in this subsection.

LADO, Robert. *Linguistics Across Cultures* (Ann Arbor: University of Michigan Press, 1957).

McRAE, Kenneth. "Belgium and Canada as Plurilingual States: Some Introductory Comparisons of Linguistic Policies." Paper presented to the American Political Science Association, 65th annual meeting, New York, September 2-6, 1969.

MURRA, J., ed. *The Soviet Linguistic Controversy* (New York: King's Crown Press, 1951). Collection of articles on the Stalin-Marr controversy.

ORNSTEIN, Jacob. "Patterns of Language Planning in the New States." World Politics 17, no. 1 (October 1964): 40-49.

POOL, Jonathan. "National Development and Language Diversity." Paper presented to The American Political Science Association, 65th annual meeting, New York, September 2-6, 1969.

RICE, Frank A., ed. *Study of the Role of Second Languages in Asia, Africa and Latin America* (Washington, D.C.: Center for Applied Linguistics of the Modern Language Association of America, 1962).

RUSTOW, Dankwart A. "Language, Modernization, and Nationhood–an Attempt at Typology." In *Language Problems of Developing Nations,* edited by Joshua A. Fishman et al. (New York: John Wiley, 1968).

SINCLAIR-DE-ZWART, H. "Linguistique et Sociologie." Paper presented to the World Congress of Sociology 6, Evian, September 4-11, 1966.

STALIN, Joseph V. *Marxism and Problems of Linguistics* (New York: Four Continent Book Corp., 1954).

TAULI, Valter. *Introduction to a Theory of Language Planning* (Uppsala: Almquist and Wiksell, 1968).

VILDOMEC, V. *Multilingualism. General Linguistics and Psychology of Speech* (Leyden: A. W. Sythoff, 1963).
VREELAND, H. H. "The Concept of Ethnic Groups as Related to Whole Societies." *In Report of the ninth annual Round Table Meeting on Linguistics and Language Studies,* edited by W. M. Austin (Washington, D.C.: Georgetown University Press, 1958).
WEINREICH, U. *Languages in Contact* (New York: Linguistic Circle of New York, 1953; The Hague: Mouton, 1963).

4.3 The role of schools and academies

ANDERSON, Charles Arnold and Mary Jean BOWMAN, eds. *Education and Economic Development* (Chicago: Aldine, 1965).
COLEMAN, James S., ed. *Education and Political Development* (Princeton: Princeton University Press, 1965). A volume in the series of the Committee on Comparative Politics.
DORE, Ronald Philip. *Education in Tokugawa Japan* (Berkeley: University of California Press, 1965).
GOOD, H. G. *A History of Western Education* (New York: Macmillan, 1966).
HEINTZ, P. "Education as an Instrument to Social Integration in Underdeveloped Countries." Paper presented to the World Congress of Sociology, Evian, September 4-11, 1966.
LEVASSEUR, E. *L'enseignement Primaire Dans les Pays Civilisés* (Paris: Berger-Lerraut, 1897).
RAMANATHAN, G. *Educational Planning and National Integration* (London: Asia Publishing House, 1965).

4.4 The role of the mass media

DEXTER, Lewis Anthony and David Manning WHITE, eds. *People, Society, and Mass Communications* (New York: Free Press, 1964).
FAGEN, Richard R. *Politics and Communication* (Boston: Little, Brown, 1966).
LERNER, D. and W. SCHRAMM, eds. *Communication and Change in Developing Countries* (Honolulu: East-West Center Press, 1967).
McLUHAN, Marshall. *The Gutenberg Galaxy* (London: Routledge, 1962).
OLIVER, Rober T. *Culture and Communication: The Problem of Penetrating National and Cultural Boundaries* (Springfield, Ill.: Thomas, 1962).
PYE, Lucian. *Communication and Political Development* (Princeton: Princeton University Press, 1963). A volume in the series of the Committee on Comparative Politics.
SCHRAMM, Wilbur. *Mass Media and National Development: The Role of Information in the Developing Countries* (Stanford: Stanford University Press, 1964).
WILDMANN, Hans. *Geschichte des Buchhandels vom Altertum bis zur Gegenwart* (History of the Booksellers' from Antiquity to the Present time) (Wiesbaden: Otto Harrassowitz, 1952).

4.5 Churches and sects as agencies of identity-building

ALBRECHT, Paul. *The Churches and the Rapid Social Change* (Garden City, N.Y.: Doubleday, 1961).

COULBORN, Rushton. *The Origin of Civilized Societies* (Princeton: Princeton University Press, 1959).

FRANZ, G. *Kulturkampf: Staat und Katholische Kirche in Mitteleuropa* (Munich: Callweg, 1954).

GLOCK, Charles Y. and Rodney STARK. *Religion and Society in Tension* (Chicago: Rand McNally, 1965).

GREEN, Robert W., ed. *Protestantism and Capitalism* (New York: D. C. Heath, 1959).

HAYES, Carlton I.H. "The Church and Nationalism—A Plea for Further Study of a Major Issue." The Catholic Historical Review 28 (April 1942): 1-12.

LAQUEUR, Walter and George L. MOSSE, eds. "Church and Politics." Journal of Contemporary History 2 (October 1967): entire issue.

LENSKI, Gerhard. *The Religious Factor: A Sociological Study of Religion's Impact on Politics, Economics, and Family Life* (Garden City, N.Y.: Doubleday, 1961).

MOODY, J. N., ed. *Church and Society* (New York: Arts Inc., 1953).

Religious Pluralism and Social Structure (Cologne: Westdeutscher Verlag, 1965).

ROSENTHAL, Erwin I.J. *Islam in the Modern National State* (London: Cambridge University Press, 1965).

SMITH, Donald E. *Religion and Political Development* (Boston: Little, Brown, 1970). Reviews the influence of Hinduism, Buddhism, Islam, and Catholicism on political development.

SWANSON, Guy E. *Religion and Regime: A Sociological Account of the Reformation* (Ann Arbor: University of Michigan Press, 1967).

WATT, W. Montgomery. *Islam and the Integration of the Society* (London: Routledge and Kegan Paul, 1961).

WEARMOUTH, Robert Fetherstone. *The Social and Political Influence of Methodism in the Twentieth Century* (London: Epworth Press, 1957).

WEBER, Max. *The Sociology of Religion* (Boston: Beacon Press, 1963). First published in German as WEBER, Max. "Religionssoziologie." In *Wirtschaft und Gesellschaft* (Tübingen: Mohr, 1922).

——— *The Protestant Ethic and the Spirit of Capitalism* (London: Allen & Unwin, 1930). Translated from "Die Protestantische Ethik, und der Geist des Kapitalismus," first published as part of Vol. I of Weber, Max. *Gesammelte Aufsätze zur Religionssoziologie.* 3 vols. (Tübingen: Mohr, 1922-23). Numerous editions.

WIJESEKERA, O. H. de A. *Buddhism and Society* (Colombo: Bauddha Sahitya Sabha, 1954).

5. ANALYTICAL STUDIES OF CONDITIONS AND TRENDS OF POLITICAL DEVELOPMENT IN MAJOR WORLD AREAS

5.1 General analyses

BRAUDEL, F. *La Méditerranée et le Monde Méditarranéen à l'Epoque de Philippe II* (Paris: Colin, 1949). A classic analysis of the links between Asia, Africa, and Europe at a crucial juncture of history.

COULBORN, Rushton, ed. *Feudalism in History* (Hamden, Conn.: Archon Books, 1965).

DEAN, Vera M. *The Nature of the Non-Western World* (New York: New American Library, 1957).

DORE, R. P. "Latin America and Japan Compared." In *Continuity and Change in Latin America,* edited by John J. Johnson, pp. 227-49 (Stanford: Stanford University Press, 1964).

EISENSTADT, Shmuel N. *The Political Systems of Empires* (New York: Free Press, 1963).

PARSONS, Talcott. *Structure and Process in Modern Societies* (Glencoe, Ill.: Free Press, 1960).

STEWARD, Julian Haynes et al. *Irrigation Civilizations: A Comparative Study* (Washington, D.C.: Pan American Union, Dept. of Cultural Affairs, Social Science Section, 1955).

TOYNBEE, Arnold J. *A Study of History.* 12 vols. (London: Oxford University Press, 1934-61). A major contribution to the philosophy of history.

5.2 The distinctiveness of European developments

BLOCH, M. *La Societé Féodale* (Paris: Albin Michel, 1939). English translation *Feudal Society* (Chicago: University of Chicago Press, 1961).

BRYCE, James. *The Holy Roman Empire* (Oxford, 1864; 3rd revised ed., London: Macmillan, 1871). Numerous editions.

BURRELL, Sidney A., ed. *The Role of Religion in Modern European History.* (New York: Macmillan, 1964).

CHRISTERN, Hermann. *Deutscher Ständesstaat und Englischer Parlamentarismus am Ende des 18. Jahrhunderts* (German Estate Régime and English Parliamentarism by the End of the 18th Century) (Munich: Beck, 1939).

CLAGETT, Marshall; Gaines POST; and Robert REYNOLDS, eds. *Twelfth-century Europe and the Foundations of Modern Society* (Madison: University of Wisconsin Press, 1961).

COUDENHOVE-KALERGI, R. N. *Die Europäische Nation* (The European Nation) (Stuttgart: Deutsche Verlags-Anstalt, 1953).

DAWSON, Christopher. *The Making of Europe* (London: Sheed and Ward, 1932; new ed., 1971).

GERHARD, Dietrich. "Regionalismus und Ständisches Wesen als ein Grundthema Europäischer Geschichte" (Regionalism and "Estatism" as a Basic Theme in European history). *Historische Zeitschrift* 174, Berlin, 1952. Reprinted in *Alte und Neue Wege der Vergleichenden Geschichtesbetrachtung* (Old Versus New Approaches to Comparative History), by Dietrich Gerhard (Göttingen: Vandenhoeck and Ruprecht, 1962).

GOODWIN, A., ed. *The European Nobility in the Eighteenth Century* (London: A. & C. Black, 1953).

GRAUS, I. "Die Entshehung des Mittelalterlichen Staates in Europa" (The Origins of the Medieval State) Historia, Prague 10 (1965): 5-65.

HAMPSON, N. *The First European Revolution, 1776-1815* (New York: Harcourt Brace, 1970).

HERAUD, G. *L'Europe des Ethnies* (Paris: Presses d'Europe, 1963). Review of information on major and minor ethnic groupings.

HROCH, M. *Die Vorkämpfer der Nationalen Bewegung bei den Kleinen Völkern Europas* (The Protagonists of the National Movement in the Small European

Nationalities) (Prague: Acta University of Carol., Philosophy and History 24, 1968).

KIERNAN, V. G. "State and Nation in Western Europe." Past and Present 31, 1965: 20-38.

KOHN, H. *Preludes to Nation-States, the French and the German Experience 1789-1815* (Princeton: Van Nostrand, 1967).

LANDES, David S. *The Unbound Prometheus* (Cambridge, Mass.: Harvard University Press, 1969). An analytical account of the Industrial Revolution in Europe.

McNEILL, William H. *The Rise of the West: A History of the Human Community* (Chicago: University of Chicago Press, 1965).

NEF, John V. *Cultural Foundations of Industrial Civilization* (Cambridge, Eng.: Cambridge University Press, 1958).

PARSONS, Talcott. *The System of Modern Societies* (Englewood Cliffs, N.J.: Prentice-Hall, 1971).

SINAI, I. Robert. *The Challenge of Modernization: The West's Impact on the Non-Western World* (London: Chatto and Windus; New York: Norton, 1964).

SMITH, C. T. *An Historical Geography of Western Europe Before 1800* (New York: Praeger, 1967).

STEINBERG, S. H. *The Thirty Years' War and the Conflict for European Hegemony, 1600-1660* (New York: Norton, 1966).

STOYE, John. *Europe Unfolding, 1648-1688* (New York: Harper, 1969).

TREVOR-ROPER, Hugh. *Religion, Reformation and Social Change* (London: Macmillan, 1967).

WHITTLESEY, Derwent Stainthorpe. *Environmental Foundations of European History* (New York: Appleton-Century-Crofts, 1949).

WILLIAMS, Ernest Neville. *The Ancien Regime in Europe: Governments and Society in the Major States, 1648-1789* (London: Bodley Head, 1970).

5.3 The Asian empires

BELLAH, Robert K., ed. *Religion and Progress in Modern Asia* (New York: Free Press, 1956). Chapters on Hinduism, Islam, and Buddhism.

BRAIBANTI, Ralph J., ed. *Asian Bureaucratic Systems Emergent from the British Imperial Tradition: Burma, Ceylon, India, Malaya, Nepal, Pakistan* (Durham, N.C.: Duke University Press, 1966).

BRECHER, Michael. *The New States of Asia* (London: Oxford University Press, 1963).

CARRERE d'ENCAUSSE, Hélène and Stuart SCHRAM. *Le Marxisme et l'Asie* (Paris: Colin, 1965). Useful collection of Marxist texts on empires and nation-building in Asia. Also in English (London: Lane, 1969).

CHEBOCSAROV, N. N. "Processes of National Consolidation in Countries of South and South-Eastern Asia." Paper presented to the World Congress of Sociology 6, Evian, September 4-11, 1966.

CLYDE, Paul Hibbert. *The Far East: A History of the Impact of the West on Eastern Asia* (Englewood Cliffs, N.J.: Prentice-Hall, 1958).

EMERSON, Rupert. "Paradoxes of Asian Nationalism" Far Eastern Quarterly 13, no. 2 (February 1954).

HAUSER, Ph., ed. *Urbanization in Asia and the Far East* (Calcutta: Unesco Research Center on the Social Implications of Industrialization in Southern Asia, 1957).

KATZ-SUCHY, Julius. "National Liberation and Social Progress in Asia." Annals of the American Academy of Political and Social Science 276 (July 1951): 48-59.

LINEBARGER, Paul M.A.; Djang CHU; and Ardath W. BURKS. *Far Eastern Government and Politics: China and Japan* (Princeton: Van Nostrand, 1967).

LYALL, Alfred. *Asiatic Studies* (London: John Murray, 1882).

MADAN, B. K., ed. *Economic Problems of Underdeveloped Countries in Asia* (New York: Russell & Russell, 1967).

ROMEIN, Jan N. *The Asian Century: A History of Modern Nationalism in Asia* (Berkeley: University of California Press, 1962).

MYRDAL, Gunnar. *Asian Drama: An Inquiry into the Poverty of Nations.* 3 vols. (New York: Twentieth Century Fund, 1968).

SMITH, Donald E., ed. *South Asian Politics and Religion* (Princeton: Princeton University Press, 1966).

WERTHEIM, W. F. *East-West Parallels: Sociological Approaches to Modern Asia* (The Hague: W. van Hoeve, 1964).

See also Section 2.2, GEERTZ.

5.4 The Moslem empires

ASAD, Muhammad. *The Principles of State and Government in Islam* (Los Angeles: University of California Press, 1961).

ASHFORD, Douglas E. "The Political Usage of 'Islam' and 'Arab culture'." Public Opinion Quarterly 25 (Spring 1961): 106-14.

BADEAU, John Stothoff. "Islam and the Modern Middle East." Foreign Affairs 38 (October 1959): 61-74.

BAER, Gabriel. *Population and Society in the Arab East* (New York: Praeger, 1964).

BERGER, Morroe. *The Arab World Today* (New York: Doubleday, 1962).

BROCKELMANN, Carl. *History of the Islamic Peoples* (New York: Capricorn Books, 1962).

DAWN, Clarence Ernest. "From Ottomanianism to Arabism: The Origin of an Ideology." Review of Politics 23 (July 1961): 378-400.

FRYE, Richard N., ed. *Islam and the West* (The Hague and New York: Lounz, 1957).

GEERTZ, Clifford. *Islam Observed: Religious Development in Morocco and Indonesia* (Chicago: University of Chicago Press, 1971).

GIBB, H.A.R. and H. BOWEN. *Islamic Society and the West, Islamic Society in the Eighteenth Century.* 2 vols. (Oxford: Oxford University Press, 1950-57).

HAIM, Sylvia, ed. *Arab Nationalism* (Berkeley: University of California Press, 1962).

HALPERN, Manfred. *The Politics of Social Change in the Middle East and North Africa* (Princeton: Princeton University Press, 1963).

HAMADY, Sania. *Temperament and Character of the Arabs* (New York: Twayne, 1960).

KEREKES, Tibor, ed. *The Arab Middle East and Muslim Africa* (New York: Praeger, 1961).

KHADOURI, Majid. *The Islamic Law of Nations: Shaybani's Siyar* (Baltimore: Johns Hopkins Press, 1966).

LAPIDUS, Ivo. *Muslin Cities in the Later Middle Ages* (Cambridge, Mass.: Harvard University Press, 1967).

LAROUI, A. *L'idéologie Arabe Contemporaine, Essai Critique* (Paris: Maspéro, 1967).

LEVY, R. *The Social Structure of Islam* (London: Cambridge University Press, 1962).

RODINSON, Maxime. *Marxisme et Monde Musulman* (Paris: Ed. du Seuil, 1971). A collection of essays on socialism and nationalism in the Arab world.

SPULER, Bertold. *The Muslim World* (Leiden: E. J. Brill, 1960).

von GRUNEBAUM, Gustave E. *Modern Islam: The Search for a Cultural Identity* (New York: Vintage, 1964).

5.5 The Anglo-Saxon settler regimes

BRYCE, James. *Modern Democracies* (New York: Macmillan, 1921).

HARTZ, Louis, et al. *The Founding of New Societies* (New York: Harcourt, Brace and World, 1964). Chapters on each of the English-speaking polities in North America, Africa, and Australia.

HARTZ, Louis. *The Liberal Tradition in America: An Interpretation of American Political Thought Since the Revolution* (New York: Harcourt Brace, 1970).

HUNTINGTON, Shmuel P. "Political Modernization: America vs. Europe." World Politics 18 (April 1966): 378-414.

LIPSET, Seymour Martin. *Revolution and Counter-revolution* (New York: Basic Books, 1968). A systematic comparison of developments in Canada and the United States.

5.6 The Iberian settler regimes

ARCINIEGAS, German. *Latin America: A Cultural History* (New York: Knopf, 1967).

BARRACLOUGH, Solon and Arthur L. DOMIKE. "Agrarian Structure in Seven Latin American Countries." Land Economics 42 (1966): 391-424.

BLANCO-FOMBONA, Rufino. *La Evolución Política y Social de Hispano-América* (The Political and Social Evolution in Spanish America) (Madrid: B. Rodriguez, 1911).

CALDERON, Francisco Garcia. *Latin America, its Rise and Progress* (New York: Charles Scribner's Sons, 1913).

FRANK, André Gunder. *Capitalism and Under-development in Latin America* (New York: Monthly Review Press, 1967).

FURTADO, Celso. *Subdesenvolvimento e Estagnacão na América Latina* (Underdevelopment and Stagnation in Latin America) (Río de Janeiro: Civilizacão Brasileira, 1968).

FURTADO, Celso. *Obstacles to Development in Latin America.* (New York: Anchor Books, 1970).

GALTUNG, Johan; Manuel MORA Y ARAUJO; and Simon SCHWARTZMAN. "El sistema Latino Americano de Naciones, un Analisis Estructural" (The Latin American System of Nations, a Structural Analysis) América Latina 9, no. 1 (1971).

GRAÑA, César. "Cultural Nationalism: The Idea of Historical Destiny in Spanish America." Social Research 29 (1962): 395-418; 30 (1963): 37-52.

HANKE, L., ed. *Do the Americas Have a Common History? A Critique of the Bolton Theory* (New York: Knopf, 1964).

HARING, Clarence H. *The Spanish Empire in America* (New York: Oxford University Press, 1947).

HUMPHREYS, R. A. and John LYNCH, eds. *The Origins of Latin American Revolutions, 1808-1826* (New York: 1965).

KAPLAN, Marcos. *Formacion del Estado Nacional en America Latina* (The Formation of National States in Latin America) (Santiago de Chile: Ed. Universitaria, 1969).

LYNCH, J. *Spanish Colonial Administration 1782-1810* (London: Athlone Press, 1958).

MORSE, R. M. "Toward a Theory of Spanish American Government." Journal of the History of Ideas 15, no. 2 (January 1954): 71-77.

PARRY, J. H. *The Spanish Seaborne Empire* (London: Hutchinson, 1966).

RIBEIRO, Darcy. *The Americas and Civilization.* Translated by L. L. Barrett and M. M. Barrett (London: Allen and Unwin, 1971).

––– *The Civilizational Process* (Washington, D.C.: Smithsonian Institute, 1969).

SARFATTI, Magali. *Spanish Bureaucratic Patrimonialism in America* (Berkeley: University of California Press, 1966).

SCOTT, Robert. "Nation-building in Latin America." In *Nation-Building,* edited by Karl W. Deutsch and William J. Foltz (New York: Atherton Press, 1963).

SILVERT, Kalman. *The Conflict Society: Reaction and Revolution in Latin America* (New Orleans: Hauser Press, 1961).

VALLIER, Ivan. *Catholicism, Social Control and Modernization in Latin America* (Englewood Cliffs, N.J.: Prentice-Hall, 1970).

WIARDA, Howard. "Toward a Framework for the Study of Political Change in the Ibero-Latin Tradition: The Corporative Model" World Politics 25, no. 2 (January 1973): 206-35.

WORCESTER, Donald E. "The Spanish-American Past, Enemy of Change." Journal of Inter-American Studies 11, no. 1 (January 1961): 66.

ZEA, Leopoldo. *The Latin American Mind* (Norman: University of Oklahoma Press, 1963). Translated from *America en la Historia* (Mexico, 1957).

See also Section 2.2, GERMANI.

5.7 The distinctiveness of conditions in Black Africa

ADE Ajayi, J. F. and Jan ESPIE, eds. *A Thousand Years of West African History* (London: Ibadan University Press, 1965).

BASCOM, William Russell and Melville J. HERSKOVITS, eds. *Continuity and Change in African Cultures* (Chicago: University of Chicago Press, 1958).

BATTEN, Thomas Reginald. *Africa, Past and Present* (London: Oxford University Press, 1959).

BATTEN, Thomas Reginald. *Problems of African Development* (London: Oxford University Press, 1964).

BUSIA, K. A. *Africa in Search of Democracy* (New York: Praeger, 1967).

COHEN, Ronald and John MIDDLETON, eds. *From Tribe to Nation in Africa: Studies in Incorporation Processes* (Scranton, Penn.: Chandler, 1970).

COLEMAN, James S. "Nationalism in Tropical Africa." In *Political Change in Underdeveloped Countries,* edited by John Kautsky (New York: John Wiley, 1962).

CROWDER, Michael. *West Africa Under Colonial Rule* (London: Hutchinson, 1968).

DAVIDSON, Basil. *A History of West Africa to the Nineteenth Century* (Garden City, N.Y.: Doubleday, 1966).

DIOP, Cheikh Anta. *L'Afrique Noire Pré-coloniale* (Paris: Présence Africaine, 1960).

DUMONT, René. *L'Afrique Noire est Mal Partie* (Paris: Ed. du Seuil, 1962).

FAGE, J. D. *An Introduction to the History of West Africa* (Cambridge, Eng.: Cambridge University Press, 1962).

FALLERS, Lloyd. "Political Sociology and the Anthropological Study of African Politics." Archives Européenes de Sociologie 4, no. 2 (1963): 311-29.

FORTES, M. and E. E. EVANS-PRITCHARD, eds. *African Political Systems* (London: Oxford University Press, 1950).

FROBENIUS, Leo. *Das Unbekannte Afrika* (The Unknown Africa) (Munich: Beck, 1923).

GIBBS, James L., ed. *Peoples of Africa* (New York: Holt, Rinehart and Winston, 1965).

GLUCKMAN, Max. *Custom and Conflict in Africa* (Oxford: Blackwell, 1956).

GOODY, Jack. *Technology, Tradition and the State in Africa* (London: Oxford University Press, 1971).

――― "Economy and Feudalism in Africa." Economic History Review 22, no. 3 (December 1969): 393-504.

GREENBERG, Joseph H. *The Languages of Africa* (Bloomington: Indiana University Press; The Hague: Mouton, 1963).

GUTKIND, Peter C.W., ed. *The Passing of Tribal Man in Africa* (Leiden: E. J. Brill, 1970).

HAILEY, Malcolm. *Native Administration and Political Development in Tropical Africa* (London: HMSO, 1942).

HERSKOVITS, M. S. *The Human Factor in Changing Africa* (New York: Knopf, 1962).

HODGKIN, Thomas Lionel. "Islam and National Movements in West Africa." Journal of African History 3 (1962): 323-28.

――― *Nationalism in Colonial Africa* (London: Muller; New York: New York University Press, 1956).

INTERNATIONAL AFRICAN INSTITUTE. *Social Implications of Industrialization and Urbanization in Africa South of the Sahara* (Paris: UNESCO, 1956).

KAMARCK, Andrew M. *The Economics of African Development* (New York: Praeger, 1967).

KUPER, Leo and M. G. SMITH, eds. *Pluralism in Africa* (Berkeley: University of California Press, 1969).

LEWIS, I. M., ed. *Islam in Tropical Africa* (London: Oxford University Press, 1966).

MARKOF, W. "La Nation en Afrique Tropicale: Notion et Structure." Paper presented to the World Congress of Sociology 6, Evian, September 4-11, 1966.

MAZRUI, Ali A. "Borrowed Theory and Original Practice in African Politics." In *Patterns of African Development,* edited by Herbert J. Spiro (Englewood Cliffs, N.J.: Prentice-Hall, 1967).

MIDDLETON, John. *The Effects of Economic Development on Traditional Political Systems in Africa South of the Sahara* (Paris: Mouton, 1961).

MIDDLETON, J. and D. TAIT. *Tribes Without Rulers. Studies in African Segmentary Systems* (London: Routledge and Kegan Paul, 1958).

MITCHELL, James Clyde. *Tribalism and the Plural Society, an Inaugural Lecture* (London: Oxford University Press, 1960).

SPIRO, Hubert J. *Patterns of African Development: Five Comparisons* (Englewood Cliffs, N.J.: Prentice-Hall, 1967).

VAN DEN BERGHE, Pierre L., ed. *Africa: Social Problems of Change and Conflict* (San Francisco: Chandler, 1965).

WESTERMANN, D. *Geschichte Afrikas: Staatenbildungen Südlich der Sahara* (History of Africa: State Formations South of the Sahara) (Cologne: Greven-Verlag, 1952).

WILSON, Godfrey and Monica WILSON. *The Analysis of Social Change, Based on Observations in Central Africa* (Cambridge, Eng.: Cambridge University Press, 1965).

WRIGLEY, C. C. "Historicism in Africa: Slavery and State Formation." African Affairs 70, no. 279 (April 1971).

See also Section 2.2, GEERTZ.

6. ANALYTICAL STUDIES OF INDIVIDUAL POLITIES

6.1 The early Western polities

BLOCH, Marc. *Les Rois Thaumaturges* (Strasbourg: Istra, 1921; new ed., Paris: Colin, 1961). Important study of kingship in England and France.

NEF, John U. *Industry and Government in France and England 1540-1640* (Philadelphia: American Philosophical Society, 1940).

PETIT-DUTAILLIS, Ch. *La Monarchie Féodale en France et en Angleterre, X-XIII s* (Paris: Renaissance du Livre, 1933). English translation, *Feudal Monarchy in France and Britain* (London: Routledge, 1936; reprinted 1964). A classic of comparative history.

6.11 Great Britain

BROWN, J. *The Un-Melting Pot. An English Town and its Immigrants* (London: Macmillan, 1970).

COUPLAND, Reginald. *Welsh and Scottish Nationalism* (London: Collins, 1954).

EDWARDS, Owen Dudley, et al. *Celtic Nationalism* (London: Routledge and Kegan Paul, 1968).

HECHTER, Michael. "Regional Inequality and National Integration in the British Isles, 1801-1921." Paper presented to the American Sociological Association, Annual Meeting, San Francisco, 1969.

JACKSON, John A. *The Irish in Britain* (London: Routledge and Kegan Paul, 1963).

ROSE, Richard. "The United Kingdom as a Multi-national Regime." In *Governing Without Consensus,* by Richard Rose, pp. 42-73 (London: Faber, 1971).

6.111 England

BINDOFF, S. T. *Tudor England* (London: Penguin, 1950).

CLARK, G. Kitson. *The Making of Victorian England* (London: Methuen, 1962).

DUBOULAY, F.R.H. "The Identity of England." In *The Age of Ambition. English Society in the Late Middle Ages,* ch. 2 (London: Nelson, 1970).

ELTON, G. R. *England Under the Tudors* (London: Methuen, 1955).

GALBRAITH, V. M. "Nationality and Language in Medieval England." Transactions of the Royal Historical Society, 4th series 23, (1941): 113-29.

JOHNSON, Paul. *The Offshore Islanders* (New York: Holt, 1972). A provocative interpretation of English nation-building *against* Europe.

KEENEY, B. C. "Military Service and the Development of Nationalism in England 1272-1327." Speculum 22 (1947): 534-49.

MAITLAND, F. W. *The Constitutional History of England* (Cambridge, Eng.: Cambridge University Press, 1963).

MATHEW, David. *Catholicism in England 1535-1935. Portrait of a Minority, Its Culture and Tradition* (London: Longmans, 1936).

PERKIN, Harold. *The Origins of Modern English Society, 1780-1880* (Toronto: University of Toronto Press, 1969).

PLUMB, J. H. *The Growth of Political Stability in England 1675-1725* (London: Macmillan, 1967).

POSTAN, M. M. "The Economic and Political Relations of England and the Hansa from 1400 to 1475." In *Studies in English Trade in the 15th Century,* edited by E. Power and M. M. Postan (London: Routledge, 1933, reprinted 1951).

READ, Donald. *The English Provinces c. 1760-1960* (London: Arnold, 1964).

ROSE, Richard. "England: A Traditionally Modern Political Culture." In *Political Culture and Political Development,* edited by L. W. Pye and S. Verba, pp. 82-129 (Princeton: Princeton University Press, 1965).

SAYLES, G. O. *Medieval Foundations of England* (Philadelphia: University of Pennsylvania Press, 1951; new ed., New York: Barnes, 1961).

TOUT, T. F. *Chapters in the Administrative History of England.* 6 vols. (Manchester: University Press, 1920-33; new ed, 1967). The classic treatise on English state-building.

WERNHAM, R. B. *Before the Armada: the Emergence of the English Nation 1485-1588* (New York: Norton, 1972).

6.112 Scotland

BUDGE, Ian and Derek W. URWIN. *Scottish Political Behavior. A Study in British Homogeneity* (London: Longmans, 1966).

CAMPBELL, R. H. *Scotland Since 1707: the Rise of an Industrial Society* (Oxford: 1965).

GIBB, Andrew Dewar. *Scottish Empire* (London: A. Maclehose, 1937).

HANHAM, H. J. *Scottish Nationalism* (London: Blackwell, 1969).

KELLAS, J. A. *The Scottish Political System* (Cambridge, Eng.: University Press, 1973).

––– *Modern Scotland* (London: Pall Mall, 1968).

MACLENNAN, R. D. "The Scottish National Movement." Virginia Quarterly Review 29 (Winter 1953): 53-67.

SCHWARZ, John E. "The Scottish National Party: Non-violent Separatism and Theories of Violence." World Politics 22, no. 4 (1970).

SMOUT, T. Christopher. *A History of the Scottish People, 1560-1830* (London: Collins, 1969).

6.113 Wales

COUPLAND, Reginald and Kenneth MORGAN. *Wales in British Politics 1868-1922* (Cardiff: University of Wales Press, 1963).

GREAT BRITAIN, BOARD of EDUCATION, COMMITTEE on WELSH in the EDUCATIONAL SYSTEM of WALES. *Welsh in Education and Life* (London: His Majesty's Stationery Office, 1927).

GRIFFITH, Llewelyn Wyn. *The Welsh and Their Country* (London: Longmans, 1946).

MASTERMAN, Neville. *The Forerunner. The Dilemmas of Tom Ellis 1859-99.* (London: C. Davis, 1972). Analysis of the ideas of an early Welsh nationalist.

MORGAN, Kenneth O. *Wales in British Politics 1868-1922.* (Cardiff: University of Wales Press, new ed., 1970).

RICHARDS, Melville. *Welsh Administrative and Territorial Units, Medieval and Modern* (Cardiff: University of Wales Press, 1969).

THOMAS, Ned. *The Welsh Extremist: a Culture in Crisis* (London: Gollanz, 1971).

WADE-EVANS, A. W. et al. *The Historical Basis of Welsh Nationalism* (Cardiff: Plaid Cymru, 1950).

WILLIAMS, David. *A History of Modern Wales* (London: Murray, 1950).

6.114 Ireland, the Irish question

ARENSBERG, Conrad and Solon T. KIMBALL. *Family and Community in Ireland* (Cambridge, Mass.: Harvard University Press, 1940; 2nd ed., 1968).

BARRITT, D. and C. CARTER. *The Northern Ireland Problem: A Study in Group Relations* (London: Oxford University Press, 1962).

BECKET, J. C. *The Making of Modern Ireland, 1603-1923* (New York: Knopf, 1966).

CHUBB, Basil. *The Government and Politics of Ireland* (Stanford: Stanford University Press, 1970).

DEVLIN, Bernadette. *The Price of My Soul* (New York: Knopf, 1969).

EDWARDS, Owen D. *The Sins of our Fathers: Roots of Conflict in Northern Ireland* (Dublin: Gill, 1970).

EVANS, E. Estyn. *The Irishness of the Irish* (Dublin: The Irish Association for Cultural, Economic and Social Relations, 1967).

FENNELL, D., ed. *The Changing Face of Catholic Ireland* (London: 1968).

GIBBON, Peter. "The Dialectic of Religion and Class in Ulster." New Left Review 55 (May/June 1969): 20-41.

HESLINGA, Marcus Willem. *The Irish Border as a Cultural Divide: A Contribution to the Study of Regionalism in the British Isles* (Assen: Van Gorcum, 1962).

KEE, Robert. *The Green Flag. The Turbulent History of the Irish National Movement* (New York: Delacorte, 1972).

LARKIN, Emmet. "Economic Growth, Capital Investment and the Catholic Church in Nineteenth Century Ireland." American History Review 72, no. 3 (1967): 852-84.

MANSERGH, Nicholas. *The Irish Question.* Rev. ed. (London: Unwin University Books, 1965).

——— *The Government of Northern Ireland: A Study in Revolution* (London: Unwin University Books, 1936).

——— *The Irish Free State: Its Government and Politics* (London: 1934).

MOODY, T. W. and F. X. MARTIN, eds. *The Course of Irish History* (Cork: Mercier Press, 1967).

O'BRIEN, Conor Cruise. *States of Ireland* (New York: Pantheon, 1972).

RAFTERY, Joseph, ed. *The celts* (Cork: Mercier Press, 1964).

ROKKAN, Stein. "The Growth and Structuring of Mass Politics." Scandinavian Political Studies 5 (1970): 65-83.

ROSE, Richard. *Governing Without Consensus. An Irish Perspective* (London: Faber, 1971). A thoroughgoing study of the legitimacy crisis in Ulster, based on a sample survey carried out *before* the onset of violence in 1969.

––– "Dynamic Tendencies in the Authority of Regimes." World Politics 21, no. 4 (1969).

SENIOR, H. *Orangeism in Ireland and Britain* (London: Oxford University Press, 1976).

SHEEHY, Michael. *Is Ireland Dying? Culture and the Church in Modern Ireland* (London: Hollis & Caster, 1958).

STEWART, A.T.Q. *The Ulster Question* (London: Faber, 1967).

STRAUSS, E. *Irish Nationalism and British Democracy* (London: Allen and Unwin, 1951).

WHYTE, J. H. *Church and State in Modern Ireland* (New York: Barnes & Noble, 1971).

6.12 France

BARZUN, Jacques. *The French Race* (New York: Columbia University Press, 1932).

BOTHEREL, Jean. *La Bretagne Contre Paris* (Paris: La Table Ronde, 1969).

BROGAN, Denis W. *The French Nation from Napoleon to Pétain* (New York: Harper, 1958) several editions.

BUISSERET, D. *Sully and the Growth of Centralized Government in France 1598-1610* (London: Eyre & Spotteswoode, 1968).

BURKE, Edmund. *Reflections on the Revolution in France* (London: 1790, numerous editions).

BUTHMAN, W. C. *The Rise of Regional Nationalism in France* (New York: Columbia University Press, 1939).

CAMPENHAUSEN, Axel von. *L'Eglise et l'Etat en France* (Paris: Ed. l'Epi, 1964).

CROZIER, Michel. *Le Phénomène Bureaucratique* (Paris: Seuil 1963). English translation *The Bureaucratic Phenomenon: An Examination of Bureaucracy in Modern Organizations and Its Cultural Setting in France* (Chicago: University of Chicago Press, 1964).

DUPEUX, Georges. *La Société Française 1789-1960* (Paris: Colin, 1964).

ELLUL, Jacques. *Histoire des Institutions de L'époque Franque à la Révolution* (Paris: Presses Universités, 1962).

FORD, Franklin L. *Robe and Sword: the Regrouping of the French Aristocracy after Louis XIV* (Cambridge, Mass.: Harvard University Press, 1953).

GRUDER, Vivian R. *The Royal Provincial Intendants: a Governing Elite in 18th Century France* (Ithaca, N.Y.: Cornell University Press, 1968).

GUENEE, Bernard. "L'histoire de l'Etat en France à la Fin du Moyen Age, Vue par les Historiens Français Depuis Cent Ans." Revue Historique 232 (1964): 331-60.

HINTZE, Hedwig. *Staatseinheit und Föderalismus im alten Frankreich und in der Revolution* (Unity and Federalism in France in the Ancien Regime and Under the Revolution) (Stuttgart: Deutsche Verlagsanstalt, 1928).

HOFFET, Fr. *Psychoanalyse de l'Alsace* (Paris: Flammarion, 1951).

HOFFMAN, Stanley, ed. *In Search of France: Economy Growing, Society Changing, Political System in Doubt* (Cambridge, Mass.: Harvard University Press, 1963).

LAFONT, Robert. *Sur la France* (Paris: Gallimard, 1968).
——— *La Révolution Régionaliste* (Paris: Gallimard, 1967).
LEWIS, P. S., ed. *The Recovery of France in the 15th Century* (London: Macmillan, 1971). Useful collection of articles on state-building processes.
LUBLINSKAYA, A. *French Absolutism: the Crucial Phase 1620-1629.* Translated from Russian (Cambridge, Eng.: Cambridge University Press, 1968).
LUETHY, Herbert. *La Banque Protestante en France de la Révocation de L'édit de Nantes à la Révolution.* 2 vols. (Paris: SEVPEN, 1959-61).
——— *Frankreichs Uhren Gehen Anders* (Zurich: Europa Verlag, 1953). Translation, *France Against Herself* (New York: Praeger, 1955).
MANDROU, Robert. *Introduction à la France Moderne. Essai de Psychologie Historique (1500-1640)* (Paris: Michel, 1961).
MARTIN, Marie Madelaine. *La Formation Morale de la France: Histoire de L'unité Française* (Paris, 1948). English translation, *The Making of France* (London: Eyre & Spotteswoode, 1952).
MUTTER, André. *L'Alsace à l'heure de l'Europe* (Paris: Ed. G.L.D., 1968).
SAGNAC, P. *La Formation de la Société Française Moderne 1661-1788.* 2 vols. (Paris: Presses Universités, 1945-46).
TILLY, Charles. *The Vendée* (Cambridge, Mass.: Harvard University Press, 1964). A lucid analysis of resistance to nation-building.
TOCQUEVILLE, A. de. *L'Ancien Régime et la Revolution* (Paris: Lévy, 1856, numerous editions; English translation, Oxford: Blackwell, 1933). The classic analysis of continuities in the structure of the French state.
WALLACE-HADRILL, I. H. and I. McMANNERS. *France: Government and Society* (London: Methuen, 1955). Chapters on all phases of French history from the times before the Roman occupation.
WEBER, Eugen. *The Nationalist Revival in France 1905-1914* (Berkeley: University of California Press, 1959).
WEDGWOOD, V. *Richelieu and the French Monarchy* (London: English University Press, 1949).

6.13 The Iberian peninsula

LIVERMORE, Harold. *The Origins of Spain and Portugal* (London: Allen and Unwin, 1971).

6.131 Spain

BRENAN, Gerald. *The Spanish Labyrinth. An Account of the Social and Political Background of the Civil War* (Cambridge, Eng.: Cambridge University Press, 1960).
CARR, Raymond. *Spain, 1808-1939* (Oxford: Clarendon, 1966).
ELLIOTT, J. H. *Imperial Spain, 1469-1716* (New York: St. Martin's Press, 1963).
——— *The Revolt of the Catalans (1558-1640)* (Cambridge, Eng.: Cambridge University Press, 1963).
——— "The Decline of Spain." Past and Present 20 (1961): 52-75.
FERNANDEZ de Castro, I. *De las Cortes de Cádiz al Plan de Desarrollo, 1808-1966, Ensayo de Interpretación Política de la España Contemporánea* (From the Cortes of Cádiz to the Development Plan, 1808-1966. An Attempt at a Political Interpretation of Contemporary Spain) (Paris: Ruédo Iberico, 1968).

LINZ, Juan J. "An Authoritarian Regime: Spain." In *Cleavages, Ideologies and Party Systems: Contributions to Comparative Political Sociology,* edited by E. Allardt and Y. Littunen (Helsinki: Westermarck Society, 1964). Also reprinted in E. ALLARDT and S. ROKKAN, eds. *Mass Politics* (New York: Free Press, 1970).

––– and Amando de MIGUEL. *Los Empresarios Ante el Poder Público* (The Entrepreneurs Facing Public Power) (Madrid: Institutio de Estudios Políticos, 1966).

––– "Within-Nation Differences and Comparisons: The Eight Spains." In *Comparing Nations,* edited by R. C. Merritt and S. Rokkan, pp. 267-319 (New Haven, Conn.: Yale University Press, 1966).

MALEFAKIS, Edward. *Agrarian Reform and Peasant Revolution in Spain. Origins of the Civil War* (New Haven, Conn.: Yale University Press, 1971).

MARAVALL, José Antonio. "The Origins of the Modern State." Journal of World History 6 (1961).

PAYNE, Stanley G. *The Spanish Revolution. A Study of the Social and Political Tensions that Culminated in the Civil War in Spain* (New York: Norton, 1970).

SANCHEZ-ALBORNOZ, Claudio. *España: un Enigma Histórico* (Spain: an Historic Enigma) (Buenos Aires: Ed. Sudamericana, 1956).

THOMAS, Hugh. *The Spanish Civil War* (New York: Harper, 1961).

VICENS VIVES, Jaime. *Aproximacion a la Historia de España* (An Approach to the History of Spain). 3rd ed. (Barcelona, 1962).

––– *Cataluña en el Siglo XIX* (Catalonia in the 19th Century) (Madrid: Rialp, 1961).

VILAR, Jean. *Histoire de L'Espagne* (Paris: Presses Universitaires de France, 1958).

VILAR, Pierre. *La Catalogne dans L'Espagne Moderns. Recherches sur les Fondements Economiques des Structures Nationales* (Paris: SEVPEN, 1962).

See also Section 6.1, Blanshard.

6.132 Portugal

BEAU, Albin E. *Die Entwicklung des Portugiesischen Nationalbewusstseins* (The Development of National Consciousness in Portugal) (Hamburg: Ger.-Amer. Institut, 1940).

KAY, Hugh. *Salazar and Modern Portugal* (New York: Hawthorn, 1970).

LIVERMORE, H. V. *A History of Portugal* (Cambridge, Eng.: Cambridge University Press, 1947; new ed., 1966).

PEREIRA DOS SANTOS, F. *Un Etat Corporatif* (Paris: Sirey, 1935).

RENARD, Ludwig. *Salazar, Kirche und Staat in Portugal* (Salazar, Church and State in Portugal) (Essen: Lindgerus, 1968).

6.2 The Northwestern Polities

6.21 The old-established nations

HOVDE, Brynjolf Jacob. *The Scandinavian Countries, 1720-1865: The Rise of the Middle Classes* (Ithaca, N.Y.: Cornell University Press, 1948).

HOMME, Lina R. *Nordisk Nykolonialisme* (Nordic Neo-Colonialism) (Oslo: Det Norske Samlaget, 1969). On the Lapps in Northern Scandinavia.

OTNES, Per. *Den Samiske Nasjon* (The Nation of the Laplanders) (Oslo: Pax, 1970).
SIMON, Erica. *Réveil National et Culture Populaire en Scandinavie* (Paris: Presses Universitaires, 1960). A comparative study of the Folk High Schools as agencies of nation-building.

6.211 Denmark

ALLEN, Carl Ferdinand. *Det Danske Sprogs Historie i Hertugdømmet Slesvig Eller Sønderjylland* (The History of the Danish Language in the Duchy of Slesvig of Soenderjylland) (Copenhagen: Reitzels, 1857-58).
BRANDT, O. *Geschichte Schleswig-Holsteins, ein Grundriss* (An Outline of the History of Schleswig-Holstein) (Kiel: Mühlau, 1925; 4th ed., 1949).
BROCK, J. *Die Vorgeschichte der Schleswig-Holsteinischen Erhebung Von 1848* (The Prelude to the Revolt of 1848 in Schleswig-Holstein) (Göttingen: Vandenhoeck, 1916; new ed., 1925).
CARR, W. *Schleswig-Holstein 1815-1848. A Study in National Conflict* (Manchester: University Press, 1963).
HAGENAK, H. *Revolution und Legitimität in der Geschichte der Erhebung Schleswig-Holsteins. Untersuchungen zur Entstehungsgeschichte und zur Politik der Provisorischen Regierung* (Revolution and Legitimacy in the History of the Revolt in Schleswig-Holstein. Inquiries into the Making and Politics of the Provisional Government) (Leipzig: Haessel, 1916).
HAUSER, Oswald. *Preussische Staatsräson und Nationale Gedanke. Auf Grund Unveröffentlichter Akten aus dem Schleswig-Holsteinischen Landesarchiv mit einem Dokumentenanhang* (The Prussian "Raison D'Etat" and the National Idea, on the Basis of Unpublished Documents in the Public Records of Schleswig--Holstein) (Neumünster: Karl Wachholtz Verl, 1960).
JESSEN, Franz de. *Manuel Historique de la Question du Slesvig. Documents, Cartes, Pièces Justificatives et Renseignements Statistiques* (Copenhague: Gyldendal, 1906).
KAMPHOVENER, Morten, ed. *Sydslesvig Gennem Tiderne* (A History of Southern Slesvig). 3 vols. (Horsens: Fonnesberg, 1946-49).
KLOSE, Olaf and Christian DEGN. *Die Herzogtümer im Gesamtstaat 1721-1830* (The Joint State of the Dukedoms 1721-1830) (Neumünster: Karl Wachholtz, 1960).
KOOPMANN, P. *Deutsch und Dänisch um die Wende des Achtzehnten Jahrhunderts. Das Völkliche Werden in den Weltanschaulichen Spannungen des Deutsch-Dänischen Gesamtstaates 1770-1814* (German and Danish at the Turn of the Eighteenth Century. The Building of the "Volk" in the Ideological Conflicts of the German-Danish Joint State) (Neumünster, 1939).
MACKEPRANG, M. *Nord-Schleswig von 1864 bis 1911* (Northern Schleswig from 1864 to 1911) (Jena, 1912).
MYKLAND, Knut. *Skiftet i Forvaltningsordningen i Danmark og Norge* (The Change in the Public Administration of Denmark and Norway, 17th Century) (Bergen, Oslo: Norwegian University Press, 1967).
OLSEN, Albert. *Danmark-Norge i Det 18. Aarhundrede* (Denmark/Norway in the 18th Century) (Copenhagen, 1936).
PEDERSEN, E. Ladewig. *The Crisis of the Danish Nobility* (Odense: University Press, (1967).
STEEFEL, Lawrence Dinkelspiel. *The Schleswig-Holstein Question* (Cambridge, Mass.: Harvard University Press, 1932).

6.212 Sweden

ABERG, Alf. *När Skane blev Svenskt* (When Scania Became Swedish) (Stockholm: LTs förlag, 1958).

ALMQUIST, J. E. "Svensk Rätts Införande i de Under 1600-talet med Sverige Inkorporerade Danska och Norska Provinserna." (The Introduction of Swedish Law in the Danish and Norwegian Provinces That Were Incorporated with Sweden During the Seventeenth Century). (Svensk Juristtidning, 1937).

BOGREN, Yngue. *Den Kyrkliga Försvenskningen av Skånelandskapen och Bohuslän* (The "Swedification" of the Church in the Provinces of Skaane and Bohuslaen) (Stockholm: Diakonistyrelsen, 1937).

CARLSSON, S. *Standssamhälle och Standspersoner 1700-1865* (Society of Estates and the Nobility 1700-1865) (Lund: Gleerup, 1949).

ELMROTH, I. *Nyrekryteringen Till de Högre Ambetena 1720-1809* (New Recruitment to Higher Offices 1720-1809) (Lund: Gleerup, 1962).

FABRICIUS, Knud. *Skaanes Overgang Fra Danmark til Sverige. Studier Over Nationalitetsskiftet i de Skaanske Landskaper i de Naermeste Slaegtled Efter Bromsebro-og Roskildefredent* (The Transfer of Scania From Denmark to Sweden. Studies on the Change of Nationality in these Provinces During the First Generations after the Settlements in Broemsebro and Roskilde) vol. 1-2 (Lund, Kbh.: Gleerups, Schultz, 1955; vol. 3, Kbh: Rosenkilde og Bagger, 1952; vol. 4, Kbh.: Gleerups, Schultz, 1958).

HERLITZ, Nils. *Svenska Statsrättens Grunder* (The Foundations of Swedish Constitutional Law) (Stockholm: Norstedt, 1940).

HUNTFORD, Roland. *The New Totalitarians* (New York: Stein & Day, 1971).

NILSSON, Martin P. "Skånes Språkliga Försvenskning." (The "Swedification" of Language in Skaane) Historisk Tidskr. (1955).

NILSSON, Sven A. *Krona och Frälse i Sverige 1523-1594. Rusttjänst, Länsväsende, Godspolitik* (Crown and Nobility in Sweden 1523-1594) (Lund: Gleerups, 1947).

ROBERTS, Michael. *The Early Vasas. A History of Sweden, 1523-1611.* (Cambridge, Eng.: Cambridge University Press, 1968).

——— *Sweden as a Great Power 1611-1697. Government, Society, Foreign Policy* (London: Edward Arnold, 1968).

ROSEN, Jerker Ingmar. *Hur Skåne Blev Svenskt* (How Scania Became Swedish) (Stockholm: Geber, 1943).

RUSTOW, D. A. *The Politics of Compromise: A Study of Parties and Cabinet Government in Sweden* (Princeton: Princeton University Press, 1955).

SCHWARZ, David, ed. *Svenska Minoriteter* (Swedish Minorities) (Sth: Aldus, 1966).

TOMASSON, Richard F. *Sweden: Prototype of Modern Society* (New York: Random House, 1970).

VEDUNG, Evert. *Unionsdebatten 1905* (The Debate Over the Dissolution of the Swedish-Norwegian Union 1905) (Uppsala: Political Science Association, 1971).

6.22 The Secession Nations

6.221 Norway

BERGSGARD, Arne. "Spørsmalet om Folkesuveraeniteten i 1814." (The question of Sovereignty in 1814) In *Hundre Ars Historisk Forskning. Utvalgte Artikler fra Historisk Tidsskrift,* pp. 230-49 (Oslo: University Press, 1970).

ECKSTEIN, Harry. *Division and Cohesion in Democracy: A Study of Norway* (Princeton: Princeton University Press, 1968).

HAUGEN, Einer. *Language Conflict and Language Planning: The Case of Modern Norwegian* (Cambridge, Mass.: Harvard University Press, 1966).

HELLE, Knut. *Norge Blir en Stat 1130-1319* (State-building in Norway) (Bergen: University Press, 1964).

OLSEN, Albert. *Danmark-Norge i Det 18. Aarhundrede* (Denmark-Norway During the Eighteenth Century) (Copenhagen, 1936).

RODNICK, David. *The Norwegians: A Study in National Culture* (Washington, D.C.: Public Affairs Press, 1955).

ROKKAN, Stein. "Geography, Religion and Social Class." In *Party Systems and Voter Alignment,* edited by S. M. Lipset and S. Rokkan (New York: Free Press, 1967).

––– "Norway: Numerical Democracy and Corporate Pluralism." In *Political Oppositions in Western Democracies,* edited by R. A. Dahl (New Haven, Conn.: Yale University Press, 1966).

––– and Henry VALEN. "Regional Contrasts in Norwegian Politics." In *Cleavages, Ideologies and Party Systems,* edited by E. Allardt and Y. Littunen (Helsinki: Westermark Society, 1964). Reprinted in E. Allardt and S. Rokkan, eds., *Mass Politics* (New York: Free Press, 1920).

SANNESS, John. *Patrioter, Intelligens og Skandinaver. Norske Reaksjoner pa Skandinavismen Før 1848* (Patriots, Intelligence and Scandinaves. Norwegian Reactions to Scandinavism Before 1848) (Oslo: University Press, 1959).

SEIP, Jens Arup. *Et Regime Foran Undergangen* (A Regime Faces its Downfall) (Oslo: Tanum, 1945). A classic analysis of the fall of the regime of the officials in the 1870s.

STEEN, Sverre. *Det Frie Norge* (Independent Norway). 5 vols. (Oslo: Cappelen, 1951-71). The fundamental treatise on state and nation-building after 1814.

STEFFENS, H. K. *Den Norske Centraladministrations Historie 1814-1914* (The History of the Norwegian Central Administration 1814-1914) (Kristiania: Stenersen, 1914).

VALEN, Henry and Stein ROKKAN. "Cleavage Structures and Mass Politics in a European Periphery: Norway." In *Comparative Electoral Behavior,* edited by R. Rose (New York: Free Press, 1973, forthcoming).

6.222 Iceland

GJERSET, K. *History of Iceland* (New York: Macmillan, 1924).

GRIMSSON, Olafur R. "Political Power in Iceland Prior to the Period of Class Politics 1845-1918." Dissertation, University of Manchester, 1970.

NORDAL, Johannes and Valdimar KRISTINSSON, eds. *Iceland 1966 Handbook* (Reykjavik: Central Bank of Iceland, 1966).

OLGEIRSSON, Einar. *Fra Aettesamfunn til Klassestat* (From Lineage Society to Class State) (Oslo: Orion, 1968).

6.223 Finland

ALLARDT, Erik. "Patterns of Class Conflict and Working Class Consciousness in

Finnish Politics." In *Cleavages, Ideologies and Party Systems,* edited by E. Allardt and Y. Littunen (Helsinki: Westermarck, 1964). Expanded as "Types of Protest and Alienation;" in *Mass Politics,* edited by E. Allardt and S. Rokkan (New York: Free Press, 1970).

DAHL, Hj. *Finlands Svenskar* (The Swedes in Finland) (Helsingfors: Schildt, 1960).

ERIKSSON, T. *Alands Självstyrelse i Kort Oversikt* (A Short Account of the Self-Government of Aaland) (Maoriehamn: Liewendal, 1964).

HAMALAINEN, Pekka Kalevi. *Nationalitetskampen och Språkstriden i Finland 1917-1939* (The National Struggle and Language Conflict in Finland 1917-1939) (Helsingfors: Holger Schildt, 1969).

HANNULA, J. O. *Finland's War of Independence* (London: Faber, 1939).

HODGSON, John H. *Communism in Finland* (Princeton: Princeton University Press, 1969).

HORNBORG, Eirik. "Den Svenska Nationalitetsidéns Födelse och Utveckling i Finland" (The Birth of the Swedish National Idea and Its Development in Finland). In *Vår Svenska Stam På Utländsk Mark. Svenska Oden och insatser i Främmande Land,* edited by Axel Boëthius and Ake Olavson, pp, 109-20 (Stockholm: Lundquist, 1952).

JAASKELAINEN, Mauno. *Die Ostkarelische Frage. Die Entstehung eines Nationalen Expansions-Programmes und die Versuche zu Seiner Verwirklichung in der Aussenpolitik Finnlands in den Jahren 1918-1920* (The Question of Eastern Karelen. The Origin of a National Program of Expansion and the Attempt to Realize it in the Foreign Policy of Finland During the Years 1918-1920) (Abo, 1965).

JANSSON, Jan Magnus. "Nationalism, Liberalism och Demokrati Under Språkstridens Första Skede i Finland" (Nationalism, Liberalism and Democracy During the First Phase of the Language Conflict in Finland) Historisk Tidsskrift 4 (1961): 357-68.

JUTIKKALA, Eino: *Finlands Historia* (The History of Finland) (London: Thames & Hudson, 1962).

LINDMAN, Sven. *The Concept of "Nationality" in Swedish-Finnish Political Thought* (Uppsala: Vetenskapssamhället, 1964).

NOUSIAINEN, I. *The Finnish Political System* (Cambridge, Mass.: Harvard University Press, 1971).

RINTALA, Marvin. *Three Generations. The Extreme Right Wing in Finnish Politics* (Bloomington: University of Indiana Press, 1962).

TORNUDD, K. *Svenska Språkets Ställning i Finland* (The Position of the Swedish Language in Finland) (Stockholm, 1960).

WAHLBACK, Frister. *Från Mannerheim Till Kekkonen* (From Mannerheim to Kekkonen) (Stockholm: Aldus, 1967).

WERNLUND, Axel. *Alands Kamp För Självhävdelse* (Aaland's Struggle for Independence) (Mariehamn: Liewendal, 1953).

WIKMAN, K. Robert V. "Den Svenska Nationalitetsrörelsen" (The Swedish Nationality Movement) In *Det Svenska Finland,* edited by G. Nickander, pp. 319-53 (Helsingfors: Schildt, 1923).

WUORINEN, John A. *A History of Finland* (New York: Columbia University Press, 1965).

――― *Nationalism in Modern Finland* (New York: Columbia University Press, 1931).

See also Section 2.4, ROKKAN, "The Growth and Structuring of Mass Politics."

6.3 The "consociational" states of Europe

Le Bilinguisme en Suisse, en Belgique et au Canada (Brussels: Fondation Charles Plisnier, 1963).

DAALDER, Hans: See Chapter 1 in Volume 2 of this work.

DUNN, James Jr. "Consociational Democracy and Language Conflict: Belgium vs. Switzerland." Comparative Political Studies 5, no. 1 (April 1972): 3-40.

LEHMBRUCH, Gerhard. *Proporzdemokratie: Politisches System und Politische Kultur in der Schweiz und in Osterreich* (Tübingen: Mohr, 1962).

LIJPHART, A. "Consociational Democracy." World Politics 21 (January 1969): 207 f.

WEIL, Gordon L. *The Benelux Nations: The Politics of Small-Country Democracies* (New York: Holt, Rinehart and Winston, 1970).

6.31 The Netherlands

BARNOUW, A. J. *The Making of Modern Holland* (New York: Norton, 1944).

BOOGMAN, J. C. *Die Suche Nach der Nationalen Identität: die Niederlande 1813-1848* (The Search for National Identity: the Netherlands 1813-48) (Wiesbaden: Steiner, 1968).

DAALDER, Hans. "The Netherlands: Opposition in a Segmented Society." In *Political Oppositions in Western Democracies,* edited by Robert A. Dahl (New Haven, Conn.: Yale University Press, 1966).

GEYL, Pieter. *The Revolt of the Netherlands 1555-1609.* 2nd ed. (London: Benn, 1958).

GEYL, Pieter. *The Netherlands in the Seventeenth Century* . 2 vols. (London: Benn, 1961-64).

LIJPHART, Arend. *The Politics of Accommodation* (Berkeley: University of California Press, 1968).

RENIER, G. J. *The Criterion of Dutch Nationhood* (London: Allen and Unwin, 1946).

––– *The Dutch Nation. An Historical Study* (London: Allen and Unwin, 1944).

VLEKKE, B.H.M. *The Evolution of The Dutch Nation* (New York: Roy, 1945).

6.32 Belgium

CHLEPNER, B. S. *Cent Ans D'Histoire Sociale en Belgique* (Brussels: Institut de Sociologie Solvay, 1956).

CLOUGH, S. B. *A History of the Flemish National Movement* (New York: R. H. Smith, 1930).

GORIS, Jan Albert, ed. *Belgium* (Berkeley: University of California Press, 1946).

HERREMANS, M. P. "Développement Economique, Social, Cultural et Politique de la Belgique en Corrélation Avec la Problématique Flamande." Syntheses 23 (1968).

KALKEN, Frans van. *La Belgique Contemporaine (1780-1949).* 2nd ed. (Paris: Colin, 1950).

KELLY, George Armstrong.. "Belgium: New Nationalism in an Old World." Comparative Politics 1, no. 3 (April 1969): 343-365.

KURTH, Godefroid. *La Nationalité Belge* (Namur: Picard-Balon, 1913).

LORWIN, Val R. "Linguistic Pluralism and Political Tension in Modern Belgium." Canadian Journal of History 5, no. 1 (1970): 1-22.

——— "Belgium: Religion, Class, and Language in National Politics." In *Political Oppositions in Western Democracies,* edited by Robert A Dahl (New Haven, Conn.: Yale University Press, 1966).

URWIN, Derek W. "Social Cleavages and Political Parties in Belgium: Problems of Institutionalization." Political Studies 18, no. 3 (1970): 320-40.

WILLEMSEN, A. W. *Het Vlaams Nationalisme, 1914-1940* (The Flemish Nationalism, 1914-1940) (Groningen: Wolters, 1958).

See also Section 4.2, McRAE.

6.33 Luxembourg

CALMES, Albert. *Histoire Contemporaine du Grand Duché de Luxembourg.* 3 vols. (Brussels: Ed. Universelles, 1932-47). This detailed history ends in 1840, just after the secession from the Netherlands.

EDWARDS, K. C. "The Grand Duchy of Luxembourg: Its Human and Economic Geography." Dissertation, University of London, 1948.

6.34 Switzerland

DEUTSCH, Karl W. and Hermann WEILENMANN. "The Social Roots of Swiss National Identity: The Conflict of Feudalism and Cantonal Self-government in the Social Order of Medieval Europe." Yale German Review 3 (Spring 1966): 23-30.

——— "The Swiss City Canton: A Political Invention." Comparative Studies in Society and History 7, no. 4 (1965): 393-408.

KOHN, Hans. *Nationalism and Liberty: the Swiss Example* (New York: Macmillan 1956).

LIEBESKIND, W. A. "La Commune dans l'Historie Politique de la Suisse." Revue de la Société des Juristes Bernois 77, no. 3 (1941): 111-16.

MARTIN, William. *Histoire de la Suisse: Essai sur la Formation d'une Confédération* (Paris: Payot, 1926; 6th ed., Lausanne: Payot, 1966).

MAYER, K. B. "International Migration, Cultural Tensions and Foreign Relations: The Case of Switzerland." Paper presented to the World Congress of Sociology, Evian, September 4-11, 1966.

——— *The Population of Switzerland* (New York: Columbia University Press, 1952).

McRAE, Kenneth. *Switzerland: An Example of Cultural Coexistence* (Toronto: Canadian Institute of International Affairs, 1964).

RUFFIEUX, Roland and B. BRONGUE. *Le Mouvement Chrétien-Social en Suisse Romande 1891-1949* (Fribourg: Imprimateur St.-Paul, 1969).

STEINER, Jürg. *Gewaltlose Politik und Kulturele Vielfalt* (Nonviolent Politics and Cultural Diversity: An Analysis of Switzerland) (Berne: Haupt, 1970).

WEILENMANN, Hermann. *Pax Helvetica: Oder die Demokratie der Kleinen Gruppen* (Pax Helvetica: or the Democracy of the Small Groups) (Erlenbach-Zurich: Rentsch Verlag, 1951).

6.4 The continental empires and their successor states

ANDERSON, Eugene N. and P. R. ANDERSON. *Political Institutions and Social Change in Continental Europe in the 19th Century* (Berkeley: University of California Press, 1967).

HARTUNG, Fritz, ed. *Das Reich und Europa* (Leipzig: Koehler, 1941).

MEYER, Henry Cord. *Mitteleuropa in German Political Thought and Action 1815-1945*. (The Hague: Mouton, 1955).

6.41 The German Reich

BARRACLOUGH, Geoffrey. *The Origins of Modern Germany* (London: Oxford University Press, 1947). A masterly interpretation of developments up to the Thirty Years War.

BRUNNER, Otto. *Land und Herrschaft. Grundfragen der Territorialen Verfassungsgeschichte Südostdeutschlands im Mittelalter* (Land and Authority. Basic Issues in the History of the Territorial Constitution of Southeast Germany in the Middle Ages) (Brünn: Rohrer, 1942; 5th ed., Vienna: Rohrer, 1965).

CONZE, W. *Die Deutsche Nation* (The German Nation) (Göttinger: Vandenhoeck, 1963).

CRAIG, Gordon A. *The Politics of the Prussian Army, 1640-1945* (Oxford: Clarendon Press, 1955).

FEHRENBACH, Elizabeth. *Wandlungen des Deutschen Kaisergedankens 1871-1918* (The Vicissitudes of the Imperial Idea 1871-1918)(Munich: Olderbourg, 1969).

FRIEDJUNG, Heinrich. *Der Kampf um die Vorherrschaft in Deutschlands 1859 bis 1870*. 7th ed. (Stuttgart: Cotta, 1907). English translation with extended preface by A.J.P. Taylor. *The Struggle for Supremacy in Germany* (London: Macmillan, 1935).

HAMEROW, Theodore. *The Social Foundations of German Unification 1858-1871*. 2 vols. (Princeton: Princeton University Press, 1969-72).

HARTUNG, Fritz. *Volk Und Staat in der Deutschen Geschichte: Gesammelte Abhandlungen* (People and State in German History: Collected Papers) (Leipzig: Koehler, 1940).

HERTZ, Frederick. *The Development of the German Public Mind: A Social History of German Political Sentiments, Aspirations and Ideas* (London: Allen and Unwin, 1962).

HINTZE, Otto. *Staat und Verfassung* (State and Constitution). 2nd ed. Collected essays, edited by Gerhard Oestreich (Göttingen: Vandenhoeck, 1962).

HOLBORN, H. *A History of Modern Germany*. 2 vols. (New York: Knopf, 1959-64).

HUGELMANN, Karl G. *Nationalstaat und Nationalitätenrecht im Deutschen Mittelalter* (Nation-State and Rights of Nationalities in Medieval Germany) (Stuttgart: Kohlhammer, 1955).

––– *Stämme, Nation und Nationalstaat im Deutschen Mittelalter* (Tribes, Nation and Nation-State in Medieval Germany) (Stuttgart: Kohlhammer, 1955).

JOACHIMSEN, Paul. *Von Deutschen Volke zum Deutschen Staat: Eine Geschichte des Deutschen Nationalbewusstsein* (From *Volk* to State: A History of German National Consciousness) (Lepizig: Teubner, 1920).

––– *Der Deutsche Staatsgedanke von Seinen Anfängen bis auf Leibnitz und Friedrich dem Grossen* (The German Idea of State From the Beginnings Until Leibniz and Frederick the Great) (Munich: Drei Masken, 1921).

MEINECKE, Friedrich. *Weltbürgertum und Nationalstaat. Studien zur Genesis des Deutschen Nationalstaats* (Munich: Oldenbourg, 1908; new eds., 1922, 1962). English translation, *Cosmopolitanism and the National State* (Princeton: Princeton University Press, 1970).

PFLANZE, Otto. *Bismarck and the Development of Germany: the Period of Unification 1815-1871* (Princeton: Princeton University Press, 1963).

PLESSNER, Hellmuth. *Die Verspätete Nation* (The Belated Nation). 2nd ed. (Stuttgart: Kohlhammer, 1959). Originally published in 1935.

SCHIEDER, Theodor. *Staat und Gesellschaft im Deutschen Vormärz* (State and Society in Germany Before the Revolution of March 1848) (Stuttgart: E. Klett, 1962).

––– *Das Deutsche Kaiserreich von 1871 als Nationalstaat* (The German Empire of 1871 as a Nation-State) (Cologne: Opladen, 1960).

––– and E. DEVERLEIN, eds. *Reichsgründung 1870-71* (Stuttgart: Kohlhammer, 1971).

SCHMIDT-VOLKMAR, E. *Der Kulturkampf in Deutschland 1871-1890* (The Struggle for National Cultural Integration) (Göttingen: Mutterschmidt, 1962).

SRBIK, Heinrich Ritter von. *Deutsche Einheit, Idee und Wirklichkeit vom Heiligen Römischen Reich bis Königgratz* (German Unity, Idea and Reality from the Holy Roman Empire to Koeniggratz). 4 vols. (Munich: Bruckman, 1936; 3rd ed., 1940). The great *grossdeutsche* interpretation.

6.411 Prussia

CARSTEN, F. L. *The Origins of Prussia* (Oxford: Clarendon, 1954).

HINRICHS, Carl. *Preussen Als Historisches Problem* (Prussia as an Historical problem) Collected essays edited by Oestreich (Berlin: de Gruyter, 1964).

HINTZE, Otto. *Die Hohenzollern und ihr Werk* (The Hohenzollern and Their Achievements). 5th ed. (Berlin: Parey, 1915).

ROSENBERG, Hans. *Bureaucracy, Aristocracy and Autocracy. The Prussian Experience 1660-1815* (Cambridge, Mass.: Harvard University Press, 1958).

6.412 Bavaria

FENSKE, Hans *Konservatismus und Rechtsradikalismus in Bayern nach 1918* (Conservatism and Right Radicalism in Baviaria after 1918) (Berlin: Gehlen, 1969).

ROVERE, Julien. *La Baviere et L'Empire Allemand* (Paris: Nouvelle Librairie Nationale, 1920).

SPINDLER, Max. *Handbuch der Bayrischen Geschichte.* 3 vols. (Munich: Beck, 1967-71).

6.42 The Habsburg Empire

AUERBACH, B. *Les Races et les Nationalités en Autriche-Hongrie.* 2nd ed. (Paris, 1917).

BAUER, Otto. *Die Nationalitaetenfrage und die Sozialdemokratie* (The National Question and the Social Democracy) (Vienna, 1907).

BEIDTEL, I. *Geschichte der Osterreichischen Staats-Verwaltung* (History of Austrian State Administration) (Innsbruch: Wagner, 1896-98).

CRANKSHAW, Edward. *The Fall of the House of Habsburg* (London: Longmans, 1963).

DEDIJER, Vladimir. *The Road to Sarajevo* (New York: Simon & Schuster, 1966).

FISCHEL, Alfred, ed. *Materialen zur Sprachenfrage in Oesterreich* (Data on the Language Question in Austria) (Brunn: F. Irrgang, 1902).

GEIST-LANYI, Paula. *Das Nationalitätenproblem auf dem Reichstag zu Kremsier 1848-49* (The Nationalities Issue at the Kremsier Reichstag) (Munich: Drei Masken, 1920).

GLAISE-HORSTENAU, E. von. *Die Katastrophe: die Zertrümmerung Oesterreichs-Ungarns und das Werden der Nachfolgestaaten* (Vienna: 1929). Condensed English version, *The Collapse of the Austro-Hungarian Empire* (London: Dent, 1930).

HANAK, Peter, ed. *Die Nationale Frage in der Oesterreichisch-Ungar. Monarchie 1900-1918* (The National Question in the Austro-Hungarian Monarchy) (Budapest: Academy of Sciences, 1966).

JASZI, Oszkar. *The Dissolution of the Habsburg Monarchy* (Chicago: University of Chicago Press, 1929; rev. ed., 1961).

KANN, Robert A. *The Habsburg Empire: a Study in Integration and Disintegration* (New York: Praeger, 1957).

——— *The Multinational Empire 1848-1918* 2 vols. (New York: Columbia University Press, 1950).

MACARTNEY, Carlile Aylmer. *The Habsburg Empire, 1790-1918* (London: Weidenfeld and Nicolson, 1968).

——— *Problems of the Danube Basin* (Cambridge, Eng.: Cambridge University Press, 1942).

——— *National States and National Minorities* (Oxford: Oxford University Press, 1934). 2nd ed. (New York: Russell & Russell, 1968).

MAY, A. J. *The Passing of the Hapsburg Monarchy* (Philadelphia: University of Pennsylvania Press, 1966).

——— *The Hapsburg Monarchy, 1867-1914.* 2nd ed. (Cambridge, Mass.: Harvard University Press, 1965).

RENNER, Karl (Rudolph Springer). *Der Kampf der Oesterreichischen Nationen um den Staat* (The Struggle of the Austrian Nations About the State) (Vienna: F. Deuticke, 1902).

TAYLOR, A.J.P.T. *The Habsburg Monarchy, 1809-1918* (London: Hamish Hamilton, 1948).

WANDRUSZKA, Adam.. *The House of Habsburg: Six Hundred Years of a European Dynasty* (Garden City, N.Y.: Doubleday, 1964).

ZEMAN, Z.A.B. *The Break-up of the Habsburg Empire: 1914-1918, A Study in National and Social Revolution* (Oxford: Oxford University Press, 1961).

ZVITTER, F. *Les Problemès Nationaux dans la Monarchie des Habsbourgs* (Belgrade, 1960).

See also Sections 1.1, SEIPEL; and 6.51, MACARTNEY and PALMER; SETON-WATSON.

6.421 Austria

ANDICS, Hellmut. *Der Staat den Keiner Wollte, Oesterreich 1918-1938* (The State No One Wanted, Austria 1918-1938) (Vienna: Molden, 1962).

BENEDIKT, Heinrich, et al. *Geschichte der Republik Oesterreich* (History of the Republic of Austria) (Munich: Oldenbourg, 1954).

BLUHM, William T. *Building an Austrian Nation* (New Haven, Conn.: Yale University Press, 1973).

——— "Nation-Building: the Case of Austria." Polity 1, no. 2 (Winter 1968).

BRAUNTHAL, Julius. *The Tragedy of Austria* (London: Gollancz, 1948).

ENGELMANN, Frederick C. "Austria: Pooling the Opposition." In *Political Oppositions in Western Democracies,* edited by Robert A. Dahl, ch. 8 (New Haven, Conn.: Yale University Press, 1966).

GOERLICH, Ernst Joseph. *Die Oesterreichische Nation und der Widerstand* (The Austrian Nation and the Opposition) (Vienna: Europa Verlag, 1967).

GULICK, Charles A. *Austria From Habsburg to Hitler* (Berkeley: University of California Press, 1948).

HANNAK, Jacques, ed. *Bestandaufnahme Oesterreich* (The State of Austria) (Vienna: 1963).

HUTER, F., ed. *Südtirol* (Vienna: Verlag f. Geschichten Politik, 1965).

MACARTNEY, C. A. *The Social Revolution in Austria* (Cambridge, Eng.: Cambridge University Press, 1926).

SHELL, Kurt. *The Transformation of Austrian Socialism* (Albany: State University of New York, 1962).

SOZIALWISSENSCHAFTLICHE STUDIENGESELLSCHAFT."Das Nationalbewusstsein der Oesterreichen" (The Austrian National Consciousness). Die Meinung, Vienna, Nos. 1-3 (1965).

STEEPLER, H. F. "Concerning the Case of Austria." Polity 1, no. 4 (Summer 1969): 520-26.

STEINER, Kurt. *Polities in Austria* (Boston, Little, Brown, 1972).

STIEFBOLD, Rodney P. "Elite-mass Opinion Structure and Communication Flow in a Consociational Democracy: Austria." Paper read at the 1968 Annual Meeting of the American Political Science Association, Washington, D.C.

——— et al., eds. *Wahlen und Parteien in Oesterreich* (Elections and Parties in Austria). 3 vols. (Vienna: Jugend und Volk, 1966).

VODOPIVEC, Alexander. *Wer Regiert in Oesterreich?* (Who Governs in Austria?). 2nd ed. (Vienna: Verlag für Geschichte und Politik, 1962).

WANDRUSZKA, Adam. "Oesterreichs Politische Struktur" (The Political Structure of Austria). In *Geschichte der Republik Oesterreich,* edited by H. Benedikt (Munich: Oldenbourg, 1954).

WEINZIERL, Erika. "Das Oesterreichische Staatsbewusstsein" (The Austrian State Consciousness). In *Der Oesterreicher und Seine Staat,* edited by Erika Weinzierl (Vienna: Herder, 1965).

——— ed. *Der Oesterreicher und Sein Staat* (The Austrian and His State) (Vienna: Herder, 1965).

See also Section 1.1, MOMMSEN.

6.4222 Czechoslovakia

BROWN, A. "Pluralistic Trends in Czechoslovakia." Soviet Studies 17 (April 1966): 453-72.

GOGOLAK, Lajos. *Die Nationswerdung der Slowaken und die Anfänge der Tschechoslowakischen Frage (1526-1790)* (The Nationbuilding of the Slovaks and the Beginnings of the Czechoslovakian Question) (Munich: R. Oldenbourg, 1963).

GRAUS, F. "The Idea of the 'Nation' in Hussite Bohemia." Historia, Prague 16 (1969): 143-248 and 17 (1969): 93-138.
MASARYK, Tomas Garrigue. *The Making of a State* (London: Allen and Unwin, 1927).
RAUPACH, Hans. *Der Tschechische Frühnationalismus* (The Early Czech Nationalism) (Essen: Essener Verlag, 1938).
SETON-WATSON, R. W. *A History of the Czechs and Slovaks* (London: Hutchinson, 1943).
——— *The New Solvakia* (London, 1929).
——— ed. *Slovakia, Then and Now* (London: Allen and Unwin, 1931).

6.423 Hungary

BARANY, George. *Stephen Szechenyi and the Awakening of Hungarian Nationalism* (Princeton: Princeton University Press, 1968).
MACARTNEY, C. A. *Hungary: A Short History* (Edinburgh: University Press, 1962).
——— *Hungary and Her Successors: The Treaty of Trianon and Its Consequences, 1919-1937* (London: Oxford University Press, 1932).
SETON-WATSON, R. W. *Racial Problems in Hungary* (London: Constable 1908).
SZEKFU, Gyula. *Etat et Nation* (Paris: Presses Universitaires, 1945).
TELEKI, P. *The Evolution of Hungary and Its Place in European History* (New York: Macmillan, 1923).
VALI, Terence Albert. *Rift and Revolt in Hungary: Nationalism vs. Communism* (Cambridge, Mass.: Harvard University Press, 1967).
WALTER, F. *Die Nationalstätenfrage im Alten Ungarn* (Nationalities in Old Hungary) (Munich: Oldenbourg, 1959).

6.43 Yugoslavia

ARNAUTOVIC, A. *De la Serbie à Yugoslavie* (Paris: Ligue des Universitaires, 1919).
BERTSCH, Gary K. *Nation-Building in Yugoslovia* (Beverly Hills: Sage, 1971).
DRIAULT, Edouard, ed. *La Question d'Orient Depuis ses Origines Jusqu'à la Paix de Sèvres (1920).* 8th ed. (Paris: Alcan, 1921).
GESTRIN, Ferdo and Vasilij MELIK. *Slovenska Zgodovina, 1813-1914* (Slovene History 1813-1914) (Ljubljana: Drzavna Zalozba Slovenije, 1950).
GROSS, M. "On Some Aspects of the Development of the National Idea During the National Renaissance in Dalmatia." Historical Review 1 (1963): 11-18.
HADROVIC, Laszlo. *Le Peuple Serve et Son Eglise Sous la Domination Turque* (Paris: Presses Universitaries, 1947).
HOFFMAN, George W. and Fred W. NEAL. *Yugoslavia and the New Communism* (New York: Twentieth Century Fund, 1962).
KALLEY, V. *Geschichte des Serbischen Aufstandes, 1807-1810* (History of the Serbian Revolt, 1807-1810) (Vienna, 1910).
KARDELJ, Edward. *Problemi Nase Socijalisticke Izgradnje* (The Problems of Our Socialist Development). 3 vols. (Belgrade: Kultura, 1954-68).
——— *The Development of the Slovenian National Question* (in Serbo-Croatian) (Ljubljana: Drzavana Zalozba Slovenije, 1957).
NOVAKOVIC, Stojan. *Die Wieder-Gebuhrt des Serbischen Staates 1804-1820* (The Rebirth of the Serbian State 1804-1820) (Sarejevo: Institute für Balkanforschung, 1912).

PAVELIC, Ante. *Aus dem Kampf um den Selbständigen Staat Kroatien* (From the Struggle for an Independent Croatian State) (Vienna, 1931).

SETON-WATSON, R. W. *The Southern Slav Question and the Habsburg Monarchy* (London: Constable, 1911). Reprinted (New York: Fertig, 1960).

SHOUP, P. *Communism and the Yugoslav National Question* (New York: Columbia University Press, 1968).

TOMASEVICH, J. *Peasants, Politics and Economic Change in Yugoslavia* (Stanford: Stanford University Press, 1955).

TROUTON, Ruth. *Peasant Renaissance in Yugoslavia 1900-1950* (London: Routledge and Kegan Paul, 1952).

VUCINICH, Wayne S. *Serbia Between East and West, the Events of 1903-08* (Stanford: Stanford University Press, 1954).

WARNIER, R. "Illyrisme et Nationalisme Croate." Le Monde Slave 13, (1935).

WENDEL, Hermann *Der Kampf der Südslawen um Freiheit und Einheit* (The Struggle of the Slavs for Freedom and Unity) (Frankfurt: Societätsdruckerei, 1925).

WEST, Rebecca. *Black Lamb and Grey Falcon* (London: Macmillan, 1942). A classic literary analysis of the Yugoslav nationalities problem.

ZANINOVITCH, M. George. *The Development of Socialist Yugoslavia* (Baltimore: Johns Hopkins Press, 1962).

6.44 Italy

ALBRECHT-CARRIE, René. *Italy From Napoleon to Mussolini* (New York: Columbia University Press, 1950).

D'ENTREVES, A. Passerin and M. LENGEREAU. "La Vallée d'Aoste, Minorité Francophone de l'Etat Italien." Paper presented to the World Congress of Sociology, Evian, September 4-11, 1966.

GOETZ, Walter. "Die Entstehung der Italienischen Nationalität." (The Rise of the Italian Nationality). In *Italien im Mittelalter* (Leipzig: Köhler and Amelang, 1942).

GREW, R. *A Sterner Plan for Italian Unity: The Italian National Society and the Risorgimento* (Princeton: Princeton University Press, 1963).

JEMOLO, A. C. *Church and State in Italy 1850-1950* (Oxford: Blackwell, 1960).

LA PALOMBARA, Joseph. *Interest Groups in Italian Politics* (Princeton: Princeton University Press, 1964).

MACK SMITH, Denis. *Victor Emanuel, Cavour and the Risorgimento* (London: Oxford University Press, 1971).

——— *Italy: a Modern History* (Ann Arbor: University of Michigan Press, 1959).

——— *Cavour and Garibaldi 1860: A Study in Political Conflict* (Cambridge, Eng.: Cambridge University Press, 1954).

SALOMONE, A. William. *Italian Democracy in the Making* (Philadelphia: University of Pennsylvania Press, 1945).

SALVADORI, Massimo. *Cavour and the Unification of Italy* (Princeton: Van Nostrand, 1961).

WEBSTER, Richard A. *The Cross and the Fasces: Christian Democracy and Fascism in Italy* (Stanford: Stanford University Press, 1960).

WHYTE, A.J.B. *The Evolution of Modern Italy, 1715-1920* (New York: Norton, 1959).

See also Section 2.4, BAYNE.

6.45 Poland and the Baltic Territories

6.45 Poland

BUELL, R. L. *Poland: Key to Europe* (New York: Knopf, 1939). (London: , 1939)
FRANKEL, H. *Poland—the Struggle for Power 1772-1939* (London: Drummond, 1946).
KAPLAN, Herbert H. *The First Partition of Poland* (New York: Columbia University Press, 1962).
KOMARNICKI, T. *The Rebirth of the Polish Republic* (London, 1957)
LESLIE, R. F. *Polish Politics and the Revolution of November 1830* (London: Athlone Press, 1950).
POLONSKY, Antony. *Politics in Independent Poland 1921-39* (Oxford: Clarendon, 1972).
ROMER, J. and J. MODZELEWSKI. *Pologne 1919-1939* (Neuchâtel, 1946).
ROSE, W. J. *The Rise of Polish Democracy* (London: Bell, 1944).
SUPER, Paul. *The Polish Tradition: An Interpretation of a Nation* (London: Allen and Unwin, 1939).

6.452 Estonia

BLEES, Jakob. *Gustav II Adolf och Estland. Kyrka, Skola och Rättsväsende* (Gustav II Adolf and Esthonia. Church, School and Law) (Norrköping: Norrköpings tidings AB, 1932).
JACKSON, J. Hampden. *Estonia.* 2nd ed. (London: Allen and Unwin, 1948).
RAUN, Linda. *The Estonians* (New Haven, Conn.: Human Relations Area Files, 1955).
UUSTALU, Evold. *The History of the Estonian People* (London: Boreas, 1952).

6.453 Latvia

BAILMANIS, A. *A History of Latvia* (Princeton: Princeton University Press, 1951).
BLOEDNIKS, Adolf. *The Undefeated Nation* (New York: Speller, 1960).
CHAMBON, Henri de. *Origines et Histoire de la Lettonie* (Lille: Bresle, 1933).
SPEKKE, A. *History of Latvia* (Stockholm: Goppers, 1951).

6.454 Lithuania

BATILLAT, René. *Origine et Développement des Institutions Politiques en Lithuanie* (Lille: Meruire, 1932).
CHAMBON, H. de. *La Lithuanie Moderne* (Paris: Revue Parlementaire, 1933).
GERUTIS, A., ed. *Lithuanias 700 Years* (New York: Maryland Books, 1969).
JURGELA, Constantine Rudyard. *History of the Lithuanian Nation* (New York: Lithuanian Cultural Institute, 1948).
STUKAS, Jack J. *Awakening Lithuania, A Study of the Rise of Modern Lithuanian Nationalism* (Madison: Florham Park Press, 1966).
VARDYS, V. Stanley, ed. *Lithuania Under the Soviets: Portrait of a Nation, 1940-1965* (New York: Praeger, 1965).

6.46 The Russian Empire

6.461 Great Russia

BLACK, Cyril E. *The Transformation of Russian Society: Aspects of Social Change Since 1861* (Cambridge, Mass.: Harvard University Press, 1960).

BILLINGTON, James H. *The Icon and the Axe: An Interpretative History of Russia* (New York: Knopf, 1965).

BLUM, Jerome. *Lord and Peasant in Russia From the 9th to the 19th Century* (Princeton: Princeton University Press, 1961).

FAINSOD, Merle. "Bureaucracy and Modernization: The Russian and Soviet Case." In *Bureaucracy and Political Development,* edited by Joseph La Palombara (Princeton: Princeton University Press, 1963).

——— *How Russia is Ruled* (Cambridge, Mass.: Harvard University Press, 1933).

FLORINSKY, Michael T. *The End of the Russian Empire* (New York: Collier Books, 1961).

——— *Russia: A History and an Interpretation* (New York: Macmillan, 1953).

GITERMANN, Valentin. *Geschichte Russlands* (History of Russia). 3 vols. (Zurich: Gutenberg, 1944-49).

HANS, N. *History of Russian Educational Policy (1701-1917)* (New York: Russell & Russell, 1964).

INKELES, Alex. *Social Change in Soviet Russia* (Cambridge, Mass.: Harvard University Press, 1968).

——— and Raymond A. BAUER. *The Soviet Citizen, Daily Life in a Totalitarian Society* (Cambridge, Mass.: Harvard University Press, 1959).

KOCHAN, Lionel. *The Making of Modern Russia* (London: Jonathan Cape, 1962; Baltimore: Penguin, 1963).

MEDIGER, Walter. *Moscaus Weg nach Europa. Der Aufsteig Russlands zum Europäischen Machtstaat im Zeitalter Friedrichs der Grossen* (Moscow's Road to Europe. The Rise of Russia to a European Power at the Time of Frederic the Great) (Brunswick: 1952).

MOORE, Barrington. *Soviet Politics: The Dilemma of Power* (Cambridge, Mass.: Harvard University Press, 1954).

MOORE, Barrington, Jr. *Terror and Progress, USSR* (Cambridge, Mass.: Harvard University Press, 1954).

MOSSE, W. E. *Alexander II and the Modernization of Russia* (London: English Universities Press, 1958).

PARES, Bernard. *A History of Russia* (London: , 1955).

——— *The Fall of the Russian Monarchy* (London: , 1939).

PIPES, Richard. *Formation of the Soviet Union* (Cambridge, Mass.: Harvard University Press, 1954).

RAUCH, Gg. von. *Russland: Staatliche Einheit und Nationale Vielfalt* (Russia: State Unity and National Plurality) (Munich: 1953).

ROGGER, Hans. *National Consciousness in Eighteenth-Century Russia* (Cambridge, Mass.: Harvard University Press, 1960).

SETON-WATSON, Hugh. *The Decline of Imperial Russia 1855-1914* (New York: Praeger, 1952).

VERNADSKY, G. V. *A History of Russia.* 5th ed. (New Haven, Conn.: Yale University Press, 1961).

6.462 Belorussia

VAKAR, N. P. *Belorussia: The Making of a Nation* (Cambridge, Mass.: Harvard University Press, 1956).

6.453 Ukraine

ALLEN, William Edward David. *The Ukraine: A History* (New York: Russell & Russell, 1963).
––– *The Ukraine* (Cambridge: , 1940).
BORYS, Jurij. *The Russian Communist Party and the Sovietization of Ukraine: A Study in the Communist Doctrine of the Self-determination of Nations* (Stockholm: Norstedt, 1960).
CHAMBERLIN, William Henry. *The Ukraine: A Submerged Nation* (New York: Macmillan, 194).
SULLIVANT, Robert S. *Soviet Politics and the Ukraine, 1917-1957* (New York: Columbia University Press, 1962).

6.464 The Russian Empire in Asia

AVTORKHANOV, Abdurankhman. "Denationalization of Soviet Ethnic Minorities." Studies of the Soviet Union 4, no. 1 (1964): 74-99.
CAROE, Olaf Kirkpatrick. *Soviet Empire: The Turks of Central Asia and Stalinism* (New York: Macmillan, 1953).
CONQUEST, Robert. *The Soviet Deportation of Nationalities* (New York: St. Martin's Press, 1960).
––– ed. *Soviet Nationalities Policy in Practice* (New York: Praeger, 1967).
DADRIAN, V. N. "The Development of the Soviet Posture on Nationalities–A Theoretical Reappraisal." Paper presented to the World Congress of Sociology, Evian, September 4-11, 1966.
DALLIN, David Julievich. *The Rise of Russia in Asia* (New Haven, Conn.: Yale University Press, 1949).
GOLDHAGEN, Erich, ed. *Ethnic Minorities in the Soviet Union* (New York: Praeger).
KOLARZ, W. *Peoples of the Soviet Far East* (London: 1954).
NOL'DE, Boris. *La Formation de L'Empire Russe* (Paris, 1953).
ORNSTEIN, Jacob. "Soviet Language Policy: Theory and Practice." Slavic and East European Journal 3 (Spring 1959): 1-24.
SMIRNOV, N. A. *Islam and Russia* (London: Central Asian Research Centre, 1950).
TOWSTER, Julian. "Soviet Federation: How the Soviets Solved the Problems of Nationalism." Current History 16 (March 1949): 131-35.
VERNADSKY, G. *Mongols and Russians* (New Haven, Conn.: Yale University Press, 1953).
WHEELER, Geoffrey. *Racial Problems in Soviet Muslim Asia* (London: Oxford University Press, 1960).
ZENKOVSKY, Serge A. *Pan-Turkism and Islam in Russia* (Cambridge, Mass.: Harvard University Press, 1960).

6.5 The Moslem Empires and their Successor and Secession States

6.51 The Balkans and the Ottoman Empire

CASSELS, Lavender. *The Struggle for the Ottoman Empire, 1717-1740* (London: Murray, 1966).

COLES, Paul. *The Ottoman Impact on Europe* (London: Thames and Hudson, 1968).

CVIJIC, Jovan. *La Peninsule Balkanique* (Paris: 1918).

DJORDJEVIC, Dimitrij. *Revolutions Nationales des Peuples Balkaniques. 1804-1914* (Belgrade: Institut d'Histoire, 1965).

ELIOT, Charles. *Turkey in Europe* (London: Arnold, 1908).

JELAVICH, C. *Tsarist Russia and Balkan Nationalism* (Berkeley: University of California Press, 1959).

LADAS, S. P. *The Exchange of Minorities Between Greece, Bulgaria and Turkey* (London: 1932).

LENIN, Vladimir. "The Balkan War and Bourgeois Chauvinism." Pravda 74 (March 29, 1913).

MACARTNEY, C. A. and A. W. PALMER. *Independent Eastern Europe: A History* (London: Macmillan, 1966).

McNEILL, William H. *Europe's Steppe Frontier, 1500-1800* (Chicago: University of Chicago Press, 1964).

OSTROGORSKY, G. *Geschichte des Byzantinischen Staates* (History of the Byzantine States) (Munich: C. H. Beck, 1952).

PITTARD, Eugene. *Les Peuples des Balkans* (Paris: Leroux, 1920).

SETON-WATSON, R. W. *The Southern Slav Question and the Habsburg Monarchy* (London, 1911).

STAVRIANOS, L. *Balkan Federation* (Northampton, Mass.: Smith College, 1944. Reprinted Hamden, Conn.: Archon, 1964).

SUGAR, Peter F. and Ivo LEDERER, eds. *Nationalism in Eastern Europe* (Seattle: Washington University Press, 1968).

WILKINSON, H. R. *Maps and Politics* (Liverpool: University Press, 1951).

WOLFF, Robert Lee. *The Balkans in Our Time* (New York: Norton, 1967).

6.511 Albania

CHEKREZI, C. A. *Albania Past and Present*

PANO, N. C. *The People's Republic of Albania* (Baltimore: Johns Hopkins Press, 1968).

SCHREIBER, Thomas. *L'Evolution Politique et Economique de la République Populaire d'Albanie (1945-1968)* (Paris: La Documentation Française, 1969).

SWIRE, J. *Albania, the Rise of a Kingdom* (London: Williams and Norgate, 1929).

6.512 Bulgaria

BLACK, C. E. *The Establishment of Constitutional Government in Bulgaria* (Princeton: Princeton University Press, 1943).

LOGIO, G. C. *Bulgaria, Past and Present* (Manchester, 1936).
SANDERS, Irwin T. *Balkan Village* (Lexington: University of Kentucky Press, 1949).

6.513 Rumania

DRAGOMIR, J. *La Transylvanie Roumaine et ses Minorités Ethniques* (Bucharest, 1934).
MITRANY, David. *The Land and the Peasant in Rumania. The War and Agrarian Reform 1917-21* (London: H. Milford, 1930).
PROKOPOWITSCH, E. *Die Rumanische Nationale Bewegung in der Bukowina* (The Rumanian National Movement in Bukowina) (Graz, 1965).
ROBERTS, H. L. *Rumania: Political Problems of an Agrarian State* (New Haven, Conn.: Yale University Press, 1951).
SETON-WATSON, R. W. *A History of the Rumanians* (Cambridge, Eng.: Cambridge University Press, 1934).
SZASZ, Z. de. *The Minorities in Roumanian Transylvania* (London: 1927). Written from the Hungarian point of view.

6.514 Greece

FINLAY, George. *A History of Greece, From Its Conquest by the Romans to the Present Time, B.C. 146 to A.D. 1864* (Oxford: Clarendon Press, 1877).
LEAGUE OF NATIONS. *The Greek Refugee Settlement* (Geneva: 1926).
MILLER, W. *A History of the Greek People, 1821-1931* (London: 1931).
SWEET-ESCOTT, Bickham. *Greece, A Political and Economic Survey, 1939-1953* (London: Royal Institute of International Affairs, 1954).
TSOUCALAS, Constantine. *The Greek Tragedy* (New York: Penguin, 1969). Mainly on developments since 1909.

6.515 Cyprus

DISCHLER, Ludwig. *Die Zypernfrage* (The Question of Cyprus) (Frankfurt am Main: Metzner, 1960).
MAYES, Stanley. *Cyprus and Makarios* (London: Putnam, 1960).
STEPHENS, Robert. *Cyprus: A Place of Arms—A Study of Power Politics and Ethnic Conflict in the Eastern Mediterranean* (London: Pall Mall, 1966).

6.516 Turkey

EREN, Nuri. *Turkey Today—and Tomorrow: An Experiment in Westernization* (New York: Praeger, 1963).
FREY, Frederick W. *The Turkish Political Elite* (Cambridge, Mass.: MIT Press, 1965).
HARRIS, George S. "The Role of the Military in Turkish Politics." Middle East Journal 19 (1965).
HERSHLAG, Z. Y. *Turkey: An Economy in Transition* (The Hague: Van Keulen, 1958).
KARPAT, Kemal H. *Turkey's Politics: The Transition to a Multi-party System* (Princeton: Princeton University Press, 1959).

LERNER, Daniel and Richard D. ROBINSON. "Swords into Plowshares: The Turkish Army as a Modernizing Force." World Politics 13, no. 1 (October 1960).

LEWIS, Bernhard. *The Emergence of Modern Turkey* (London: Oxford University Press, 1961).

MARDIN, Serif. "Center-Periphery Relations: A Key to Turkish Politics." Daedalus 102, no. 1 (Winter 1973): 169-90.

――― *The Genesis of Young Ottoman Thought: A Study in the Modernization of Turkish Political Ideas* (Princeton: Princeton University Press, 1962).

NALBANDIAN, Louise. *The Armenian Revolutionary Movement: The Development of Armenian Political Parties Through the Nineteenth Century* (Berkeley: University of California Press, 1963).

ORGA, Irfan. *Phoenix Ascendant: The Rise of Modern Turkey* (London: Robert Hale, 1958).

RAMSAUR, E. E., Jr. *The Young Turks: Prelude to the Revolution of 1908* (Princeton: Princeton University Press, 1957).

ROBINSON, Richard D. *The First Turkish Republic* (Cambridge, Mass.: Harvard University Press, 1963).

RUSTOW, Dankwart A. "The Army and the Founding of the Turkish Republic." World Politics 11 (1959): 513-52.

TACHAU, Frank. "The Face of Turkish Nationalism as Reflected in the Cyprus Dispute." Middle East Journal 13 (Summer 1959): 262-72.

WARD, Robert E. and Dankwart A. RUSTOW, eds. *Political Modernization in Japan and Turkey* (Princeton: Princeton University Press, 1964).

YALMAN, Nur. "Islamic Reform and the Mystic Tradition in Eastern Turkey." European Journal of Sociology 10, no. 1 (1969): 41-61.

6.52 The Eastern Sultanates

6.521 The Arab Middle-East

BINDER, Leonard. *The Ideological Revolution in the Middle East* (New York: John Wiley, 1964).

BONNE, Alfred. *State and Economics in the Middle East. A Society in Transition* (London: 1955).

FISHER, Sydney N., ed. *The Military and the Middle East: Problems in Society and Government* (Columbus: Ohio State University Press, 1963).

――― *Social Forces in the Middle East* (Ithaca, N.Y.: Cornell University Press, 1955).

FISHER, William Bayne. *The Middle East: A Physical, Social, and Regional Geography*. 4th ed. (London: Methuen, 1961).

FLORY, Maurice and Robert MANTRAN. *Les Regimes Politiques des Pays Arabes* (Paris: Presses Universitaires de France, 1968).

HAIM, Sylvia G. *Arab Nationalism. An Anthology* (Berkeley: University of California Press, 1967).

LABIB, Subhi. "Nationsbildung im Arabischen Orient" (Nationbuilding in the Arab Orient). Saeculum 15 (1964): 350-64.

LAQUEUR, Walter Z. *Communism and Nationalism in the Middle East* (New York: Praeger, 1956).

――― ed. *The Middle East in Transition* (New York: Praeger, 1958).

LEIDEN, C., ed. *The Conflict of Traditionalism and Modernism in the Muslim Middle East* (Austin: University of Texas Press, 1968).

LEWIS, Bernard. *The Middle East and the West* (Bloomington: Indiana University Press, 1964).

MACDONALD, Robert W. *The League of Arab States: A Study in the Dynamics of Regional Organization* (Princeton: Princeton University Press, 1965).

POLK, W. R. and R. L. CHAMBERS, eds. *Beginnings of Modernization in the Middle East: The Nineteenth Century* (Chicago: University of Chicago Press, 1968).

RIVLIN, B. and J. S. SZYLIOWICZ. *The Contemporary Middle East. Tradition and Innovation* (New York: Random HOuse, 1965).

RUSTOW, Dankwart A. "Southwest Asia." In *Modern Political Systems: Asia,* edited by Robert E. Ward and Roy C. Macricis, pp. 367-441 (Englewood Cliffs, N.J.: Prentice-Hall, 1963).

——— *Politics and Westernization in the Near East* (Princeton: Center of International Studies, 1956).

SAUVAGET, J. *Introduction à L'Histoire de L'Orient Musulman.* 2nd ed. revised by Cl. Cohen (Paris: 1961). English translation, *Introduction to the History of the Muslim East* (Berkeley and Los Angeles: University of California Press, 1965).

SHARABI, Hisham B. *Nationalism and Revolution in the Arab World* (Princeton: Van Nostrand, 1965).

SMITH, Wilfred Cantwell. *Islam in Modern History* (Princeton: Princeton University Press, 1957).

WARRINER, Doreen. *Land Reform and Development in the Middle East: A Study of Egypt, Syria and Iraq* (London: Oxford University Press, 1962).

ZEINE, N. *Arab-Turkish Relations and the Emergence of Arab Nationalism* (Beirut: Khayat's, 1958).

6.522 Egypt

ABDEL-MALEK, A. *Egypte Société Militaire* (Paris: Seuil, 1962). English translation (New York: Random House, 1968).

BERGER, Morroe. *Bureaucracy and Society in Modern Egypt* (Princeton: Princeton University Press, 1957).

DODWELL, Henry. *The Founder of Modern Egypt: A Study of Muhammed Ali,* (Cambridge, Eng.: Cambridge University Press, 1931).

HARRIS, Christina Phelps. *Nationalism and Revolution in Egypt: The Role of the Muslim Brotherhood* (The Hague: Mouton, 1964).

HEAPHEY, James. "The Organization of Egypt: Inadequacies of a Nonpolitical Model for Nation-Building." World Politics 18 (January 1966): 177-93.

LACOUTURE, Jean and Simonne Lacouture. *Egypt in Transition* (New York: Criterion Books, 1958).

MARLOWE, John. *A History of Egypt and Anglo-Egyptian Relations, 1800-1953* (New York: Praeger, 1954).

NASSER, Gamal Abdul. *Egypt's Liberation: The Philosophy of the Revolution* (Washington, D.C.: Public Affairs Press, 1955).

PALMER, Monte. "The United Arab Republic: An Assessment of its Failure." Middle East Journal 20 (Winter 1966): 50-67.

SAFRAN, Nadav. *Egypt in Search of Political Community: An Analysis of the Intellectual and Political Evolution of Egypt 1804-1952* (Cambridge, Mass.: Harvard University Press, 1961).

TIGNOR, Robert L. *Modernization and British Colonial Rule in Egypt, 1882-1914* (Princeton: Princeton University Press, 1966).
VATIKIOTIS, P. J. *The Egyptian Army in Politics: Pattern for New Nations?* (Bloomington: Indiana University Press, 1961).
WAKIN, Edward. *A Lonely Minority: The Modern Story of Egypt's Copts* (New York: William Morrow, 1963).

6.523 Iraq

CARACTACUS (pseud.). *Revolution in Iraq: An Essay in Comparative Public Opinion* (London: Victor Gollancz, 1959).
GANTHER, Serge. "Le Mouvement National Kurde." Orient 9 (1965): 29-120.
GAVAN, S. S. *Kurdistan, Divided Nation of the Middle East* (London: Lawrence and Wisharg, 1958).
HARRIS, George L. *Iraq: Its People, Its Society, Its Culture* (New Haven, Conn.: Human Relations Area Files, 1958).
KHADDURI, Majid. *Independent Iraq 1932-1958*. 2nd ed. (London: Oxford University Press, 1960).
LONGRIGG, Stephen Hemsley. *Iraq 1900-1950: A Political, Social and Economic History* (New York: Oxford University Press, 1954).
PENROSE, E. F. "Essai sur L'Irak." Orient 35 (1965): 35-64.
QUBAIN, Fahim. *The Reconstruction of Iraq* (New York: Praeger, 1958).
SHWADRAN, Benjamin. *The Power Struggle in Iraq* (Elmont, N.Y.: Council on Middle Eastern Affairs, 1961).

6.524 Jordan

ABIDI, Agil H.H. *Jordan, A Political Study, 1948-1957* (New York: Asia Publishing House, 1965).
HARRIS, George Lawrence. *Jordan: Its People, Its Society, Its Culture* (New York: Grove Press, 1958).
PATAI, Raphael. *The Kingdom of Jordan* (Princeton: Princeton University Press, 1958).
SHWADRAN, Benjamin. *Jordan: A State of Tension* (Elmont, N.Y.: Council on Middle Eastern Affairs, 1959).
SPARROW, J. G. *Modern Jordan* (London: 1961).

6.525 Saudi Arabia

BERREBY, J. J. *La Péninsule Arabique* (Paris: 1958).
BROWN, E. H. *The Saudi Arabia, Kuwait, Neutral Zone* (Beirut: 1964).
LIPSKY, George Arthur and Ani MOUKHTAS. *Saudi Arabia* (New Haven, Conn.: Human Relations Area Files, 1959).
NOLTE, Richard H. "From Nomad Society to New Nation: Saudi Arabia." In *Expectant Peoples: Nationalism and Development,* edited by K. H. Silvert (New York: Random House, 1963).
SOULIE, G.J.L. and L. CHAMPENOIS. *Le Royaume d'Arabie Séoudite Face à L'Islam Révolutionaire* (Paris: 1966).

6.526 Aden, Yemen, and the Gulf States

AL-ATTAR, Mohammad Said. *Le Sous-Développement Economique et Social du Yemen. Perspectives de la Révolution Yéménite* (Paris: 1965).

BROWN, E. H. *The Saudi Arabia, Kuwait, Neutral Zone* (Beirut: 1964).

CENTRAL OFFICE OF INFORMATION. *Aden and South Arabia* (London: HMSO, 1965).

HAKKIMA, A. A. *The Rise and Development of Bahrein and Kuwait* (Beirut: 1964).

HEYWORTH-DUNNE, G. E. *Al-Yemen. Social, Political and Economic Survey* (Cairo: 1952).

INGRAMS, Harold. *The Yemen: Imams, Rulers, and Revolutions* (New York: Praeger, 1964).

KING, G. *Imperial Outpost Aden* (New York: 1964).

6.53 The Maghreb states

AMIN, Samir. *The Maghreb in the Modern World: Algeria, Tunisia, Morocco* (New York: Penguin, 1970).

——— *L'Economie du Maghreb* (Paris: Maspéro, 1965).

ASHFORD, Douglas. *Second and Third Generation Elites in the Maghreb* (Washington, D.C.: Government Printing Office, 1964).

BARBOUR, Nevill, ed. *A Survey of North West Africa (The Maghrib)* (London: Oxford University Press, 1959).

BERQUE, Jacques. *Le Maghreb Entre Deux Guerres* (Paris: 1962).

——— *Les Arabes d'Hier à Demain* (Paris: 1960).

——— *Structures Sociales du Haut Atlas* (Paris: Presses Universitaries, 1955).

FAVRET, J. "La Segmentarité au Maghreb." L'Homme, Revue Française d'Anthropologie 6, no. 2 (1966).

GAUTIER, E. F. *Le Passé de l'Afrique du Nord* (Paris: Payot, 1952).

GELLNER, E. *Saints of the Atlas* (London: Weidenfeld, 1969).

HAHN, Lorna. *North Africa: Nationalism to Nationhood* (Washington, D.C.: Public Affairs Press, 1960).

LACOUTURE, Jean. *Cinq Hommes et la France* (Paris: Editions du Seuil, 1961).

LAROUI, Abdullah. *L'Histoire du Maghreb* (Paris: Maspéro, 1970).

MOORE, Clement Henry. *Politics in North Africa* (Boston: Little, Brown, 1970).

TIANO, André. *Le Maghreb entre les Mythes* (Paris: 1968).

TOURNEAU, Roger le. *Evolution Politique de l'Afrique du Nord Musulmane (1920-1961)* (Paris: A. Colin, 1962).

VALENSI, Lucette. *Le Maghreb Avant la Prise d'Alger* (Paris: Flammarion, 1969).

ZGHAL, Abdelkader. "La Participation de la Paysannerie Maghrébine à la Construction Nationale." Revue Tunisienne des Sciences Sociales 22 (July 1970).

6.531 Algeria

ANDREWS, William George. *French Politics and Algeria: The Process of Policy Formation, 1954-1962* (New York: Appleton-Century-Crofts, 1962).

BOUDIAF, Mohamed. *Où Va l'Algérie?* (Paris: Librairie de l'Etoile, 1964).

BOURDIEU, B. Pierre and Abdelnalek SAYAD. *Le Déracinement: La Crise de l'Agriculture Traditionelle en Algérie* (Paris: Editions de Minuit, 1964).

BUY, Françoise. *La République Algérienne Démocratique et Populaire* (Paris: Librairie Française, 1965).

FAVRET, J. "Relations de Dépendance et Manipulation de la Violence en Kabylie." L'Homme, Revue Française d'Anthropologie 8, no. 4 (1968).

GORDON, David C. *The Passing of French Algeria* (London: Oxford University Press, 1966).

KNIGHT, H. M. "The Algerian Revolt: Some Underlying Factors." Middle East Journal 10 (Autumn 1956): 355-67.

KRAFT, Joseph. "Settler Politics in Algeria." Foreign Affairs 39 (July 1961): 591-600.

――― *The Struggle for Algeria* (Garden City, N.Y.: Doubleday, 1961).

LACHERAF, M. *L'Algérie: Nation et Société* (Paris: Maspéro, 1965).

LACOSTE, Y.; A. NOUSCHI; and A. PRENANT. *L'Algérie, Passé et Présent* (Paris: Editions Sociales, 1960).

NORA, Pierre. *Les Français d'Algérie* (Paris: Julliard, 1961).

NOUSCHI, André. *La Naissance du Nationalisme Algérien 1914-1954* (Paris: 1962).

MINER, Horace Mitchell and George DE VOS. *Oasis and Casbah: Algerian Culture and Personality in Change* (Ann Arbor: University of Michigan Press, 1960).

PICKLES, Dorothy. *Algeria and France: From Colonialism to Cooperation* (New York: Praeger, 1963).

SICARD, E. "Essai d'Analyse Sociologique Schématique sur la Construction Nationale Algérienne." Revue de l'Institut de Sociologie, Brussels 2, no. 3 (1967): 487-512.

6.532 Libya

EVANS-PRITCHARD, E. E. *The Sanusi of Cyrenaica* (Oxford: 1949).

KHADDURI, Majid. *Modern Libya, A Study in Political Development* (Baltimore: Johns Hopkins Press, 1963).

KUBBAH, Abdul Amir. *Libya, Its Oil Industry and Economic System* (Bagdad-Beirut: 1964).

MARTHELOT, Pierre. "La Révolution du Pétrole dans un Pays Insuffisamment Développé: la Libye." Cahiers d'Outre-Mer, January-March 1965.

NORMAN, John. *Labor and Politics in Libya and Arab Africa* (New York: Bookman, 1965).

RIVLIN, Benjamin. "Unity and Nationalism in Libya." Middle East Journal 3 (June 1949): 31-54.

ROSSI, Pierre. *Libye* (Lausanne: Edition Rencontre, 1965).

6.533 Morocco

ASHFORD, Douglas E. *Political Change in Morocco* (Princeton: Princeton University Press, 1961).

――― "Local Reform and Social Change in Morocco and Tunisia." In *Emerging Africa,* edited by William H. Lewis (Washington, D.C.: Public Affairs Press, 1963).

AYACHE, A. *Le Maroc, Bilan d'une Colonisation* (Paris: Editions Sociales, 1956).

COHEN, Mark I. and Lorna HAHN. *Morocco: Old Land, New Nation* (New York: Praeger, 1966).

FOGG, Walter. "Village, Tribal Markets, and Towns: Some Considerations Concerning Urban Development in the Spanish and International Zones of Morocco." *Sociological Review* 32 (April 1940): 85-107.

GELLNER, E. "Patterns of Rural Rebellion in Morocco: Tribes as Minorities." *European Journal of Sociology* 3, no. 2 (1962):

HALSTEAD, J. P. *Rebirth of a Nation: The Origins and Rise of Moroccan Nationalism, 1912-1944* (Cambridge, Mass.: Harvard University Press, 1967).

HEINEMEYER, W. F. *Nationale Integratie en Regionale Diversiteit* (National Integration and Regional Diversity) (Amsterdam: de Bezige Bij., diss., 1968).

LACOUTURE, Jean and Simon LACOUTURE. *Le Maroc à l'Epreuve* (Paris: Seuil, 1958).

LAHBABI, Mohamed. *Le Gouvernement Marocain à l'Aube du XXe Siècle* (Rabat: Editions Techniques Nord-Africaines, 1968).

LEWIS, William H. "Feuding and Social Change in Morocco." *Journal of Conflict Resolution* 5 (March 1961): 43-59.

――― "Les Lignes de Force du Maroc Moderne." *Politique Etrangère* 20 (August-September 1955): 393-424.

MONTAGNE, R. *Les Berbères et le Makhzen dans le Sud du Maroc. Essai sur la Transformation Politique des Berbères Sédentaires (Groupe Chleuh)* (Paris: Alcan, 1930).

――― ed. *Naissance du Proletariat Marocain* (Paris: Peyronnet, 1952).

MONTEIL, Vincent. *Le Maroc* (Paris: 1962).

TOURNEAU, Roger le. *Le Nationalisme Marocain* (Alger: Faculté de Lettres, 1955).

VINOGRADOV, A. and John WATERBURY. "Situations of Contested Legitimacy in Morocco: An Alternative Framework." *Comparative Studies in Society and History* 43, no. 1 (January 1971): 52-59.

WATERBURY, John. *The Commander of the Faithful. The Moroccan Political Elite. A Study of Segmented Politics* (London: Weidenfeld and Nicholson, 1970).

YATA, Ali. *Les Problèmes Actuels de la Révolution Nationale Démocratique au Maroc* (Casablanca: 1966).

ZARTMAN, I. William. *Destiny of a Dynasty: The Search for Institutions in Morocco's Developing Society* (Columbia: University of South Carolina Press, 1964).

――― *Morocco: Problems of New Power* (New York: Atherton, 1964).

See also Section 5.4, Geertz.

6.534 Tunisia

ASHFORD, Douglas E. "Local Reform and Social Change in Morrocco and Tunisia." In *Emerging Africa,* edited by William H. Lewis (Washington, D.C.: Public Affairs Press, 1963).

BOURGUIBA, Habib. *La Tunisie et la France. Vingt-cinq Ans de Lutte Pour une Coopération Libre* (Paris: R. Julliard, 1954).

――― "The Tunesian Way." *Foreign Affairs* 44 (April 1966): 480-88.

GARAS, Félix. *Bourguiba et la Naissance d'une Nation* (Paris: R. Julliard, 1956).

MICAUD, Charles A.; Clement H. MOORE; and C. BROWN. *Tunisia: The Politics of Modernization* (New York: Praeger, 1964).

MOORE, Clement Henry. *Tunisia Since Independence. The Dynamics of One-party Government* (Berkeley: University of California Press, 1965).

RAYMOND, André. *La Tunisie* (Paris: "Que Sais-je? ", 1961).

RIVLIN, Benjamin. "The Tunesian Nationalist Movement: Four Decades of Evolution." Middle East Journal 6 (Spring 1952): 167-93.

SEBAG, P. *La Tunisie: Essai de Monographie* (Paris: Editions Sociales, 1951).

ZERAFFA, Michel. *La Tunisie* (Paris: 1955).

ZGHAL, Abdelkader. "Construction Nationale et Nouvelles Classes Sociales en Tunisie." Révue de l'Institut de Sociologie 2, no. 3 (1967).

ZIADAH, Nicolas. *Origina of Nationalism in Tunisia* (Beirut: American University of Beirut, 1962).

6.6 Asian empires and states

PANIKKAR, K. *Asia and Western Dominance* (London: Allen and Unwin, 1953).

WEIDNER, Edward W., ed. *Development Administration in Asia* (Durham, N.C.: Duke University Press, 1970).

WERTHEIM, W. F. *East-West Parallels: Sociological Approaches to Modern Asia* (The Hague: W. van Hoeve, 1964).

6.61 Near Eastern polities

BERGER, Earl. *The Covenant and the Sword: Arab-Israeli Relations 1948-56* (London: Routledge and Kegan Paul, 1965).

HOURANI, Albert H. *Syria and Lebanon* (London: Oxford University Press, 1946).

KIMCHE, Jon and David KIMCHE. *A Clash of Destinies: The Arab-Jewish War and the Founding of the State of Israel* (New York: Praeger, 1960).

LONGRIGG, Stephen A. *Syria and Lebanon Under French Mandate* (London: Oxford University Press, 1958).

ZIADEH, Nicola. *Syria and Lebanon* (New York: Praeger, 1957).

6.611 Israel

BADI, J. *Religion in Israel Today: The Relationship Between State and Religion* (New York: Bookman, 1959).

DESHEN, Shlomo A. "A Case of Breakdown of Modernization in an Israeli Immigrant Community." Jewish Journal of Sociology 7 (1965): 63-91.

EISENSTADT, Samuel N. *Israeli Society* (London: Weidenfeld and Nicholson, 1967).

――― *The Absorption of Immigrants: A Comparative Study Based Mainly on the Jewish Community in Palestine and the State of Israel* (Glencoe, Ill.: Free Press, 1955).

FEIN, Leonard J. *Politics in Israel* (Boston: Little, Brown, 1967).

FRIEDMANN, Georges. *Fin du Peuple Juif* (Paris: Gallimard, 1965).

HALPERN, Ben. *The Idea of the Jewish State* (Cambridge, Mass.: Harvard University Press, 1961).

MATRAS, Judah. *Social Change in Israel* (Chicago: Aldine, 1965).

TELLER, Judd. *The Jews: A Biography of a People* (New York: Bantam Books, 1966).

VAUX, Roland de. *Ancient Israel* (New York: McGraw-Hill, 1966).
WILLNER, D. *Nation-Building and Community in Israel* (Princeton: Princeton University Press, 1969).

Lebanon

ABOU, Selim. *Le Bilinguisme Arabo-Français au Liban* (Paris: 1962).
BINDER, Leonard, ed. *Politics in Lebanon* (New York: John Wiley, 1966).
CROW, Ralph E. "Religious Sectarianism in the Lebanese Political System." Mimeographed. Paper presented at the Fifth World Congress, International Political Science Association, 1961.
HUDSON, Michael C. *The Precarious Republic: Political Modernization in Lebanon* (New York: 1968).
MEO, Leiler M.T. *Lebanon: Improbably Nation* (Bloomington: University of Indiana Press, 1965).
POLK, William R. *The Opening of South Lebanon, 1788-1840: A Study of the Impact of the West on the Middle East* (Cambridge, Mass.: Harvard University Press, 1963).
QUBAIN, Fahim. *Crisis in Lebanon* (Washington, D.C.: Middle East Institute, 1961).
SALIBI, Kamal S. *The Modern History of Lebanon.* (New York: Praeger, 1965).
SULEIMAN, M. *Political Parties in Lebanon: The Challenge of a Fragmented Culture* (Ithaca, N.Y.: Cornell University Press, 1967) .

6.613 Syria

SEALE, Patrick. *The Struggle for Syria: A Study of Post-War Arab Politics* (London: Oxford University Press, 1965).
TORREY, G. H. *Syrian Politics and the Military, 1945-1958* (Columbus: Ohio State University Press, 1964).

6.62 Iran

BANANI, Amin. *The Modernization of Iran, 1921-1941* (Stanford: Stanford University Press, 1961).
BINDER, Leonard. *Iran: Political Development in a Changing Society* (Berkeley: University of California Press, 1962).
COTTAM, Richard. *Nationalism in Iran* (Pittsburgh: University of Pittsburgh Press, 1964).
GASTIL, Raymond D. "Middle Class Impediments to Iranian Modernization." Public Opinion Quarterly 22 (Fall 1958): 325-29.
LENCZOWSKI, George. *Russia and the West in Iran* (Ithaca, N.Y.: Cornell University Press, 1949).
VREELAND, Herbert H. *Iran* (New Haven, Conn.: Human Relations Area Files, 1957).
WILBER, Donald N. *Contemporary Iran* (New York: Praeger, 1963).
——— *Iran: Past and Present.* 4th ed. (Princeton: Princeton University Press, 1958).

See also Section 2.2, BAYNE.

6.63 The Indian empires, their successors and neighbours

FERGUSON, Charles A. and J. J. GUMPERZ, eds. *Linguistic Diversity in South Asia* (Bloomington: Indiana University Research Center in Anthropology, Folklore, and Linguistics, 1960).

WEINER, Myron. *Political Change in South Asia* (Calcutta: Mukhopadhyay, 1963).

WILSON, Patrick, ed. and compiler. *Government and Politics of India and Pakistan, 1885-1955: A Bibliography of Works in Western Languages* (Berkeley: University of California Press).

6.631 Afghanistan

BLEIBER, Fritz. "Afghanistan und Paschtunistan." Zeitschrift Fuer Geopolitik 24 (February 1953): 88-96.

DUPREE, Louis. "Tribalism, Regionalism, and National Oligarchy: Afghanistan." In *Expectant Peoples: Nationalism and Development,* edited by K. H. Silvert (New York: Random House, 1963).

SYKES, Percy M. *A History of Afghanistan* (New York: Macmillan, 1940).

WATKINS, Mary Bradley. *Afghanistan: Land in Transition* (Princeton: Van Nostrand, 1963).

WILBER, N. *Afghanistan* (New Haven, Conn.: Taplinger, 1956).

6.632 Ceylon (Sri Lanka)

ARASARATNAM, Sinnappah. *Ceylon* (Englewood Cliffs, N.J: Prentice-Hall, 1965).

——— *Dutch Power in Ceylon, 1658-1687* (Amsterdam: Netherlands Institute for International Cultural Relations, 1958).

Ceylon. Report of the Select Committee of the State Council on Sinhalese and Tamil as Official Languages (Colombo: Government Press, 1946).

FARMER, B. H. *Ceylon: A Divided Nation* (London: 1963).

GOONEWARDENA, Karunadada Wijesiri. *The Foundation of Dutch Power in Ceylon, 1638-1658* (Amsterdam: Djambatan, 1958).

KEARNEY, Robert N. *Communalism and Language in the Politics of Ceylon* (Durham, N.C.: Duke University Press, 1967).

LUDOWYK, E.F.C. *The Modern History of Ceylon* (New York: Praeger, 1966).

MASON, Philip, ed. *India and Ceylon: Unity and Diversity* (New York: Oxford University Press, 1967).

PAKEMAN, Sidney A. *Ceylon* (London: Benn, 1964).

RANGNEKAR, D. K. "Racialism and National Integration in Ceylon." United Asia 10 (October 1959): 391-97.

SINGER, Marshall R. *The Emerging Elite: A Study of Political Leadership in Ceylon* (Cambridge: MIT Press, 1964).

WEERAWARDANA, I.D.S. "Minority Problems in Ceylon." Pacific Affairs 25 (September 1952): 278-87.

WRIGGINS, William Howard. "Impediments to Unity in New Nations: The Case of Ceylon." American Political Science Review 55, no. 2 (June 1961): 313-20.

6.633 India

AHMAD, Aziz. *Islamic Modernization in India and Pakistan 1857-1965* (London: Oxford University Press, 1967).

AIYER, Chetpat Pattabhisag Ramaswami. *Disintegration: How to Avert It?* (Bombay: Bharatiya Vidya Bhavan, 1961).

AMBEDKAR, Bhimrao Ramjo. *States and Minorities: What are Their Rights and How to Secure Them in the Constitution of Free India* (Bombay: Thacker, 1947).

BAILEY, F. G. *Tribe, Caste and Nation. A Study of Political Activity and Political Change in Highland Orissa* (Manchester: Manchester University Press, 1960).

BARNOUW, Victor. "The Sindhis, Mercantile Refugees in India: Problems of Their Assimilation." Phylon 27 (1966): 40-49.

BASHAM, A. L. *The Wonder That Was India: A Survey of the Culture of the Indian Sub-continent Before the Coming of the Muslims* (London: Sidgwick and Jackson, 1954).

BOSE, Nemai Sadhan. *The Indian Awakening and Bengal* (Calcutta: Mukhopadhyay, 1960).

BOSE, Nirmal Kumar. *Problems of National Integration* (Simla: Indian Institute of Advanced Study, 1967).

BRASS, Paul R. *Factional Politics in an Indian State: The Congress Party in Uttar Pradesh* (Berkeley: University of California Press, 1965).

BROWN, W. Norman. "India's Pakistan Issue." Proceedings of the American Philosophical Society 91 (April 1947): 162-80.

COHEN, Stephen P. *The Indian Army: Its Contribution to the Development of a Nation* (Berkeley: University of California Press, 1971).

COUPLAND, Reginald. *The Indian Problem: Report on the Constitutional Problem in India* (London: Oxford University Press, 194).

DANGE, P. A. *India From Primitive Communism to Slavery* (Bombay: People's Publishing House, 1949).

DAS GUPTA, J. *Language Conflict and National Development: Group Policies and National Language Policy in India* (Berkeley: University of California Press, 1970).

DESAI, A. R. *Rural India in Transition* (Bombay: Popular Book Depot, 1961).

——— *Social Background of Indian Nationalism* (Bombay: Oxford University Press, 1948).

DREKMEIER, Charles. *Kinship and Community in Early India* (Stanford: Stanford University Press, 1962).

DUMONT, Louis. "Nationalism and Communalism." Contributions to Indian Sociology 8 (March 1964): 30-70.

GOKHALE, Balkrishna Govind. *The Making of the Indian Nation* (Bombay: Asia Publishing House, 1958).

GRIFFITHS, Percival Joseph. *The British Impact on India* (London: Macdonald, 1952).

HARRISON, S. *India: The Most Dangerous Decades* (Princeton: Princeton University Press, 1960).

HEESTERMAN, J. C. "Tradition in Modern India." Bijdragen Tot de Taal, Land en Volkenkunde 119 (1963): 237-55.

HEIMSATH, Charles. *Indian Nationalism and Hindu Social Reform* (Princeton: Princeton University Press, 1967).

KARUE, Irawati Karmarkas. *Hindu Society: An Interpretation* (Poona: Deccan College, 1961).

KEITH, A. B. *A Constitutional History of India, 1600-1935.* 2nd ed. (London: Methuen, 1936).

KHAN, Rahat Nahi. "La Communauté Musulmane Indienne et les Problèmes de la Partition." Politique Etrangère 31 (1966): 44-64.

KOSAMBI, Damodar Dharmanad. *Myth and Reality: Studies in the Formation of Indian Culture* (Bombay: Popular Prakashan, 1962).

KOTHARI, Rajni. *Politics in India* (Boston: Little, Brown, 1970; New Delhi: Orient Longmans, 1970).

––– and Bashiruddin Ahmed. "Social Mobilisation and Politicization: India's Pattern of Interaction." Mimeograph. Centre for the Study of Developing Societies.

LEWIS, John P. *Quiet Crisis in India* (Washington, D.C.: Brookings Institution, 1962).

MANDELBAUM, David G. *Society in India.* 2 vols. (Berkeley: University of California, 1970).

MARRIOTT, McKim, ed. *Village India: Studies in the Little Community* (Chicago: University of Chicago Press, 1955).

MASON, Philip, ed. *India and Ceylon: Unity and Diversity* (New York: Oxford University Press, 1967).

MENON, V. P. *The Transfer of Power in India* (Princeton: Princeton University Press, 1957).

––– *The Story of the Integration of the Indian States* (New York: Macmillan, 1956).

MISRA, B. B. *The Administrative History of India 1834-1947* (Bombay: Oxford University Press, 1970).

MOOKERJI, Radakumud. *The Fundamental Unity of India* (London: Longmans, 1914).

MOON, Penderel. *Divide and Quit: Ending of British Rule in India* (Berkeley: University of California Press, 1961).

MUKERJI, Nirod. *Standing at the Cross-roads: An Analytical Approach to the Basic Problems of Psychological Integration* (Bombay: Allied Publishers, 1964).

MUKHERJEE, Ramkrishna. *The Sociologist and Social Change in India Today* (New Delhi: Prentice-Hall of India, 1965).

––– *The Rise and Fall of the East India Company* (Berlin: Verlag der Wissenschaften, 1958).

––– *The Dynamics of a Rural Society* (Berlin: Akademie-Verlag, 1957).

NAMBOODRIPAD, E. M. S. *Kerala Yesterday, Today and Tomorrow* (Calcutta: National Book Agency, 1967).

––– *The National Question in Kerala* (Bombay: People's Publishing House, 1952).

NEHRU, Jawaharlal. *India's Freedom* (New York: Barnes and Noble, 1962).

ORENSTEIN, Henry. *Gaon: Conflict and Cohesion in an Indian Village* (Princeton: Princeton University Press, 1965).

PARK, Richard L. "India." In *Modern Political Systems: Asia,* edited by Robert E. Ward and Roy C. Macridis, pp. 217-94 (Englewood Cliffs, N.J.: Prentice-Hall, 1963).

RICHTER, William L. "The Politics of Language in India." Ph.D. dissertation, University of Chicago, 1968.

RUDOLPH, Lloyd I and Suzanne Hoeber RUDOLPH. "The Political Role of India's Caste Associations." Pacific Affairs 33 (March 1960): 5-22.

SCOTT, Michael. *The Nagas. India's Problem—Or the World's* (New York: McKay, 1966).

SHARMA, Rambilas. *The Question of an Obligatory State Language in India* (Bombay: People's Publishing House, 1954).

SHILS, Edward. *The Intellectual Between Tradition and Modernity: The Indian Situation* (The Hague: Mouton, 1961).

SINGER, Milton, ed. *Traditional India: Structure and Change* (Philadelphia: American Society, 1959).

SMITH, Donald Eugene. *India as a Secular State* (Princeton: Princeton University Press, 1963).

SMITH, William R. *Nationalism and Reform in India* (New Haven, Conn.: Yale University Press, 1938).

SOVANI, N. V. and V. M. DANDEKAR, eds. *Changing India* (Bombay: Asia Publishing House, 1961).

SRINIVAS, M. N. *Caste in Modern India and Other Essays* (Bombay: Asia Publishing House, 1962).

"The Story of Goa (Past, Present and Future of the Portuguese State in India)." British Survey, Main Series (N.S.), November 1954, pp.12-24.

TANGRI, Shanti S. "Intellectuals and society in 19th century India, Comparative Studies in Society and History 3, July 1961: 368-

THIRTHA, N. V. *National Integration* (Delhi: University Publishers, 1964).

THOMPSON, Edward and G. T. GARRETT. *Rise and Fulfillment of British Rule in India* (London: Macmillan, 1934).

THORNER, Daniel. *Investment in Empire: British Railway and Steam Shipping Enterprise in India, 1825-1849* (Philadelphia: University of Pennsylvania Press, 1950).

TINKER, H. *Experiment With Freedom* (New York: Oxford University Press, 1967).

WEBER, Max. *The Religion of India* (Glencoe, Ill.: Free Press, 1958). Original title, *Hinduismus und Buddhismus.* Gesammelte Aufsätze zur Religionssoziologie, vol. 2 (Tübingen: Mohr, 1922-23).

WEINER, Myron. *Party Building in a New Nation: The Indian National Congress* (Chicago: University of Chicago Press, 1966).

——— *The Politics of Scarcity: Public Pressure and Political Response in India* (Chicago: University of Chicago Press, 1962).

——— *Party Politics in India* (Princeton: Princeton University Press, 1957).

WOLPERT, Stanley A. *Tilak and Gokhale: Revolution and Reform in the Making of Modern India* (Berkeley: University of California Press, 1962).

WOODRUFF, Philip. *The Men Who Ruled India.* 2 vols. (London: Jonathan Cape, 1953-54).

ZINKIN, Taya. *Challenges in India* (New York: Walker, 1967).

6.634 Kashmir

BRECHER, Michael. *The Struggle for Kashmir* (New York: Oxford University Press, 1953).

FERGUSON, James. *Kashmir, an Historical Introduction* (London: Centaur Press, 1961).

KORBEL, Josef. *Danger in Kashmir* (Princeton: Princeton University Press, 1954).

6.635 Nepal

GUPTA, Anirudha. *Politics in Nepal* (Bombay: Allied Publishers, 1964).

JOSHI, Bhuwan Lal and Leo E. ROSE. *Democratic Innovations in Nepal: A Case Study of Political Acculturation* (Berkeley and Los Angeles: University of California Press, 1966).

6.636 Pakistan

AHMAD, Mushtag. *Government and Politics in Pakistan.* 2nd ed. (Karachi: Pakistan Publishing House, 1963).

ANDERSON, David D. "Pakistan's Search for National Identity." Yale Review 55 (June 1966): 552-69.

BESSAIGNET, Pierre, ed. *Social Research in East Pakistan* (Dacca: Asiatic Society of Pakistan, 1960).

BINDER, Leonard. *Religion and Politics in Pakistan* (Berkeley: University of California Press, 1961).

BIRKHEAD, Guthrie S., ed. *Administrative Problems in Pakistan* (New York: Syracuse University Press, 1966).

BRAIBANTI, Ralph. *Research on the Bureaucracy of Pakistan: A Critique of Sources, Conditions and Issues, With Appended Documents* (Durham: Duke University Press, 1966).

CALLARD, Keith. *Pakistan: A Political Study* (London: Allen and Unwin, 1957).

EISTER, Allan W. "Perspective on Functions of Religion in a Developing Country: Islam in Pakistan." Journal for the Scientific Study of Religion 3 (1964): 227-38.

GOODNOW, Henry Frank. *The Civil Service in Pakistan: Bureaucracy in a New Nation* (New Haven, Conn.: Yale University Press, 1964).

KUREISHI, R. *The Nation of Pakistan* (Oxford, N.Y.: Pergamon Press, 1969).

RUSHBROOK-WILLIAMS, L. F. *The State of Pakistan* (London: Faber & Faber, 1962).

SYMONDS, Richard. *The Making of Pakistan* (London: Faber, 1950).

VORYS, Karl *Political Development in Pakistan* (Princeton: Princeton University Press, 1965).

WEEKES, Richard V. *Pakistan: Birth and Growth of a Muslim Nation* (Princeton: Van Nostrand, 1964).

WILCOX, W. A. *Pakistan and the Consolidation of a New Nation* (New York: Columbia University Press, 1963).

ZIRING, Lawrence. *The Ayub Khan Era: Politics in Pakistan, 1958-1969* (New York: Syracuse University Press, 1971).

6.637 Bangladesh

JAHAN, R. *Pakistan: Failure in National Integration* (New York: Columbia University Press, 1972).

LAMBERT, Richard D. "Factors in Bengali Regionalism in Pakistan." Far Eastern Survey 28 (April 1959): 49-58.

MARON, Stanley O. "The Problem of East Pakistan." Pacific Affairs 28 (June 1955): 132-44.

PARK, Richard L. "East Bengal: Pakistan's Troubled Province." Far Eastern Survey 23 (May 1954): 70-74.

RAHMAN, M. Akhlagur. *Partition, Integration, Economic Growth, and Interregional Trade: A Study of Interwing Trade in Pakistan, 1948-1959* (Karachi: Institute for Development Economics, 1963).

RISLEY, H. H. *The Tribes and the Castes of Bengal* (Calcutta: Bengal Secretariat Press, 1891).

6.64 Southeast Asia

BECHERT, Heinz. *Buddhismus, Staat und Gesellschaft* (Buddhism, State and Society) (Frankfurt: Schriften des Instituts fuer Asienkunde in Hamburg, 1966).

BUTWELL, Richard A. *Southeast Asia Today—And Tomorrow: Problems of Political Development* (New York: Praeger, 1969).

CADY, John F. *Southeast Asia: Its Historical Development* (New York: McGraw-Hill, 1964).

CHATTERJIE, Bujam Raj. "The Role of the Armed Forces in Politics in Southeast Asia." International Studies 2 (January 1961): 221-33.

DOBBY, E.H.G. *Southeast Asia.* 6th ed. (London: University of London Press, 1958).

DuBOIS, Cora. *Social Forces in Southeast Asia* (Cambridge: Harvard University Press, 1959).

EMERSON, Rupert. "Indo-China." Yale Review 44 (September 1954): 51-63.

EVERS, Hans-Dieter, ed. *Modernisation in Southeast Asia* (New York: Oxford University Press, 1972).

GIAP, The Siauw. "Religion and Overseas Chinese Assimilation in Southeast Asian Countries." Revue de Sud-est Asiatique 2 (1965): 67-84.

GOLAY, Frank H., et al. *Underdevelopment and Economic Nationalism in Southeast Asia* (Ithaca, N.Y.: Cornell University Press, 1969).

GORDON, Bernard. *The Dimensions of Conflict in Southeast Asia* (Englewood Cliffs, N.J.: Prentice-Hall, 1966).

HALL, D.G.E. *A History of Southeast Asia* (London: 1955).

HICKEY, Gerald C. and John K. MUSGRAVE, eds. *Ethnic Groups of Mainland Southeast Asia* (New Haven: Conn.: Human Relations Area Files).

KAHIN, George McTurnan, ed. *Governments and Politics of Southeast Asia* (New York: Cornell University Press, 1959).

KUNSTADTER, Peter, ed. *Southeast Asian Tribes, Minorities, and Nations.* 2 vols. (Princeton: Princeton University Press, 1967).

MARYANOV, Gerald S. *Conflict and Political Development in Southeast Asia: An Exploration in the Internal Political Implications of Comparative Theory* (Ohio University: Center for International Studies, 1969).

McALISTER, John T. *Southeast Asia: The Politics of National Integration* (New York: Random House, 1973).

MEHDEN, Fred. R. van der. *Religion and Nationalism in Southeast Asia* (Madison: University of Wisconsin Press, 1963).

MILLS, Lenox A. *Southeast Asia: Illusion and Reality in Politics and Economy* (Minneapolis: University of Minnesota Press, 1964).

PYE, Lucian W. *Southeast Asia's Political Systems* (Englewood Cliffs, N.J.: Prentice-Hall, 1967).

——— "Southeast Asia." In *Modern Political Systems: Asia,* edited by Robert E. Ward and Roy C. Macridis, pp. 297-364 (Englewood Cliffs: Prentice-Hall, 1963).

SINGHAL, D. P. "Nationalism and Communism in Southeast Asia: A Brief Survey." Journal of Southeast Asian History, no. 34 (March 1962), pp. 59-66.

THAYER, Phillip W., ed. *Southeast Asia in the Coming World* (Baltimore: Johns Hopkins Press, 1953).

TILMAN, Robert C., ed. *Man, State and Society in Contemporary Southeast Asia* (New York: Praeger, 1969).

6.641 Burma

CADY, John F. *A History of Modern Burma* (Ithaca, N.Y.: Cornell University Press, 1958).

FURNIVALL, John S. "Communism and Nationalism in Burma." The Eastern Survey 18 (1949): 193-97.

––– *Colonial Policy and Practice: A Comparative Study of Burma and Netherlands India* (London: Cambridge University Press, 1948).

HOBBS, Cecil. "Nationalism in British Colonial Burma." Far Eastern Quarterly 6 (1947): 113-21.

LANDON, K. P. "Burmese Nationalism." Far Eastern Quarterly 2 (1943): 141-44.

LEACH, Edmund. "The Political Future of Burma." In *Futuribles,* edited by Bertrand de Jouvenel (Geneva: Droz, 1963).

––– *Political Systems of Highland Burma: a Study of Kachin Social Structure* (Cambridge, Mass.: Harvard University Press, 1954).

PYE, Lucian W. *Politics, Personality and Nation-Building: Burma's Search for Identity* (New Haven: Yale University Press, 1962).

SILVERSTEIN, Josef. "Burma." In *Governments and Politics of Southeast Asia,* edited by George M. Kahin (Ithaca, N.Y.: Cornell University Press, 1959).

SMITH, Donald Eugene. *Religion and Politics in Burma* (Princeton: Princeton University Press, 1965).

SPIRO, Melford E. *Buddhism and Society: A Great Tradition and its Burmese Vicissitudes* (London: Allen and Unwin, 1971).

THET, Vyan. "Burma: The Political Integration of Linguistic and Religious Minorities." In *Nationalism and Progress in Free Asia,* edited by P. Thayer (Baltimore: Johns Hopkins Press, 1956).

TINKER, Hugh. *The Union of Burma: A Study of the First Years of Independence.* 2nd ed. (London: Oxford University Press, 1959).

TRAGER, Frank Newton. *Burma: From Kingdom to Republic* (New York: Praeger, 1966).

WOODMAN, Dorothy. *The Making of Burma* (London: Cresset Press, 1962).

6.642 Malaysia

FREEDMAN, Maurice. "The Growth of a Plural Society in Malaya." Pacific Affairs 33 (June 1960): 158-68.

GINSBURG, Norton and Chester F. ROBERTS, JR. *Malaya* (Seattle: University of Washington Press, 1958).

GULLICK, J. M. *Malaya* (New York: Praeger, 1963).

HANNA, Willard A. *Sequel to Colonialism: The 1957-1960 Foundations for Malaysia* (New York: American Universities Field Staff, 1965)

——— *The Formation of Malaysia: New Factor in World Politics* (New York: American Universities Field Staff, 1964).

MILLS, Lennox A. *Malaya: A Political and Economic Appraisal* Minneapolis: University of Minnesota Press, 1958).

MILNE, R. S. *Government and Politics in Malaysia* (Boston: Houghton Mifflin, 1967).

NESS, Gayl D. "Modernization and Indigenous Control of the Bureaucracy in Malaysia." Asian Survey 5 (September 1965): 467-73.

PURCELL, Victor William. *The Chinese in Modern Malaya* (Singapore: Donald Moore, 1956).

——— *Malaysia* (London: Pall Mall, 1965).

PYE, Lucian W. *Guerrilla Communism in Malaya, Its Social and Political Meaning* (Princeton: Princeton University Press, 1956).

ROFF, Thomas Henry. *Towards a Malayan Nation* (Singapore: Far Eastern Universities Press, 1961).

TILMAN, Robert O. *Bureaucratic Transition in Malaya* (Durham, N.C.: Duke University Press, 1964).

TREGONNING, K. G. *North Borneo* (London: H.M.S.O., 1960).

WANG, Gungwu, ed. *Malaysia: A Survey* (New York: Praeger, 1964).

6.643 Singapore

BOYCE, Peter. "Singapore as a Sovereign State." Australian Outlook 19 (December 1965): 259-71.

CHAN Heng-Chee *Singapore: The Politics of Survival 1965-1967* (Singapore: Oxford University Press, 1971).

6.644 Indonesia

ALISJAHBANA, S. Takdir. *Indonesia: Social and Cultural Revolution* (Kuala Lumpur: Oxford University Press, 1966).

BENDA, Harry J. "Decolonization in Indonesia: The Problem of Continuity and Change." American Historical Review 70, no. 4 (July 1965): 1058-73.

——— *The Pattern of Administrative Reforms in the Closing Years of Dutch Rule in Indonesia.* Reprint Series, no. 16 (New Haven, Conn.: Southeast Asia Studies, Yale University, 1965).

——— *The Crescent and the Rising Sun: Indonesian Islam Under the Japanese Occupation, 1942-1945* (The Hague and Bandung: Van Hoeve, 1958).

BONE, R. C., Jr. "Will Indonesia Disintegrate?" Foreign Policy Bulletin 36 (May 1, 1957): 125-27.

FEITH, Herbert, "Indonesia's Political Symbols and Their Wielders." World Politics 16 (October 1963): 79-97.

——— *The Decline of Constitutional Democracy in Indonesia* (Ithaca, N.Y.: Cornell University Press, 1962).

FURNIVALL, J. S. *Colonial Policy and Practice: A Comparative Study of Burma and Netherlands India* (London: Cambridge University Press, 1948).

——— *Netherlands India: A Study of Plural Economy* (Cambridge, Mass.: Cambridge University Press, 1939).

GEERTZ, Clifford. *The Religion of Java* (Glencoe, Ill.: Free Press, 1960).

KAHIN, George McT. *Nationalism and Revolution in Indonesia* (Ithaca, N.Y.: Cornell University Press, 1952).

KROEF, Justus van der. *The Communist Party of Indonesia* (Vancouver: University of British Columbia Press, 1965).

——— "The Arabs in Indonesia." Middle East Journal 7 (Summer 1953): 300-23.

——— "The Eurasian Minority in Indonesia." American Sociological Review 18 (October 1953: 484-93.

LEGGE, John David. *Central Authority and Regional Autonomy In Indonesia: A Study in Local Administration, 1950-1960* (Ithaca, N.Y.: Cornell University Press, 1961).

LIDDLE, R. William. *Ethnicity, Party and National Integration: An Indonesian Case Study* (New Haven, Conn.: Yale University Press, 1970).

McVEY, Ruth T., ed. *Indonesia* (New Haven, Conn.: Human Relations Area File, 1963).

MUSKENS, M.P.M. *Indonesië: Ein Strijd om Nationale Identiteit* (A Struggle for National Identity) (Bussum: Brand, 1970).

PEACOCK, James. *Rites of Modernization: Symbols and Social Aspects of Indonesian Proletarian Drama* (Chicago: University of Chicago Press, 1968).

SKINNER, G. W., ed. *Local, Ethnic, and National Loyalties in Village Indonesia.* Cultural Series 8. (New Haven, Conn.: Yale University, 1959).

VLEKKE, Bernard H. M. *Nusantara: A History of Indonesia.* Rev. ed. (Chicago: Quadrangle Books, 1960).

WERTHEIM, W. F. *Indonesian Society in Transition: A Study of Social Change.* 2nd rev. ed. (The Hague/Bandung: W. van Hoeve, 1959).

WILLMOTT, Donald E. *The National Status of the Chinese in Indonesia* (Ithaca, N.Y.: Cornell University Press, 1961).

6.645 Thailand

BENEDICT, Ruth. *Thai Culture and Behavior.* Mimeographed. (New York: 1943).

BLANCHARD, Wendell; Henry C. AHALT; et al. *Thailand: Its People, Its Society, Its Culture* (New Haven, Conn.: Taplinger Publishing, Human Relations Area Files, 1968).

COUGHLIN, Richard J. *Double Identity: The Chinese in Modern Thailand* (New York: Oxford University Press, 1961).

EVERS, Hans-Dieter. *Higher Thai Civil Servants, Social Mobility and Attitudes Towards Their Own Cultural Tradition* (Freiburg: Arnold Bergstraesser Institute, 1964).

——— ed. *Loosely Structured Social Systems: Thailand in Comparative Perspective* (New Haven, Conn.: Yale University Press, 1969).

RIGGS, Fred. *Thailand: the Modernization of a Bureaucratic Polity* (Honolulu: East-West Center Press, 1966).

SILCOCK, T. M., ed. *Thailand: Economic and Social Studies in Development* (Canberra: Australian National University Press, 1969).

SKINNER, George William. "Chinese Assimilation and Thai Politics." Journal of Asian Studies 16 (February 1957): 237-50.

——— *Chinese Society in Thailand: An Analytical Study* (Ithaca, N.Y.: Cornell University Press, 1957).

WILSON, David. *Politics in Thailand* (Ithaca, N.Y.: Cornell University Press, 1962).

6.646 Laos

CHAMPASSAK, Sisnouk Na. *Storm Over Laos, A Contemporary History* (New York: Praeger, 1961).
FALL, Bernard B. *Laos: Background of a Conflict* (Washington: Public Affairs Press, 1961).
HALPERN, Joel M. "The Role of Religion in Government and Politics in Laos." *Government, Politics and Social Structure in Laos.* Monograph no. 4 (New Haven: Yale South East Asian Studies, 1966).
LeBAR, Frank M., ed. *Laos: Its People, Its Society, Its Culture* (New York: Taplinger Publishing, Human Relations Area Files, 1960).

6.647 Cambodia

HERZ, Martin F. *A Short History of Cambodia* (New York: Praeger, 1958).
OLIVIER, G. and J. MOULLEC. *Anthropologie des Cambodgiens* (Paris: Ecole Française d'Extrême-Orient, 1968).
OSBORNE, Milton E. "History and Kingship in Contemporary Cambodia." Journal of Southeast Asian History 7 (March 1966): 1-14.
STEINBERG, David, ed. *Cambodia: Its People, Its Society, Its Culture* (New York: Tapliner Publishing, Human Relations Area Files, 1959).
THIERRY, Solange. *Les Khmers* (Paris: Seuil, 1964).

6.648 Vietnam

BUTTINGER, Joseph. *Vietnam: A Dragon Embattled.* 2 vols. (New York: Pall Mall Press, 1967).
CHESNEAUX, J. *Contribution à l'Histoire de la Nation Vietnamienne* (Paris: Editions Sociales, 1955).
DUNCANSON, Dennis J. "Vietnam as a Nation-State." Modern Asian Studies 3, no. 2 (1969).
FALL, Bernard B. *The Two Vietnams: A Political and Military Analysis* (New York: Praeger, 1964).
——— *Le Viet-Minh, La République Démorcratique du Viet-Nam, 1945-60* (Paris: Colin, 1960).
FITZGERALD, Frances. *Fire in the Lake: The Vietnamese and the Americans in Vietnam* (Boston: Little, Brown, 1972).
ISOART, Paul. *Le Phenomène National Vietnamien de l'Independance Unitaire à l'Independance Fractionée* (Paris: Cie. Générale de Droit et de Jurisprudence, 1961).
McALISTER, John T. and Paul MUS. *The Vietnamese and Their Revolution* (New York: Harper, 1970).
MUS, P. *Vietnam: Sociologie d'une Guerre* (Paris: Seuil, 1952). Important study of sources of identity.
PIKE, Douglas. *Viet Cong: The Organization and Techniques of the National Liberation Front* (Cambridge: MIT Press, 1966).
SCIGLIANO, Robert. *South Vietnam: Nation Under Stress* (Boston: Houghton Mifflin, 1963).
VAN CHI, Hoang. *From Colonialism to Communism: A Case History of North Vietnam* (New York: Praeger, 1964).

WOODSIDE, Alexander. *Vietnam and the Chinese Model* (Cambridge, Mass.: Harvard University Press, 1970).

6.649 Philippines

BERNSTEIN, David. *The Philippine Story* (New York: Farrar, Straus & Cudahy, 1947).

FRIEND, Theodore. *Between Two Empires: The Ordeal of the Philippines, 1929-1946* (New Haven, Conn.: Yale University Press, 1965).

GOLAY, Frank. *The Philippines: A Study in National Economic Development* (Ithaca, New York: Cornell University Press, 1961).

HUNT, Chester Leigh. "Moslem and Christian in the Philippines." Pacific Affairs 28 (December 1955).

MAHAJANI, U. *Philippine Nationalism, 1565-1946* (St. Ancia: University of Queensland Press, 1971).

QUIRINO, Eliseo, ed. *Nepa: Objectives of Protectionism in the Philippines. Essays on Political Economy* (Manila: Bookman, 1960).

SMITH, Robert Aura. *Philippine Freedom, 1946-1958* (New York: Columbia University Press, 1958).

6.65 The Chinese empire and its neighbours

FAIRBANK, John K.; Edwin O. REISCHAUER; and Albert M. CRAIG. *East Asia: The Modern Transformation* (Boston: Houghton Mifflin, 1965).

REISCHAUER, Edwin O. and John K. FAIRBANK. *East Asia: The Great Tradition* (Boston: Houghton Mifflin, 1958).

6.651 China

BALAZS, Etienne. *Chinese Civilization and Bureaucracy: Variations on a Theme* (New Haven: Yale University Press, 1964).

BARY, William Theodore de; Burton WATSON and Wing-tuit CHAN. *Sources of Chinese Tradition* (New York: Columbia University Press, 1960).

BECKMANN, George M. *The Modernization of China and Japan* (New York: Harper & Row, 1962).

BIANCO, Lucien. *The Origins of the Chinese Revolution, 1915-1949* (Stanford: Stanford University Press, 1971).

CALLIS, Helmut G. *China, Confucian and Communist* (New York: Holt, 1969).

CHOW, Tse-Tung. *The May Fourth Movement: Intellectual Revolution in Modern China* (Cambridge: Harvard University Press, 1960).

FRANCIS, J. de *Nationalism and Language Reform in China* (Princeton: Princeton University Press, 1950).

GRAY, Jack and Patrick CAVENDISH. *Chinese Communism in Crisis: Maoism and the Cultural Revolution* (New York: Praeger, 1968).

HO, Ping-ti and Tang TSOU. *China in Crisis: China's Heritage and the Communist Political System.* 3 vols. (Chicago: University of Chicago Press, 1968).

HOUN, Franklin W. *To Change a Nation: Propaganda and Indoctrination in Communist China* (New York: Free Press of Glencoe, 1961).

HU, Ch'ang-tu. *China: Its People, Its Society, Its Culture* (New Haven, Conn.: Human Relations Area Files, 1960).

KOTOV, Konstantin Flagontovich. *Autonomy of Local Nationalities in the Chinese People's Republic* (New York: Joint Publications Research Service, 1960).

LATOURETTE, K. S. *The Chinese, Their History and Culture* (New York: Macmillan, 1946).

LEVENSON, J. R. *Confucian China and Its Modern Fate* (Berkeley: University of California Press, 1958).

LINDBECK, John. *China: Management of a Revolutionary Society* (Seattle: Washington University Press, 1971).

MAO Tse-tung. *On the Correct Handling of Contradictions Among the People* (Peking: Foreign Language Press, 1957).

MILLS, H. C. "Language Reform in China." Far Eastern Quarterly 15 (1955-56).

NEEDHAM, Joseph. *Science and Civilization in China.* 4 vols. (Cambridge, Eng.: Cambridge University Press, 1954-71).

PYE, Lucian. *The Spirit of Chinese Politics. A Psycho-Cultural Study of the Authority Crisis in Political Development* (Cambridge, Mass.: MIT Press, 1968).

SCHRAM, Stuart R. *The Political Thought of Mao Tse-tung* (New York: Frederick A. Praeger, 1963).

SCHURMANN, Franz. *Ideology and Orgnaization in Communist China* (Berkeley: University of California Press, 1966).

TANG, Peter S. H. *Communist China as a Developmental Model for Underdeveloped Countries* (Washington: Research Institute of the Sino-Soviet Bloc, 1966).

TAWNEY, R. H. *Land and Labor in China* (London: Allen and Unwin, 1932).

WHITING, Allen S. "China." pp. 117-214 In *Modern Political Systems: Asia,* edited by Robert E. Ward and Roy C. Macridis (Englewood Cliffs, N.J.: Prentice-Hall, 1963).

——— "Nationality Reforms in Sinkiang." Far Eastern Survey 25, (January 1956): 8-13.

YANG, C. K. *Chinese Communist Society: The Family and the Village* (Cambridge, Mass.: MIT Press, 1959).

6.652 Korea

HENDERSON, Gregory. *Korea: The Politics of the Vortex* (Cambridge, Mass: Harvard University Press, 1968).

LEE, Chong-sik. *The Politics of Korean Nationalism* (Berkeley: University of California Press, 1963).

LEE, Hahn-been. *Korea: Time, Change, and Administration* (Honolulu: East-West Center Press, 1968).

OH, John Kie-Chiang. *Korea: Democracy on Trial* (Ithaca: Cornell University Press, 1968).

REEVE, W. D. *The Republic of Korea: A Political and Economic Study* (London: Oxford University Press, 1963).

RUDOLPH, Philip. *North Korea's Political and Economic Structure* (New York: Institute of Pacific Relations, 1959).

SCALAPINO, Robert, ed. *North Korea Today* (New York: Praeger, 1963).

WEEMS, Clarence Norwood. *Korea: Dilemma of an Underdeveloped Country* (New York: Foreign Policy Association, 1960).

6.653 Mongolia

BAWDEN, C. R. *The Modern History of Mongolia* (London: Weidenfeld and Nicolson, 1968).

LATTIMORE, Owen. *Nationalism and Revolution in Mongolia* (New York: Oxford University Press, 1955).

MONTAGU, Ivor. *Land of Blue Sky* (London: Dobson, 1956).

MURPHY, George G. S. *Soviet Mongolia: A Study of the Oldest Political Satellite* (Berkeley: University of California Press, 1966).

6.654 Tibet

CARRASCO, P. *Land and Polity in Tibet* (Seattle: University of Washington Press, 1959).

GINSBURGS, George and Michael MATHOS. *Communist China and Tibet: The First Dozen Years* (The Hague: Nijhoff, 1964).

MORAES, Frank R. *The Revolt in Tibet* (New York: Macmillan, 1960).

RICHARDSON, H. E. "Tibet Since 1950." India Quarterly 17 (April-June 1961): 128-39.

STEIN, Rolf Alfred. *La Civilisation Tibetaine* (Paris: Dunod, 1962).

THOMAS, Lowell, Jr. *The Silent War in Tibet* (Garden City, N.Y.: Doubleday, 1959).

6.655 Taiwan

GODDARD, W. G. *Formosa. A Study in Chinese History* (London: Macmillan, 1966).

MANCALL, Mark, ed. *Formosa Today* (New York: Praeger, 1963).

6.66 Japan

ANESAKI, Masaharu. *History of Japanese Religion* (London: Paul, Trench, Trubner, 1930).

BEARDSLEY, R. K.; J. W. HALL; and R. E. WARD. *Village Japan* (Chicago: University of Chicago Press, 1959).

BECKMANN, George M. *The Modernization of China and Japan* (New York: Harper & Row, 1962).

BELLAH, Robert N. "Continuity and Change in Japanese Society." In *Stability and Social Change* edited by Bernard Barber and Alex Inkeles, pp. 377-407 (Boston: Little, Brown, 1971).

——— *Tokugawa Religion: The Values of Preindustrial Japan* (Glencoe, N.Y.: Fress Press, 1957).

BENEDICT, Ruth. *The Chrysanthemum and the Sword: Patterns of Japanese Culture* (Boston: Houghton Mifflin, 1946).

BROWN, D. M. *Nationalism in Japan: An Introductory Historical Analysis* (Berkeley: University of California Press, 1955).

COLE, A. B. *Japanese Society and Politics* (Boston: Boston University Press, 1956).

CROWLEY, James B. *Japan's Quest for Autonomy: National Security and Foreign Policy, 1930-1938* (Princeton: Princeton University Press, 1966).

DORE, R. P. *Education in Tokugawa Japan* (Berkeley: University of California Press, 1965).
——— "Latin America and Japan Compared." In *Continuity and Change in Latin America,* edited by John J. Johnson, pp. 227-49 (Stanford: Stanford University Press, 1964).
EARL, David M. *Emperor and Nation in Japan—Political Themes of the Tokugawa Period* (Seattle: University of Washington Press, 1964).
HARTOONIAN, H. D. *Toward Restoration: The Growth of Political Consciousness in Tokugawa Japan* (Berkeley: University of California Press, 1970).
IKE, Nobutaka. *The Beginnings of Political Democracy in Japan* (Baltimore: Johns Hopkins Press, 1950).
INOUE, Mitsusada. *Nihon Kikka no Kigen* (The Origin of the Japanese State) (Tokyo: Iwanami Shoten, 1960).
LOCKWOOD, William W. "Japan's Response to the West: The Contrast with China." World Politics 9 (1956).
McLAREN, W. W. *A Political History of Japan During the Meiji Era, 1867-1912* (London: Scribners, 1916).
MARUYAMA, Masao. *Thought and Behavior in Japanese Politics.* Expanded ed. (London: Oxford University Press, 1969).
MENDEL, Douglas H., Jr. "Japan as a Model for Developing Nations." Paper prepared for the Annual Meeting, American Political Science Association, September 8, 1965.
MITCHELL, Richard Hanks. *The Korean Minority in Japan, 1910-1963* (Berkeley: University of California Press, 1966).
NORMAN, Herbert E. *Japan's Emergence as a Modern State: Political and Economic Problems of the Meiji Period* (New York: Institute of Pacific Relations, 1940).
PYLE, Kenneth B. *The New Generation in Meiji Japan: the Problem of Cultural Identity 1885-1895* (Stanford: Stanford University Press, 1969).
SCALAPINO, Robert A. *Parties and Politics in Contemporary Japan* (Berkeley: University of California Press, 1962).
"A Symposium on Japanese Nationalism." Journal of Asian Studies 30, no. 1 (November 1971): 5-63.
VOS, George de and Hiroshi WAGATSUMA. *Japan's Invisible Race* (Berkeley: University of California Press, 1966).
WARD, Robert E. "Japan: The Continuity of Modernization." In *Political Culture and Political Development,* edited by L. W. Pye and S. Verba, pp. 27-82 (Princeton: Princeton University Press, 1965).
——— "Japan." In *Modern Political Systems: Asia,* edited by Robert E. Ward and Roy C. Macridis, pp. 17-114 (Englewood Cliffs, N.J.: Prentice-Hall, 1963).
——— ed. *Political Development in Modern Japan* (Princeton: Princeton University Press, 1968).
——— and Dankwart A. Rustow, eds. *Political Modernization in Japan and Turkey* (Princeton: Princeton University Press, 1964).
YANAGA, Chitoshi. *Japanese People and Politics* (New York: John Wiley, 1956).

6.67 Oceanian polities

DAVIDSON, J. W. *Damoa mo Samoa: the Emergence of the Independent State of Western Samoa* (Melbourne: Oxford University Press, 1967).

FISK, E. K., ed. *New Guinea on the Threshold: Aspects of Social, Political, and Economic Development* (Pittsburgh: University of Pittsburgh Press, 1968).

FORCE, Roland W. *Leadership and Culture Change in Palau* (Chicago: Chicago Natural History Museum, 1960).

GATTY, Roland. "Fiji Colony in Transition." Pacific Affairs 26 (June 1953): 118-30.

HANCOCK, William K. *Politics in Pitcairn and Other Essays* (London: Macmillan, 1947).

KEESING, Felix M. and Marie M. KEESING. *Elite Communication in Samoa: A Study of Leadership* (Stanford: Stanford University Press, 1956).

KOUWENHOVEN, Willem Jan Hendrik. *Nimboran: A Study of Social Change and Social Economic Development in a New Guinea Society* (The Hague: Voorhoeve, 1956).

KROEF, Justus Maria van der. "Nationalism and Politics in West New Guinea." Pacific Affairs 34 (Spring 1961): 38-53.

LIJPHART, Arend. *The Trauma of Decolonization: The Dutch and West New Guinea* (New Haven, Conn.: Yale University Press, 1966).

MAKER, Robert Francis. *New Men of Papua: A Study in Cultural Change* (Madison: University of Wisconsin Press, 1960).

MAYER, Adrian. *Indians in Fiji* (New York: Oxford University Press, 1963).

ROBSON, Nancy. "French Oceania Takes Stock." Pacific Affairs 26 (March 1953): 24-43.

SUGGS, Robert Carl. *The Island Civilizations of Polynesia* (New York: New American Library, 1960).

WEST, Francis James. *Political Advancement in the South Pacific: A Comparative Study of Colonial Practice in Fiji, And American Samoa* (Melbourne: Oxford University Press, 1961).

6.7 The English-speaking settler nations
6.71 The United States

ADAMIC, Louis. *A Nation of Nations* (New York: Harper, 1945).

BERTHOFF, Robert. *An Unsettled People: Social Order and Disorder in American History* (New York: Harper, 1971).

BESTOR, Arthur. "The American Civil War as a Constitutional Crisis." American Historical Review 69 (January 1964).

BROWN, Robert E. *Middle-Class Democracy and the Revolution in Massachusetts, 1691-1780* (Princeton: Princeton University Press, 1960).

BRYCE, James. *The American Commonwealth* (London and New York: Macmillan, 1888).

BURNHAM, Walter Dean. "The Changing Shape of the American Political Universe." American Political Science Review 59 (1965): 7-28.

CHARLES, Joseph. *The Origins of the American Party System* (New York: Harper Torchbooks, 1956).

DAHL, Robert A. *Pluralist Democracy in the United States: Conflict and Consent* (Chicago: Rand McNally, 1967). New ed., *Democracy in the United States,* 1972.

DINNERSTEIN, Leonard and Frederic Cople JAHER, eds. *The Aliens: A History of Ethnic Minorities in America* (New York: Appleton-Century-Crofts, 1970).

DODD, William Edward. *The Cotton Kingdom: A Chronicle of the Old South* (New Haven, Conn.: Yale University Press, 1919).

DRAPER, Theodore. *The Rediscovery of Black Nationalism* (New York: Viking, 1970).

GLAZER, Nathan and Daniel Patrick MOYNIHAN. *Beyond the Melting Pot: The Negroes, Puerto Ricans, Jews, Italians, and Irish* (Cambridge, Mass.: MIT Press and Harvard University Press, 1963).

GORDON, Milton Myron. *Assimilation in American Life: The Role of Race, Religion and National Origins* (New York: Oxford University Press, 1964).

GREEN, Constanse Winsor. *American Cities in the Growth of the Nation* (New York: J. de Groff, 1957).

HARTMANN, Edward George. *The Movement to Americanize the Immigrant* (New York: Columbia University Press, 1948).

HAUGEN, Einar. *The Norwegian Language in America: A Study in Bilingual Behavior.* 2 vols. (Philadelphia: University of Pennsylvania Press, 1953).

KARIEL, Henry S. *The Decline of American Liberalism* (Stanford: Stanford University Press, 1961).

KEY, V. O., Jr. *Southern Politics in State and Nation* (New York: Alfred Knopf, 1949).

LIPSET, S.M. *The First New Nation: The United States in Historical and Comparative Perspective* (New York: Basic Books, 1963).

MERRITT, R. L. *Symbols of American Community, 1735-1775* (New Haven, Conn.: Yale University Press, 1966).

MITCHELL, William C. *The American Polity* (New York: Free Press, 1962).

MORPUGO, J. E. and Russell B. NYE, eds. *A History of the United States.* 2 vols. (Harmondsworth: Penguin, 1956).

TOCQUEVILLE, Alexis de. *La Démocratie en Amérique* (Paris: Gosselin, 1835). Numerous editions. English translation by H. Reeve. *Democracy in America.* 4 vols. (London: Saunders and Otley, 1835-40).

WILLIAMS, Robin Murphy. *American Society. A Sociological Interpretation.* 2nd rev. ed. (New York: Knopf, 1960).

6.72 Canada

BERGER, C., ed. *Imperialism and Nationalism, 1884-1914* (Toronto: 1969).

Le Bilinguisme en Suisse, en Belgique et an Canada (Brussels: Foundation Charles Plisnier, 1963).

BRADY, Alexander. *Democracy in the Dominions.* 2nd ed. (Toronto: University of Toronto Press, 1952).

BREBNER, J. B. *North Atlantic Triangle: The Interplay of Canade, The United States and Great Britain* (New Haven, Conn.: 1945).

BRUNET, Michel. *La Présence Anglaise et les Canadiens, Etudes sur l'Histoire et la Pensée des Deux Canadas* (Montreal: Beauchemin, 1958).

CLARK, Samuel D. "The Religious Factor in Canadian Economic Development." Journal of Economic History, Supplement 7 (1947): 89-103.

COATS, R. H. and M. C. MacLEAN. *The American-Born in Canada: A Statistical Interpretation* (Toronto and New Haven: 1943).

CREIGHTON, D. G. *British North America at Confederation* (Ottawa: Queen's Printer, 1963).

——— *Commercial Empire of the St. Lawrence, 1760-1850* (New Haven, Conn.: Yale University Press, 1937).

DAWSON, Robert MacGregor, ed. *The Development of Dominion Status, 1900-1936* (London, New York, and Toronto: Oxford University Press, 1937).

FARR, David M. L. *The Colonial Office and Canada, 1967-1887* (Toronto: University of Toronto Press, 1955).

FREGAULT, Guy. *Canadian Society in the French Regime.* Brochures Historiques, no. 3 (Ottawa: Société Historique du Canada, 1954).

GARNER, J. *The Franchise And Politics in British North America, 1755-1867* (Toronto: 1969).

HANSEN, Marcus L. *The Mingling of the Canadian and American Peoples* (New Haven, Conn.: Yale University Press, 1940).

HOROWITZ, G. "Conservatism, Liberalism and Socialism in Canada: An Interpretation." Canadian Journal of Economics and Political Science 32 (1966): 143-171.

HUGHES, E. C. *French Canada in Transition* (Chicago: University of Chicago Press, 1943).

LOWER, Arthur Reginald Marsden. *Canadians in the Making: A Social History of Canada* (Toronto: Longmans, Green, 1958).

MacKIRDY, K. A. "Problems of Adjustment in Nation-Building: The Maritime Provinces and Tasmania." Canadian Journal of Economics and Political Science 20 (February 1954): 27-43.

MARTIN, Chester B. *Empire and Commonwealth. Studies in Governance and Self-Government in Canada* (Oxford: Clarendon, 1929).

MATTHEWS, Roy A. "Canada, the International Nation." Queen's Quarterly 72 (Autumn 1965): 499-523.

MELESE, Pierre. *Canada: Deux Peuples, Une Nation* (Paris: Hachette, 1959).

MORTON, W. L. *The Canadian Identity* (Madison: University of Wisconsin Press, 1962).

PORTER, J. *The Vertical Mosaic* (Toronto: University of Toronto Press, 1965). A study of the ethnic composition of Canadian elites.

QUINN, Herbert Furlong. *The Union Nationale: A Study in Quebec Nationalism* (Toronto: University of Toronto Press, 1963).

RIDDELL, Walter Alexander. "The Rise of Ecclesiastical Control in Quebec." Ph.D. dissertation, Columbia University, 1916.

ROYAL COMMISSION ON BILINGUALISM AND BICULTURALISM. *Preliminary Report,* Ottawa 1965. *Report,* Ottawa 1967-70. 4 vols.

SCHWARTZ, Mildred A. *Public Opinion and Canadian Identity* (Berkeley: University of California Press, 1967).

SMILEY, Donald V. *The Canadian Political Nationality* (Toronto and London: Methuen, 1967).

SMITH, Goldwin. *Canada and the Canadian Question* (London, New York, and Toronto: Macmillan, 1891).

SOCIAL RESEARCH GROUP. *"A Study of Interethnic Relations in Canada."* 6 vols. Mimeographed. (Montreal, 1965).

STACEY, Charles P. *Canada and the British Army, 1846-1871.* Rev. ed. (Toronto: University of Toronto Press, 1963).

Statement of the Government of Canada on Indian Policy, 1969. Ottawa, 1969.

UNDERHILL, Frank H. *The Image of Confederation* (Toronto: Canadian Broadcasting Corp., 1964).

URQUHART, M. C., ed. *Historical Statistics of Canada* (Toronto: Macmillan, 1965).

WADE, Mason. *The French Canadians, 1760-1945* (Toronto: Macmillan, 1955; rev. and enlarged ed., 1968).

––– ed. *Canadian Dualism: La Dualité Canadienne: Studies of French-English Relations* (Toronto and Quebec: University of Toronto Press, 1960).

WHITELAW, William Menzies. *The Maritimes and Canada Before Confederation* (Toronto: Oxford University Press, 1934; rev., 1966).

WRONG, George McKinnon. *Canada and the American Revolution: The Disruption of the First British Empire* (New York: Macmillan, 1935).

See also Section 4.2, McRAE.

6.73 Australia

BLACKTON, C. S. "Australian Nationality and Nationalism: The Imperial Federationist Interlude, 1885-1901." *Historical Studies, Australia and New Zealand* 7, no. 25 (November 1955).

DAVIES, Alan Fraser. *Australian Democracy, An Introduction to the Political System* (London: Longmans, Green, 1958).

––– and S. ENCEL, eds. *Australian Society: A Sociological Introduction.* 2nd ed. (Melbourne: F. W. Cheshire, 1970).

HANCOCK, William Keith. *Australia* (London: E. Benn, 1945).

MAYER, H., ed. *Australian Politics.* 2nd ed. rev. and enlarged (Melbourne: F. W. Cheshire, 1967).

NADEL, George Hans. *Australia's Colonial Culture: Ideas, Men And Institutions in Mid-Nineteenth Century Eastern Australia* (Melbourne: F. W. Cheshire, 1957).

PHILLIPS, Arthur Angell. *The Australian Tradition: Studies in a Colonial Culture* (Melbourne: F. W. Cheshire, 1958).

ROSECRANCE, R. N. "The Radical Tradition in Australia: An Interpretation." The Review of Politics 22, no. 1 (1960): 115-132.

TRUMAN, Tom C. "Catholics and Politics in Australia." Western Political Quarterly 12 (June 1959): 527-34.

WARD, Russel Braddock. *The Australian Legend* (Melbourne: Oxford University Press, 1958).

6.74 New Zealand

CONDLIFFE, John Bell. *New Zealand in the Making. A Survey of Economic and Social Development* (London: Allen and Unwin, 1930).

FORSTER, John, ed. *Social Processes in New Zealand* (Auckland: Paul Longman, 1969).

HAWTHORN, H. B. *The Maori: A Study in Acculturation* (Menasha: American Anthropological Association Memoir 64, 1944).

LIPSON, Leslie. *The Politics of Equality: New Zealand's Adventures in Democracy* (Chicago: University of Chicago Press, 1948).

METGE, Joan. *A New Maori Migration* (London: Athlone Press, 1964).

POCOCK, J.G.A., ed. *The Maori and New Zealand Politics* (Auckland: Blackwood and Janet Paul, 1965).

SCHWIMMER, Eric. *The World of the Maori* (Wellington, Auckland and Sydney: Reed, 1966).

SINCLAIR, Keith. *A History of New Zealand* (Harmondsworth: Penguin, 1959).

WILLIAMS, J. A. *Politics of the New Zealand Maori: Protest and Cooperation, 1891-1909* (Seattle: University of Washington Press, 1969).

6.8 The Central and South American empires and their successor states

AGUILAR, A. *Pan-Americanism From Monroe to the Present: A View from the Other Side.* Rev. ed. (New York: Monthly Review Press, 1968).

ALBA, Victor. *The Latin Americans* (New York: Praeger, 1969).

——— *Nationalists Without Nations: The Oligarchy Versus the People in Latin America* (New York: Praeger, 1968).

ALEXANDER, Robert J. *Organized Labor in Latin America* (New York: Free Press, 1965).

ALONSO, Isidoro. *La Iglesia en America Latina: Estructuras Eclesiásticas* (The Church in Latin America: Ecclesiastical Structure) (Fribourg, Switzerland: Oficina Internacional de Investigaciones Sociales de FERES, 1964).

ANDERSON, Charles. *Politics and Economic Change in Latin America: The Governing of Restless Nations* (Princeton: Van Nostrand, 1967).

ANDRESKI, Stanislaw. *Parasitism and Subversion: The Case of Latin America* (New York: Pantheon Books, 1966).

BAGU, Sergio. *Estructura Social de la Colonia: Ensayo de Historia Comparada de América Latina* (The Social Structure of the Colony: Essay on the Comparative History of Latin America) (Buenos Aires: Ateneo, 1952).

BEYER, Glenn H., ed. *The Urban Explosion in Latin America: A Continent in Process of Modernization* (Ithaca, N.Y.: Cornell University Press, 1967).

BONILLA, Frank. *The Politics of Change in Latin America.* 2 vols. (Cambridge, Mass.: MIT Press, forthcoming).

BOURRICAUD, François. *Le Problème des Capitales en Amerique Latine* (Paris: Editions du C.N.R.S., 1965).

CABEZAS de G., Betty. *América Latina: Una y Múltiple* (Latin America: One And Many) (Santiago de Chile: Desal, 1968: Barcelona: Editorial Herder, 1968).

CAMPOS, Roberto de Oliveira. *Reflections on Latin American Development* (Austin: University of Texas Press, 1967).

CARDOSO, Fernando Henrique. *Mudanças Sociais na América Latina.* (Social Change in Latin America) (São Paulo: Diffusão Européia do Livro, 1969).

——— and Enso FALETTO. *Dependencia y Desarollo en América Latina* (Dependency and Development in Latin America) (Mexico: Siglo XXI, 1969).

CARDOSO, F. H. and F. WEFFORT, eds., *America Latina: Ensayos de Interpretación Sociologica-Politica* (Santiago: Editorial Universitaria, 1970).

COCKCROFT, James D., André Gunder FRANK; and Dale L. JOHNSON. *Dependence and Underdevelopment—Latin America's Political Economy* (New York: Anchor Books, 1972).

CORNBLIT, O. "Politics in New Nations: A Model of Social Change for Latin America." Paper presented to the World Congress of Sociology 6, Evian, September 4-11, 1966.

D'ANTONIO, William V. and Frederick B. PIKE, eds. *Religion, Revolution and Reform: New Forces for Change in Latin America* (New York: Praeger, 1964).

DONGHI, Tulio Halperin. *Historia Contemporanea de América Latina* (Contemporary History of Latin America) (Madrid: Alianza Editorial, 1969).

DUNCAN, W. Raymond and James Nelson GOODSELL, eds. *The Quest for Change in Latin America: Sources for a Twentieth-Century Analysis* (New York: Oxford University Press, 1070).

FITZGIBBON, Russell and Kenneth JOHNSON. "Measurement of Latin American Political Change." In *The Dynamics of Change in Latin American Politics,* edited by John Martz (Enlgewood Cliffs, N.J.: Prentice-Hall, 1965).

FRANK, André G. *Capitalism and Underdevelopment in Latin America. Historical Studies of Chile and Brazil* (New York: Monthly Review Press, 1967).

GERASSI, John. *The Great Fear: The Reconquest of Latin America by Latin Americans* (New York: Macmillan, 1963).

GERMANI, Gino. *Sociologica de la Modernizacion. Estudios Teoricos, Methodologicos y Aplicados en America Latina* (Buenos Aires: Paidos, 1969).

——— and K. H. SILVERT. "Politics. Social Structure and Military Intervention in Latin America." Archives Européennes de Sociologie 2 (1961): 62-81.

GOLDENBERG, Boris. *The Cuban Revolution and Latin America* (New York: Praeger, 1965).

HAAS, Ernst B. and Phillipe C. SCHMITTER. *The Politics of Economics in Latin American Regionalism* (Denver: University of Denver Press, 1965).

HAMILL, Hugh M., Jr., ed. *Dictatorship in Latin America* (New York: Knopf, 1965).

HANKE, Lewis. *Modern Latin America, Continent in Ferment.* 2 vols. (Princeton: Van Nostrand, 1959).

——— ed. *History of Latin American Civilization: Sources and Interpretations* (Boston: Little, Brown, 1967).

HEATH, Dwight B. and Richard N. ADAMS, eds. *Contemporary Cultures and Societies of Latin America* (New York: Random House, 1965).

HERNANDEZ ARREGUI, J. J. *Quie es el Ser Nacional? La Conciencia Historico Latinoamericano* (Buenos Aires: Hachea, 1962).

HIRSCHMAN, Albert O. *Journeys Toward Progress: Studies of Economic Policy-Making in Latin America* (New York: Twentieth Century Fund, 1963).

HOROWITZ, Irving Louis, ed. *Masses in Latin America* (New York: Oxford University Press, 1970).

——— ; Josue de CASTRO; and John GERASSI, eds. *Latin American Radicalism: A Documentary Report on Left and Nationalist Movements* (New York: Random House, 1969).

HOUTART, François and Emile PIN. *The Church and the Latin American Revolution* (New York: Sheed and Ward, 1965).

HUMPHREYS, R. A. *Tradition and Revolt in Latin America and Other Essays* (London: Weidenfeld and Nicholson, 1969).

——— *The Evolution of Modern Latin America* (London: Oxford University Press, 1946).

——— and John LYNCH, eds. *The Origins of the Latin American Revolutions, 1808-1826* (New York: Knopf, 1965).

IRELAND, Gordon. *Boundaries, Possessions and Conflicts in Central and North America and the Caribbean* (Cambridge, Mass.: Harvard University Press, 1941).

JAGUARIBE, Helio. *La Dependencia Politico-Economica de la America Latina.* (Mexico D.F.: Siglo XXI, 1969).

JOHNSON, John J. *Political Change in Latin America: The Emergence of the Middle Sectors* (Stanford: Stanford University Press, 1958; new ed., 1965).

——— *The Military and Society in Latin America* (Stanford: Stanford University Press, 1964).

——— ed. *Continuity and Change in Latin America* (Stanford: Stanford University Press, 1964).

KAPLAN, Marcos. *Formación del Estado Nacional en América Latina* (The Formation of the National State in Latin America) (Santiago: Editorial Universitaria, 1969).

LAMBERT, Jacques. *Amérique Latine* (Paris: Presses Universitaires de France, 1963). English translation, *Latin America: Social Structure and Political Institutions* (Berkeley: University of California Press, 1967).

LANDSBERG, Henry A. *Latin American Peasant Movements* (Ithaca, N.Y.: Cornell University Press, 1969).

——— ed. *The Church and Social Change in Latin America* (Notre Dame: University of Notre Dame Press, 1970).

LIEUWEN, Edwin. *Arms and Politics in Latin America* (New York: Praeger, 1960).

LIPSET, S. M. and Aldo SOLARI, eds. *Elites in Latin America* (New York: Oxford University Press, 1967).

MANDER, John. *The Unrevolutionary Society. The Power of Latin American Conservatism in a Changing World* (New York: Knopf, 1969).

MANNONI, O. *Prospero and Caliban: A Study of the Psychology of Colonization* (New York: Praeger, 1964).

MARTINS, Luciano. *Industrializacão, Burguesia Nacional e Desenvolvimento* (Industrialization, the National Bourgeoisie and Development) (Rio: Saga, 1968).

MECHAM, J. Lloyd. *Church and State in Latin America: A History of Politico-Ecclesiastical Relations* (Chapel Hill: University of North Carolina Press, 1966). Originally published in 1934.

MERCIER VEGA, Luis. *Guerillas in Latin America: The Technique of the Counter State* (New York: Praeger, 1969).

——— *Mécanismes du Pouvoir en Amerique Latine* (Paris: Ed. Universitaires, 1967). English translation, *Roads to Power in Latin America* (New York: Praeger, 1968).

MOERNER, Magnus. *Race Mixture in the History of Latin America* (Boston: Little, Brown, 1967).

MOOG, V. *Bandeirantes and Pioneers* (New York: Braziller, 1964; originally published in Portuguese, Rio: Ed. Globo, 1961).

MORSE, Richard. "Primacia, Regionalizacion, Dependencia: Enfoques Sobre las Ciudades Latinoamericanos en el Desarrollo Nacional." Desarrollo Economico 11, no. 41 (1971): 55-85.

——— "Recent Research on Latin American Urbanization: A Selective Survey with Commentary." Latin American Research Review 1, no. 1 (1965): 35-74.

——— "The Heritage of Latin America." In *The Founding of New Societies,* edited by Louis Hartz et al., pp. 123-77 (New York: Harcourt, 1964).

NEEDLER, Martin C. *Political Development in Latin America: Instability, Violence and Evolutionary Change* (New York: Random House, 1968).

NUN, Jose. *Latin America: The Hegemonic Crisis and the Military Coup* (Berkeley: Institute of International Studies, University of California, 1969).

PENDLE, George. *A History of Latin America* (Baltimore: Penguin, 1963).

PETRAS, James and Maurice ZEITLIN. *Latin America Reform or Revolution? A Reader* (New York: Gettleman, Fawcett, 1968).

PIKE, Fredrick B. *The Conflict Between Church and State in Latin America* (New York: Knopf, 1964).

PUTNAM, Robert D. "Toward Explaining Military Intervention in Latin American Politics." World Politics 10 (October 1967): 101-02, 106.

REDFIELD, Robert and Sol TAX. *Heritage of Conquest* (Glencoe, Ill.: Free Press, 1952).

RUIZ, Ramon Eduardo, ed. *Interpreting Latin American History from Independence to Today* (New York: Holt, Rinehart and Winston, 1970).

SOARES, Glaucio Dillon. "Desenvolvimento Economico e Radicalismo Politico" (Economic Development and Political Radicalism) *America Latina* 5 (1962): 65-83.

SODRE, Nelson Werneck. *A Ideologia do Colonialismo* (The Ideology of Colonialism) (Rio: ISEB, 1961).

SOLBERG, Carl. *Immigration and Nationalism: Argentina and Chile, 1890-1914.* (Austin: University of Texas Press, 1970).

STAVENHAEREN, Rodolfo, ed. *Agrarian Problems and Peasant Movements in Latin America* (New York: Anchor Books, 1970).

STEPAN, Alfred. "Political Development Theory: the Latin American Experience." *Journal of International Affairs* 20 (1966).

SZULC, Tad. *The Winds of Revolution: Latin America Today and Tomorrow* (New York: Praeger, 1963).

TANNENBAUM, Frank. *Ten Keys to Latin America* (New York: Knopf, 1962).

VEKEMANS, Roger E. and J. L. SEGUNDO. "Essay on the Socio-economic Typology of the Latin American Countries." In *Social Aspects of Economic Development in Latin America,* edited by Egbert de Vries and José Medina Echavarria, pp. 67-93 (Paris: UNESCO, 1963).

VELIZ, Claudio. "Centralism amd Nationalism in Latin America." *Foreign Affairs* 47, no. 1 (October 1968): 68-83.

――― ed. *The Politics of Conformity in Latin America* (London: Oxford University Press, 1967).

――― *Obstacles to Change in Latin America* (New York: Oxford University Press, 1965).

VRIES, Egbert de and José Medina ECHEVARRIA, eds. *Social Aspects of Economic Development in Latin America* (Paris: UNESCO, 1963).

WAGLEY, Charles and Marvin HARRIS. "A Typology of Latin American Subcultures." *American Anthropologist,* New Series 57 (1955): 428-51.

WEHNER, F. "Der Konflikt Zwischen Spanischer und Liberaler Staatsauffassung in Hispano-America." (The Conflict Between the Iberian and the Liberal Conception of the State in Hispano-America) *Verfassung und Recht in Ubersee* 2, no. 1 *(1969): 41-54.*

WHITAKER, Arthur P. and D. C. JORDAN. *Nationalism in Contemporary Latin America* (New York: Free Press, 1966).

ZEA, Leopoldo. *America en la Historia* (America in History) (Mexico: 1957).

6.81 The West Indies, the Caribbean and Guyana

BELL, Wendell, ed. *The Democratic Revolution in the West Indies: Studies in Nationalism, Leadership and the Belief in Progress* (Cambridge, Mass.: Schenkman, 1967).

BELL, Wendell and Ivar OXAAL. *Decisions of Nationhood: Political and Social Development in the British Caribbean* (Denver: University of Denver, 1965).

JONES, Chester Lloyd. *Costa Rica and Civilization in the Caribbean* (Madison: 1935).

LEIRIS, Michel. *Contacts de Civilisations en Martinique et en Guadeloupe* (Paris: UNESCO, Gallimard, 1955).

LIER, R.A.J. van. *The Development and Nature of Society in the West Indies* (Amsterdam: Royal Institute for the Indies, 1950).

LOWENTHAL, David. *The West Indian Federation: Perspectives on a New Nation* (New York: Columbia University Press, 1961).

MITCHELL, Harold P. *Contemporary Politics and Economics in the Caribbean* (Athens: Ohio University Press, 1968).

––– *The Policies of Great Britain, France and the Netherlands Towards Their West Indian Territories* (Edinburgh: Constable, 1963).

NEWTON, Arthur P. *The European Nations in the West Indies: 1493-1688* (London: Black, 1933).

PROCTOR, Jesse Harris, Jr. *Constitutional Defects and the Collapse of the West Indian Federation* (Durham: Duke University Commonwealth Studies Center, 1964).

RUBIN, Vera. "Approaches to the Study of National Characteristics in a Multicultural Society." International Journal of Social Psychiatry 5 (1959): 20-26.

–––,ed. "Social and Cultural Pluralism in the Caribbean." Annals of the New York Academy of Sciences 83 (January 1960).

––– *Caribbean Studies: A Symposium* (Mona, Jamaica: Institute of Social and Economic Research, University College of the West Indies, 1957).

SMITH, M. G. *The Plural Society in the British West Indies* (Berkeley: University of California Press, 1965).

TAYLOR, Douglas. "New Languages for Old in the West Indies." Comparative Studies in Society and History 3 (1961): 277-288.

WILGUS, A. Curtis, ed. *The Caribbean: Its Political Problems* (Gainesville, Fla.: University of Florida Press, 1956).

WILLIAMS, Eric. *Capitalism and Slavery* (Chapel Hill: University of North Carolina Press, 1944).

6.811 British Honduras

WADDELL, David A. G. *British Honduras: A Historical and Contemporary Survey* (London: 1961).

6.812 Cuba

DEWART, Leslie. *Christianity and Revolution: The Lesson of Cuba* (New York: 1963).

DRAPER, Theodore. *Castroism: Theory and Practice* (New York: Praeger, 1965).

––– *Revolution: Myths and Realities* (New York: Praeger, 1962).

FAGEN, Richard R. *The Transformation of Political Culture in Cuba* (Stanford: Stanford University Press, 1969).

GUERRA Y SANCHEZ, Ramiro. *Sugar and Society in the Antilles: An Economic History of Cuban Agriculture* (New Haven, Conn.: Yale University Press, 1964).

HENNESY, C. A. M. "The Roots of Cuban Nationalism." International Affairs 39 (July 1963): 346-58.

IGLESIAS, Jose. *In the Fist of the Revolution: Life in a Cuban Town* (New York: 1968).

JENKS, Leland H. *Our Cuban Colony* (New York: 1928).
MacGAFFEY, Wyatt and Clifford R. BARNETT. *Twentieth-Century Cuba* (New York: 1965).
NELSON, Lowry. *Rural Cuba* (Minneapolis: University of Minnesota Press, 1950).
ORTIZ, Fernando. *Cuban Counterpoint: Tobacco and Sugar* (New York: 1947). Spanish version originally published in 1940.
SEARS, Dudley, ed. *Cuba, the Economic and Social Revolution* (Chapel Hill: 1964).
SMITH, Robert Freeman, ed. *Background to Revolution. The Development of Modern Cuba* (New York: Knopf, 1966).
SWEEZY, Paul and Les HUBERMAN. *Cuba: Anatomy of a Revolution* (New York: Monthly Review Press, 1961).

6.813 Dominican Republic

LOGAN, R. W. *Haiti and the Dominican Republic* (New York: Oxford University Press, 1968).
WIARDA, H. J. *The Dominican Republic: Nation in Transition* (New York: Praeger, 1969).
––– *Dictatorship and Development: The Methods of Control in Trujillo's Dominican Republic* (Gainesville: University of Florida Press, 1968).

6.814 Guyana

COLLINS, B.A.N. "Acceding to Independence: Some Constitutional Problems of a Poly-ethnic Society (British Guiana)." Civilisations 15 (1965): 376-403.
DESPRES, Leo A. *Cultural Pluralism and Nationalist Politics in British Guiana* (Chicago: Rand McNally, 1967).
––– "The Implications of Nationalist Policies in British Guiana for the Development of Cultural Theory." American Anthropologist 66 (October 1964): 1051-77.
"Guyana Independence Issue." New World, Demerara, Guiana, May 1966.
JAYAWARDENA, Chandra. "Religious Belief and Social Change: Aspects of the Development of Hinduism in British Guiana." Comparative Studies in Society and History 8 (1966): 211-40.
LANDIS, J. B. "Race and Politics in Guyana." Ph.D. dissertation, Yale University, 1971.
NEWMAN, Peter. *British Guiana: Problems of Cohesion in an Immigrant Society.* (New York: Oxford University Press, 1964).
New World Associates "Working Notes Towards the Unification of Guyana." (Georgetown, British Guiana) 1 (March 1963): 1-81.
SMITH, Raymond T. *British Guiana* (London: Oxford University Press, 1962).
––– *The Negro Family in British Guiana* (London, 1956).

6.815 Haiti

BASTIEN, R. "Haiti: Clases y Prejuicio de Color" (Haiti: Classes and Color Prejudice). Aportes 9 (1968): 4-25.
BELLEGARDE, Dantès. *La Nation Haitienne* (Paris: 1938).
DIEDERICH, Bernard. *Papa Doc: The Truth About Haiti Today* (New York: McGraw-Hill, 1969).
FLEISCHMAN, V. *Aspekte der Sozialen und Politischen Entwicklung Haitis* (Stuttgart: Klett, 1971).

LOGAN, R. W. *Haiti and the Dominican Republic* (New York: Oxford University Press, 1968).

6.816 Jamaica

BELL, Wendell. *Jamaican Leaders: Political Attitudes in a New Nation* (Berkeley: University of California Press, 1964).
EISNER, Gisela. *Jamaica, 1830-1930: A Study in Economic Growth* (Manchester: Manchester University Press, 1961).
NETTLEFORD, Rex. "National Identity and Attitudes to Race in Jamaica." Race 7, no. 1 (1965): 59-72.
NORRIS, Katrin. *Jamaica: The Search for an Identity* (London: Oxford University Press, 1962).

6.817 Puerto Rico

LEWIS, Gordon K. *Puerto Rico: Freedom and Power in the Caribbean* (New York: Monthly Review Press, 1963).
STEWARD, Julian H. *The People of Puerto Rico* (Urbana: University of Illinois Press, 1956).
TUGWELL, R. G. *The Stricken Land: The Story of Puerto Rico* (New York: Greenwood Press, 1968).
TUMIN, M. M. and A. S. FELDMAN. *Social Class and Social Change in Puerto Rico* (Princeton: Princeton University Press, 1961).
WELLS, H. *The Modernization of Puerto Rico: A Political Study of Changing Values and Institutions* (Cambridge, Mass.: Harvard University Press, 1969).

6.818 Trinidad and Tobago

KLASS, Morton. *East Indians in Trinidad: A Study of Cultural Persistence* (New York: 1961).
WOOD, D. *Trinidad in Transition: The Years After Slavery* (London: Oxford University Press, 1968).
WILLIAMS, E. *History of the People of Trinidad and Tobago* (Port of Spain, Trinidad: P.N.M. Publishing, 1962).

6.82 Central America

ADAMS, Richard N. *Cultural Surveys of Panama-Nicaragua-Guatemala-El Salvador-Honduras* (Washington, D.C.: Pan-American Sanitary Bureau, 1957).
DUNCAN, Julian S. "Demographic Factors and Economic Integration in Central America." Journal of Inter-American Studies 5, no. 2 (April 1963).
GRUBB, Kenneth. *Religion in Central America* (London: 1937).
LOOMIS, Charles P. et al. *Turrialba: Social Systems and the Introduction of Change* (Glencoe, Ill.: Free Press, 1953).
MARTZ, John D. *Central America—The Crisis and the Challenge* (Chapel Hill: University of North Carolina Press, 1959).
MUNRO, Dana G. *The Five Republics of Central America: Their Political and*

Economic Development and Their Relations With the United States (New York: 1918).
RODRIGUEZ, Mario. *Central America* (Englewood Cliffs, N.J.: Prentice-Hall, 1965).

6.821 Costa Rica

BUSEY, James L. *Notes on Costa Rican Democracy* (Boulder: 1962).
NUNLEY, Robert E. *The Distribution of Population in Costa Rica* (Washington, D.C.: 1960).

See also Section 6.81, JONES.

6.822 El Salvador

ANDERSON, Charles W. "El Salvador: The Army as a Reformer." In *Political Systems of Latin America,* edited by Martin C. Needler (Princeton: Van Nostrand, 1964).
ANDERSON, Thomas P. *Matanza. El Salvador's Communist Revolt of 1932* (Lincoln: University of Nebraska Press, 1971).
RAYNOLDS, D. R. *Rapid Development in Small Economies: The Example of El Salvador* (New York: Praeger, 1967).

6.823 Guatemala

ADAMS, Richard N., ed. *Political Changes in Guatemalan Indian Communities. A Symposium* (New Orleans: 1957).
COLBY, B. N. and P. L. van den BERGHE. *Ixil Country: A Plural Society in Highland Guatemala* (Berkeley: University of California Press, 1969).
HOLLERAN, Mary P. *Church And State in Guatemala* (New York: 1949).
INMAN, Samuel Guy. *A New Day in Guatemala, A Study of the Present Social Revolution* (Wilton, Conn.: 1951).
JONES, Chester Lloyd. *Guatemala, Past and Present* (Minneapolis: 1940).
NASH, Manning. "Political Relations in Guatemala." Social and Economic Studies 7, no. 1 (March 1958): 65-75.
——— "The Multiple Society in Economic Development: Mexico and Guatemala." American Anthropologist 59, no. 5 (October 1957): 825-38.
NEWBOLD, Stokes. "Receptivity to Communist Fomented Agitation in Rural Guatemala." Economic Development and Cultural Change 5 (1958-59).
ROSENTHAL, Marie. *Guatemala: The Story of an Emergent Latin-American Democracy* (New York: Twayne, 1962).
ROZZOTTO, Jaime Díaz. *El Carácter de la Revolución Guatemalteca* (The Character of the Guatemalean Revolution) (Mexico: 1958).
SILVERT, Kalman H. *A Study in Government: Guatemala* (New Orleans: 1954).
TAX, Sol. *Penny Capitalism, A Guatemala Indian Economy* (Washington, D.C.: 1953).
TOLEDO, M. Monteforte. *Guatemala* (Mexico: Monografía Sociólogica, 1959).
WHETTEN, Nathan L. *Guatemala—The Land and the People* (New Haven, Conn.: Yale University Press, 1961).

6.824 Honduras

PAREDES, Luces. *Liberalismo y Nacionalismo* (Tegucigalpa: Honduras, 1963).
STOKES, William S. *Honduras, an Area Study in Government* (Madison: University of Wisconsin Press, 1950).

6.825 Mexico

BEALS, Carleton. *Mexico: An Interpretation* (New York: 1923).
BRANDENBURG, Frank. *The Making of Modern Mexico* (Englewood Cliffs, N.J.: Prentice-Hall, 1964).
CAMARA, Francisco López. *La Estructura Económica y Social de México en la Epoca de la Reforma* (The Economic and Social Structure of Mexico at the Time of the Reform) (Mexico: Siglo XXI, 1967).
CASANOVA, Pablo Gonzales. *La Democracia en Mexico* (Democracy in Mexico) (Mexico: 1965).
——— "Sociedad Plural y Desarrollo: El Caso de México" (Plural Society and Development: the Case of Mexico). *América Latína* 5, no. 4 (1962).
CLINE, Howard. *Mexico: Revolution to Evolution: 1940-1960* (New York: Oxford University Press, 1962).
CORNELIUS, Wayne A., Jr. "Crisis, Coalition-Building, and Political Entrepreneurship in the Mexican Revolution: The Politics of Social Reform Under Lázaro Cárdenas." Project on Historical Crises and Political Development, Department of Political Science, Stanford University, July 1969.
CUMBERLAND, Charles C. *Mexico: The Struggle for Modernity* (New York and London: 1968).
MONTEVERDE, Alonso Aguilar. *Dialéctica de la Economía Mexicana* (The Dialectics of the Mexican Economy) (México: Editorial Nuestro Tiempo, 1968).
NASH, Manning. "The Multiple Society in Economic Development: Mexico and Guatemala." American Anthropologist 59, no. 5 (October 1957): 825-38.
RUIZ, Ramon Eduardo. *Mexico: The Challenge of Poverty and Illiteracy* (San Marino, Calif.: Huntington Library, 1963).
SCOTT, Robert. "Mexico: The Established Revolution" in *Political Culture and Political Development,* edited by L. Pye and S. Verba (Princeton: Princeton University Press, 1966).
——— *Mexican Government in Transition* (Urbana: University of Illinois Press, 1959).
SIMPSON, Lesley B. *The Encomienda in New Spain: The Beginning of Spanish Mexico.* Rev. and enlarged ed. (Berkeley: University of California Press, 1966). Originally published, 1929.
SOUSTELLE, Jacques. "Religion and the Mexican State." Diogenes 34 (Summer 1961): 1-15.
TANNENBAUM, Frank. *Mexico: The Struggle for Peace and Bread* (New York: Knopf, 1950).
——— *Peace by Revolution: An Interpretation of Mexico* (New York: 1933).
VERNON, Raymond. *The Dilemma of Mexico's Development* (Cambridge, 1963).
WEYL, Nathaniel and Sylvia WEYL. *The Reconquest of Mexico: The Years of Lázaro Cárdenas* (London: Oxford University Press, 1939).
WIONCZEK, Miguel S. *El Nacionalismo Mexicano y la Inversion Extranjera* (Mexican Nationalism and Foreign Investment) (Mexico: Siglo XXI, 1967).

WOMACK, John, Jr. *Zapata and the Mexican Revolution* (Cambridge, Mass.: Harvard University Press, 1969).

6.826 Nicaragua

MACAULAY, Neill. *The Sandino Affair* (Chicago: Quadrangle, 1967).
NOGALES Y MENDEZ, R. *The Looting of Nicaragua* (New York: Arno Press, 1970). Originally published, 1928.

6.827 Panama

GOLDRICH, Daniel. *Radical Nationalism: The Political Orientations of Panamanian Law Students* (East Lansing: Bureau of Social and Political Research, Michigan State University, 1962).
MATERNO, Vásquez, J. *Teoría Particular del Estado Panameño* (A Specific Theory of the Panamanian State) (Panamá: Estrella de Panamá, 1969).
PORRAS DE LA GUARDIA, J. R. *El Multipartidismo de Panamá* (The Multiparty System in Panama) (Bogotá: Pontifica Universidad Javeriana, 1968).

6.83 Spanish South America

6.831 Argentina

BAILY, Samuel L. *Labor, Nationalism, and Politics in Argentina* (New Brunswick: Rutgers University Press, 1967).
BLANKSTEN, George I. *Peron's Argentina* (Chicago: University of Chicago Press, 1953).
CANTON, Dario. "The Argentine Revolution of 1966 and the National Project." Paper presented at the Rio de Janeiro Round Table of Political Science, IPSA, October 1969.
CORNBLIT, O. *Imigrantes y Empresarios en la Politica Argentina* (Immigrants and Entrepreneurs in Argentine Politics) (Buenos Aires: Instituto Di Tella, 1966).
CORTES CONDE, Roberto and Ezequiel GALLO. *La Formacion de la Argentina Moderna* (The Formation of Modern Argentina) (Buenos Aires: Ed. Paidós, 1967).
DI TELLA, Torcuato S. *El Sistema Politico Argentino y la Clase Obrera* (The Argentinian Political System and the Working Class) (Buenos Aires: Eudeba, 1964).
——— Gino Germani; et al. *Argentina, Sociedad de Masas* (Argentina, Mass Society) (Buenos Aires: Instituto Di Tella, 1965).
FERRER, Aldo. *La Economia Argentina: Las Etapas de su Desarrollo y Problemas Actuales* (The Economy of Argentina: The Stages of Development and Present Problems). 2nd ed. (Mexico: Fondo de Cultura Economica, 1965).
GERMANI, Gino. *Estructura Social de la Argentina* (The Social Structure of Argentina) (Buenos Aires: Paidos, 1955).
HERNANDEZ ARREGUI, J. J. *La Formación de la Conciencia Nacional 1930-1960* (Buenos Aires: Hachea, 1968).
IMAZ, José Luis de. *Los Que Mandan* (Those Who Command) (Buenos Aires: Editorial Eudeba, 1964).

KENNEDY, John Joseph. *Catholicism, Nationalism, and Democracy in Argentina* (Note Dame, Ind.: University of Notre Dame Press, 1958).

NUN, Jose. "The Argentine variant." In *Latin America: The Hegemonic Crisis And the Military Coup* (Berkeley: Institute of International Studies, University of California, 1969).

ORTIZ, Ricardo M. *Histótia Económica de la Argentina* (Economic History of Argentina) (Buenos Aires: Raigal, 1955).

ROMERO, José Luis. *Argentina: Imágenes y Perspectivas* (Argentina: Images and Perspectives) (Buenos Aires: Raigal, 1956).

SARMIENTO, Domingo Faustino. *Facundo.* (Santiago, Chile, 1845, numerous editions). English translation, *Life in the Argentine Republic in the Days of the Tyrants.* (New York, 1868; paperback, Macmillan, 1961). A classic analysis of the urban-rural conflict in nation-building.

SCOBIE, James R. *Argentina: A City and a Nation* (New York: Oxford University Press, 1964).

SMITH, Peter H. *Politics and Beef in Argentina: Patterns of Conflict and Change* (New York: Columbia University Press, 1969).

See also Section 6.8, SOLBERG.

6.832 Bolivia

ALEXANDER, Robert J. *The Bolivian National Revolution* (New Brunswick: Rutgers University Press, 1958).

ARNADE, Charles W. *The Emergence of the Republic of Bolivia* (Gainesville: University of Florida Press, 1957).

CESPEDES, Augusto. *El Dictator Suicida: 40 Anos de Historia de Bolivia* (The Suicide Dictator: 40 Years of Bolivian history) (Santiago: Editorial Universitaria, 1956).

KLEIN, Herbert S. *Parties and Political Change in Bolivia, 1800-1952.* (Cambridge, Eng.: Cambridge University Press, 1969).

OSBORNE, Harold. *Bolivia, A Land Divided* (London: Royal Institute of International Affairs, 1955).

PATCH, R. W. "Peasantry and National Revolution: Bolivia." In *Expectant Peoples: Nationalism and Development* edited by Kalman Silvert (New York: Random House, 1963).

6.833 Chile

GIL, Frederico G. *The Political System of Chile* (Boston: 1966).

HALPERIN, Ernst. *Nationalism and Communism in Chile* (Cambridge: MIT Press, 1965).

LEHMANN, David. "Political Incorporation Versus Political Stability: the Case of the Chilean Agrarian Reform, 1965-70." Journal of Development Studies, no. 4 (July 1971).

NEELY, Carlos. *Cambios Políticos para el Desarrollo: El Caso de Chile* (Political Change and Development: The Case of Chile) (Santiago: Editorial Universitaria, 1968).

PETRAS, James. *Politics and Social Forces in Chilean Development.* 2nd. ed. (Berkeley: University of California Press, 1969, 1972).

––– and Maurice ZEITLIN. "Miners and Agrarian Radicalism." In *Latin America Reform or Revolution ̂ A Reader,* edited by James Petras and Maurice Zeitlin (New York: Gettleman, Fawcett, 1968).

PIKE, Frederick B. *Chile and the United States, 1880-1962: The Emergence of Chile's Social Crisis and the Challenge to United States Diplomacy* (Notre Dame, Ind.: University of Notre Dame Press, 1963).

PINTO, Anibal. *Chile, Una Economia Difícil* (Mexico: 1964).

SILVERT, K. H. "Some Propositions on Chile." In *Latin American Politics: Studies of the Contemporary Scene,* edited by Robert D. Tomasek (Garden City, N.Y.: Doubleday, 1966).

SUNKEL, Oswaldo. "Change and Frustration in Chile." In *Obstacles To Change in Latin America,* edited by Claudio Véliz (New York: Oxford University Press, 1965).

ZEITLIN, Maurice. "The Social Determinants of Political Democracy in Chile." In *Latin America Reform or Revolution ̂ A Reader,* edited by James Petras and Maurice Zeitlin (New York: Gettleman, Fawcett, 1968).

6.834 Colombia

BUSHNELL, David. *The Santander Regime in Gran Colombia* (Newark, Del.: 1954).

DIX, Robert H. *Colombia: The Political Dimensions of Change* (New Haven, Conn.: Yale University Press, 1967).

DUMONT, Jacques J. "Le Conflict 'Sociétal et le Processus de Changement Politique et Economique. Le Cas de la Violencia en Columbie."

FALS BORDA, Orlando. *La Subversión en Colombia: El Cambio Social en la Historia* (Subversion in Colombia: Social Change in History) (Bogotá: Tercer Mundo, 1967).

––– "Violence and the Break-up of Tradition in Colombia." In *Obstacles to Change in Latin America,* edited by Claudio Véliz, pp. 188-205 (London: Oxford University Press, 1965).

FLAHARTY, Vernon Lee. *Dance of the Millions: Military Rule and the Social Revolution in Colombia, 1930-1956* (Pittsburgh: University of Pittsburgh Press, 1957).

GILMORE, Robert L. "Federalism in Colombia, 1910-1848." Ph.D. dissertation, University of California, 1949.

GUZMAN, C. Germán; Eduardo Umaña LUNA; and Orlando FALS BORDA. *La Violencia en Colombia.* Monografías Sociologicas 12 (Bogota: Facultad de Sociología, Universidad Nactional de Colombia, 1962).

HALGUERA, J. Leon. "The Changing Role of the Military in Colombia." Journal of Inter-America Studies, July 1961, pp. 351-57.

HOLT, Pat M. *Colombia Today – And Tomorrow* (New York: Praeger, 1964).

HUNTER, John Merlin. *Emerging Colombia* (Washington, D.C.: Public Affairs Press, 1962).

MARTZ, John D. *Colombia – A Contemporary Political Survey* (Chapel Hill: University of North Carolina Press, 1962).

PAYNE, J. L. *Patterns of Conflict in Colombia* (New Haven, Conn.: Yale University Press, 1968).

PEREZ, Gustavo. *El Problema Sacerdotal en Colombia* (The Problem of Religion in Colombia) (Madrid: Editorial Rivadeneira, 1962).

PEREZ RAMIREZ, Gustavo and Isaac WUST. *La Iglesia en Colombia: Estructuras Eclesiásticas* (The Church in Colombia: Ecclesiastical Structure) (Bogota: Oficina Internacional de Investigaciones Sociales de FERES, 1961).

SHAW, Jr., Carey. "Church and State in Colombia, as Observed by American Diplomats, 1834-1906." *Hispanic American Historical Review* 31, November 1941, pp. 577-613.

WILLIAMSON, Robert C. "Toward a Theory of Political Violence: The Case of Rural Colombia." *Western Political Quarterly*, March 1965, pp. 35-44.

6.835 Ecuador

BLANKSTEN, George I. *Ecuador: Constitutions and Caudillos* (Berkeley: University of California Press, 1951).

LINKE, Lilo. *Ecuador, Country of Contrasts* (London: 1954).

PAREJA DIEZ CANSECO, Alfredo. *Historia del Ecuador.* 2 vols. (Quito: 1958).

6.836 Paraguay

BAUDIN, Louis. *Une Théocratie Socialiste: l'Etat Jesuite de Paraguay* (Paris: Genin, 1962).

LOTT, Leo B. *Venezuela and Paraguay: Political Modernity and Tradition in Conflict* (New York: Holt, Rinehart and Winston, 1972).

PENDLE, George. *Paraguay: A Riverside Nation* (New York: Royal Institute of International Affairs, 1954).

WARREN, Harris Gaylord. *Paraguay, An Informal History* (Norman: University of Oklahoma Press, 1949).

6.837 Peru

ASTIZ, Carlo. *Pressure Groups and Power Elites in Peruvian Politics* (Ithaca, N.Y.: Cornell University Press, 1969).

BOURRICAUD, F. *Pouvoir et Société dans le Pérou Contemporain* (Paris: Colin, 1967; English translation, London: Faber, 1970).

CHAPLIN, David. "Peruvian Stratification and Mobility–Revolutionary and Developmental Potential." In *Structural Social Inequality: A Reader in Comparative Social Stratification,* edited by Celia S. Heller (New York: Macmillan, 1969).

COTLER, Julio. "La Mecanica de la Dominacion Interna y del Cambio Social en el Peru." *America Latina* 11, no. 1 (January-March 1968): 72-105.

GOLDRICH, Daniel; Raymond B. PRATT; and C. R. SCHULLER. "The Political Integration of Lower-Class Urban Settlements in Chile and Peru." *Studies in International Comparative Development* 3, no. 1 (1967-68).

HILLIKER, Grant. *The Politics of Reform in Peru: The Aprista and Other Mass Parties* (Baltimore: Johns Hopkins Press, 1971).

KANTOR, Harry. *The Ideology and Program of the Peruvian Aprista Movement* (Berkeley: University of California Press, 1953).

MAR, J. Matos. "Les 'Barriadas' de Lima: Un Example d'Intégration à la Vie Urbaine." In *L'Urbanisation en Amerique Latine* (Paris: UNESCO, 1962).

OWENS, Ronald Jerome. *Peru* (New York: Oxford University Press, 1963).

PAYNE, James L. "Peru: The Politics of Structured Violence." *Journal of Politics,*

May 1965, pp. 362-74. Reprinted in *Latin American Politics. Studies of the Contemporary Scene,* 2nd ed. rev and updated, edited by Robert D. Tomasek (Garden City, N.Y.: Doubleday, 1970).

——— *Labor and Politics in Peru: the System of Political Bargaining* (New Haven, Conn.: Yale University Press, 1965).

6.838 Uruguay

DEVOTO, Juan E. Pivel and Alcira Ranieri de Pivel DEVOTO. *Historia de la República Oriental del Uruguay (1830-1030)* (Montevideo: Editorial Medina, 1945).

FITZGIBBON, Russell H. *Uruguay: Portrait of Democracy* (New Brunswick, N.J.: Rutgers University Press, 1954).

PENDLE, George. *Uruguay: South America's First Welfare State* (New York: Royal Institute of International Affairs, 1952).

RAMA, Carlos. "La Crisis Politica Uruguaya." Ciencias Politicas e Sociales 16, pp. 233-412.

SOLARI, Aldo E. *Estudios Sobre la Socieda Uruguaya* (Montevideo, 1964).

6.839 Venezuela

BETANCOURT, Rómulo. *Venezuela: Política y Petróleo* (Venezuela: Politics and Petroleum) (Mexico: Fondo de Cultura Economico, 1956).

BONILLA, Frank and José A. SILVA MICHELENA, eds. *Strategy of Research on Social Policy: Politics of Change in Venezuela,* Vol. I. (Cambridge, Mass.: MIT Press, 1968).

BONILLA, Frank and J. A. SILVA MICHELENA. *Studying the Venezuelan Polity* (Cambridge, Mass.: MIT, 1966).

FRIEDMAN, John. *Venezuela: From Doctrine to Dialogue* (Syracuse, N.Y.: Syracuse University Press, 1965).

——— *Regional Development Policy: A Case Study of Venezuela* (Cambridge, Mass.: MIT Press, 1965).

LIEUWEN, Edwin. *Venezuela* (London: Oxford University Press, 1961).

LOTT, Leo B. *Venezuela and Paraguay: Political Modernity and Tradition in Conflict* (New York: Holt, Rinehart and Winston, 1972).

MARTZ, John D. *Accion Democratica: Evolution of a Modern Political Party in Venezuela* (Princeton: Princeton University Press, 1966).

MIJARES, Augusto. *La Evolucion Politica de Venezuela, 1810-1960* (The Political Evolution of Venezuela, 1810-1960) (Buenos Aires: Ed. Universitaria, 1967).

PICON-SALAS, Mariano et al. *Venezuela Independiente, 1810-1960* (Caracas, 1962).

6.84 The Portuguese Empire: Brazil

AGUIAR, Manoel Pinto de. *Brasil: Integraçao e Desenvolvimento Economico* (Brazil: Integration and Economic Development) (Salvador: Progresso, 1958).

BAER, Werner. *Industrialization and Economic Development in Brazil* (New Haven, Conn.: Yale University Press, 1965).

BONILLA, Frank. "Brazil: A National Ideology for Development." In *Expectant Peoples: Nationalism and Development,* edited by Kalman Silvert et al. (New York: Random House, 1963).

CARDOSO, Fernando Henrique. *Empresario Industrial e Desenvolvimento Economico no Brasil* (Industrial Enterprise and Economic Development in Brazil) (São Paulo: Difusão Européia do Livro, 1964).

CORBISIER, Roland. *Formação e Problema da Cultura Brasileira* (Formation and Problems of Brazilian Culture) (Rio: ISEB, 1960).

CUNHA, Euclides da. *Os Sertões* (Rio de Janeiro: F. Alves, 1911). English translation, *Rebellion in the Backlands* (Chicago: University of Chicago Press, 194). A classic study of the rural peripheries.

DEAN, Warren. *The Industrialization of São Paulo, 1880-1945* (Austin: University of Texas Press, 1969).

DEBRUN, Michel. "Nationalisme et Politique du Développement du Brasil." Sociologie du Travail, 1964, vol. 6, no. 4, pp. 235-59; vol. 7, no. 2, pp. 351-80.

FAORO, Raymundo. *Os Donos do Poder-Formação do Patronato Politico Brasiliero* (Porto Alegre: Editora Globo, 1958).

FREYRE, Gilberto. *Casa Grande e Senzala: Formação da Familia Brasileira sob o Regimen de Economia Patriarchal.* 2nd. ed. (Rio de Janeiro: Schmidt, 1936). English translation, *The Masters and the Slaves: A Study in the Development of Brazilian Civilization,* 2 vols. (New York: Knopf, 1946). French translation, *Maitres et Esclaves* Paris: Gallimard, 1952).

FUJII, Yukio and T. Lynne SMITH. *The Acculturation of the Japanese Immigrants in Brazil* (Gainesville: University of Florida Press, 1959).

FURTADO, Celso. *Diagnosis of the Brazilian Crisis* (Berkeley: University of California Press, 1965).

——— *Political Obstacles to Growth in Brazil* (London: Oxford University Press, 1965).

——— *The Economic Growth of Brazil: A Survey from Colonial to Modern Times* (Berkeley: University of California Press, 1963).

——— *The New Colonial Economy and its Mechanisms of Defense—A Economia Brasileira* (Rio: Edit. A Noite, 1954).

GRAHAM, Richard. *Britain and the Onset of Modernization in Brazil, 1850-1914* (Cambridge, Eng.: Cambridge University Press, 1968).

HOROWITZ, Irving Louis. *Revolution in Brazil: Politics and Society in a Developing Nation* (New York: E.P.Dutton, 1964).

IANNI, Octavio. *Estado e Capitalismo: Estrutura Social e Industrializacâo do Brasil* (State and Capitalism: Social Structure and Industrialization in Brazil) (Rio de Janeiro: Civilizaçao Brasileira, 1965).

JAGUARIBE, Felio. "The Dynamics of Brazilian Nationalism." In *Obstacles to Change in Latin America,* edited by Claudio Véliz, pp. 162-87 (New York: Oxford University Press, 1965).

——— *Desenvolvimento Politico—Desenvolvimento Economico* (Political Development—Economic Development) (Rio: F.C.E., 1962).

——— *O Nacionalismo na Atualidade Brasileira* (Nationalism in the Brazilian Present) (Rio: ISEB, 1958).

LAUBERT, Jacques. *Le Brésil* (Paris: Colin, 1953).

LEFF, Nathaniel H. *Economic Policy—Making and Development in Brazil—1947/1964* (New York: John Wiley, 1968).

LOVE, Joseph L. *Rio Grande do sul and Brazilian Regionalism, 1882-1930* (Stanford: Stanford University Press, 1971).

MENDES, Candido. "O Governo Castelo Branco—Paradigm e Prognose." (The Castelo Branco Government—Paradigm and Prognosis). Dados 2, no. 3 (1970) 63-111.

——— "Sistema Politico e Modelos de Poder no Brasil." (The Political System and Models of Power in Brazil). Dados 1 (1969): 7-41.

——— "The Parameter of Centralization in Elites of Power, Democracy and Development—An Attempt at Model Building for the Brazilian Patterns of Power Since 1964." Dados 1 (1969): 6.

——— "The Emergence of the Brazilian Intelligentsia." Mimeographed. Paper presented at the University of California, Los Angeles/Riverside Symposium on Brazil—Portunguese Africa, February 1968.

——— Memento Dos Vivos, Emergência da Cultura Popular (Memento of the Living: The Emergence of Popular Culture) (Rio: Tempo Brasileiro, 1966).

——— Memento of the Living—The Catholic Left in Brazil—Church and Order in the Colonia Regimes (Rio: Tempo Brasileiro, 1966).

——— "Elites de Poder, Democracia e Desenvolvimento." (Power Elites, Democracy and Development). Dados 6, pp. 57-90.

PEREIRA, L. C. Bresser. Desenvolvimento e Crise no Brasil (Development and Crisis in Brazil) (Rio: Zahar, 1968).

PINTO, Alvaro Vieira. Consciência e Realidade Nacional (Conscience and National Reality) (Rio: ISEB, 1961).

RANGEL, Ignacio. Dualidade Básica de Economia Brasileira (Fundamental Dualism of the Braziliam Economy) (Rio: ISEB, 1957).

RODRIGUES, José Albertino. Sindicato e Desenvolvimento no Brasil (The Labor Movement and Development in Brazil) (São Paulo: Difusão Européia do Livro, 1969).

SCHMITTER, Philippe C. Interest Conflict and Political Change in Brazil (Stanford: Stanford University Press, 1971).

SMITH, Thomas Lynn. Brazil: People and Institutions (Baton Rouge: Louisiana State University Press, 1963).

SOARES, Glaucio A. Dillon. "A Nova Industrialização e o Sistema Político Brasileiro." (The New Industrialization and the Political System of Brazil). Dados 2, no. 3 (1970): 32-51.

SODRE, Nelson Werneck. Formacão Historica do Brasil (Buenos Aires: Ed. Universitaria, 1964).

——— Historória da Burgesia Brasileira (History of the Brazilian Boureoisie) (Rio de Janeiro: Civilizaçâ Brasileira, 1964).

WEFFORT, Francisco C. "State and Mass in Brazil." Studies in Comparative International Development 2, no. 12 (1966).

See also Section 3.8, Kuznets.

6.9 Tropical Africa

ADU, A. L. The Civil Service in the New African States (New York: Praeger, 1965).

AGBLEMAGNON, N'Sougan. "Interprétation Sociologique la Décolonisation: le Cas de l'Afrique Noire." Paper presented to the World Congress of Sociology 6, Evian, September 4-11, 1966.

AMIN, Samir. Le Mali, La Guinée et la Ghana: Trois Expériences Africaines de Développement (Paris: Presses Universitaires, 1965).

APTHORPE, Raymond, ed. From Tribal Rule to Modern Government. Proceedings of the 13th conference of the Rhodes-Livingstone Institute, Lusaka, 1959.

BADIAN, Seydou. *Les Dirigeants d'Afrique Noire Face à Leur Peuple* (Paris: Maspéro, 1965).

BALANDIER, G. *Sociologie Actuelle de l'Afrique Noire* (Paris: Presses Universitaires, 1955). English translation, *The Sociology of Black Africa* (London: Deutsch, 1969; New York: Praeger, 1969).

BERG, Elliot J. "Socialism and Economic Development in Tropical Africa." Quarterly Journal of Economics 78 (November 1964): 549-73.

BURKE, Fred G. *Africa's Quest for Order* (Englewood Cliffs, N.J.: Prentice-Hall, 1965).

CARTER, Gwendolyn, ed. *National Unity and Regionalism in Eight African States* (Ithaca: Cornell University Press, 1966).

——— *Politics in Africa: Seven Cases* (New York: Harcourt, Brace and World, 1966).

——— *African One-Party States* (Ithaca, N.Y.: Cornell University Press, 1964).

——— *Five African States: Responses to Diversity: The Congo, Dahomey, the Cameroon, Federal Republic of Rhodesia and Nyasaland, and South Africa* (Ithaca, N.Y.: Cornell University Press, 1963).

——— and William O. BROWN, eds. *Transition in Africa: Studies in Political Adaptation* (Boston: Boston University Press, 1958).

CARTEY, Wilfred and Martin KILSON, eds. *The Africa Reader.* 2 vols. (New York: Vintage Books, 1970).

CERVENKA, Zdenek. *The Organisation of African Unity and Its Charter* (London: C. Hurst, 1969).

CHALIAND, Gerard. *Armed Struggle in Africa* (New York: Monthly Review Press, 1969).

COLEMAN, James S. "The Politics of Sub-Saharan Africa." In *The Politics of Developing Areas,* edited by G. A. Almond and J. S. Coleman (Princeton: Princeton University Press, 1960).

——— and Carl ROSBERG, eds. *Political Parties and National Integration in Tropical Africa* (Berkeley: University of California Press, 1964).

COWAN, L. Gray. *The Dilemmas of African Independence* (New York: Walker, 1965).

——— ; James O'CONNELL; and David G. SCANLON, eds. *Education and Nation-Building in Africa* (New York: Praeger, 1965).

COX, Richard. *Pan-Africanism in Practice* (London: Oxford University Press, 1964).

CURRIES, David P. *Federalism and the New Nations of Africa* (Chicago: University of Chicago Press, 1967).

CURTIN, Phillip D. *The Image of Africa: British Ideas and Action, 1780-1850* (Madison: University of Wisconsin Press, 1964).

DAVIDSON, Basil. *The Africans* (New York: International Publishing Service, 1969).

DIA, Mamadou. *The African Nations and World Solidarity* (New York: Praeger, 1961).

DOOB, Leonard W. *Communication in Africa: A Search for Boundaries* (New Haven, Conn.: Yale University Press, 1961).

EMERSON, Rupert. "Nation-Building in Africa." In *Nation-Building,* edited by Karl W. Deutsch and William J. Foltz (New York: Atherton Press, 1963).

——— "The Problem of Identity, Selfhood and Image in New Nations: the Situation in Africa." Contemporary Politics 1, no. 3 (April 1969): 297-312.

——— and Martin Kilson, eds. *The Political Awakening of Africa* (Englewood Cliffs, N.J.: Prentice-Hall, 1965).

FITZGERALD, Walter. *Africa: A Social, Economic, and Political Geography of its Major Regions.* Rev. ed. (London: Methuen, 1957).

FOLTZ, William J. "Political Opposition in Single-Party States of Tropical Africa." In *Regimes and Oppositions,* edited by Robert A. Dahl (New Haven, Conn.: Yale University Press, 1973).

––– "Psychanalyse des Armées Sud-Sahariennes." Revue Française d'Etudes Politiques Africaines 14 (February 1967).

FORDE, Daryll and P. M. KABERRY, eds. *West African Kingdoms in the Nineteenth Century* (London, 1967).

FRIEDLAND, William H. and Carl G. ROSBERG, Jr., eds. *African Socialism* (Stanford: Stanford University Press, 1964; new ed. 1967).

GANN, L. H. and Peter DUIGNAN. *White Settlers in Tropical Africa* (Harmondsworth: Penguin, 1962).

GIFFORD, P. and W. R. LOUIS, eds. *Britain and Germany in Africa: Imperial Rivalry and Colonial Rule* (New Haven, Conn.: Yale University Press, 1967).

HATCH, John. *Africa: The Rebirth of Self-Rule* (London: Oxford University Press, 1967).

HAZELWOOD, Arthur, ed. *African Integration and Disintegration: Case Studies in Economic and Political Union* (London: Oxford University Press, 1967).

KASFIR, Nelson. "Prismatic Theory and African Administration." World Politics 21, no. 2 (January 1969): 295-314.

KIEWIET, Cornelis Willem de. "The Revolution that Disappeared." Plural Societies 2, no. 1 (1971): 3-15.

KITCHEN, Helen A., ed. *The Educated African: A Country-by-Country Study of Educational Development in Africa* (New York: Praeger, 1962).

LEE, J. M. *African Armies and Civil Order* (New York: Praeger, 1969).

LEMARCHAND, René. "Political Clientelism and Ethnic Solidarities in Tropical Africa." Amer. Pol. Sci. Rev. 66, no. 1 (March 1972): 68-90.

LEWIS, L. J. *Education and Political Independence in Africa* (London: Nelson, 1962).

LEWIS, W. Arthur. *Politics in West Africa* (London: Allen and Unwin, 1965).

LLOYD, P. C., ed. *The New Elites of Tropical Africa* (London: Oxford University Press, 1966).

LYSTAD, R. A., ed. *The African World: A Survey of Social Research* (New York: Praeger, 1965).

MAFEJE, Archie. "The Ideology of Tribalism." Journal of Modern African Studies 9, no. 2 (January 1967): 190-217.

MAGUBANE, B. "Pluralism and Conflict Situations in Africa: A New Look." African Social Research 7 (June 1969): 529-54.

MAZRUI, Ali A. *Violence and Thought: Essays on Social Tensions in Africa* (London: Longmans, 1969).

MEISTER, Albert. *L.Afrique, Peut-Elle Partir?* (Paris, Ed. du Seuil, 1966).

MINER, Horace, ed. *The City in Modern Africa* (London: Pall Mall, 1967).

MORRISON, Donald and H. M. STEVENSON. "Integration and Instability: Patterns of African Political Development." American Political Science Review 66, no. 3 (September 1972): 902-27.

MURDOCK, George Peter. *Africa: Its Peoples and Their Culture History* (New York: McGraw-Hill, 1959).

MUSHKERT, M. "La Nature du Colonialisme et du Nationalisme Post-Colonial en

Afrique." Paper presented to the World Congress of Sociology, Evian, September 4-11, 1966.

N'DIAYE, J. P. *Elites Africaines et Culture Occidentale: Assimilation ou Résistance* (Paris: Présence Africaine, 1969).

NKRUMAH, Kwame. *New-Colonialism: The Last Stage of Imperialism* (New York: International Publishers, 1966).

——— *Africa Must Unite* (New York: Praeger, 1963).

NYERERE, Julius K. *Freedom and Unity: Uhuru Na Umoja: A Selection from Writings and Speeches 1952-65* (London: Oxford University Press, 1967).

PANIKKAR, K. Madhu. *The Serpent and the Crescent* (Bombay: Asia Publishing House, 1963).

PERHAM, Margery. *The Colonial Reckoning* (London: Collins, 1961).

RENCONTRES INTERNATIONALES DE BOUAKE. *Traditions et Modernisme en Afrique Noire* (Paris: Seuil, 1965).

RICHARDSON, Sam S. *The Evolving Public Service in Africa* (Madison: Institute of Governmental Affairs, University of Wisconsin, 1964).

RIVKIN, Arnold. *Nation-Building in Africa: Problems and Prospects* (New Brunswick: Rutgers University Press, 1969).

——— ed. *Nations by Design. Institution-Building in Africa* (Garden City, N.Y.: Doubleday, 1968).

ROSBERG, Carl S., Jr. "Democracy and the New African States." In *African Affairs: Number Two,* edited by Kenneth Kirkwood (London: Chatto and Windus, 1963).

ROTBERG, Robert I. and Ali A. MAZRUI, eds. *Protest and Power in Black Africa* (London: Oxford University Press, 1970).

SCANLON, David G., ed. *Church, State and Education in Africa* (New York: Teachers College Press, 1966).

SENGHOR, Léopold Sédar. "Négritude et Arabisme." Présence Africaine, 1961.

——— *African Socialism: A Report to the Constitutive Congress of the Party of African Federation* (New York: American Society of African Culture, 1959).

——— ed. *On African Socialism* (New York: Praeger, 1964).

SITHOLE, Ndabaningi. *African Nationalism* (London: Oxford University Press, 1959; 2nd ed. 1968).

SKLAR, Richard L. "Political Science and National Integration—A Radical Approach." Journal of Modern African Studies 5, no. 1 (1967): 1-11.

SPENCER, John, ed. *Language in Africa* (Cambridge, Eng.: Cambridge University Press, 1963).

SPIRO, H. J. *Politics in Africa: Prospects South of the Sahara* (Englewood Cliffs, N.J.: 1962).

STEVENSON, Robert F. *Population and Political Systems in Tropical Africa* (New York: Columbia University Press, 1968).

TEVOEDJRE, Albert. *Pan-Africanism in Action: An Account of the UAM.* Occasional Paper 11 (Cambridge, Mass.: Harvard University Center for International Affairs, 1965).

TRIMINGHAM, John Spencer. *A History of Islam in West Africa* (London and New York: Oxford University Press, 1962).

TURNBULL, Colin M. *Tradition and Change in African Tribal Life* (New York: World Publishing Company, 1966).

TURNER, V. W., ed. *Profiles of Change: The Impact of Colonialism on African Societies* (London: Cambridge University Press, 1969).

WALLERSTEIN, Immanuel. *Africa: The Politics of Unity* (New York: Random House, 1967).
――― *Africa: The Politics of Independence, An Interpretation of Modern African History* (New York: Vintage Books, 1961).
――― "Ethnicity and National Integration in West Africa." Cahiers d'Etudes Africaines 1 (1960): 129-39.
WILLS, A. J. *An Introduction to the History of Central Africa* (London: Oxford University Press, 1967).
WODDIS, Jack. *Africa: The Roots of Revolt* (London: Lawrence and Wishart, 1960).
ZIEGLER, Jean. *Le Pouvoir Africain* (Paris: Ed. du Seuil, 1971).
――― *Sociologie de la Nouvelle Afrique* (Paris: Gallimard, 1964).
ZOLBERG, Aristide. "The Structure of Political Conflict in the New States of Tropical Africa." American Political Science Review 62 (March 1968): 70-87.
――― *Creating Political Order: The New Party States of West Africa* (Chicago: Rand McNally, 1967).
――― "Patterns of National Integration." Journal of Modern African Studies 10, no. 4 (December 1967): 449-67.

6.91 British Africa

ADU, A. L. *The Civil Servant in Commonwealth Africa: Development and Transition* (London: Allen and Unwin, 1969).
COHEN, Sir Andrew. *British Policy in Changing Africa* (London: Routledge and Kegan Paul, 1959).
HAILEY, William Malcolm. *Native Administration in the British African Territories* (London: Her Majesty's Stationary Office, 1952).
HANCOCK, W. K. *Problems of Nationality 1918-1936. Survey of British Commonwealth Affairs, Vol. I* (London: Oxford University Press, 1937).
LUGARD, Frederick. *The Dual Mandate in British Tropical Africa* (Edinburgh, 1922).
PERHAM, Margery. *Colonial Sequence 1949-1969* (London: Methuen, 1970).
SYMONDS, Richard. *The British and Their Successors* (Evanston: Northwestern University Press, 1966).

6.911 British West Africa

GAILEY, Harry A. *A History of the Gambia* (New York: Praeger, 1965).
RICE, B. *Enter Gambia―The Birth of an Improbable Nation* (Boston: Houghton Mifflin, 1967).

6.9112 Ghana

AFRIFA, A. A. *The Ghana Coup* (London: Frank Cass, 1968).
APTER, David. *Ghana in Transition* (New York: Athenum, 1962).
――― "The Role of Traditionalism in the Political Modernization of Ghana and Uganda." World Politics 13 (October 1960): 45-68.
AUSTIN, Dennis. *Politics in Ghana, 1946-1960* (London: Oxford University Press, 1964).

BOURRET, Florence Mabel. *Ghana: The Road to Independence, 1919-1957* (Stanford: Stanford University Press, 1960).

BUSIA, K. A. "The Present Situation and Aspiration of Elites in the Gold Coast." International Social Science Bulletin 8 (1956): 413-23.

——— *The Position of the Chief in the Modern Political System of Ashanti: A Study of the Influence of Contemporary Social Changes on Ashanti Political Institutions* (London: Oxford University Press, 1951).

FOSTER, Philip J. *Education and Social Change in Ghana* (Chicago: University of Chicago Press, 1965).

GOODY, Jack. "Consensus and Dissent in Ghana." Political Science Quarterly 83 (1968): 337-352.

GREAT BRITAIN, CENTRAL OFFICE OF INFORMATION, Reference Division. *The Making of Ghana* (London: Her Majesty's Stationary Office, 1956).

HARVEY, William Burnett. *Law and Social Change in Ghana* (Princeton: Princeton University Press, 1966).

JAHODA, Gustav. *White Man: A Study of the Attitudes of Africans to Europeans in Ghana Before Independence* (New York: Oxford University Press, 1961).

NKRUMAH, Kwame. *Dark Days in Ghana* (New York: International Publishers, 1968).

——— *Ghana* (New York: Nelson, 1957).

OCRAN, A. K. *A Myth is Broken: An Account of the Ghana Coup d'Etat* (London, 1968).

PADMORE, George. *The Gold Coast Revolution: The Struggle of an African People From Slavery to Freedom* (London: Dobson, 1953).

6.9113 Nigeria

ABERNETHY, David B. *The Political Dilemma of Popular Education: An African Case* (Stanford: Stanford University Press, 1969).

AKIWOWO, A. "The Sociological Relevance of Tribalism to the Building of the Nigerian Nation." Paper presented to the World Congress of Sociology 6, Evian, September 4-11, 1966.

ARIKPO, Okoi. *The Development of Modern Nigeria* (Harmondsworth: Penguin, 1967).

AWOLOWO, Obafemi. *Path to Nigerian Freedom* (London: Faber, 1966).

——— *Awo* (Cambridge, Eng.: Cambridge University Press, 1960).

AZIKIWE, Nnandi. *Zik: Selected Speeches* (Cambridge, Eng.: Cambridge University Press, 1961). A major advocate of federalism.

BRAND, J. A. "The Mid-West State Movement in Nigerian Politics: A Study in Party Formation." Political Studies 13 (October 1965): 346-65.

BRETTON, Henry L. *Power and Stability in Nigeria: The Politics of Decolonization* (New York: Praeger, 1962).

BUCHANAN, Keith M. and John Charles PUGH. *Land and People in Nigeria: The Human Geography of Nigeria and its Environmental Background* (London: University of London Press, 1958).

COLEMAN, James S. *Nigeria: Background to Nationalism* (Berkeley: University of California Press, 1958).

CROWDER, Michael. *The Story of Nigeria* (London: Faber, 1962; Rev. and expanded ed., 1966).

DIAMOND, Stanley. *Nigeria: Model of a Colonial Failure* (New York: A.C.A., 1967).

FORDE, Daryll and G. I. JONES. *The Ibo and Ibibio-Speaking People of South-Eastern Nigeria* (London: International African Institute, 1962).

JOHNSTON, H. A. S. *The Fulani Empire of Sokoto* (London, 1967).

KIRK-GREENE, A. H. M. *Crisis and Conflict in Nigeria* (London: Oxford University Press, 1971).

KOPYTOFF, Jean Herskovitz. *A Preface to Modern Nigeria: The 'Sierra Leonians' in Yoruba, 1830-1890* (Madison: University of Wisconsin Press, 1965).

LAST, Murray. "Aspects of Administration and Dissent in Hausaland, 1800-1968." *Africa* 40, no. 4 (October 1970): 345-357.

LUCKHAM, Robin. *The Nigerian Military: A Sociological Analysis of Authority and Revolt, 1960-67* (Cambridge, Eng.: Cambridge University Press, 1971).

MACKINTOSH, John P. *Nigeria: The Biafran War* (Pretoria: Africa Institute of South Africa, 1969).

——— et al. *Nigerian Government and Politics* (London: Allen and Unwin, 1966).

MELSON, R. and H. WOLFE, eds. *Nigeria: Modernization and the Politics of Colonialism* (East Lansing: Michigan State University Press, 1971).

PANTER-BRICK, S. K., ed. *Nigerian Politics and Military Rule: Prelude to the War* (London: Athlone Press, 1969).

PERHAM, Margery. *Lugard: Makers of Modern Nigeria* (London: Collins, 1956-60).

——— *Native Administration in Nigeria* (London, 1937).

SCHWARZ, Frederick A. O., Jr. *Nigeria: The Tribes, The Nation, or the Race—The Politics of Independence* (Cambridge: MIT Press, 1965).

SCHWARZ, Walter. *Nigeria* (London: Pall Mall, 1968).

SKLAR, Richard L. "Nigerian Politics: The Ordeal of Chief Awolowo, 1960-65." In *Politics in Africa: 7 Cases,* edited by G. C. Carter (New York: Harcourt, Brace and World, 1966).

——— "Contradictions in the Nigerian Political System." Journal of Modern African Studies 3, no. 2 (1965): 201-13.

——— *Nigerian Political Parties: Power in an Emergent African Nation* (Princeton: Princeton University Press, 1963).

SMITH, M. G. *Government in Zazzau* (London: Oxford University Press, 1960). A major analysis of the Northern emirate.

SMOCK, Audrey C. *Ibo Politics: The Role of Ethnic Unions in Eastern Nigeria* (Cambridge, Mass.: Harvard University Press, 1971).

SMYTHE, H. H. and M. M. SMYTHE. *The New Nigerian Elites* (Stanford: Stanford University Press, 1960).

TILMAN, Robert O. and Taylor COLE, eds. *The Nigerian Political Scene* (Durham, N.C.: Duke University Press, 1962).

WHITAKER, C. S., Jr. *The Politics of Tradition: Continuity and Change in Northern Nigeria, 1946-1966* (Princeton: Princeton University Press, 1970).

6.9114 Sierra Leone

ALLEN, Christopher. "Sierra Leone Politics Since Independence." African Affairs 67 (1968): 305-29.

COX, Herbert. *Sierra Leone Report of Commission of Inquiry into the Disturbances in the Provinces, November 1955-March 1956* (London: 1956).

FYFE, Christopher. *A History of Sierra Leone* (London: Oxford University Press, 1962).

KILSON, Martin. *Political Change in a West African State: A Study of the Modernization Process in Sierra Leone* (Cambridge, Mass.: Harvard University Press, 1966).

LITTLE, Kenneth. "Structural Change in the Sierra Leone Protectorate." Africa 25, no. 3 (June 1955): 217-34.

PORTER, Arthur T. *Creoledom* (London: Oxford University Press, 1963).

6.912 British East Africa

DELF, George. *Asians in East Africa* (London, 1963).

DIAMOND, Stanley and Fred G. BURKE, eds. *The Transformation of East Africa: Studies in Political Anthropology* (New York: Basic Books, 1966). Papers written for a seminar on problems of nation-building in East Africa as part of the program of East African Studies, Syracuse University.

GHAI, Dharam P., ed. *Portrait of a Minority: Asians in East Africa* (New York: Oxford University Press, 1966).

GULLIVER, P. H., ed. *Tradition and Transition in East Africa: Studies of the Tribal Element in the Modern Era* (Los Angeles: University of California Press, 1969; London: Routledge and Kegan Paul, 1969).

HOLLINGSWORTH, L. W. *The Affairs of East Africa* (New York, 1960).

HUGHES, Anthony. *East Africa: The Search for Unity. Kenya, Tanganyika, Uganda and Zanzibar* (Harmondsworth: Penguin Books, 1963).

NYE, Joseph S. Jr. *Pan-Africanism and East African Integration* (Cambridge, Mass.: Harvard University Press, 1965).

RICHARDS, Audrey I. *The Multicultural States of East Africa* (Nairobi: East African Publishing House, 1968).

ROTHCHILD, Donald, ed. *Politics of Integration: An East African Documentary* (Nairobi: East African Publishing House, 1968).

"Tribe and Nation in East Africa: Separatism and Regionalism." Round Table 52 (June 1962): 252-58.

TRIMMINGHAM, J. S. *Islam in East Africa* (London, 1964).

WHITELY, W. H., ed. *Language Use and Social Change: Problems of Multi-Lingualism with Special Reference to Eastern Africa* Studies presented and discussed at the ninth International African Seminar at University College, Dar es Salaam, 1968. (London: International African Institute, 1971).

6.9121 Kenya

BENNETT, George. *Kenya: A Political History. The Colonial Period* (London: Oxford University Press, 1963).

CASTAGNO, A. A. "The Somali-Kenya Controversy." Journal of Modern African Studies 2 (1964): 165-88.

COLONY AND PROTECTORATE OF KENYA. *Historical Survey of the Origins and Growth of Mau Mau* (The Corfield Report) (Nairobi, 1960).

COX, Richard. *Kenyatta's Country* (New York: Praeger, 1965).

DILLEY, Ruth. *British Policy in Kenya Colony* (New York: Thomas Nelson, 1937).

GERTZEL, Cherry. *The Politics of Independent Kenya 1963-8* (Nairobi: East African Publishing House, 1970).

––– Maure GOLDSCHMIDT; and Don ROTHCHILD, eds. *Government and Politics in Kenya* (Nairobi: East African Publishing House, 1969).

GHAI, Y. P. and J.P.W.B. McAUSLAN. *Public Law and Political Change in Kenya* (Nairobi, London: Oxford University Press, 1970).

GOLDS, J. M. "African Urbanization in Kenya." Journal of African Administration 13 (1961): 24-28.

HUXLEY, Elspeth. *White Man's Country: Lord Delaware and the Making of Kenya* 2 vols. (London: Chatto and Windus, 1935).

——— and Margery PERHAM. *Race and Politics in Kenya* (London: Faber & Faber, Revised edition, 1955).

KENYATTA, Jomo. *Facing Mount Kenya* (London: Secker and Warburg, 1953).

KILSON, M. L. "Land and Politics in Kenya: An Analysis of African Politics in a Plural Society." Western Political Quarterly 10 (1957): 559-81.

LEAKEY, L.S.B. *Defeating Mau Mau* (London: Methuen, 1954).

MARRIS, Peter and Anthony SOMERSET. *African Business: A Study of Entrepreneurship and Development in Kenya* (London: Routledge and Kegan Paul, 1971).

MASON, Philip. "The Plural Society of Kenya." In *Ethnic and Cultural Pluralism in Intertropical Countries,* pp. 325-37 (Brussels: INCIDI, 1957).

OGOT, B. A. "British Administration in the Central Nyanza District of Kenya." Journal of African History 4 (1963): 249-74.

PANKHURST, Richard K. P. *Kenya: The History of Two Nations* (London: Independent Publishing, 1955).

ROSBERG, Carl G., Jr., and John NOTTINGHAM. *The Myth of "Mau Mau": Nationalism in Kenya* (New York: Praeger, 1966).

SOJA, Edward W. *The Geography of Modernization in Kenya. A Spatial Analysis of Social, Economic, and Political Change* (Syracuse, N.Y.: Syracuse University Press, 1968).

WOOD, Susan. *Kenya: The Tensions of Progress* (London: Oxford University Press for Institute of Race Relations, 1960).

6.9122 Malawi

CLUTTON-BROCK, Guy. *Dawn in Nyasaland* (London: Hodder and Stoughton, 1959).

DEBENBAUM, Frank. *Nyasaland: The Land of Lake* (London: HMSO, Carone Library, 1955).

HAZELWOOD, A. and P. O. HENDERSON. *Nyasaland: The Economics of Federation* (Oxford: Basil Blackwell, 1960).

PIKE, John G. *Malawi: A Political and Economic History* (London: Pall Mall, 1968).

ROTBERG, Robert I. *The Rise of Nationalism in Central Africa: The Making of Malawi and Zambia, 1873-1964* (Cambridge, Mass.: Harvard University Press, 1966).

6.9123 Rhodesia

ARRIGHI, G. *The Political Economy of Rhodesia* (The Hague: Mouton, 1967).

BARBER, James. *Rhodesia. The Road to Rebellion* (London: Oxford University Press, 1967).

BULL, Theodor. *Rhodesian Perspective* (London: Joseph, 1967).

GANN, L. H. *A History of Southern Rhodesia* (London, 1965).

LEYS, Golin. *European Politics in Southern Rhodesia* (Oxford: Clarendon, 1959).

NKOMO, Joshua. *Rhodesia: The Case for Majority Rule* (New Delhi, 1966).

RANGER, Terence. "African Politics in Twentieth-Century Southern Rhodesia." In *Aspects of Central African History* edited by T. O. Ranger (London, 1968).

6.9124 Somalia

CASTAGNO, A. A. "The Somali-Kenya Controversy." Journal of Modern African Studies 2 (1964): 165-88.

LEWIS, I. M. *The Modern History of Somaliland* (London: 1965).

SHARMARKE, Abdirashid Ali. "Preface." In *The Somali Peninsula: A New Light on Imperial Motives* (Mogadiscio: Information Service of the Somali Government, 1962).

"La Somalie Indépendante." Présence Africaine 38 (1961): 73-237.

TOUVAL, Saadia. *Somali Nationalism: International Politics and the Drive for Unity in the Horn of Africa* (Cambridge, Mass.: Harvard University Press, 1963).

6.9125 Sudan

BESHIR, Mohamed Omer. *Sudan: Nationalism and Revolution* (London: Pall Mall, 1972).

––– *The Southern Sudan: Background to Conflict* (London, 1968).

DUNCAN, J.S.R. *The Sudan's Path to Independence* (Edinburgh: Blackwood, 1957).

EVANS-PRITCHARD, E. E. *The Nuer* (London: Oxford University Press, 1949).

GRAY, Richard. *A History of the Southern Sudan, 1839-1889* (London: Oxford University Press, 1961).

HENDERSON, K.D.D. *Sudan Republic* (London: Ernest Benn, 1965).

HILL, Richard Leslie. *Egypt in the Sudan, 1820-1881* (London: Oxford University Press, 1959).

HOLT, Peter Malcolm. *The Mahdist State in the Sudan, 1881-1898.* 2nd ed. (Oxford: Clarendon Press, 1970).

––– *A Modern History of the Sudan, From the Funj Sultanate to the Present Day* (London: Weidenfeld and Nicolson, 1961).

MUDDATHIR, 'Abd al-Rahim. *Imperialism and Nationalism in the Sudan* (London: Oxford University Press, 1969).

ODUHO, Joseph and William DENG. *The Problem of the Southern Sudan* (London: Oxford University Press, 1963).

RIFE, David C. and John R. RANDALL. "The Peoples of the Sudan." Middle East Journal 7 (Spring 1953): 165-81.

SUDAN REPUBLIC. *Report of the Commission to Inquire into the Disturbances in the Southern Sudan* (Khartoum, 1956).

WARBURG, Gabriel. *The Sudan Under Wingate* (London: Frank Cass, 1971).

6.9126 Tanzania

AUSTEN, Ralph A. *Northwest Tanzania Under German and British Rule: Colonial Policy and Tribal Politics, 1889-1939* (New Haven, Conn.: Yale University Press, 1968).

BIENEN, Henry. *Tanzania: Party Transformation and Economic Development* (Princeton: Princeton University Press, 1967).

HOPKINS, Raymond F. *Political Roles in a New State: Tanzania's First Decade* (New Haven, Conn.: Yale University Press, 1971).

LOFCHIE, Michael F. "The Zazibari Revolution: African Protest in a Racially Plural Society." In *Protest and Power in Black Africa* edited by Robert I. Rotberg and Ali A. Mazrui (London: Oxford University Press, 1970).

——— *Zanzibar: Background to Revolution* (Princeton: Princeton University Press, 1965).

MacDONALD, Alexander. *Tanzania: Young Nation in a Hurry* (New York: Hawthorn, 1966).

OKELLO, John. *Revolution in Zanzibar* (Nairobi: East African Publishing House, 1967).

6.9127 Uganda

APTER, David. *The Political Kingdom in Uganda: A Study in Bureaucratic Nationalism* (Princeton: Princeton University Press, 1961).

——— "The Role of Traditionalism in the Political Modernization of Ghana and Uganda." World Politics 13 (October 1960): 45-68.

BEATTIE, John. *Bunyoro: An African Kingdom* (New York: Holt, Rinehart and Winston, 1962).

BURKE, Fred George. *Local Government and Politics in Uganda* (Syracuse, N.Y.: Syracuse University Press, 1964).

EDEL, M. M. "African Tribalism: Some Reflections on Uganda." Political Science Quarterly 80 (1965): 357-72.

FALLERS, Lloyd A. *The King's Men: Leadership and Status in Buganda on the Eve of Independence* (New York: Oxford University Press, 1964).

——— "Ideology and Culture in Uganda Nationalism." American Anthropologist 63, no. 4 (August 1971): 677-86.

INGRAMS, William Harold. *Uganda: A Crisis of Nationhood* (London: Her Majesty's Stationary Office, 1960).

LEE, J. M. "Buganda's Position in Federal Uganda." Journal of Commonwealth Political Studies 3 (November 1965): 165-81.

LOW, D. A. and R. Cranford PRATT. *Buganda and British Overrule* (London, 1962).

MAZRUI, Ali A. "Leadership in Africa: Obote of Uganda." International Journal, Summer 1970.

——— "Privilege and Protest as Integrative Factors: The Case of Buganda's Status in Uganda." In *Protest and Power in Black Africa,* edited by Robert I. Rotberg and Ali A. Mazrui, pp. 1027-87 (London: Oxford University Press, 1970).

MORRIS, H. S.; Julian PITT-RIVERS; and Ernest GELLNER, eds. *The Indians in Uganda: Caste and Sect in a Plural Society* (Chicago: University of Chicago Press, 1968).

MUKHERJEE, Ramkrishna. *The Problem of Uganda* (Berlin: Akademie-Verlag, 1956).

OBERG, K. "The Kingdom of Ankole in Uganda." In *African Political Systems,* edited by M. Fortes and E. E. Evans-Pritchard (London: Oxford University Press, 1950).

WRIGLEY, C. C. "The Christian Revolution in Buganda." Comparative Studies in Society and History 2 (October 1959): 48f.

6.9128 Zambia

CAPLAN, Gerald L. *The Elites of Barotseland 1878-1969: A Political History of Zambia's Western Province* (Berkeley: University of California Press, 1970).

GANN, L. H. *A History of Northern Rhodesia: Early Days to 1953* (London: Chatto and Windus, 1964).

——— *The Birth of a Plural Society: The Development of Northern Rhodesia Under the British South African Company, 1894-1914* (Manchester: Manchester University Press, 1958).

GELFAND, M. *Northern Rhodesia in the Days of the Charter: A Medical and Social Study, 1878-1924* (Oxford: Basil Blackwell, 1961).

HALL, Richard. *Zambia* (New York: Praeger, 1965).

KAUNDA, Kenneth. *Zambia Shall Be Free* (London: Heineman, 1962).

ROTBERG, Robert I. *The Rise of Nationalism in Central Africa: The Making of Malawi and Zambia, 1873-1964* (Cambridge, Mass.: Harvard University Press, 1966).

——— *Christian Missionaries and the Creation of Northern Rhodesia, 1880-1924* (Princeton: Princeton University Press, 1965).

——— "The Lenshina Movement of Northern Rhodesia." In *Human Relations in British Central Africa* (March, 1961).

WOOD, Anthony St. John. *Northern Rhodesia, The Human Background* (London: Pall Mall, 1961).

6.913 Mauritius

BENEDICT, B. *Indians in a Plural Society: A Report on Mauritius* (London: HMSO, 1961).

BLOOD, Sir Hilary. "Ethnic and Cultural Pluralism in Mauritius." In *Ethnic and Cultural Pluralism in Intertropical Countries*, pp. 356-62 (Brussels: INCIDI, 1957).

HAZEERSINGH, K. "The Religion and Culture of Indian Immigrants in Mauritius and the Effect of Social Change." Comparative Studies in Society and History 8, no. 2 (January 1966): 241-57.

6.92 British-Dutch South Africa

DAVIS, J. A. and J. K. BAKER, eds. *Southerm Africa in Transition* (New York: Praeger, 1965).

STEVENS, Richard P. *Lesotho, Botswana, and Swaziland: The Former High Commission Territories in Southern Africa* (London: Pall Mall, 1967).

THOMPSON, Leonard M. *African Societies in Southern Africa: Historical Studies* (New York: Praeger, 1969).

6.921 South Africa

ADAM, Heribert. *Modernizing Racial Domination: The Dynamics of South African Politics* (Berkeley: University of California Press, 1971).

BREYTENBACH, W. J. "The Multi-National Population Structure of South Africa." Plural Societies 2, no. 1 (1971): 53-68.

BRUWER, J. P. van S. *Die Bantu van Suid-Afrika* (The Batu of South Africa) (Johannesburg: APB, 1963).

CALPIN, G. H. *There Are No South Africans* (London, 1941).

CARTER, G. M. *The Politics of Inequality: South Africa Since 1948* (New York, 1958).

CLOETE, Stuart. *South Africa, The Land, Its People and Achievements* (Johannesburg: Da Gama, n.d.).

HANCOCK, W. K. *Are There South Africans?* (Johannesburg, 1966).

HILL, Christopher. *Bantustan: The Fragmentation of South Africa* (London and New York: Oxford University Press, 1964).

KIEWIET, C. W. de. *A History of South Africa, Social and Economic* (London: Oxford University Press, 1942).

KRUEGER, Daniel Wilhelmus. *The Making of a Nation: A History of the Union of South Africa 1910-61* (Johannesburg, 1969).

KUPER, Leo. *An African Bourgeoisie: Race, Class and Politics in South Africa* (New Haven, Conn.: Yale University Press, 1965).

LOUBSER, Jan. "Calvinism, Equality and Inclusion: The Case of Africaaner Calvinism." In *The Protestant Ethic and Modernization,* edited by S. N. Eisenstadt (New York: Basic Books, 1968).

MANSERGH, Nicholas. *South ·Africa 1906-1961: The Price of Magnanimity* (New York: Praeger, 1962).

MARQUARD, Leo. *The Peoples and Policies of South Africa.* 4th ed. (London: Oxford University Press, 1969).

MBEKI, Govan. *South Africa: The Peasants' Revolt* (Baltimore: Penguin, 1964).

NIDDRIE, David L. *South Africa: Nation or Nations* (Princeton: Van Nostrand, 1968).

OMER-COOPER, J. D. *The Zulu Aftermath—A Nineteenth Century Revolution in Bantu Africa* (London: Longmans, 1960).

PATON, Alan. *The Long View* (New York, 1968).

RHOODIE, Eschel. *The Third Africa* (Cape Town: Nas. Boekhandel, 1968).

SCHAPERA, I. *The Koisan Peoples of South Africa* (London, 1930).

SUNDKLER, B.G.M. *Bantu Prophets in South Africa* (London, 1948).

THOMPSON, Leonard M. *Politics in the Republic of South Africa* (Boston: Rand McNally, 1966).

WILSON, Monica and Leonard THOMPSON, eds. *The Oxford History of South Africa.* 2 vols. (Oxford: Clarendon Press, 1971).

6.922 Botswana

CERVENKA, Sdenek. *Republic of Botswana: A Brief Outline of its Geographical Setting, History, Economy and Policies* (Uppsala: Scandanavian Institute of African Studies, 1970).

MITCHISON, N. "Tribal Values in Botswana." Phylon 28, no 3 (1967): 261-66.

MUNGER, Edwin S. *Bechuanaland: Pan-African Outpost or Bantu Homeland* (New York: Oxford University Press, 1965).

6.923 Lesotho

ASHTON, Hugh. *The Basuto: A Social Study of the Traditional and Modern Lesotho* (London: International African Institute, 1952; 2nd ed. 1967).

PROCTOR, J. H. "Building Constitutional Monarchy in Lesotho." Civilisations 19, no. 1 (1969): 64-83.

SPENCE, J. E. *Lesotho: The Politics of Dependence* (London: Oxford University Press, 1968).

WYK, A. J. van. *Lesotho: A Political Study* (Pretoria: Africa Institute, 1967).

6.924 Southwest Africa (Namibia)

BLEY, Helmut. *Kolonialherrschaft und Sozialstruktur in Deutsch-Sudwestafrika, 1894-1914* (Colonial Administration and Social Structure in German Southwest Africa, 1894-1914) (Hamburg, 1968).

OLIVIER, M. J. "Ethnic Relations in South West Africa." Plural Societies 2, no. 1 (1971): 31-42.

SEGAL, Ronald and Ruth SEGAL, eds. *Southwest Africa: A Travesty of Trust* (New York: Andre Deutsch, 1967).

6.925 Swaziland

HOLLEMAN, J. F., ed. *Experiment in Swaziland* (Cape Town, 1964).

KUPER, Hilda. *The Swazi* (London: International African Institute, 1952).

——— *The Uniform of Colour: A Study of White-Black Relationships in Swaziland* (Johannesburg: University of Witwatersrand Press, 1947).

6.93 French Africa

BERG, Elliot. "The Economic Basis of Political Choice in French West Africa." American Political Science Review 44 (June 1960): 391-405.

DELAVIGNETTE, Robert. *L'Afrique Noire Française et son Destin* (Paris: Gallimard, 1962).

——— *Freedom and Authority in French West Africa* (London, 1950).

DE LUSIGNAN, Guy. *French-Speaking Africa Since Indpendence* (London: Pall Mall, 1969).

FANON, Frantz. *Les Damnés de la Terre* (paris: Maspéro, 1961). English edition, *The Wretched of the Earth* (New York: Grove Press, 1965; Harmondsworth: Penguin, 1967).

FOLTZ, William J. *From French West Africa to the Mali Federation* (New Haven, Conn.: Yale University Press, 1965).

GRIMAL, Henri. *La Décolonisation, 1919-1963* (Paris: Armand Colin, 1965).

LeVINE, Victor. *Political Leadership in Africa: Post-Independence Generational Conflict in Upper Volta, Senegal, Niger, Dahomey, Central African Republic* (Stanford: Hoover Institution on War, Revolution, and Peace, 1967).

MAUNIER, René. *Sociologie Coloniale* (Paris: Domat-Montchrestien, 1932). English translation, *The Sociology of Colonies* (London: Routledge and Kegan Paul, 1949).

MORGENTHAU, Ruth Schachter. *Political Parties in French-Speaking West Africa* (Oxford: Clarendon Press, 1964).

SEURIN, Jean-Louis. "Elites Sociales et Partis Politiques d'AOF." Annales Africaines, Dakar, 1958.

6.931 French West Africa

6.9311 Dahomey

CORNEVIN, R. "Les Militaires au Dahomey et au Togo." Revue Française d'Etudes Politiques Africaines 36 (December 1968): 65-84.
——— Histoire du Dahomey (Paris: Berger-Levrault, 1962).
HERSKOVITS, M. J. Dahomey: An Ancient West African Kingdom (New York: J. J. Augustin, 1938; Reprint ed., 1967, 2 vols).
RONEN, Don. "Is National Integration Essential to Modernization? An Enquiry Into Regionalism in Dahomey." Paper presented to the Midwest Political Science Association Conference, Chicago, April 30-May 2, 1970.

6.9312 Guinea

AMEILLON, B. La Guinée, Bilan d'une Indépendence (Paris: Maspéro, 1964).
DECKER, H. de. Nation et Developpement Communautaire en Guinée et au Senegal (Paris: Mouton, 1967).
NENEKHALY-CAMARA, C. "Guinée: Révolution et Culture." Tricontinental 3 (1967): 124-39.
TOURE, Sekou. La Révolution Guinéenne et le Progrès Social (Conakry: Imprimérie Nationale, 1962).

6.9313 Ivory Coast

AMIN, Samir. Le Développement du Capitalisme en Côte d'Ivoire (Paris: Ed. de Minuit, 1965).
CLIGNET, Remi and Philip FOSTER. The Fortunate Few. A Study of Secondary Schools and Students in the Ivory Coast (Evanston, Ill.: Northwestern University African Studies 18, 1966).
DRAKE, Lyman M., III. "The Anxious Gneration: Ivory Coast Youth Look at Work and Politics." Ph.D. dissertation, MIT, 1968.
HOLAS, Bohumil. Changements Sociaux en Côte d'Ivoire (Paris: Presses Universitaires de France, 1961).
ZELLER, C. Elfehbeinkueste. Ein Entwicklungsland auf dem Wege Zur Nation (The Ivory Coast: A Developing Country on its Way to a Nation) (Freiburg i. B., 1969).
ZOLBERG, Aristide. One-Party Government in the Ivory Coast (Princeton: Princeton University Press, 1964).
——— "Mass Parties and National Integration: The Case of the Ivory Coast." Journal of Politics 25 (February 1963): 36-48.

6.9314 Mali

BRASSEUR; G. Les Etablissements Humains au Mali (Dakar: Institut Fondamental d'Afrique Noire, 1968).
HOPKINS, N. S. "Socialism and Social Change in Mali." Journal of Modern African Studies 7, no. 3 (October 1969): 457-68.

MEILLASSOUX, C. *Urbanization of an African Community: Voluntary Associations in Bamako* (Seattle: University of Washington Press, 1968).

MONTEIL, C. *Les Empires du Mali. Etude d'Histoire et de Sociologie Soudanaises* (Paris: G.P. Maisonneuve–larose, 1968).

SNYDER, Francis G. *One-Party Government in Mali. Transition Toward Control* (New Haven, Conn.: Yale University Press, 1965).

6.9315 Mauritania

BAL, M. B. "Les Communes en Mauritanie." Revue Juridique et Politique 22, no. 2 (1968): 391-98.

GERTEINY, Alfred G. *Mauritania* (London: Pall Mall, 1967).

6.9316 Niger

CLAIR, Andrée. *Le Niger: Pays à Découvrir* (Paris: Hachette, 1965).

GUILLOU, J. M. and B. HERNANDEZ. "Dogondoutchi, Petit Centre Urbain du Niger." Revue de Géographie Alpine 56, no. 2 (1968): 297-358.

6.9317 Senegal

BEHRMAN, Lucy C. *Muslim Brotherhoods and Politics in Senegal* (Cambridge, Mass.: Harvard University Press, 1970).

COTTINGHAM, Clement. "Political Consolidation in Centre-Local Relations in Senegal." Canadian Journal of African Studies 4, no. 1 (1970): 101-20.

CROWDER, Michael. *Senegal: A Study in French Assimilation Policy* (London: Oxford University Press, 1962).

DECKER, H. de. *Nation et Développement Communautaire en Guinée et au Senegal* (Paris: Mouton, 1967).

FOLTZ, William J. "Le Parti Africain de l'Indépendence." Revue Française d'Etudes Politiques Africaines 45 (September 1969): 8-35.

GELLAR, Sheldon. *The Politics of Dependency: The Senegal Case* (Bloomington: Indiana University Press, 1972).

KLEIN, Martin. *Islam and Imperialism in Senegal: Sine-Saloum* (Stanford: Stanford University Press, 1968).

MARKOVITZ, Irving L. *Leopold Sedar Senghor and the Politics of Negritude* (New York: Atheneum, 1969).

6.9318 Togo

CORNEVIN, R. "Les Militaires au Dahomey et au Togo." Revue Française d'Etudes Politiques Africaines 36 (December 1968): 65-84.

––– *Histoire du Togo* (Paris: Berger-Levrault, 1959).

QUASHIE, L. "La Commune Togolaise." Revue Juridique et Politique 22, no. 2 (1968): 397-406.

6.9319 Upper Volta

SKINNER, Elliot P. *The Mossi of Upper Volta* (Stanford: Stanford University Press, 1964).

6.932 French Central Africa

THOMPSON, V. and R. ADLOFF. *The Emerging States of French Equatorial Africa* (Stanford: Stanford University Press, 1960).

6.9321 Cameroun

GARDINIER, David E. *Political Behavior in the Community of Douala, Cameroon: Reactions of the Douala People to Loss of Hegemony, 1940-1955* (Athens: Ohio University, Center for International Studies, 1966).
––– *Cameroun: United Nations Challenge to French Policy* (London: Oxford University Press, 1963).
JOHNSON, Willard R. *The Cameroon Federation: Political Integration in a Fragmentary Society* (Princeton: Princeton University Press, 1970).
LeVINE, Victor T. *The Cameroons from Mandate to Independence* (Berkeley: University of California Press, 1964).
RUBIN, Neville. *Cameroun: An African Federation* (London: Pall Mall, 1971).
STOECKER, Helmuth, ed. *Kamerun Unter Deutscher Kolonialherrschaft. Studien* (The Cameroons Under German Colonial Administration. Studies). 2 vols. (Berlin: Instituts fuer Allgemeine Geschichte an der Humboldt-Universitaet Berlin, 1960-68).

6.9322 Central African Republic

KALCK, Pierre. *Central African Republic: A Failure of De-Colonisation* (New York: Praeger, 1971).

6.9323 Chad

DIGUIMBAYE, G. and R. LANGUE. *L'Essor du Tchad* (Paris: Presses Universitaires de France, 1969).
LeBEUF, Annie M. D. *Les Populations du Tchad* (Paris: Presses Universitaires de France, 1959).
Le CORNEC, Jacques. *Histoire Politique du Tchad de 1900 à 1962* (Paris: Librairie Générale de Droit et de Jurisprudence, 1963).
––– *Les Chefferies du Tchad et l'Evolution Politique* (Paris: Librairie Générale de Droit et de Jurisprudence, 1963).

6.9324 Congo (Br.)

AMIN, Samir and Catherine COQUERY-VIDROVITCH. *Histoire Economique du Congo 1880-1968* (Paris: Ed. Anthropos, 1969).

6.9325 Gabon

FERNANDEZ, J. W. *"Redistributive Acculturation and Ritual Reintegration in Fang Culture."* Ph.D. dissertation, Northwestern University, 1963.
WEINSTEIN, Brian. *Gabon: Nation-Building on the Ogooué* (Cambridge, Mass.: MIT Press, 1966).

6.933 Malagasy

BOITEAU, Pierre. *Contribution à l'Histoire de la Nation Malgache* (Paris: Editions Sociales, 1958).

HESELTINE, Nigel. *Madagascar* (London: Pall Mall, 1971).

KENT, Raymond K. *From Madagascar to the Malagasy Republic* (New York: Praeger, 1962).

LAPIERRE, J. W. "Tradition et Modernité à Madagascar." Paper presented to the World Congress of Sociology, Evian, September 4-11, 1966.

RAMANDRAIVONONA, Desire. *Le Malgache: Sa Langue, Sa Religion* (Paris: Présence Africaine, 1959).

THOMPSON, Virginia and Richard ADLOFF. *The Malagasy Republic: Madagascar Today* (Stanford: Stanford University Press, 1965).

6.94 Spanish and Portuguese Africa

ABSHIRE, David M., and Michael A. SAMUELS, eds. *Portuguese Africa: A Handbook* (London: Pall Mall, 1969).

DUFFY, James. *Portuguese Africa* (Cambridge, Mass.: Harvard University Press, 1959).

HAMMOND, R. J. *Portugal and Africa, 1815-1910: A Study in Uneconomic Imperialism* (Stanford: Stanford University Press, 1966).

6.941 Angola

DUFFY, James. "The Portuguese Presence in Angola, 1483-1960." Présence Africaine 41 (1962).

EGERTON, F. Clement C. *Angola in Perspective: Endeavor and Achievement in Portuguese West Africa* (London: Routledge and Kegan Paul, 1957).

MARCUM, John. *The Angolan Revolution, Vol. I, The Anatomy of an Explosion, 1950-1962* (Cambridge, Mass.: MIT Press, 1969).

OKUMA, Thomas Masaji. *Angola in Ferment: The Background and Prospects of Angolan Nationalism* (Boston: Beacon Press, 1962).

PELISSIER, R. "Nationalismes en Angola." Revue Française de Science Politique 19, no. 6 (December 1969): 1187-215.

WHEELER, Douglas L. and René PELISSIER. *Angola* (London: Pall Mall, 1971).

6.942 Guinée-Bissau

CABRAL, Amilcar. *Revolution in Guinea* (New York: Monthly Review Press, 1970).

DAVIDSON, Basil. *The Liberation of Guinée. Aspects of an African Revolution* (Harmondsworth: Penguin, 1969).

6.943 Mosambique

MONDLANE, Eduardo C. "FRELIMO: The Struggle for Independence in Mozambique." In *Southern Africa in Transition,* edited by John A. Davis and James K. Baker (New York, 1966). Reprinted in *The Africa Reader: Independent Africa,* edited by Wilfred Cartey and Martin Kilson (New York: Vintage, 1970).

6.95 Belgian Africa

6.951 Burundi

LEMARCHAND, René. *Rwanda and Burundi* (London: Pall Mall, 1970).

6.952 Congo (Zaire)

LEMARCHAND, René. *Political Awakening in the Congo* (Berkeley: University of California Press, 1964).
MERRIAM, Alan P. *Congo, Background of Conflict* (Evanston, Ill.: Northwestern University Press, 1961).
LUMUMBA, Patrice. *Congo, My Country* (London: Pall Mall, 1962).
SLADE, Ruth M. *King Leopold's Congo: Aspects of the Development of Race Relations in the Congo Independent State* (London: Oxford University Press, 1962).
STENGERS, Jean. "King Leopold's Imperialism." In *Studies in the Theory of Imperialism,* edited by R. Owen and B. Sutliffe, pp. 248-76 (London: Longmans, 1972).
VERHAEGEN, Benoit. *Rebellions au Congo* (Brussels: CRISP, 1966).
WILLAME, Jean-Claude. "Politics and Power in Congo Kinshasa." Africa Report 16, no. 1 (January 1971): 14-17.
YOUNG, Crawford. "Rebellion in the Congo." In *Protest and Power in Black Africa,* edited by Robert I. Rotberg and Ali A. Mazrui (London: Oxford University Press, 1970).
——— *Politics in the Congo: Decolonization and Independence* (Princeton: Princeton University Press, 1965).

6.953 Rwanda

GRAVEL, P. B. *Remera. A Community in Eastern Ruanda* (The Hague: Mouton, 1968).
LEMARCHAND, René. *Rwanda and Burundi* (London: Pall Mall, 1970).

6.96 Italian Africa

CUMMING, D. C. "British Stewardship of the Italian Colonies: An Account Rendered." International Affairs 29 (January 1953): 11-21.

6.961 Somalia
See Section 6.9124.

6.97 Ethiopia

ABIR, M. *Ethiopia: The Era of the Princes. The Challenge of Islam and the Reunification of the Christian Empire 1769-1855* (London, 1968).
GREENFIELD, Richard. *Ethiopia: A New Political History* (London: Pall Mall, 1965).
HESS, Robert L. *Ethiopia: The Modernization of Autocracy* (Ithaca, N.Y.: Cornell University Press, 1970).

JESMAN, Czeslaw. *The Ethiopian Paradox* (London: Oxford University Press, 1963).

LEVINE, David. *Wax and Gold: Tradition and Innovation in Ethiopian Culture* (Chicago: University of Chicago Press, 1965).

LEWIS, William H. "The Ethiopian Empire: Progress and Problems." Middle East Journal 10 (Summer 1956): 257-68.

LIPSKY, George A. *Ethiopia* (New Haven, Conn.: Human Relations Area Files, 1962).

PERHAM, Margery. *The Government of Ethiopia* (London: Faber and Faber, 1947).

6.98 Liberia

CLOWER, Robert W.; George DALTON; Mitchell HARWITZ; and A. A. WALTERS. *Growth Without Development: An Economic Survey of Liberia* (Evanston, Ill.: Northwestern University Press, 1966).

FRAENKL, Merran. *Tribe and Class in Monrovia* (London: Oxford University Press, 1964).

LIEBENOW, J. Gus *Liberia: The Evolution of Privilege* (Ithaca, N.Y.: Cornell University Press, 1969).

RICHARDSON, Nathaniel R. *Liberia's Past and Present* (London: Diplomatic Press and Publishing, 1959).

TAYLOR, Wayne C. *The Case Study of the Firestone Operation in Liberia* (Washington, D.C.: Washington National Planning Association).

YANCY, Ernest Jerome. *The Republic of Liberia* (London: Allen and Unwin).

7: Data resources for comparative research on national development

Atlas Narodov Mira *(Atlas of the Peoples of the World)* (Moscow, 1964). A useful source for information on language distribution.

BANKS, A. S. *Cross-Polity Time Series Data* (Cambridge, Mass.: MIT Press, 1971). Historical data for a great number of countries since 1815.

——— "Political Characteristics of Nation-States: A Longitudinal Analysis." Mimeographed. Center for Comparative Political Research, State University of New York at Binghamton, 1971.

——— and Robert TEXTOR. *A Cross-Polity Survey* (Cambridge: MIT Press, 1966). Codings for characteristics of all independent politics: machine readable.

BAUER, R. A., ed. *Social Indicators* (Cambridge: MIT Press, 1966). A series of papers on problems of establishing broad batteries of indicators.

BORNSCHIER, V.; H. B. DECHMANN; and M. DECHMANN. "Towards a General Typology of Nations." Mimeographed. Universität Zürich, 1968. Based on data-bank developed at the University of Zurich under the direction of Peter Heintz.

DAVIS, Kingsley. *Basic Data for Cities, Countries and Regions. World Urbanization 1950-1970,* Vol. I (Berkeley: University of California, 1969).

DOGAN, Mattei and Stein ROKKAN, eds. *Quantitative Ecological Analysis in the Social Sciences* (Cambridge: MIT Press, 1969).

FEIERABEND, Ivo and Rosalind FEIERABEND. "Cross National Data Bank of Political Instability Events." (Ann Arbor: Inter-University Consortium, n.d.).

GILLESPIE, John and Betty NESVOLD, eds. *Cross-National Research: Macro-Quantitative Analysis* (Beverly Hills: Sage, 1970).

GINSBURG, Norton, ed. *Atlas of Economic Development* (Chicago: University of Chicago Press, 1961).

HARBISON, Frederick H.; Joan MARUHNIC; and Jane R. RESNICK. *Quantitative Analysis of Modernization and Development* (Princeton: Princeton University, Industrial Relations Section, 1970).

––– "Indices of Development for Selected Latin American and Middle African Countries." (Princeton: Princeton University, Industrial Relations Section, 1969). Unpublished UNESCO working paper.

JANDA, Kenneth. *A Conceptual Framework for the Comparative Study of Political Parties* (Beverly Hills: Sage, 1970).

KUHNLE, Stein. "Time-Series Data for Eleven Smaller European Democracies. A Survey of Data Resources for Cross-National Time-Series Analysis." Paper presented to the ISSC-ECPR Workshop on Indicators of National Development, University of Lausanne, 9-14 August 1971.

LeROY LADURIE, Emmanuel and Paul DUMONT. "Quantitative and Cartographic Exploitation of French Military Archives, 1819-1926." Daedalus (Spring 1971): 397-441.

LORWIN, Val R. and Jacob PRICE. *The Dimensions of the Past* (New Haven, Conn.: Yale University Press, 1972). A collection of essays on data resources for quantitative history. Major contributions by Charles and Louise Tilly on French data, and Juan Linz on Spanish data.

MITCHELL, Robert Edward. "A Social Science Date Archive for Asia, Africa and Latin America." Social Science Information 4 (September 1970): 85-103.

NAROLL, Raoul. "A Holonational Bibliography." Comparative Political Studies 5, no. 2 (July 1972): 211-30. Review of statistical analyses using whole nations as units.

––– *Data Quality Control: A New Research Technique* (New York: Free Press, 1962). Important discussion of problems of statistical inference from whole-nation data.

REQUA, Eloise and Jane STETHAM. *The Developing Nations: A Guide to Information Sources* (New York: Gale Research, 1965).

ROACH, John, comp. *A Bibliography of Modern History* (Cambridge, Eng.: Cambridge University Press, 1968). A companion to the New Cambridge Modern History.

ROKKAN, Stein, ed. *Data Archives for the Social Sciences* (The Hague: Mouton, 1966).

––– and Jean MEYRIAT, eds. *International Guide to Electoral Statistics.* National elections in Western Europe, Vol. I (The Hague and Paris: Mouton, 1969).

ROKKAN, Stein and Frank AAREBROT. "The Norwegian Archive of Historical Ecological Data." Social Science Information 8 (1968): 77-84.

RUMMEL, R. J. *Dimensions of Nations* (Beverly Hills: Sage, 1972). Summary of numerous reports on major data and analysis operations using dyads of nations-states as the basis.

RUSSETT, Bruce et al. *World Handbook of Political and Social Indicators* (New Haven, Conn.: Yale University Press, 1964). First edition of useful collection of aggregate statistics by nation.

SINGER, J. D., ed. *Quantitative International Politics: Insights and Evidence* (New York: Free Press, 1968).

SINGER, J. David and Melwin SMALL. *The Wages of War 1816-1965: A Statistical Handbook* (New York: John Wiley, 1973).

——— "The Composition and Status Ordering of the International System 1815-1940." World Politics 18, no. 2 (January 1966).

STUDENSKI, Paul. *The Income of Nations* (New York: New York University Press, 1958).

TAYLOR, Charles Lewis and Michael C. HUDSON. *World Handbook of Political and Social Indicators. 2nd ed.* (New Haven, Conn.: Yale University Press, 1972). Expanded and improved version of RUSSETT, above.

THRUPP, Sylvia. "Diachronic Methods in Comparative Politics." In *The Methodology of Comparative Research,* edited by R. T. Holt and J. Turner, ch. 8 (New York: Free Press, 1970).

UNESCO. *Progress of Literacy in Various Countries: A Preliminary Study of Available Census Data Since 1900* (New York: Columbia University Press, 1953).

——— *Basic Facts and Figures: Illiteracy, Education, Libraries, Books, Newspapers, Newsprint, Films and Radio* (Paris: UNESCO, 1952).

UNITED NATIONS STATISTICAL OFFICE. *Compendium of Social Statistics* (New York: U.N. Statistical Service, 1963).

WOYTINSKY, W. S. *Die Welt in Zahlen.* 7 vols. (Berlin: R. Mosse, 1925-28).

——— and E. S. WOYTINSKY. *World Commerce and Governments* (New York: Twentieth Century Fund, 1955).

——— *World Population and Production* (New York: Twentieth Century Fund, 1953).

ZAPF, W. and P. FLORA. "Some Problems of Time-Series Analysis in Research on Modernization." Social Science Information 10, no. 3 (1971): 53-102. Reprinted as Chapter 6 of Volume 1 of this work.